SYRIAN JEWRY IN TRANSITION

T0373446

THE LITTMAN LIBRARY OF
JEWISH CIVILIZATION

Dedicated to the memory of
LOUIS THOMAS SIDNEY LITTMAN
*who founded the Littman Library for the love of God
and as an act of charity in memory of his father*
JOSEPH AARON LITTMAN
and to the memory of
ROBERT JOSEPH LITTMAN
who continued what his father Louis had begun
יהא זכרם ברוך

'*Get wisdom, get understanding:
Forsake her not and she shall preserve thee*'

PROV. 4: 5

*The Littman Library of Jewish Civilization is a registered UK charity
Registered charity no.* 1000784

SYRIAN JEWRY IN TRANSITION
1840–1880

◆

YARON HAREL

Translated by
DENA ORDAN

The Littman Library of Jewish Civilization
in association with Liverpool University Press

The Littman Library of Jewish Civilization
in association with Liverpool University Press
4 Cambridge Street, Liverpool L69 7ZU, UK

www.liverpooluniversitypress.co.uk/littman

Managing Editor: Connie Webber

Distributed in North America by
Oxford University Press Inc., 198 Madison Avenue,
New York, NY 10016, USA

First published in Hebrew 2003 © The Zalman Shazar Centre for Jewish History

English translation © The Littman Library of Jewish Civilization 2010
First published in paperback 2014

Catalogue records for this book are available from the
British Library and the Library of Congress

ISBN 978-1-906764-56-2

Publishing co-ordinator: Janet Moth
Copy-editing: Gillian Somerscales
Proof-reading: Agnes Erdos
Index: Bonnie Blackburn
Design: Pete Russell, Faringdon, Oxon.
Typeset by John Saunders Design & Production, Eastbourne

Printed and bound by CPI Group (UK) Ltd, Croydon, CR0 4YY

Preface to the English Edition

THIS volume is an updated translation of my Hebrew book *By Ships of Fire to the West: Changes in Syrian Jewry during the Period of Ottoman Reform (1840–1880)* (Jerusalem: Shazar, 2003). The impetus to undertake the original study came in part from the changed social and academic climate in Israel towards the Jews of Islamic lands. Whereas formerly the historical study of these communities suffered from lack of interest on the part of their members, and Israeli culture's emphasis on the 'melting pot' and the creation of a 'new Jew' discouraged preservation of their ways, recent years have seen both the emergence of communal pride on the part of the communities themselves and a shift away from the Eurocentric bias of academic research into Jewish history. In addition, the branching out of the discipline of history beyond the political sphere into social, economic, and cultural fields has provided scholars with a new spectrum of topics considered worthy of research, notable among them the past of those Jewish communities hitherto seen as ancillary to the central historical narrative of the Jewish people. Further impetus for the study of the historical symbiosis between the Jews of Islam and the surrounding society is provided by recognition that better knowledge of the Middle East will improve the state of Israel's ability to function in Muslim space. All of these factors both fuelled my original study and shaped the present volume.

Impressive advances have been made in the study of the Middle Eastern Jewish communities in recent years, with almost every important community receiving scholarly attention. However, this activity has only emphasized the absence of a comprehensive historical study of the Jewish communities of Syria, one devoted to their political, social, economic, and cultural history in recent generations. Generally, the Syrian Jewish communities have been treated by scholars in the overall context of Jewish communities in the Ottoman empire, and then in a marginal fashion. Even if current studies include some entirely, or almost entirely, devoted to Syrian Jewry, for the most part these studies are restricted to a narrow aspect of the life of these communities or rely on a limited number of sources. On the other hand, although Syria has a place of honour in Middle Eastern studies, most scholars of Syrian society pay little attention to its Jewish aspect. Almost all of the few references to Jews made in their studies are based on a small number of external sources and not on the Jewish sources themselves.

This book, grounded in archival study, undertakes a comprehensive examination of the changes in the life of the Syrian Jewish communities, both within those communities and in their relationships with others, over the forty-year period of Ottoman reform. In order to achieve this aim, and to provide a broad, multifaceted view of events, processes, and developments, I have made use of a wide range of Jewish, Ottoman, local Christian Arab, Muslim Arab, and European sources, including consular reports, travel accounts, the contemporary press, and reports by emissaries of the Alliance Israélite Universelle. In the course of preparing the English edition, I also had the opportunity to consult up-to-date studies that examine new and old issues from original perspectives, and to reconsider past conclusions.

It is important to stress that this book focuses not on Syrian history as a whole but on the Jewish minority in Syria, and on its apperception of events within its own community and in the surrounding society during the period of Ottoman reform (Tanzimat). One significant issue to which the study of Syria and of its Jews can contribute is that of how the Middle Eastern Jewish communities confronted westernization and modernization, providing a clearer picture of how these processes affected Jewish communities living in the centre of the Muslim world.

Regrettably, Israeli researchers still cannot visit Syria. I sincerely hope that publication of this study will make a modest contribution towards bringing Syria and the state of Israel closer until the establishment of full peace between them, which can only be advantageous to both nations. After all, Jews were and still are an inseparable part of Syrian history.

*

Many individuals stood by my side during the long years devoted to the writing of this book. Some agreed with me, and some did not; all, however, aimed to enhance my research. It is my pleasant task to thank Professors Shimon Schwarzfuchs, Norman Stillman, Abraham Marcus, Zvi Zohar, Shmuel Feiner, Jacob Barnai, Moshe Ma'oz, Kais Firro, Yaron Zur, Nahem Ilan, Dr Leah Makovetsky, and Dr Yitzchak Kerem, and to mark the contribution of the late Professors Jonathan Frankel, Walter P. Zenner, and Joshua Kaniel, among many others.

I owe special appreciation to the devoted librarians in the various libraries and archives I visited while engaged in researching and writing this book: at the Jewish National and University Library of Israel, the Central Archives for the History of the Jewish People, Yad Ben-Zvi, and the Bar-Ilan Library. Invaluable aid was provided by staff at the British National Archives in London, the archives of the French Foreign Office in Paris and Nantes, and the Austrian State Archives in Vienna, and those at the archive of the Alliance Israélite Universelle in Paris, first and foremost my dear friend Jean-Claude Kuperminc.

My many trips abroad for the purposes of this research were made possible by generous support from the French government. It is my pleasant duty to thank the French cultural attachés Claude Domenach, Jean Soler, Jean Claude Jacq, and Alexander Defay, who did everything in their power to assist me.

My research also received support from the Memorial Foundation for Jewish Culture, Bar-Ilan University, the Israeli Ministry of Education, and the World Center for Aleppo Jews' Traditional Culture.

I also owe profound thanks to all those who assisted in the creation of this English edition. Without the generous support of Mr Joe Dwek, who encouraged me from the time that he first heard of this study, this English translation would not have become a reality. Words do not suffice to express my appreciation for all his efforts on my behalf. Thanks are also due to Mr Alain Farhi for the initial introduction to Joe Dwek. I extend warm thanks to the translator, Dena Ordan, whose comments and insights contributed to the quality of this study, and to the devoted staff at the Littman Library, first and foremost Connie Webber and Ludo Craddock, and the copy-editor, Gillian Somerscales, who did everything in their power to bring this project to a successful conclusion.

Last but not least, I thank my wife Tammy, to whom this book is dedicated, and my children Snir, Marva, Asa, and Nitai, who fill my life with delight.

August 2009   GIVAT ZEEV

This book was published in English thanks to a generous contribution from

MR JOE DWEK CBE

of Manchester, through the Aleppo Jewish Heritage Center (Halab) in Israel

Contents

Note on Transliteration and Conventions Used in the Text

THE transliteration of Hebrew in this book reflects consideration of the type of book it is, in terms of its content, purpose, and readership. The system adopted therefore reflects a broad approach to transcription, rather than the narrower approaches found in the *Encyclopaedia Judaica* or other systems developed for text-based or linguistic studies. The aim has been to reflect the pronunciation prescribed for modern Hebrew, rather than the spelling or Hebrew word structure, and to do so using conventions that are generally familiar to the English-speaking reader.

In accordance with this approach, no attempt is made to indicate the distinctions between *alef* and *ayin*, *tet* and *taf*, *kaf* and *kuf*, *sin* and *samekh*, since these are not relevant to pronunciation; likewise, the *dagesh* is not indicated except where it affects pronunciation. Following the principle of using conventions familiar to the majority of readers, however, transcriptions that are well established have been retained even when they are not fully consistent with the transliteration system adopted. On similar grounds, the *tsadi* is rendered by 'tz' in such familiar words as barmitzvah, mitzvot, and so on. Likewise, the distinction between *ḥet* and *khaf* has been retained, using *ḥ* for the former and *kh* for the latter; the associated forms are generally familiar to readers, even if the distinction is not actually borne out in pronunciation, and for the same reason the final *heh* is indicated too. As in Hebrew, no capital letters are used, except that an initial capital has been retained in transliterating titles of published works (for example, *Shulḥan arukh*).

Since no distinction is made between *alef* and *ayin*, they are indicated by an apostrophe only in intervocalic positions where a failure to do so could lead an English-speaking reader to pronounce the vowel-cluster as a diphthong—as, for example, in *ha'ir*—or otherwise mispronounce the word.

The *sheva na* is indicated by an *e*—*perikat ol*, *reshut*—except, again, when established convention dictates otherwise.

The *yod* is represented by *i* when it occurs as a vowel (*bereshit*), by *y* when it occurs as a consonant (*yesodot*), and by *yi* when it occurs as both (*yisra'el*).

Names have generally been left in their familiar forms, even when this is inconsistent with the overall system.

ARABIC

A simplified system has also been used for Arabic transliteration. *Hamza* and *'ayn* are indicated by ' and ' respectively (apart from initial *hamza*, which is omitted), but otherwise no special signs are used. Long vowels are not indicated, and there is no differentiation in print between soft and hard *t*, breathed and unbreathed *h*, *sin* and *sad*, *dal* and *dad*, or *zayn* and *za'*. The letter *tha'* is indicated by *th*, *dhal* by *dh*, *kha'* by *kh*, and *shin* by *sh*. The definite article is represented throughout as *al-*, with no attempt to indicate elision, either following a vowel or preceding a sun letter. *Ta' marbuta* is indicated by *a*, except in the construct (*idafa*), when it is represented as *at*. All Arabic words, apart from proper names standing alone, are italicized. When proper names occur within a transliterated phrase, they are italicized and written with the initial letter in lower case.

Arabic sources listed in the references are cited with their full transliterated Arabic title following the English translation of the title. In the notes, they are referred to by this English translation (sometimes shortened), followed by (Arab.).

List of Abbreviations

AAIU	Archives de l'Alliance Israélite Universelle, Paris
ACRI	Archives of the Chief Rabbinate, Istanbul
AECADN	Affaires Etrangères [France], Centre des Archives Diplomatiques de Nantes
AECCC	Archives du Ministère des Affaires Etrangères, Paris, Correspondance Consulaire et Commerciale
AECPC	Archives du Ministère des Affaires Etrangères, Paris, Correspondance Politique du Consul
AENS	Archives du Ministère des Affaires Etrangères, Paris, Nouvelle Série
AIU	Alliance Israélite Universelle
BAIU	*Bulletin de l'Alliance Israélite Universelle*
BofD	Board of Deputies of British Jews
CAHJP	Central Archives for the History of the Jewish People, Jerusalem
CZA	Central Zionist Archives, Jerusalem
DA	Department of Archives, National Library of Israel, Jerusalem
FO	Foreign Office, London
HHSTA	Österreichischen Staatsarchiv, Vienna, Haus-, Hof-, und Staatsarchiv
HHSTA, Adm. Reg.	Österreichischen Staatsarchiv, Vienna, Haus-, Hof-, und Staatsarchiv, Administrative Registratur
HHSTA, PA	Österreichischen Staatsarchiv, Vienna, Haus-, Hof-, und Staatsarchiv, Politisches Archiv
IMHM	Manuscripts Department and Institute of Microfilmed Hebrew Manuscripts, National Library of Israel, Jerusalem
JC	*Jewish Chronicle*
JTSL	Jewish Theological Seminary Library, New York
MC	Montefiore Collection, Jews' College, London
NLIS	National Library of Israel, Jerusalem

INTRODUCTION

THE EIGHTEENTH century saw a massive penetration of the Ottoman empire by European powers and ideas. In the nineteenth, according to Albert Hourani, the Arabs were swept into a new world created in western Europe.[1] Other scholars have studied the broad processes fostering the entry of the Ottoman empire into modernity, as embodied by the period of mid-nineteenth-century administrative reform known as the Tanzimat era; this book focuses on how one sector of the variegated Ottoman mosaic—its Syrian Jewish community—experienced the changes sweeping the empire during those years.

Any consideration of Ottoman modernization must take note of its distinctive nature as compared to the European process. Eurocentric divisions of history into the ancient, medieval, and modern periods are of questionable applicability to the Middle East, itself a European-defined term.[2] More pertinent to this study is the historical framework proposed by Albert Hourani in the study mentioned above, which designates the sixteenth- to eighteenth-century history of the Arab peoples as the 'Ottoman Age', and the period that opens in the early nineteenth century and ends on the eve of the Second World War as the 'Age of European Empires'.

Underlying the decision to open this book with a look at the eighteenth-century exposure of Aleppine Jews to western influences is the recognition that each of the eras identified by Hourani both preserves elements of the preceding period and contains harbingers of the one to follow. In the case of the Ottoman empire, as Hourani and others note, the eighteenth century can be identified as a transitional phase containing traditional and new elements, which eventually gave way to more thoroughgoing westernization and modernization in the nineteenth. In his characterization of the eighteenth-century Ottoman empire, Hourani refers to transitions in both the internal and external balance of power: a shift in influence from the sultan's court to a small group of upper-level civil servants, and significant changes in the empire's relations with Europe. Earlier, the European–Ottoman relationship had been grounded in military and diplomatic equality; now a shift took place in which the technologically and scientifically advanced, economically

---

[1] Hourani, *A History of the Arab Peoples*, 249–64.
[2] See Lewis, *The Jews of Islam*, 107–8.

flourishing, and militarily newly strengthened European powers began to demand priority. Losing its primacy on the European political scene, the Ottoman empire was slowly pushed to the sidelines. The deepening European penetration into the various regions of the Ottoman empire in the eighteenth century gave rise to an enhanced awareness of western conceptions on the part of the empire's inhabitants, preparing the ground for significant change in the nineteenth century.

Hourani is not alone in his perception of the eighteenth century as a pivotal age for the Ottoman empire. Bernard Lewis agrees, but adopts a slightly different emphasis. For him, the shift from old to new is encapsulated in the changing relations between Christian Europe and the Islamic world, whose roots he identifies in various events that took place as the seventeenth century ended and the eighteenth began—first and foremost, the Treaty of Carlowitz between the Ottoman and Habsburg empires signed on 26 January 1699, which significantly diminished Turkish influence in eastern and central Europe and altered the balance of power in the relationship between Christianity and Islam.[3]

One study more specifically related to the Syrian milieu, Abraham Marcus's incisive examination of eighteenth-century Aleppo, characterizes the eighteenth-century Middle East, and Aleppo in particular, as poised 'on the eve of modernity'.[4] His comprehensive portrait of this city notes the active beginning of the processes of internal and external change that facilitated the penetration of the Middle East by modernizing influences at the next turn of the century, from the eighteenth to the nineteenth. Among the new features that emerge strongly in the nineteenth century, he cites disaffection with the receptivity of traditional institutions to European ideas, the emergence of the state as a leading agent of change, and the evolution of a westernized class committed to reform.[5]

The present study follows in the footsteps of these scholars and similarly identifies the eighteenth century as a pivotal period. After an introductory consideration of eighteenth-century Jewish Aleppo, it focuses on the forty-year period of Ottoman reforms from 1840 to 1880. In constructing its portrayal of the changes, both internal and external, experienced by the Syrian Jewish community over these four decades, this enquiry drew primarily on a wide range of archival material, including Jewish, Christian Arab, and Muslim Arab sources, Ottoman and European documents, consular reports, travel accounts, and reports from the contemporary press and by emissaries to Syria of the French Alliance Israélite Universelle. Rabbinic sources, such as responsa and halakhic works, open a window on to Syrian Jewish life and concerns, and the many letters consulted serve to round out the picture obtained from printed

---

[3] Lewis, *The Middle East*, 276–7.   [4] Marcus, *The Middle East on the Eve of Modernity*.
[5] Ibid. 26. For further discussion of this topic, see Philipp, 'Bilad al-Sham in the Modern Period'.

works. One archive of outstanding importance is that of the chief rabbinate in Istanbul, which houses dozens of letters from the leaders of the Damascus and Aleppo Jewish communities to the *ḥakham bashi* (chief rabbi), requesting his intervention with the Sublime Porte on their behalf. These and the additional sources consulted reflect an attempt to provide a broad, multifaceted perspective on events and processes.

The blood libel of 1840 known as the Damascus affair temporarily placed Syrian Jewry in the spotlight of Jewish history. The accusation at its heart galvanized western Jewish communities and played an important role in bringing the Middle Eastern Jewish question to western Jewish consciousness, in the rise of Jewish newspapers and of organized Jewish public opinion in Europe, and in the creation of modern secular Jewish solidarity. Some scholars mark it as the first sign of active involvement of western Jews in promoting internal change in the Middle Eastern Jewish communities.[6] Yet once the episode was over the Syrian Jewish communities no longer occupied centre stage, and the following years saw them pushed to the margins of historical interest.

This study begins in 1840 not because of the Damascus affair but because of a political event—the re-establishment of Ottoman rule over Syria in late 1840 after a hiatus of some eight years. This point is chosen in recognition that the return of Ottoman rule and the ensuing implementation of reforms in the region marked the beginning of a new era in Syrian Jewish history. Within the broader framework of the Ottoman empire, the Tanzimat era is seen as an essential base for its subsequent modernization. The reforms brought the entire empire, albeit slowly, from the old order to a new one dominated by modern western ideas.

This process did not bypass Syrian Jewry; indeed, in some respects exposure to western ideas came earlier to Syrian Jews than to the general Syrian population. Among the forces influencing the Syrian Jewish response to these changes we must consider the arrival in the eighteenth century of Jewish traders from Europe, who introduced western ideas to the traditional local community; the role of European consular representatives and their protégés in changing the structure of Jewish society; the effects of Ottoman economic decline on Jewish occupations; the impact of the reforms on traditional Jewish autonomy and the communal administration; the penetration of western education in the form of schools run by the Alliance Israélite Universelle; local Muslim opposition to granting equality to minorities; the changing relationships between the three points of the Muslim–Christian–Jewish triangle; and, ultimately, how the confluence of these processes resulted in a western inclination on the part of the Syrian Jewish communities which culminated in large-scale emigration to the West.

[6] See Frankel, *The Damascus Affair*; id., '"Ritual Murder" in the Modern Era'.

Up to the 1870s the Syrian Jewish communities were in a condition of growth, flourishing both economically and politically; but at the same time they were creating ties with Jewish communities in the West, in the developing recognition that their future lay in the new world overseas. Three events mark the beginning of decline in the history of Syrian Jewry: the opening of the Suez Canal in 1869; the bankruptcy of the Ottoman empire in 1875; and the suspension of the Ottoman constitution in 1878, which ended the period of reform. From that point on, for Syrian Jews, the future was vested in the West, not the East. From the early 1880s the Syrian Jewish communities began to dwindle, mostly because of a stream of emigration, first to Egypt and then overseas.

In order to understand how the Syrian Jewish community is defined in this study, a brief examination of Syria's geographical and administrative status in the Ottoman imperial context is necessary. From the eighth century to the early twentieth, the region designated as Syria was not, in either theory or actuality, an independent political entity subject to strong centralized rule. Throughout this lengthy period Syria belonged to various large empires, governed from distant centres, that conquered it, ruled it, and divided it into districts; the Ottoman empire, which ruled Syria for centuries until its defeat by the Egyptian ruler Muhammad 'Ali in 1831–2, was no exception to this pattern. When Ottoman rule was restored in late 1840, the administrative division of Syria into three main districts—Aleppo, Damascus, and Sidon (Saida)—as a means of implementing centralized control was likewise reinstated. The Aleppo district remained virtually unchanged, except for two measures that later proved burdensome to Aleppine merchants and to the local rulers, and indirectly affected the region's Jewish communities. The first was the severing of Aleppo's natural port, Alexandretta, from the district of Aleppo and its annexation to the district of Adana. Nevertheless, the Jews of Alexandretta continued to identify themselves as part of the Syrian Jewish community, primarily because most of them were of Aleppine origin. The second was the annexation of the non-Arab Urfa to the Aleppo district, which led to the migration of Jewish families between Aleppo and Urfa. Even though Urfa, with a mixed, largely Kurdish population, was not definitively Syrian, Aleppine Jewish influence on Urfa's Jewish community was so compelling that its economic, social, and intellectual development must be viewed in the context of Aleppine Jewry.

In the Ottoman restructuring the Damascus district or *wilaya* retained its traditional component elements of Homs, Hama, and the area east of the Jordan. On its western border, the Lebanon valley was added to this *wilaya*, but the area of Palestine was annexed to the Sidon district, as was Tripoli, once an independent district. The Sidon *wilaya*, and its new capital Beirut, which replaced the former capital of Acre in early 1841, swiftly achieved a level of importance almost matching that of the Damascus *wilaya*. Their development

—and in particular that of Beirut, which became a major Syrian city—differed from that of other provinces, particularly after Lebanon became an autonomous district in 1861. The 1864 Wilaya Law divided Syria into two large provinces: Aleppo and Damascus. Aleppo received additional Anatolian territory, whereas the Damascus province incorporated areas such as Tripoli and Sidon, and was known from that time as the Suriyya *wilaya*. Lebanon remained an autonomous district with a special status.[7]

For its geographical definition of 'Syria', this study makes use of the Ottoman administrative division in order to include Urfa, but otherwise ignores the borders between the various provinces. It encompasses mainly the Jewish communities that viewed themselves as Syrian, thereby excluding the area defined as Lebanese, which covers the communities of Beirut, Tripoli, Hasbayah, Aley, Sidon, and Deir al-Qamar, as well as the regions of Transjordan and Palestine, each of which merits independent study by virtue of its unique features.

Another feature of the Ottoman empire germane to this study is the relationship between the imperial centre and its outlying provinces. Within the broad framework of the Ottoman regime, the Syrian province was of lesser strategic and economic importance than other regions such as Anatolia and the Balkans. Nonetheless, Syria did have considerable religious, economic, and strategic significance in the imperial context. Ottoman control of Syria greatly enhanced the sultan's status in the Muslim world, for the *mahmal*—the yearly caravan to Mecca—left from Damascus, drawing masses of pilgrims from various locations worldwide. As *amir al-mu'minin* (commander of the faithful), the sultan was responsible for overseeing the organization of the caravan and for guaranteeing its safety on the journey to and from Mecca.[8] Syria's economic importance derived from its location on the crossroads of East–West trade, with Aleppo and Damascus serving as points of departure for the large commercial caravans heading for Baghdad, Persia, and India. Although the importance of this trade was declining by the beginning of the nineteenth century, some commerce with the east continued along the traditional routes across the middle of Syria.[9] Finally, Syria's strategic importance to the Ottoman empire as a defensive front towards Egypt came to the fore as the empire's military prowess declined, peaking in the early part of the nineteenth century when Syria constituted the final barrier to the invasion of Turkey by the army of the rebellious Egyptian ruler Muhammad 'Ali.

[7] On the administrative division of Syria and its place in Ottoman strategy, see Ma'oz, *Ottoman Reform*, 31–3; Tibawi, *A Modern History of Syria*, 136; Gross, 'Ottoman Rule in the Province of Damascus', 1–20. On the existence of a Syrian territorial identity in the Ottoman context as early as the seventeenth century, see Gerber, '"Palestine" and Other Territorial Concepts'.

[8] See Ma'oz, *Ottoman Reform*, 13–30.

[9] On Aleppo's economic importance prior to the Ottoman era, see Bruce Masters, 'Aleppo'. For commercial activity in Aleppo in the early nineteenth century, see al-Hasani, *Economic History of Syria* (Arab.), 173 ff.

The declining strength of the Ottoman empire in the first decades of the nineteenth century had an adverse effect on the fortunes of Syrian Jewry. The waning of the sultan's authority at times left Syria's Jewish population at the mercy of rebellious local rulers. Strongmen such as Jazzar Pasha either protected or abused the Jewish public at their whim. Even those individual Jews who held high office in local administrations were at the mercy of, and dependent upon, the local rulers.[10] Jewish vulnerability to the caprice of individual leaders was also evident in varying levels of enforcement of discriminatory legislation. Thus, on the eve of the Egyptian incursion into Syria, discriminatory laws governing the colour of the clothing worn by Jews were once again enforced.[11] In 1832, with the completion of the takeover by Muhammad 'Ali, the position of the Jews took a turn for the better. Seeking to curry favour with the European powers, Muhammad 'Ali instituted measures to improve the status of the non-Muslim minorities under his rule, the Christians in particular. Yet it was in the final days of Muhammad 'Ali's rule in Syria that the Damascus affair erupted, when Jews were accused of murdering a Christian monk and his servant for ritual purposes; at this point only the active intervention and lobbying of European Jewish communities saved the Jews of Syria from the worst consequences of this blood libel. The period just prior to the reinstatement of Ottoman rule in Syria was one of Syrian Jewry's darkest hours, in which the community, impoverished by burdensome taxes and isolated from other Jewish centres, was humiliated and persecuted by the surrounding Muslim and Christian communities.

Following an opening consideration of the eighteenth-century Aleppine Jewish community, this book treats four main areas of Syrian Jewish life during the forty-year period of Ottoman reform: the internal conduct of the Syrian Jewish community; the legal status of the Jews; relations between Muslims, Jews, and Christians; and the shift to a westward inclination and emigration. This fourfold analysis provides insight into the distinctive dynamics of how one minority group experienced the changes sweeping Ottoman society, showing how the seeds of change planted in the eighteenth century, fed by the Ottoman attempts at reform, bore fruit and reached their culmination over the course of the nineteenth.

[10] See e.g. Philipp, 'The Farhi Family'.
[11] AECADN, Damas, 01, Cote A/18/54, Beaudin à Guys, 30 Dec. 1830.

PART I

THE SEEDS OF CHANGE

ONE

FIRST SIGNS OF
WESTERNIZATION

T HE perception of the eighteenth century as nurturing the seeds of change for the Ottoman empire as a whole applies especially strongly to the Syrian Jewish community. The arrival of Italian Jewish merchants in eighteenth-century Aleppo—attracted by flourishing French mercantile activity—fostered significant changes in the socio-economic fabric of the long-standing Jewish community: changes that set in motion Syrian Jewry's later transition from an old to a new order.

The roots of the uninterrupted Syrian Jewish settlement, the diaspora closest to Erets Yisra'el, lie in antiquity. Over the course of the centuries this community experienced cycles of growth and decline and changes in its pattern of settlement. The arrival in the late fifteenth century of several families of Spanish exiles was followed by an economic and intellectual flowering that continued into the sixteenth century, when Syria, like the rest of the eastern Mediterranean basin, came under Ottoman rule.[1] In the eighteenth century the most significant force for change in the Syrian Jewish community was the extended exposure of Aleppo's Jews to new European Jewish settlers in that city. By creating reference groups outside the existing traditional context, these European Jews altered the communal and economic structure of Aleppine Jewry and ultimately affected other Syrian Jewish centres as well.

The Arrival of the Francos

Our starting point is the late 1730s, the conjectured date for the arrival in Aleppo of Hillel ben Samuel Picciotto of Leghorn (Livorno).[2] This Italian Jewish merchant, like other of his compatriots, had visited Aleppo before; now he decided to settle there, and to found a permanent mercantile base in the city. The product of complex economic and political considerations, this move was primarily grounded in Picciotto's perception that a window of economic opportunity was opening in Syria, and more particularly in his chosen destination, Aleppo.

---

[1] Harel, 'Conflict and Agreement' (Heb.).
[2] Le Calloc'h, 'La Dynastie consulaire', 136–8.

Aleppo had functioned as an important centre of international east–west trade for centuries, since Venetian merchants had founded the first European mercantile houses in the region in the period of the later crusades. The Venetians' commercial activity peaked in the fourteenth and fifteenth centuries; the Dutch, who used the land route to Baghdad on their way to India, subsequently overtook them, to be followed by the English, who next took the lead in setting up mercantile houses in Aleppo. These establishments closed in the early seventeenth century, when the British and Dutch East India trading companies began to use the more profitable sea route around the Cape of Good Hope.

In the late seventeenth century several developments brought French mercantile houses on to the scene. In 1669 Marseilles gained a valuable tax exemption; in 1670 the French Levant Company was founded; and the capitulations and confirmatory treaties of 1673 between France and the Ottoman empire confirmed France's position as protector of all European citizens lacking their own consular representation and reduced the customs rate applied to French traders to that already enjoyed by the Dutch and English. With this increasing French activity came a change in the nature of Aleppine trade. Whereas in earlier periods the goods imported to Europe had come from the Far East, Persia, and India, now they came mainly from the regions close to Syria. Camel caravans originating in Baghdad unloaded their goods in Damascus and Aleppo, making these cities significant centres of import–export commerce. In Aleppo, most of this enormously profitable business was funded by the great mercantile houses of Marseilles.[3] Operating under the aegis of France, whose consul extended his protection to the Jewish colony in the city, Italian Jewish merchants such as Hillel Picciotto became increasingly involved in the Ottoman trade,[4] and the colony expanded;[5] some Italian Jewish immigrants also settled in Damascus, where they rose to positions of social and economic prominence.

Against this background of brisk commercial activity, the Picciotto mercantile house in Aleppo prospered, quickly becoming one of the most important trading establishments in the region. Its success attracted additional European Jewish settlers, on whom the local community bestowed the honorific 'Signores Francos'. It was this expanded European Jewish colony in Aleppo that opened the way for the penetration of modernization to the Syrian Jewish communities. Several main avenues can be identified through which change was to occur

[3] AECCC, Alep, vol. 30, Deval, Alep, 25 Feb. 1838; see also Marcus, *The Middle East on the Eve of Modernity*, 148–9. On French economic interests in Syria, see Rayyan, 'French Economic Interests in Syria' (Arab.). For a comprehensive study of Aleppo's place in occidental trade until the mid-eighteenth century, see Masters, *The Origins of Western Economic Dominance*.

[4] Rozen, *In the Mediterranean Routes* (Heb.), 54. See also Makovetski, 'The Jewish Economic Elite in Aleppo'.

[5] See Lutzky, 'The "Francos"' (Heb.), 46–76. See also Rozen, 'The Archives of the Chamber of Commerce of Marseilles' (Heb.); Schwarzfuchs, 'La "Nazione Ebrea" Livornaise au Levant', 711–12; Philipp, 'French Merchants and Jews in the Ottoman Empire', 318.

in the nineteenth century: alterations in the social composition of the Jewish communities, along with criticism and reform of communal institutions, and movement from villages to cities, culminating in the beginning of emigration overseas; the incorporation of many local Jews into the international trading businesses of the Francos, the widening of lending on credit, and entry into new realms of economic activity; the introduction of modern European-style education into local Jewish communities, transforming the world-view of students; a worsening of relations between Jews and Christians, alongside a degree of improvement in relations between Muslims and Jews; a turning of Jewish communities to the West, with the acquisition of foreign protection and a reliance on western Jewish communities; and an improvement in the legal status of Jews as a result of the Ottoman reforms.

The Ottoman Imperial Context

The eighteenth-century social environment of Syrian Jews, like that of other Levantine Jewish communities, differed from that of European Jewry. In each European state Jews lived as a minority in a realm under sole Christian domination. In contrast, in the Ottoman region Jews lived alongside a Sunni Muslim majority and a Christian minority—in former Byzantine areas, a substantial minority—as well as dozens of other religious, ethnic, and language groups. Up until the early nineteenth century, relations between the Christian and Jewish minorities, themselves divided into smaller distinctive groups, may be characterized as 'correct'—which is to say, each virtually ignored the other's existence. Thereafter, however, an element of hostility entered the relationship, fostered by the economic success of the Francos. The Picciottos aroused the jealousy both of (Christian) French traders, who saw themselves as the primary victims of their success, and of French consular representatives in Aleppo and Damascus. This resentment, fanned by Catholic religious envoys from Europe, gave rise to anti-Jewish feelings among the local Christian population as well, laying the foundation for tense relations between Syria's Jewish and Christian communities throughout the nineteenth century (see Chapter 9 below).

Until the late eighteenth century all parties accepted the arrangement governing the relationships between Muslims and Christians, and between Muslims and Jews, within which the non-Muslim minorities, known as *ahl al-dhimma*, were granted certain rights in return for their acceptance of certain obligations. Relations between the Ottoman imperial authorities and the minority groups were conducted through the respective religious authorities of imam, priest, and rabbi. In exchange for payment of the *jizya* tax and submission to certain restrictions that highlighted their inferiority to the Muslim majority, Jews and Christians were tolerated and enjoyed substantial autonomy in their internal affairs. They were empowered to choose their own leaders, and to maintain independent tax-collection, judicial, and school systems, virtually without government interference. Within the religious mosaic of urban life in the Ottoman empire, each religious community was subject to the authority of its particular leader.[6] In practice, the Ottoman authorities recognized and supported the Jewish leadership, so that this leader functioned in a dual capacity: not only was he the Jewish community's representative to the Ottoman authorities, he was also an agent of the Ottoman authorities to the Jewish community. But the rabbi did not operate on his own; he was assisted by a public leadership body comprising seven officials known as *parnasim*. The loyalty of these men, selected from the hereditary aristocracy or the moneyed elite, to communal Jewish values and the welfare of their religious community was taken for granted. The rabbi and the *parnasim* were interdependent: the rabbi needed their financial means, and they needed the rabbi's halakhic and moral backing for their actions.[7]

The authority of the Jewish communal leadership, with the rabbi at the apex of the pyramid, was grounded not only in the community's consent to it on religious grounds, but also in its de facto recognition by the Ottoman authorities. Preferring to deal with the group rather than the individual, the Ottoman authorities strengthened the leadership of the *dhimmi*s, seeking thereby to maintain peace throughout an empire that encompassed a multitude of religious and ethnic groups. In Syria, as in Europe, the internal stability of the Jewish community, with the rabbi at its head, depended on the identification in the Jewish public mind of communal with religious existence. One important expression of this stability—which, as we shall see, was undermined by the Francos—was the hereditary nature of the office of the chief rabbi.

Although to the outside observer at the time of the Francos' arrival the Aleppine Jewish community might have appeared to be a homogeneous unit operating under a single leadership, in fact it consisted of two groups: Mustaribun (local Jews, whose families had lived in Syria for a long time, some even from before the expulsion of the Jews from Spain in 1492), and Sephardis (who had settled in Syria after the Spanish expulsion). Over the centuries following the Sephardis' arrival in Syria, many of the differences between the two groups had disappeared, so that they seemed destined to merge into one. But the arrival of the Francos, mainly from Leghorn and Venice, and with them the forgotten language of Judaeo-Spanish and the old Sephardi *minhagim*, strengthened Sephardi identity, delaying the process of amalgamation between the two sectors of the Jewish population.

The budding European Jewish merchant colony in Aleppo, which consisted of six primary households and dozens of other families, had unique features

[6] For a more comprehensive discussion, see Lewis, *The Jews of Islam*, 125–6.

[7] See Levi, 'Changes in the Leadership of the Main Spanish Communities' (Heb.), 242.

that distinguished it both from the European merchant colony and from the wider Jewish community.[8] On the whole, the members of the city's European merchant colony, even those of long standing, did not see themselves as Aleppine; rather, they retained their European identity and identification, considering themselves temporarily resident in Aleppo for business purposes only. Most never learned Arabic, and only a minority brought their wives or families to Aleppo or married local women. They even lived apart from the local residents, in a separate quarter.[9] European Jewish merchants likewise resided outside the Jewish quarter, and their primary affiliation was with the European colony rather than with the local Jewish community. Not subject to the Ottoman discriminatory laws that applied to local Jews, they operated under the protection of European powers, in particular of France.[10] Nonetheless, there were differences between European Jewish merchants and their non-Jewish counterparts. Although initially they too viewed themselves as only temporary residents in Aleppo, over time the Francos, to whom the local Jewish customs were not altogether unfamiliar, began to participate in local Jewish religious life; many of them also married local women and raised their families in Aleppo. Thus, in due course, they in fact became permanent residents of the city.[11] Even so, by virtue of their dress, their clean-shaven faces, and their attitude towards and treatment of women, the Francos remained distinct from the surrounding Jewish society and brought elements of European culture to Middle Eastern Jewry.[12]

Throughout the eighteenth century this elitist, wealthy group, who identified socially not with the local Jews—who were on the fringes of Aleppine society—but with the high-status European colony, developed alongside the local Jewish community. Notwithstanding their autonomous status, the Francos did not found a separate communal and religious framework, but rather relied on the local communal institutions to meet their religious needs, as exemplified first and foremost by their joining the local community in prayer. The Francos also engaged voluntarily in philanthropic activity on behalf of the community, making generous donations to local charitable institutions, *talmudei torah* (schools) and scholars, serving as treasurers of the *bikur ḥolim* (communal health) and *gemilut ḥasadim* (charitable) funds, and seeing to the importation of the Four Species for the Sukkot holiday, among other things. On the

---

[8] The major households were those of the Picciotto, Silvera, Ancona, Lofez, Belilios, and Altaras families. See Harel, 'The Overthrow of the Last Aleppan Chief Rabbi' (Heb.), 123.

[9] Marcus, *The Middle East on the Eve of Modernity*, 45–6.

[10] For a comprehensive discussion, see Harel, 'The Status and Image of the Picciotto Family' (Heb.), 173.

[11] See R. Laniado, *Beit dino shel shelomoh*, 501, 'Ḥoshen mishpat', no. 39; Kassin, *Maḥaneh yehudah*, i, introd., 1*b*.

[12] On the significant role played by the Francos in the modernization of Jewish communities in the central Ottoman empire, see Rodrigue, *French Jews, Turkish Jews*, 39–40.

other hand, they refused to be bound by the local communal regulations (*takanot*) or by the authority of the local Jewish communal institutions.[13]

This maintenance of an identity separate and apart from the local Jewish community was significant in the context of the Ottoman state, for it released the Francos from the burdensome measures associated with *dhimmi* status as well as from subjection to the authority of the local Jewish administration. Yet because the Francos participated in the local Jewish religious framework, the presence of this elite did not immediately pose a threat to the local Jewish community. Rather, its existence and growth benefited the community—first and foremost economically, by creating new job opportunities for local Jews as translators, clerks, financiers, intermediaries, warehouse supervisors, workers, and servants in its mercantile enterprises. Not only did local employees help to open their home markets to European traders, they also supplied important insight into the local mentality. Naturally, European Jewish merchants in Aleppo preferred to employ their co-religionists. But good pay and high status were not the sole benefits accruing from employment by the Francos; another significant, sought-after advantage was the privilege of exemption from Ottoman law.[14] As a means of extending their spheres of influence, European consuls bestowed protection on various officials in their employ, primarily the guides and interpreters known as dragomen, freeing them from Ottoman law and authority; in addition, as a means of raising capital, foreign consulates adopted the practice of selling consular protection to various individuals for hefty fees and then fictitiously recording these individuals as consular employees.[15]

With Raphael Picciotto's appointment as head of the Austrian diplomatic representation in Aleppo in 1784, and later as Austrian consul in 1798, Jewish access to consular protection widened.[16] At this time a process becomes apparent whereby the local employees of foreign merchants and consulates, Jews and Christians alike, sought to create a new identity for themselves, apart from their original communities, and to achieve official recognition from the Ottoman authorities, hoping by these means to obtain official release from the lower status and heavy taxes imposed on the *dhimmi*. Ultimately, the Francos' presence in Aleppo spawned the rise of another elite, this time within the local Jewish community, whose members had more far-reaching goals. Not only did they seek to throw off the yoke of Ottoman law, by virtue of being protégés of foreign powers they also sought to avoid payment of internal taxes to their

[13] For a summation of the social status of the Francos within the Jewish community, see Lutzky, 'The "Francos"' (Heb.), 64–72.

[14] R. Laniado, *Beit dino shel shelomoh*, 482–3, 'Ḥoshen mishpat', no. 35.

[15] For the number of dragomans in the various consulates, see al-Yashu'i, *Historical Documents about Aleppo* (Arab.) (Beirut, 1958–62), i. 104–5. See also al-Tunji, 'Social Interaction between the Ottomans and the Arabs' (Arab.); Cunningham, 'Dragomania'.

[16] See Harel, 'The Status and Image of the Picciotto Family' (Heb.), 177–9. See also HHSTA, Türkei, II/129, de Testa au Comte de Colloredo, Pera de Consple, 25 July 1802.

original communities. For some, this aspiration blossomed into denial of the right of their communal heads to represent them.[17] It was primarily this local nouveau riche elite, which sought to detach itself from the Jewish community, that posed a significant threat to Jewish communal unity and strength. The traditional status quo was further undermined by the presence of *parnasim* in this new economic stratum, which provided them with a reference group outside the long-standing Jewish community. The nouveau riche and the local *parnasim* began to question and disparage the old order, which bestowed preferential status on the scholarly class in setting communal norms. In the late eighteenth century these developments gave rise to an increasingly bitter debate concerning the authority of the Jewish communal leadership over the Francos, and more particularly over their employees, resulting in a marked weakening of the status and authority of the chief rabbi of the time, Raphael Solomon Laniado.

Friction between Old and New

As long as the Francos were perceived to be temporary residents in Aleppo, the Jewish communal leadership ignored the question of whether they were subject to communal regulations and taxes, particularly in the light of their generosity to communal institutions and their support of the community and of individual Jews in times of trouble. But as it became clear that the Francos were settling in Aleppo, the issue of whether or not they were bound by communal regulations began to trouble the Jewish leadership. Had it not been for the further question of whether or not their local Jewish employees should also enjoy exemption from communal obligations, this issue might have been either overlooked or settled through compromise. As it turned out, the dispute surrounding the status of the Francos, which began in the late 1760s or early 1770s, and the further controversy over that of their employees which followed swiftly on its heels, lasted for over fifteen years.

One significant result of this dispute, which was inherently linked to radical changes taking place in the Jewish communal structure in Aleppo and later in Damascus, was opposition to, and the ending of, the practice of the office of chief rabbi passing from father to son. This in turn undermined the status of the chief rabbi as a sole halakhic authority (*posek*) for his co-religionists; indeed, it was during the course of this controversy that we find for the first time full-blown opposition to local communal authority in the form of refusal to obey a chief rabbi's verdict or to appear before the local Jewish court presided over by the chief rabbi.[18]

[17] Marcus, *The Middle East on the Eve of Modernity*, 46.
[18] For a detailed study of this controversy, see Yaron Harel, 'The Controversy over Rabbi Ephraim Laniado's Inheritance'.

Laniado, as chief rabbi of Aleppo during these years, was not alone in strongly opposing the privileges claimed by the widening circle of protected, tax-exempt individuals such as the Francos' employees. The Ottoman authorities took a dim view of the resultant reduction in their income, and they too initiated a campaign to withdraw these privileges from the numerous favoured employees and consular protégés. Moreover, the emergence of this protected class was not only undermining and weakening the authority of the chief rabbi as leader of the Jewish community; it also affected the traditional relationship between the Muslim majority and the Christian minority. The increased involvement of foreign consulates in the empire's internal affairs, in attempting to assist individuals under their protection, disrupted the delicate intercommunal balance, promoting Muslim distrust, fear, and even hatred of Christians.[19]

The dispute in Aleppo had its origin in a disagreement between a husband and wife, both Francos.[20] In seeking to impose his will on his wife, the husband asked Laniado whether or not the Francos were subject to local Jewish communal regulations. Laniado's response was unequivocal: the Francos were indeed bound by all community regulations and ordinances, and could not adjudicate for themselves; moreover, their wives were subject to the local customs governing women's behaviour. This drew an angry reaction from the leading members of the Franco community, who claimed that Laniado was using a marital quarrel as a pretext to alter the status quo. Ultimately, Laniado found himself isolated, facing opposition not only from the Francos but also from the entire scholarly stratum of the Jewish community, which sided with the Francos against him. The scholars feared that this controversy would lead to a permanent rift and to withdrawal of Franco financial support and philanthropic activity. This was not their sole concern, however; they were also troubled by the possibility that such a split would lead to financial losses by local Jews in the Francos' employ. In their opposition to Laniado, Aleppo's Jewish scholars were supported by the leading Jerusalem and Damascus sages, and the eventual outcome of the dispute was never really in question. Overwhelming backing by Aleppine and other scholars for the continued exemption of the Francos from communal regulations, and their unique status as foreign nationals, freed the Francos from the yoke of Jewish communal regulations for years to come.

But the repercussions of this dispute extend beyond a simple exemption of a newly prominent elite from communal obligations. Not only did the emergence of these new and powerful elements significantly alter the internal power

[19] Marcus, *The Middle East on the Eve of Modernity*, 47. On the decreased imperial revenues as a result of foreign protection and the reaction of the Ottoman authorities, see Masters, 'The Sultan's Entrepreneurs', 579–97.

[20] For an in-depth treatment, see Harel, 'The Controversy over Rabbi Ephraim Laniado's Inheritance'; Lutzky, 'The "Francos"' (Heb.), 73–7; and Cohen-Tawil, 'The Francos in Aleppo' (Heb.).

structure of the Aleppine Jewish community; the fact that their influence was grounded in external political factors, namely the capitulation agreements and the protection of foreign consulates, and not in internal communal structures, ultimately lessened overall Jewish dependence on the Ottoman authorities for the upholding of Jewish autonomy.

The creation of fresh economic opportunities by the Franco businessmen, and the ensuing emergence of a new wealth-based oligarchy alongside the long-standing lineage-based one, provided the basis for the growth of a Jewish middle class in Aleppo which eventually came to dominate the Jewish community there. These changes in the communal structure constitute the first signs of alteration in a world-view hitherto centred on the principles of communal cohesion and mutual responsibility. By the latter half of the eighteenth century, the established Jewish community was no longer the sole locus of social life for the Aleppine Jew.[21] Although Jews were by no means fully integrated into non-Jewish society, there were new social contacts with non-Jews, albeit predominantly with members of the European Christian colony rather than with the local Muslim population. This intercourse facilitated the introduction of modern European social ideas into Aleppo's Jewish community.

The first traditional principle to suffer from this altered balance of power in the Jewish communal structure was the enjoyment of greater privileges and social status by the hereditary aristocracy. Once accepted without question, this stratum's claim to absolute status lost ground. Another time-honoured practice to come under challenge was that of handing over spiritual leadership from father to son—a practice in accordance with the conventions of the Muslim East that was now viewed as clashing with newly introduced western social norms.[22] Certain sectors of the Jewish community began to question the automatic conformism and obedience to the communal leadership more generally. Their refusal to accept the jurisdiction of the Jewish court represented a wider lack of confidence in the communal framework and in its leadership, and posed a challenge to the entire institutional structure. In the past, the individual Jew had bowed to the dictates of Jewish society, there being no alternative protective framework; now, however, we see increased tension emerging between individual needs and communal obligations. By refusing to submit to the authority of the chief rabbi and to communal regulations, the Francos sought to limit rabbinical authority to its religious functions, and so to prevent the rabbi from interfering with their increasing involvement with, and integration into, non-Jewish society and adherence to European norms. On the other hand, it should be noted that the Francos made no attempt either to restrict or to supervise the rabbinate with respect to its religious functions. The extant

---

[21] These new affiliations found expression in shared gatherings and celebrations. See e.g. Attiah, *Bigdei yesha*, 31a.

[22] See Grossman, 'From Father to Son' (Heb.), 199–200.

sources neither testify, nor even allude, to any effort to reshape the rabbinate along modern, west European lines.

The Francos' presence in Aleppo also impinged on the status of the scholarly rabbinic class, primarily by their provision of financial support. It is more than likely that the scholars' backing for their benefactors in the latters' struggle against the chief rabbi was prompted by gratitude as well as by the aspiration to strengthen the status of the entire scholarly stratum, even though this essentially meant thwarting its leader.

For its part, the long-standing leadership class of past and present *parnasim*, many of whose members were becoming integrated into the new socio-economic order, remained largely indifferent to the struggle between Laniado and the Francos, deterred from supporting the chief rabbi by their economic involvement with the latter. In effect, the *parnasim* too had begun to look outwards, beyond their traditional community; indeed, their neglect of communal affairs created a leadership vacuum, which was filled by the Francos. Despite, perhaps even because of, their detachment, the Francos began to demonstrate an ever-increasing level of involvement in the internal affairs of the Jewish community, to whose regulations and ordinances they were not even subject. Thus, in the years following the dispute mentioned above we find the Jewish community asking the Francos to assume responsibility for estimating the individual level of the communal tax, a task formerly performed by a committee of *parnasim* from which the Francos were totally divorced. This changed balance of power in the community potentially strengthened the newly prominent 'secular' elements of the Jewish community at the expense of the long-established 'rabbinic' authorities, posing a particular threat to the chief rabbi's status as head of the communal institutions. The danger arose that the traditional communal frameworks would be dissolved as an alternative community emerged led by the Francos.

Chief Rabbi Laniado evidently felt that any signs of weakness or compromise on his part would not only accelerate communal disintegration but also indirectly lower his status. However, he misjudged the power accrued by the Francos in the community at large and in particular among the scholarly class that they supported. In attempting to force the Francos to accept his authority, Laniado sought to return the balance of power within Aleppine Jewish society to its traditional pattern. Naturally, there had been disagreements, crises, and conflict between rabbis and *parnasim* in the past; but these had been resolved according to the model with which Laniado was familiar, namely through halakhic means, at times including such extreme measures as excommunication or semi-ostracism. By applying traditional administrative and religious tools in his attempt to resolve this crisis, Laniado perhaps hoped simultaneously to suppress the Francos and curb their local employees, who had begun to weaken the communal administration from within.

Laniado's defeat at the hands of the scholarly class created a crisis of confidence that filtered down to other strata of the community, now exposed for the first time to an unconditional rout of the absolute rabbinic authority by the open opposition of the scholarly class. In essence, there was a rupture in Laniado's leadership. Though he correctly identified the signs of social unrest in the community, he failed to grasp the nature of the new socio-economic and political forces at work. Raphael Picciotto's position as head of the Austrian diplomatic representation in Aleppo from 1784 enabled him to place a greater number of individuals under Austrian protection: in consequence, an increasing number of Jews sought to avoid not only their obligations to the Ottoman authorities but also their obligations to the Jewish community. Thus the foundation was laid for a perceptual shift on the part of many Syrian Jews, who now sought to divest themselves of their Ottoman citizenship to become protégés of Christian powers.

The Francos also fanned the flames of opposition to Laniado's insistence that his son Ephraim inherit his post as chief rabbi during his lifetime. Notwithstanding both the widespread opposition to this step and his own admission that the community had in its midst scholars more erudite than his son, Raphael Laniado continued to defend his son's appointment on halakhic grounds until his death in December 1793. The bitterness aroused by his uncompromising stance on both this issue and the application of communal regulations to the Francos increased after his son's appointment in 1787. Although certainly aware of the new forces in Aleppine Jewish society, Raphael Laniado refused to accept that the Laniado dynasty that had headed the city's Jewish community by virtue of inheritance would end with him. A typical product of the traditional value system in which his position and status, and those of his son, were vested, Laniado was unable to respond effectively to the challenge to this tradition's validity.[23]

Laniado may have won this particular battle, but the dynasty ultimately lost the war. Tempers cooled after Raphael Laniado's death and Ephraim Laniado continued to serve as chief rabbi until he in turn died in January 1805. As Ephraim had no surviving sons, Aleppo's scholars were now free to choose someone outside the Laniado family as their head, as first among equals. Thus ended not only the Laniado dynasty of chief rabbis of Aleppo, but also the practice of bequeathing the office of the city's chief rabbinate from father to son. None of the rabbis who subsequently headed the Aleppo Jewish community was succeeded by his son. Moreover, this episode's influence was not restricted to Aleppo: soon after these events dynastic inheritance of the chief rabbinate also ended in Damascus, where members of the Galante family had

---

[23] A definitive expression of Laniado's firmly held view on this matter is exemplified by his sermon 'Lema'alat morish kitro liveno ('On bequeathing his crown to his son'), published many years prior to the dispute in his *Hama'alot lishelomoh*, 170a–172b.

held this post. The criteria for choosing the chief rabbis in Damascus now underwent radical change as the principle of heredity was replaced by a process of election.

Nonetheless, the controversy over the succession to Raphael Laniado in Aleppo did not immediately affect the image of the early-nineteenth-century rabbinate in Syria. The winds of change had not yet blown up into a call for a rabbi with other qualities or even different, more modern training. Because modifications in the Ottoman administrative structure were in their infancy, a modern, well-formulated conception of the status and authority of the chief rabbi within the imperial apparatus had not yet emerged. In practice, the chief rabbi's status remained unaltered and he continued to serve as the recognized head of the community in the eyes both of its members and of the Ottoman authorities. Harbingers of alterations in the chief rabbi's status and function in the Syrian Jewish communities, and in other Jewish communities throughout the Ottoman empire, become evident only towards the mid-nineteenth century, as the spread of the Haskalah encouraged the growth and consolidation of an enlightened middle class, and after the implementation of the 1865 Jewish millet decree.

Nevertheless, the Laniado episode does mark an important moment in the history of the Syrian Jewish communities, a turn away from the old world towards modernity. It is worth taking a moment to examine this episode within the broader context of eighteenth-century Syria—an environment in which change and modernization took place in many spheres of life, even though the impact was in some cases not visible until the nineteenth century. Abraham Marcus persuasively argues that, despite the broad spectrum of changes he charts, eighteenth-century Aleppo 'was clearly not a society in a state of transition toward Western-inspired modernity'.[24] This was, however, only partly true of Aleppo's Jewish society, which differed from Muslim society by virtue of its absorption of European Jews, bearers of European culture to the Middle East. The resulting penetration of the new world and its values into the Jewish community from outside, and the spread of these ideas within the Syrian Jewish community, pre-dated by fifty years the famous European invasion of Egypt by Napoleon Bonaparte, priming these communities for change. Although the French invasion—the first military incursion of the modern West into the Middle East—shook Muslim complacency, providing the initial impetus for westernization and reform, a new state of affairs had already been created among Syrian Jewry by the earlier arrival of the Francos. Their differentiation from, and their socio-cultural influence on, the established Jewish community had begun to open up cracks in the hitherto absolute identification of the Jewish community with its religious and cultural structures. Whereas in the past the

---

[24] Marcus, *The Middle East on the Eve of Modernity*, 330.

community had been the accepted unifying force for all Jewish individuals in a particular locale, Aleppo's Jews in the latter half of the eighteenth century witnessed the beginning of a new order, different from the familiar historical one, in which it was now possible to remain outside the community legally—by virtue of exemption from communal *takanot*—and physically—by residing outside the Jewish quarter—and yet, at the same time, to exercise significant influence on the community. That the Francos did not necessarily view their primary social affiliation as Jewish was a revelation for their local co-religionists; and the appointment of members of the Picciotto family as consular representatives of Christian European powers came as a surprise to Jews and non-Jews alike.

During the episode of opposition to dynastic inheritance of the rabbinate, Aleppine Jews also experienced a new situation: disruption of the traditional interdependence of rabbi and *parnasim*, with the communal leadership—*parnasim* and scholars alike—openly opposing the chief rabbi's wishes. The Francos, having from the start refused to recognize or bow to the hegemony of the local rabbinate, constituted an important element in this new balance of power, emerging as a new natural leadership. Their residence outside the Jewish quarter, their lack of formal ties to the community, their challenge to the chief rabbi's status, and their penetration of, rather than separation from, the surrounding society, all constitute clear signs of the beginning of a transformation in the behaviour of the Jewish community to suit it to functioning in the modern world. These developments, not yet accompanied by abandonment of religious observance, did not constitute an ideological threat to the foundations of traditional Judaism, but did set Syrian Jewry on the path to modernization. Proceeding with caution, we can then argue that the path into a 'new era' for Aleppo's Jewish community was laid with the arrival of the Francos in the first half of the eighteenth century and widened in the conflict over the dynastic inheritance of the Aleppo rabbinate in the latter part of the century, and in the cessation of this practice in Damascus as well.

The eventual outcome—namely, the actual entry of the Syrian Jewish communities into the modern world—was the result of a long, slow process. It was the Francos who continued to carry the banner of progress, westernization, and modernization in the Syrian Jewish communities throughout the nineteenth century. As we shall see in later chapters, by providing their children with a modern western education they paved the way for the educational activity of the Alliance Israélite Universelle. But change in Jewish society was slow, and until the mid-nineteenth century the Francos were ahead of their time. In contrast to Christian Europe, where administrative and social life was opened up to the Jews—albeit on condition that they relinquished the characteristic clothing and language that distinguished them from others—the conservative Middle Eastern Muslim administrative and social milieux did not encourage change either for themselves or for their non-Muslim minorities.

The process sparked by the arrival of the Francos in the eighteenth century continued to reverberate and deepen in the nineteenth, accelerating with the enactment of reforms by the Ottomans upon the renewal of their rule in the Syrian region in late 1840. In telling the story of how the Syrian Jewish community experienced the Ottoman attempts at reform, I shall begin in the next chapter with an examination of life within that community during the nineteenth century, covering its demography, social stratification, occupational structure, and educational systems. Primarily focused on the large Jewish communities of Aleppo and Damascus, this analysis will show that each of these communities had distinctive features affecting the nature and speed of its response to the Tanzimat.

PART II

INTERNAL JEWISH LIFE

THE JEWISH POPULATION
OF SYRIA

THOUGH various difficulties confront the historian attempting to arrive at an accurate depiction of Jewish life in nineteenth-century Syria, a broad picture can be drawn of a largely urban pattern of settlement, concentrated in two main, distinct centres: Damascus and Aleppo. This part of the book examines the Jewish population's geographical distribution and demography, the defining characteristics of Jewish social identity and stratification, the role of Jews in the local economy, the nature of the Jewish leadership and the communal administration, and Jewish education, both traditional and modern, comparing and contrasting the two main communities and their individual responses to change during the Tanzimat era.

The Geographical Distribution of Settlement: Central and Satellite Communities

The distribution of Jewish settlement in Syria was not influenced by the dictates of the Muslim majority, which regarded the presence of the small Jewish minority as natural. Though unable to own land, Jews were not legally barred from settlement in any rural or urban areas in Syria, and it was internal Jewish considerations—primarily related to security, economic opportunity, and social and religious requirements—that determined the largely urban character of Syrian Jewish settlement and its concentration in the main centres of Aleppo and Damascus. Compared to rural areas and outlying towns, which were more vulnerable to attack by robbers or local militias, these cities, with their gubernatorial seats and military barracks, provided a greater degree of personal safety. The predominance of urban settlement also reflected the extremely limited involvement of Jews in agriculture, in consequence of the Islamic ban on Jewish landowning. Moreover, as way stations in east–west trade and important commercial centres, Damascus and Aleppo offered Jews a variety of commercial and financial opportunities. Finally, Syrian Jews typically sought to live in a supportive Jewish environment with a full range of communal services, such as a prayer quorum (*minyan*), a ritual bath, kosher food, a *talmud torah* (school), and a cemetery; nowhere in Syria do we find isolated settlements of single Jewish families, or even groups too small to provide a quorum within a non-Jewish setting. There were, however, smaller satellite communities in the towns surrounding Aleppo and Damascus, and these for the most part relied on the mother communities to meet their religious needs—for decisions on halakhic questions, for spiritual leadership, and for the provision of Jewish functionaries.[1]

Although Syrian Jewry lacked any regional umbrella organization, even of an ad hoc nature, this does not mean that individual settlements were isolated. The Aleppo and Damascus communities were linked to one another by marital as well as extensive economic and commercial ties, and by halakhic interchanges, even though physical travel between communities was not easy. Roads were poorly maintained, inhibiting both current travel and the introduction of modern means of transport such as carriages and trains; indeed, the time it took to travel from one community to the other remained virtually unchanged from earlier centuries. As late as 1883 the trip by mule from Damascus to Aleppo via Hama took twelve days; from Aleppo, it took three days to get to Antioch, one day to get to Kilis, and three days to get to ʿAyntab. In 1875, five years after work began on the new road from Aleppo to Alexandretta, it was still a difficult three-day journey from one to the other.[2] Until the early 1860s the postal system relied on a route that traversed the distances between Aleppo, Damascus, Beirut, Tripoli, Homs, and Hama once or twice a week. It was not until 1861 that Damascus and Aleppo were joined by a telegraph line.[3]

Traditions linking particular places to ancient events and figures, emphasizing the antiquity of the Jewish presence in Syria, also played a role in determining patterns of settlement. Aleppine Jews claimed a venerable past for their synagogue, attributing its construction to Joab ben Zeruiah (son of King David's sister Zeruiah and commander of his armies); the synagogue in the village of Tadef near Aleppo was sanctified by a tradition of a miracle performed there by Ezra the Scribe; and the synagogue in the village of Jobar near Damascus was reputedly built over a cave in which the prophet Elijah hid. Another tradition identified Urfa with Ur of the Chaldeans, Abraham's birthplace, and its inhabitants pointed out the local spring as the place where Abraham was thrown into the fiery furnace. The Jews in Antioch maintained that a grave located near the city was that of Hannah and her seven sons, martyred for their refusal to obey Antiochus Epiphanes' command to bow to idols.[4]

---

[1] For examples of this dependence, see A. Dayan, *Zikaron lanefesh*, 65; Neumark, *A Journey in the Old Land* (Heb.), 69; M. Dayan, *Yashir mosheh*, introd. to the Davidic genealogy.

[2] Neumark, *A Journey in the Old Land* (Heb.), 53, 56; Schur, *Maḥazot haḥayim*, 8. On the condition of the roads in Syria and their improvement, see Fawaz, 'The Beirut–Damascus Road'.

[3] Maʾoz, *Ottoman Reform*, 167; Rogan, 'Instant Communication'.

[4] For the traditions associated with various locations, see Sutton (ed.), *Aleppo, City of Scholars*,

Demographic Data

Any attempt to determine the number of Jews in the different Syrian Jewish communities must acknowledge that the numerous sources available are all based upon estimates rather than upon precise data. The results of the first official Ottoman census in Syria, from 1848, like those of earlier censuses held elsewhere in the empire, are incomplete; moreover, even contemporary observers questioned the extent to which this census reflected demographic reality.[5] The censuses carried out from 1881–2 to 1893, although more comprehensive and accurate than previous ones, by no means provide definitive data with regard to the non-Muslim minorities.[6]

Up until 1856 at least, the main purpose of the Ottoman censuses was to enhance tax collection by setting the list of taxpayers. Even when Ottoman censuses began to be conducted more in line with western aims and procedures, with a view to establishing the population's needs as well as their revenue-generating potential, the minority communities continued to regard them with suspicion. Seeking to reduce the number of taxpaying members on the list, which in turn would reduce the payment required to obtain release from army service, the Jewish and Christian communities tried to hide their true numbers. Attempts to arrive at a fuller demographic picture are also hampered by the lack of internal Jewish records of births and deaths, and of the death toll from the frequent, severe epidemics that swept across Syria until the mid-nineteenth century, when improved sanitation reduced fatalities.[7]

Another phenomenon affecting the Syrian Jewish population for which we have neither complete nor consecutive demographic data is migration, both external and internal. Although Syria was not a prominent destination for immigration, and the Jewish communal demographic structure in the country remained largely static, there is evidence for Jewish migration to and from Syria as well as movement from cities to towns and vice versa within Syria.

9–12; Neumark, *A Journey in the Old Land* (Heb.), 57; Schur, *Maḥazot haḥayim*, 16; Braslavy, 'Elijah Caves from Cairo to Aleppo' (Heb.), 54–5; Kestelmann, *Expeditions of the Emissary* (Heb.), 22; Hamway, *Zeman beit din*, 2b; Ben-Zvi, *Remnants of Ancient Jewish Communities* (Heb.), 484–90, 578–81.

[5] For descriptions of the 1848 census, see AECPC, Turquie, Damas, vol. 2, 23–30, Vattier-Bourville, Damas, 2 Mar. 1848; Porter, *Five Years in Damascus*, i. 138–9; Karpat, *Ottoman Population*, 26–30; Stanford J. Shaw, 'The Ottoman Census System'.

[6] On these censuses, see Karpat, *Ottoman Population*, 33–4; id., 'Ottoman Population Records', 237–74.

[7] From 1840 to 1880 there were many outbreaks of disease. See AECCC, Damas, vol. 2, 209, Edmond Combes, 14 Aug. 1848; Benjamin, *Eight Years in Asia and Africa*, 44–51; FO 195/800, Skene to Bulwer, Aleppo, 16 Oct. 1865; Jessup, *Fifty-three Years in Syria*, ii. 443; *JC*, 16 July 1875, p. 254.

One area from which Jews did migrate to Syria during this period was Algeria. Starting after the French invasion of Algeria in 1830 and increasing in 1848, Jews leaving Algeria for economic and social reasons joined thousands of Muslim Algerians heading for Syria. The emir ʿAbd al-Qadir, leader of the anti-French revolution, who himself left Algeria for Syria in 1848, sought permission for a large number of Algerians to do likewise and thereby escape humiliation under the yoke of Christian French rule.[8] An estimated thirty Algerian Jewish families were living in Damascus in 1847; by the end of the century that number had increased to eighty.[9] There is also evidence of settlement in Syria by several Ashkenazi families from Europe, most from Poland and Russia, though precisely how many is uncertain. The estimated twenty European Ashkenazi families who lived in Syria in the second half of the nineteenth century, mainly in Damascus, made no effort to preserve a separate identity and were absorbed by the long-standing local Jewish community. Finally, during the nineteenth century, motivated by economic factors or by the desire to escape persecution, Jews from Persia, the Uzbek cities of Bukhara and Samarkand, India, and Iraq also migrated to Syria.[10] However, Syria's declining status in international trade over the course of the century and its limited economic potential made it less attractive to those migrating on economic grounds. The consequent absence of large-scale immigration of Jews of different cultural backgrounds contributed to Syrian Jewish communal cohesion.

As for internal migration, many sources indicate that Jews relocated within Syria. The general trend, rooted in economic factors, was from villages and small towns to the cities, though there was movement between the large cities as well. In 1822 a destructive earthquake sparked a wave of relocation from Aleppo to Damascus, apparently swelling the number of Jews in Damascus from approximately three thousand to five thousand.[11] The disappearance of the Hama Jewish community under Egyptian rule with the conversion of its last Jew to Islam, and the later disbanding of the Jewish community of Hasbayah, probably as a result of the 1860 war between Christians and Druzes in Lebanon, also swelled the Damascus Jewish community.[12] In the region around

[8] For a comprehensive treatment of the Algerian migration, see Bardin, *Algériens et Tunisiens*; Schwarzfuchs, 'Aliyah from North Africa' (Heb.). See also Harel, 'The Citizenship of the Algerian-Jewish Immigrants'.

[9] See AECCC, Damas, vol. 1, 019–023, Ratti-Menton, 21 Dec. 1839; 072, Ratti-Menton, 22 Feb. 1842; 117, Devoize, 8 Mar. 1843; vol. 2, 146, 'Tableau des protégés qui se sont presentés à la chancellerie du Consulat de France à Damas pour y connaître leur titres. Conformément à l'avis du 1er Septembre 1847'; AECPC, Turquie, Damas, vol. 2, 23–30, Vattier-Bourville, 2 Mar. 1848.

[10] See e.g. *JC*, 1 Jan. 1869, p. 3.

[11] See Paton, *The Modern Syrians*, 39; Antebi, *Yoshev ohalim*, author's introd. For a detailed description of the earthquake of 13 Aug. 1822, which occurred at 21.50, see AECCC, Alep, vol. 26, 169–80.

[12] Abulafia, *Penei yitshak*, ii, 36b. On Aslan ibn Yaʾqub, the last Jew in Hama to convert to Islam, see Douwes, *The Ottomans in Syria*, 194 n. 16.

Aleppo, too, economic forces played the primary role in migration between the city itself and the surrounding Jewish communities. Towards the late 1870s, as the economic situation deteriorated, a clear trend developed of migration from Damascus, Aleppo, and their satellite towns to Beirut and overseas, which eventually resulted in the almost total abandonment of the smaller communities and the contraction of the larger ones.[13]

Up to the end of the nineteenth century Erets Yisra'el, although close to Syria, fairly easily accessible, and governed by the same regime, did not attract large numbers of Syrian Jewish immigrants. In fact, Syria's geographical proximity to the Holy Land made it feasible to visit briefly and return to Syria, while its partial halakhic parity with Erets Yisra'el meant that Syria's Jews felt less need to migrate and settle there. Even more significantly, unlike Jews in more distant communities, whose image of the Holy Land was coloured by its description in the Bible and rabbinic literature as a land flowing with milk and honey, Syrian Jews harboured no illusions about the conditions in their poorer southern neighbour, also under Ottoman rule.[14] Thus throughout the period in question we find Syrian Jews travelling back and forth between their homes and Erets Yisra'el, primarily for pilgrimage and not for settlement,[15] as described by Rabbi Isaac Abulafia: 'I reside here in Damascus, may the Lord found it well, behind our wall, the Western Wall, and caravans go daily from here to there and from there to here. Also the government mail service . . . and ships of fire [steamships] are constantly going back and forth.'[16] Those who did settle permanently in Palestine were usually the elderly, or individuals (mainly from the scholarly class) who wished to end their days and to be buried in Jerusalem. Others emigrated in response to particular economic or political pressure.[17]

The difficulties noted above in establishing accurate demographic data for the Syrian Jewish population apply to other sectors of the Syrian population as well. In the second half of the nineteenth century, estimates of the Muslim population of Damascus range from 70,000 to 150,000,[18] and of that of Aleppo

[13] See e.g. I. Dayan, *Imrei no'am*, 34*b*, no. 22; 40*b*; Saul Dweck Hakohen, *Emet me'erets*, 12*a*, no. 2. On Jewish emigration to Beirut, see Gagin, *Yismaḥ lev*, 39*b*, 'Even ha'ezer', no. 17; *JC*, 23 Nov. 1866, p. 8. For the development of Beirut and why it attracted immigrants, see Dahir, 'The Settlement Movement in the Arab East' (Arab.), 461–76.

[14] On Syria's halakhic status, see e.g. I. Dayan, *Zeh ketav yadi*, 422, 'Yoreh de'ah', no. 13; Tawil, *Et sofer*, 8*b*, 'Yoreh de'ah', no. 5; Moses Sutton, *Kehilat mosheh*, 43*a*; Bar-Deroma, *A Unique Conquest* (Heb.); Adler, *Jews in Many Lands*, 159.

[15] See Wilson, *The Lands of the Bible*, ii. 331–2. See also Jacob Saul Dweck Hakohen, *Derekh emunah*, author's introd., 9. On pilgrimage by the few Jews living in the town of Latakia, see Harel, 'Latakia' (Heb.), 62.

[16] Abulafia, *Lev nishbar*, 60*a*, no. 7.

[17] I. Dayan, *Imrei no'am*, 47*a*, 'Ḥoshen hamishpat', no. 30; Altaras, *Yitsḥak yeranen*, 2; Sasson, *Keneset yisra'el*, pt. 1, introd. Abraham Sasson.

[18] See FO 195/965, Burton to Elliot, Damascus, 1 Sept. 1870.

from 50,000 to 83,500.[19] Damascus' Christian population was estimated at anything from 13,000 to 18,000 individuals and that of Aleppo at between 16,000 and 20,000.[20]

The Syrian Jewish population figures for the main settlements also vary widely. Wide discrepancies between reports from the same year, in conjunction with annual variations, make it impossible to arrive at any precise figure for the Syrian Jewish population during the period under consideration. Nor can we establish definitively whether or to what extent specific Jewish communities in Syria experienced growth or decline, or what factors promoted these shifts. The data from the available sources are summarized in Table 2.1. However, using the more trustworthy results of the 1882/3–93 census (summarized in Table 2.2) it is possible to arrive at a relatively reliable assessment of general demographic trends among the Syrian Jewish communities between 1840 and 1880.

The demographic picture that emerges from these data shows that, for most of the period, the Aleppo Jewish community was larger than that of Damascus. Both communities showed a consistent rate of growth, as a result of a high birth rate and a decrease in mortality from a reduction of epidemics, whereas the satellite communities tended to lose population. In the 1880s, as mass migration overseas was just beginning, there were approximately 20,000 Jews in Syria.

Social Stratification

To an outside observer, the nineteenth-century Jewish Syrian communities may appear at first glance to be homogeneous. Indeed, nearly all the new arrivals, from the Spanish expellees to the few Ashkenazis, were absorbed by the long-standing Mustarib Jewish population and did not retain a separate identity. Heightening this first impression are the overwhelmingly urban nature of Syria's Jewish population, its concentration in a separate quarter of each town or city, and its unitary political and social establishment.

Yet the autonomous organization of a group with shared social and religious characteristics does not necessarily imply uniformity within that group. In actuality, the Jewish communities were not homogeneous but were divided internally: to a small extent by virtue of a few remaining heterogeneous elements, but mainly through social stratification, defined both economically (rich vs poor) and culturally (modern/western vs conservative/eastern orientation). In drawing a profile of the Syrian Jewish community it is also necessary to look beyond economic and cultural divisions to consider both other status-conferring criteria—wealth, lineage, scholarship, membership of the Francos, consular protection—and the role of women, both in general and

---

[19] See Murray, *Handbook for Travellers*, ii. 578.
[20] See FO 195/965, Burton to Elliot, Damascus, 1 Sept. 1870; Murray, *Handbook*, ii. 443, 578; AECCC, Alep, vol. 36, Destrée, 25 Feb. 1879.

Table 2.1. Population figures for Syrian Jewry

Place	Year	Population	Place	Year	Population
Damascus	1841	5,000	Aleppo	1847	3,500
	1842	4,850		1848	9,000
	1843	5,000		1855	5,500
	1847	3,000		1858	4,000
	1848	4,000/7,000		1859	8,500
	1855	5,000		1862	8,000
	1856	4,630/7,000		1865	8,000
	1857	5,000		1866	5,000
	1859	3,000/9,000		1868	3,500/6,600
	1866	6,000		1870	4,000/8,500
	1868	6,000		1872	8,500
	1870	4,000/7,000		1873	8,500
	1874	7,000		1875	10,000
	1881	7,000		1876	9,000
				1877	9,000/12,000
				1878	9,000
				1879	5,500/9,000
				1880	10,410
				1881	10,200
Urfa	1848	700	'Ayntab	1855	500
	1855	200		1860	180
	1875	700		1862	250
	1877	700		1875	900
				1877	750
Idlib	1862	700	Kilis	1848	250
				1855	750
				1860	180
				1862	400
Antioch	1848	650	Tadef	1848	90
	1855	250		1862	150
	1856	250			
	1860	180			
	1862	200			
	1879	300			
Alexandretta	mid-19th c.	20 families			

Sources: The various sources for demographic data on Syrian Jewry are as follows, by year: 1841—Paton, *The Modern Syrians*, 39; 1842—FO 78/498, Wood to Canning, Damascus, 19 May 1842; AECCC, Damas, vol. 1, 092, Statistique Religieux du Pachalik de Damas, 1842; 1843—Wilson, *Lands of the Bible*, ii. 356; 1847—Basili, *Memories from Lebanon* (Heb.), 330; 1848—Benjamin, *Eight Years in Asia and Africa*, 40–54; 1855—Wortabet, *Syria and the Syrians*, 198; 1856—Frankl, *The Jews in the East*, i. 291; Abraham Dayan, *Vayosef avraham*, 104a, no. 16; 1857—*JC*, 28 May 1858, p. 187; 1858—FO 78/1389, Skene to Earl of Malmesbury, Aleppo, 17 June 1858; 1859—*JC*, 21 Oct. 1859, p. 7; 1860—Kestelmann, *Expeditions of the Emissary* (Heb.), 22, 35; 1862—FO 78/1869, report of Skene, Aleppo, 5 June 1862; 1865—*JC*, 13 Jan. 1865, p. 2. 1866—Reischer, *Sha'arei yerushalayim*, 19; 1868—FO 78/2052, report of Skene, Aleppo, 25 Apr. 1868; 1870—AAIU, Syrie, III.E, Alep, 21, Behar, 22 Aug. 1870; FO 78/2260, Burton to Granville, Damascus, 28 Nov. 1870; FO 195/965, Burton to Elliot, Damascus, 1 Sept. 1870; Jean A. Bost, *Souvenirs d'Orient*, 71; I. Burton, *The Inner Life of Syria*, i. 105; 1872—*BAIU*, 2ème sem. 1871—1er sem. 1872, 128; 1873—*BAIU*, 1er sem. 1873, 1130 2ème sem. 1873, 116; 1874—AAIU, Syrie, XI.E, 94, Damas, Halfon et Belilios, 26 Aug. 1874; 1875—Schur, *Maḥazot haḥayim*, 8–16; 1876—*BAIU*, 2ème sem. 1877, 37; 1878—*BAIU*, 2ème sem. 1878, 19; 1879—AAIU, Syrie, II.E, Alep, 11, Altaras; AECCC, Alep, vol. 36, 013, Destrée, 25 Feb. 1879; *BAIU*, 1er et 2ème sem. 1879, 36; 1880—FO 195/1305, report of Henderson, Alep, 28 Aug. 1880l 1881—*BAIU*, 1er sem. 1881, 72, 74.

Table 2.2. Syrian Jewish population according to the 1882/3–1893 census[a]

	Damascus		Aleppo	
	City	Wilaya	City	Wilaya
Men	3,177	3,184	4,659	4,932
Women	3,088	3,093	4,697	4,981

[a] For the census results in tabular form, see Karpat, *Ottoman Population*, 263–5.

within each of the male-defined strata. Closer examination of each of these strata reveals significant structural differences between the two largest Syrian Jewish communities.

Economic Strata: Rich and Poor

In Damascus the Jewish community was polarized between a small group of about ten wealthy families and the overwhelming impoverished majority. The palatial residences of Damascus' affluent Jews were famed not only in the East but in Europe as well, and became tourist attractions for western travellers in Syria. One visitor commented: 'The beauty of these houses is unsurpassed even by those I saw in England for they are covered with gold and each and every courtyard has fountains and trees.'[21] Many eyewitness accounts note the hospitality of these families and the almost unrestricted access they offered to tourists wishing to see their homes.[22] This surprising openness, motivated largely by the householders' desire to display their wealth and to enjoy their guests' admiring exclamations, may also have served as a means of demonstrating their western orientation and differentiating themselves from the local population. This elite also displayed their prosperity and high status by daily trips on summer afternoons, mounted on white donkeys, to the nearby resort town of Jobar.[23] Their wealth endowed these families with considerable influence in the communal leadership; nonetheless, as we shall see, this influence was at times undermined by the rivalry that frequently surfaced between them.

Sharply contrasting with this handful of enormously wealthy Jewish families were the vast majority of the Damascene Jewish community, who lived in poverty. The class chasm was immediately visible to the visitor:

As opposed to a small number of enormously wealthy individuals, there are thousands of poor, who due to lack of work and employment literally die of starvation.

---

[21] Shneour, *Zikhron yerushalayim*, 18*b*. Other detailed descriptions of the palaces and their contents are found in scores of travel books. See e.g. Ashworth, *Walks in Canaan*, 277; Tilt, *The Boat and the Caravan*, 410–11; Woodcock, *Scripture Lands*, 37–8; M. Margoliouth, *A Pilgrimage to the Land of my Fathers*, ii. 244–5; Wilson, *The Lands of the Bible*, ii. 337–8; Burton, *The Jew, the Gypsy and el Islam*, 40–1, 171–2.

[22] See e.g. Wood, *An Eastern Afterglow*, 482; Murray, *Handbook for Travellers*, ii. 464–71.

[23] Kestelmann, *Expeditions of the Emissary* (Heb.), 16; Porter, *The Giant Cities of Bashan*, 340.

The wealthy live in marble palaces while the poor dwell in holes and burrows, a heartbreaking sight. The wives of the wealthy walk with mincing steps and rouged faces, their heads adorned with sapphires; the wives of the poor have nothing with which to cover their naked children, who faint from hunger at every street corner.[24]

In Aleppo, the gap between rich and poor was less pronounced. Although both social extremes were in evidence, here the majority of the Jewish population belonged to the middle class, which was almost non-existent in the Damascus Jewish community. Even the Aleppine rich were not as outstandingly or as ostentatiously wealthy as their Damascus counterparts, a difference noted by travellers to both cities.[25] Nonetheless, wealthy Aleppine Jews too had servants and took holidays in the mountain resorts near Antioch and Alexandretta or in Lebanon, or closer at hand in spots such as Tadef or ʿAyntab. At the other end of the spectrum, many Aleppine Jews could not afford meat, even on the sabbath and holidays.[26] But the gulf between these extremes was less noticeable than in Damascus, filled as it was with the city's large middle class.

Inequality between the affluent and the indigent was not confined to the large Jewish communities, being found also in smaller settlements, such as the town of Urfa. In 1875 a visitor to this largely poor town reported that members of the Dayan family were building large stone houses furnished with 'tables and chairs for sitting, and with utensils such as spoons, knives, and forks, things not found elsewhere in the Orient'.[27] This branch of an eminent Aleppo family had probably relocated to Urfa for business purposes.

Prominent Families: Hereditary and other Elites

Wealth or its absence was by no means the sole determinant of social position in the Syrian Jewish community; distinguished lineage conferred status quite separately from economic criteria, and Damascus and Aleppo alike boasted illustrious families. Outstanding among these was the Aleppine Dayan family, which claimed Davidic descent. A member of the Dayan family had for centuries served as chief rabbi and head of the court (*dayan* meaning 'judge'), and as the communal representative to the Ottoman authorities. The *dayan* derived not only honour but also a good income from his position.[28]

Some tension emerged in the sixteenth century between Jews arriving from Spain, whence they had been expelled, and the local Jews (Mustaribun), who sought to subordinate the Sephardis to the authority of the house of Dayan. Eventually the two communities amalgamated, with the Sephardis adopting

---

[24] *Hamagid*, 22, 9 June 1869, p. 172.

[25] See Neumark, *A Journey in the Old Land* (Heb.), 65–6.

[26] See Antebi, *Ḥokhmah umusar*, 34*b*–35*a*, 138*b*. For additional information on the behaviour of the rich, see J. A. D. Sutton, *Magic Carpet*, 179.

[27] Schur, *Maḥazot haḥayim*, 18.

[28] For details see M. Dayan, *Yashir mosheh*, introd. to the Davidic genealogy.

local customs and vice versa, so that with the exception of isolated practices nothing distinguished the two groups. A Sephardi was appointed chief rabbi, which united the community under a single leadership; the scions of the Dayan family, although no longer heading the rabbinic court, retained their other privileges.[29] Over time, the symbolic responsibilities of the Dayan family came to represent the preservation of the past and the depth of Syrian Jewish roots, for Sephardis and Mustaribun alike. The maintenance of respect for, and the privileges of, the Dayan family also reflected Jewish hopes for future redemption linked to the house of David.[30]

On the other hand, the entire community took pride in its Spanish roots, as the British consul Henderson noted in an 1880 report on the Aleppine community:

The Jews of Aleppo boast of being descended from those who were expelled from Spain in the beginning of the 16th century after having done so much for the prosperity and enlightenment of that country. They talk with pride of Isaac of Cordova, of Benjamin of Tudela, Hasdai the friend of Abd erahman [*sic*] the greatest of the Moorish kings of Spain and many other distinguished Israelites of Granada. They brought to the Levant that commercial activity and intelligence the loss of which was so much felt in the Western heart of the Mediterranean. In his religion the Aleppo Jew is, as St Paul says of himself before his conversion, a Hebrew of the Hebrews, and his traditional pertinacity on the subject of genealogies goes so far as to show the greatest respect for a poor family at Aleppo [the Dayan family] which is asserted to be lineally descended in the male line from King David.[31]

In Damascus, it was the Farhi family that enjoyed particular eminence. Although this status had no official form, and was not institutionalized by special communal privileges as was the case for the Dayans in Aleppo, as holders of senior posts in service to the rulers of Damascus the Farhis came to symbolize the power and status enjoyed by Syrian Jews of the previous century.[32]

---

[29] For a detailed consideration, see Harel, 'Conflict and Agreement' (Heb.), 122–9. On Aleppine customs, see Ades, *Derekh erets*. The fact that the additional clauses in Sephardi *ketubot* granted more favourable conditions to women perhaps underlies the demand by local women to introduce at least some of these clauses in their *ketubot*. See Antebi, *Mor ve'oholot*, 40a, 'Oraḥ ḥayim', no. 4; 56b, 'Oraḥ ḥayim', no. 12. See also M. Labaton, *Nokhaḥ hashulḥan*, 12b, 'Oraḥ ḥayim, no. 11; 24a, 'Oraḥ ḥayim', no. 15.

[30] M. Dayan, *Yashir mosheh*, introd. to Davidic genealogy.

[31] FO 195/1305, Henderson, explanatory memorandum to accompany approximate return of population of Vilayet of Aleppo, Aleppo, 28 Aug. 1880.

[32] The Farhis received attention both from their contemporaries and from later researchers. See e.g. Philipp, 'The Farhi Family'. For more recent studies containing many references to primary and secondary sources, see Shochetman, 'The Murder of the "Minister"' (Heb.); id., 'New Sources' (Heb.). For additional sources, including some in Arabic and some not mentioned in the studies cited above, see al-Dimashqi, *History of Events in Syria* (Arab.); Mishaqa, *Murder, Mayhem, Pillage and Plunder*, 64–7, 105–7. See also al-Qattan, 'The Damascene Jewish Community', 208–10; Bouchain, *Juden in Syrien*; Wilson, *The Lands of the Bible*, ii. 339.

Despite the fact that some family members became impoverished and lost their political influence, the members of the Jewish community continued to look up to the Farhis. Whenever a Farhi was chosen to fill some official position in the local Ottoman administration, Damascus Jews felt renewed hope for the renewal of their community's golden age, when its members held key positions in the corridors of power.[33]

The Francos, whose arrival in Aleppo was described in Chapter 1, comprised another elite. Unlike the Spanish exiles who were absorbed by the Mustaribun, the Francos maintained their distinct identity and status within the Jewish community. Over time, as its members were appointed consular representatives of various European powers, this group also acquired political power. Nevertheless, in spite of their social and economic detachment from the Jewish community, grounded in their foreign nationality and special commercial privileges, even in the nineteenth century the Francos did not establish a separate communal framework. Nor did Aleppo's commercial decline affect the standing of the Francos as a separate sector. Indeed, although their numbers dwindled, the Francos—the Picciotto, Altaras, Ancona, Belilio, Lofez, and Silvera families— both dominated and remained separate from the community and its institutions until the late nineteenth century.[34]

How did this group manage to remain separate from the local Jewish community some two centuries after its arrival in the Middle East? The answer to this question lies in the consular role of the Francos, and in particular of the Picciotto family. As long as members of this family held consular office, serving as official representatives of European countries, the Francos clung to the European habits and predominantly western orientation that differentiated them from the local Jewish population, despite their long-standing residence in Aleppo and their adoption of some eastern practices. It was for this reason that the independent framework of the Francos disappeared earlier in Damascus and other cities than in Aleppo.

It was perhaps in response to the erosion of their special status over the course of the nineteenth century that we find greater efforts among some of the Francos to preserve their prestige as a social elite—efforts which found expression mainly in the promotion of modern education and in the activity of the Alliance Israélite Universelle in Aleppo. It was the Francos who initiated contact with the Alliance with an eye to persuading it to open an elitist school in Aleppo for their children and for other upper-class children in the community.[35] As we shall see in the discussion of education in Chapter 5 below, this class snobbery aroused

[33] Wilson, *The Lands of the Bible*, ii. 341.

[34] AAIU, Syrie, III.E., Alep, 21, Behar, 13 Nov. 1869. See also Harel, 'The Overthrow of the Last Aleppan Chief Rabbi' (Heb.), 122–3.

[35] For an evaluation of the role of the Francos in the penetration of western education to the central Ottoman empire, see Rodrigue, *French Jews, Turkish Jews*, 39.

opposition within both Aleppo's Jewish community and the Alliance itself, further exacerbating the Francos' loss of status within the Jewish community.

The mid-nineteenth century saw the emergence of another elite stratum in the Jewish community, when European powers began to grant protection to a wider circle of individuals, including local residents, as part of their effort to broaden their sphere of influence in Syria. This new elite was particularly prominent in Damascus. Unlike the Francos in Aleppo, the new consular protégés were part and parcel of the Jewish community, although increasing contacts with western culture led to the adoption of some European habits and attitudes. Drawn in the main from the local wealthy, these individuals sought to use foreign protection to avoid both the Ottoman tax and judicial systems and Jewish communal regulations, in particular those related to communal taxation and summonses to appear before the rabbinical court.[36]

The members of this moneyed Jewish elite under foreign protection enjoyed not only increased status and influence within the Jewish community, but heightened importance in the eyes of prominent visitors from those European powers under whose aegis they lived.[37] Their local social contacts reached beyond the bounds of the Jewish community: they hosted parties and balls at their homes, and attended events sponsored by the foreign consuls in their homes or at the consulates.[38] The wealth, status, and connections of these Jewish consular protégés—those under British protection in particular—led the chief rabbis to name those of them in Damascus 'the elite of the Israelite nation'.[39] It was these individuals who set the tone for their community and acted as its mainstay.

The Scholarly Class

Status within the Jewish community was also conferred by rabbinic scholarship. In nineteenth-century Jewish Damascus and Aleppo, those recognized and approved by the community as Torah scholars numbered between forty and sixty individuals in each community, constituting a unique socio-religious elite.[40] Travel accounts up to 1875 testify to the existence of numerous yeshivas, many of which were located in the homes of affluent Jews. Indeed, maintaining a yeshiva and scholars in one's home was an important status symbol for the wealthy.[41]

[36] See e.g. NLIS, DA, V-736/72, Hillel Ezra de Picciotto to Abraham Hayim Gagin, Aleppo, 27 Heshvan 1843.
[37] See e.g. the descriptions of the visits of the Prince of Wales and of Prince Adalbert of Prussia to Damascus in *JC*, 23 May 1862, p. 5; see also M. E. Poujade, *Le Liban et La Syrie*, 213–14.
[38] Martineau, *Eastern Life*, 463.
[39] FO 78, vol., 2259, letter of Rabbis Aaron Jacob and Jacob Peretz to Rabbi Nathan Adler in London, 17 Elul 1870.
[40] See Laniado, *For the Sake of the Holy Ones* (Heb.), 167–8; Benayahu Collection, *Ḥet* 79, *Pinkas ḥalab*, 'Funding for rabbis, 1868–9'.
[41] Kestelmann, *Expeditions of the Emissary*, 13–14.

The scholarly class had its own internal hierarchy. At the apex of the pyramid were the chief rabbis and the members of the rabbinical court; below them were the various levels of teachers and religious functionaries; and at the base were the scholars who held no public posts.[42] The scholarly class as a whole enjoyed special privileges, pertaining mostly to exemptions from taxes, both communal and governmental. Because Torah scholarship was held to be fundamental to the Jewish community's spiritual existence, the community was obliged to support those who engaged in it, an arrangement regularized in halakhically grounded communal regulations.[43] The scholarly class also received additional financial support, provided in the main by the affluent members of the community. Such generosity was fostered by the notion that the divine reward for Torah study would be divided between the practitioner and the wealthy man who provided him with financial support, thereby releasing him from material concerns. Not only did these wealthy benefactors equip their yeshivas with extensive libraries (at considerable expense), they also awarded the scholars a weekly stipend.[44] In addition, every self-respecting man of means had a scholar-in-residence in his home, with whom he and his sons studied.[45] The prosperous members of the community also funded the publication of scholarly works written by members of the rabbinic class.[46] Another source of income for scholars derived from funds and property endowments (*hekdeshot*) from within the community or further afield, earmarked for the benefit of the scholars. Aleppo, for example, had a central fund administered by the scholars themselves, which disbursed stipends to some forty rabbis.[47] In Damascus there were several funds for scholars, some of which were administered by members of this group independently from the communal authority of the *parnasim*.[48]

Despite its relatively low economic standing, the scholarly class enjoyed high social status by virtue of its senior position in the communal institutional hierarchy as the group responsible—in the eyes of both its members and the Ottoman government—for the Jewish community's religious, legal, and educational infrastructure. Public gestures of respect for scholars, who were distinguished by their dress, speech, and manner of walking, included standing

---

[42] For a comprehensive treatment, see Zenner, 'Jews in Late Ottoman Syria', 175.

[43] Antebi, *Mor ve'oholot*, 100b, 'Ḥoshen mishpat', no. 13.

[44] NLIS, DA, V-736/218, Joseph Halfon Attiah, Elijah Laniado, and Moses Attiah to Abraham Hayim Gagin, Damascus, 1847; 13; Y. Abadi, *Kol rinah viyeshuah*, author's introd.

[45] Thus, for example, prior to becoming the chief rabbi of Damascus, Rabbi Jacob Peretz served as rabbi in Mordecai Farhi's home. See Wilson, *The Lands of the Bible*, ii. 338. For more examples, see NLIS, DA, V-736/215, Nissim Harari[?] to Abraham Gagin, Aleppo, Erev Shavuot 1847; NLIS, DA, V-736/28, 5 Sivan 1847.

[46] For a comprehensive treatment, see Harel, *The Books of Aleppo* (Heb.), 20–5.

[47] See Laniado, *For the Sake of the Holy Ones* (Heb.), 166–70; Hadaya, *Shalom la'am*, 34a.

[48] Abulafia, *Penei yitshak*, iii. 59b–60a, no. 13.

when a scholar passed by in the street: 'even those sitting in stores, with their legs folded under them in the Ishmaelite fashion, bow down and greet them'.[49] Among the masses, respect for scholars was enhanced by the popular belief in their power to bless or to curse.[50] Scholarly preaching, and the belief in the power of these sermons to elevate the souls of the dead, represented another fruitful source of income for the scholars, who were invited to speak on occasions such as memorial days for the dead, circumcisions, and weddings.[51]

At times, however, even these varied sources of income did not suffice to meet the needs of the entire scholarly class, forcing young scholars with families to abandon their studies in order to seek employment. This angered the chief rabbis and halakhists. However, recognizing that the fault did not always lie with the miserliness of the rich, the rabbinic authorities also encouraged scholars to acquire a profession so that they could be self-supporting.[52] A minority of scholars refused on principle to benefit from the communal treasury, or to be supported by prosperous Jews, and earned their own living from commerce or craft work.[53]

Rabbinic scholars had defined roles in the daily life of the Jewish community, some of which generated income. In addition to teaching and providing halakhic guidance, they oversaw the observance of *kashrut* regulations; [54] they were also paid for drawing up legal documents. Furthermore, the *dayanim* were entitled to receive an 'attendance allowance' from those appearing before the court.[55] Poor scholars earned their living by teaching in the *talmudei torah* (schools), although many parents neglected to pay the school fees, leaving the *melamedim* (teachers) with no means of support.[56] This forced the teachers not only to demean themselves by visiting the parents' homes to seek payment, but also to resort to other ways of earning small sums, such as the practice of going from house to house on the eve of Rosh Hashanah and Yom Kippur in order to release women from vows for a fee.[57] The situation improved somewhat with the opening of Alliance schools in Syria, when the teaching of Jewish subjects was kept in the hands of local scholars to appease conservative elements

[49] *Halevanon*, 7, 13 Nisan 1866, p. 102.

[50] For further detail, see Zenner, 'Jews in Late Ottoman Syria', 174–5; Zohar, *Tradition and Change* (Heb.), 61.

[51] *Halevanon*, 7, 13 Nisan 1866, p. 102.   [52] Antebi, *Ḥokhmah umusar*, 39b.

[53] Of these, the most outstanding was Rabbi Menasheh Sutton. See his *Maḥberet pirḥei shoshanim*, with an introduction by the author's grandson.

[54] For examples of the everyday role of scholars in the community, see e.g. Tarab, *Milei de'ezra*, 5b–7b, 'Oraḥ ḥayim', no. 6; 35b, 'Yoreh de'ah', no. 26; 56a, 'Yoreh de'ah', no. 36. See also id., *Sha'arei ezra*, 19a, 'Oraḥ ḥayim', no. 20; M. Abadi, *Ma'ayan ganim*, 107, 'Oraḥ ḥayim', no. 12; Sutton, *Vayelaket yosef*, 30a; Hamway, *Beit habeḥirah*, 27b.

[55] Benayahu Collection, Ḥet 86, *Pesakim*.

[56] Hamway, *Beit el*, 7b. On the failure of parents to pay tuition, see e.g. Abraham Dayan, *Zikaron lanefesh*, 37–8.

[57] On this custom, see J. Yadid Halevi, *Yemei yosef batra*, 132, 'Yoreh de'ah', no. 8.

in the community. For their part, the *melamedim* preferred to be hired by the Alliance than to be at the mercy of their pupils' parents.

Although always distinct from the rest of the population, until the 1880s the scholars made no attempt to organize as a class, either to establish common privileges or to provide for its members. Up to that time, the existence of a thriving wealthy elite made it worthwhile for a talented young scholar to devote himself to his studies, because this gave him access to a high-status social group and promised at least minimal financial support. When the bankruptcy of the Ottoman empire in 1875 impoverished even the wealthy Jews, this support evaporated, reducing the scholars in Aleppo, and even more so those in Damascus, to the level of the most indigent.

Changes in Ottoman regulations introduced as the processes of secularization and modernization took hold also impinged on the status of the Jewish scholarly class. In the mid-1870s the Aleppine authorities introduced taxes on property or residences owned by scholars, who had previously been exempt from such payments.[58]

As a result of these threatening developments, in the late nineteenth century Jewish scholars began to take steps to protect and regularize their status. One such step was to issue regulations securing their place in the community, both on the organizational level—to assert their role in the communal leadership and the communal obligation to support them, as in the past—and on the ideo-logical and religious plane.[59]

Social Mobility

From the above discussion, it appears that Syrian Jewish male society was neither closed nor rigidly stratified. Despite the contrasts between immense affluence and extreme indigence, between scholars and their wealthy supporters, between Ottoman citizenship and foreign protection, between the hereditary aristocracy and the masses, Jewish society did not bar the passage of individuals from one group to another. In principle, the poor could acquire wealth and join the affluent aristocracy; intellectual ability could make anyone a scholar; ties of marriage could confer prestige; and foreign protection could be purchased by almost anyone. Nonetheless, in practice the ability to move from class to class was limited. The elites who controlled the community's wealth also held the top communal leadership positions. The most striking way in which class boundaries were crossed arose from the desire of prosperous Jews to marry their daughters to scholars, even those without money. As a

---

[58] At that time a tax was also levied on religious institutions such as synagogues and study houses. See ACRI, TR/Is-162a, Aleppine rabbis to Rabbi Moses Halevi, Aleppo, 12 Shevat 1874; Rosh Hodesh Tamuz 1874.

[59] For further detail, see Harel, 'The Overthrow of the Last Aleppan Chief Rabbi' (Heb.), 129–30.

result, some scholars became exceedingly rich, whereas others remained desperately poor. The ability to devote time to Torah study depended upon the individual's economic status and means of support. For most Syrian Jews, forced to work for their livelihoods, becoming a scholar was not an option; nor did they have the means to purchase consular protection. Thus, in practice, the polarization between those in possession of the privileges associated with wealth, lineage, scholarship, and foreign protection, and those who lived under the burdens imposed by poverty, lack of education, and Ottoman citizenship, remained largely in effect throughout the nineteenth century. Because the communal leadership was in the hands of the affluent, it was they who continued to set the tone for the Jewish community as a whole.

Women

Syrian women, including Syrian Jewish women, enjoyed fewer rights than men. In the monogamous patriarchal family structure that prevailed in nineteenth-century Syria, the Jewish woman had a single task: running the household and caring for the family unit, serving her husband and children. Husbands generally enjoyed greater rights in any joint property; wives' prerogatives to make use of this property were limited. From birth, sons enjoyed a higher status than daughters, and some families even regarded the birth of a daughter as a burden.[60] Fathers aspired to marry off their daughters as soon as they were of age to someone who could relieve them of the responsibility for their financial support. Marriage and childrearing represented the pinnacle of a woman's role, her self-fulfilment. In essence, being married was understood as a woman's natural state. Jewish society encouraged single women, divorcees, and widows to marry so that they would not constitute a drain on the communal coffers and to reduce the incidence of sexual laxity and prostitution. Women, however, rarely had a say in choosing their mates. Marriage was part of the patriarchal system: finding suitable husbands for his daughters was a father's responsibility and fell under the scope of his authority. Love, physical attraction, and feelings of intimacy were not recognized preconditions for marriage; if such feelings developed, this usually occurred after marriage.

Both the lower and the scholarly classes perceived women as the most ignorant in society and repeatedly criticized both their beliefs and their behaviour.[61] Notwithstanding their exclusion on principle from the ritual and intellectual parts of Jewish life, faith played a central role in women's lives; theirs was not a faith grounded in scriptural study, but rather one based on folkloristic traditions handed down from mother to daughter. Often intermingled with superstition, these traditions extended to the performance of

---

[60] On the 'burden of a daughter', see Lamdan, *A Separate People*, 24–57.
[61] Abraham Dayan, *Holekh tamim*, 55a, 57b.

rituals based on pagan customs, such as the Aleppine practice of *indolico*, the curing of illness by making ceremonial offerings to 'demons'.[62] Indisputably, the foundations of this ignorance lay in the fact that women received no schooling and consequently did not know how to read or write. It is also possible that the exclusion of women from any role in the ritual framework impelled them to find an outlet for their religious impulses in quasi-religious activity such as magic.

In spite of women's generally low status and exclusion from any positions of public influence, the communal rabbis did make attempts to improve their status, in the family nucleus at least. This trend was grounded in the rabbis' recognition of the changing social reality, genuine concern for women, and their desire to preserve the stability of the family unit. Male superiority remained the rule within the family setting, and was absolute in the communal order and its leadership. Nonetheless, the latter half of the nineteenth century saw the promulgation of communal regulations aimed at improving the status of women, particularly in relation to their husbands. Thus women were granted the opportunity to insert into their marriage contracts clauses providing certain protections. To existing and accepted conditions such as those requiring her consent to a divorce or to her husband taking a second wife, new conditions, specifically related to the processes affecting Syrian Jewish society, were added. One particular example is linked to the trend of emigration from Syria. In marriage contracts from this period we find clauses forbidding a husband to force his wife to leave her home town and thereby cut her off from her extended family.[63] In addition, although the practice was not widespread, the rabbis spoke out sharply against the marriage of young girls to elderly widowers.[64] Another phenomenon against which the rabbis battled was that of physical abuse within the family. For example, the Damascus rabbinical court had no qualms about throwing abusive husbands into gaol, even though wife-beating was accepted as normal in Syrian society as a whole.[65]

The situation of Jewish women in Syria as outlined above did not apply to the thin layer of wealthy Jews—that distinct stratum of aristocratic women in Jewish society composed of the wives of the Francos and of other wealthy members of the community. On the contrary, indeed, it seems that the conventions of high society influenced the passing of regulations aimed at improving the

---

[62] See the 1852 regulation of the Aleppine rabbis against this phenomenon, cited by Sutton, *Kenesiyah leshem shamayim*, 75b–76a. See also M. Abadi, *Ma'ayan ganim*, 277, 'Yoreh de'ah', no. 11. For a comprehensive treatment of the practice of offering sweets to demons, known as *indolico*, see Gaon, *The Sages of Jerusalem* (Heb.), 136–43. See also Zimmels, *Magicians, Theologians, and Doctors*, 84–5, 140, 146.

[63] See e.g. Antebi, *Mor ve'oholot*, 146b, 'Oraḥ ḥayim', no. 13; Abulafia, *Penei yitsḥak*, i. 75a, no. 15.

[64] See M. Abadi, *Melits na'im*, 7, no. 102; 30, no. 245; Abraham Dayan, *Tuv ta'am*, 196.

[65] *Halevanon*, 23, 13 Kislev 1865, p. 362. On the status of women in the Muslim court in the seventeenth and eighteenth centuries, see Tucker, *In the House of the Law*.

status of Jewish women in general. There is ample evidence that the aristocratic Jewish women of Damascus, who had no real role even within their own households, spent their time dressing up, smoking water-pipes, and attending social gatherings. This was certainly unusual behaviour in the Middle East: these women dressed boldly and revealingly, remained at their husbands' side in the presence of European guests, and even took part in the conversation and smoking.[66] Moreover, they were invited to parties and balls in the homes of foreigners, including European consuls, where they appeared in their unique attire and danced before the guests bedecked in their jewels.[67] European guests were generally both startled and impressed by these women: alongside expressions of surprise at their manner of dress and use of cosmetics, and amazement at the opulence of their jewellery, several travellers expressed their astonishment that, as opposed to Muslim women, Jewish women in Damascus were not isolated from participation in society. They noted not only that these women had graciousness and manners that would not embarrass European nobility, but also that they were capable of conversing intelligently on matters of religion. These upper-class Jewish women were certainly aware, moreover, of the generally low social status of women, for there is evidence that they discussed the subject with European visitors.[68]

In Aleppo, the wives of the Francos constituted a similar modern Jewish female aristocracy, and their status differed from that of other Jewish women. They wore European clothing and walked about the city streets either unaccompanied or in the company of men.[69] It is possible that their influence led to the abandoning of the practice of face-covering by all Jewish women, whereas Muslim and Christian women continued to adhere to this custom.[70] In Aleppo and Damascus the majority of Jewish women did not generally leave their homes at all:

The custom is that women do not leave their houses for the market or the street in order to make purchases; their honour is to stay within . . . And it is the husband's role to bring home all the necessities; even if he is extremely wealthy no shame attaches to his shouldering a sack, and going to the market to purchase the household necessities, from bread to meat and vegetables.[71]

---

[66] See e.g. Wilson, *The Lands of the Bible*, ii. 337; Lynch, *Narrative*, 492–3.

[67] Martineau, *Eastern Life*, 463; I. Burton, *The Inner Life of Syria*, i. 142–3. In this practice, they did not differ from upper-class Turkish women. See Fanny Davis, *The Ottoman Lady*, 131–55.

[68] See Wilson, *The Lands of the Bible*, ii. 330, 337–8; I. Burton, *The Inner Life of Syria*, i. 142–3; Lynch, *Narrative*, 492–3; Martineau, *Eastern Life*, 463; *JC*, 11 June 1858, p. 202; Woodcock, *Scripture Lands*, 44–6; M. Margoliouth, *A Pilgrimage to the Land of my Fathers*, ii. 260. For more negative impressions, see e.g. George W. Curtis, *The Howadji in Syria*, 264–7.

[69] See Harel, 'The Controversy over Rabbi Ephraim Laniado's Inheritance', 90.

[70] Antebi, *Ḥokhmah umusar*, 116b–117a; Guys, *Voyage en Syrie*, 279.

[71] Kestelmann, *Expeditions of the Emissary* (Heb.), 19–20.

There was one exception, however. Upper-class Jewish women in Aleppo and Damascus, and, in their wake, other Jewish women, went to the bazaars on their own in order to purchase items of clothing. This flew in the face of the accepted convention in the East, in which the husband made all purchases for his wife's needs, and angered many rabbis:

And in the glorious city of Damascus . . . it is the custom that the women go on their own to the bazaar to purchase clothing for themselves whenever they like, and not via their husbands. And they bargain more than men do. Even respectable women do so, and this is a widespread affliction.[72]

The behaviour of the wealthy, aristocratic women of Aleppo had its influence on the city's middle-class women, many of whom adopted a conspicuously ostentatious and wasteful lifestyle, even leading to bankruptcy in some cases, as Rabbi Abraham Antebi described:

And we are witness to the phenomenon that even he who is not wealthy spends more than his means on fine clothing and jewellery for his wife. He is forced against his will to fulfil all of his wife's desires, for each woman is jealous of her neighbour. When she sees her neighbour wearing handsome garments she is seized by a fit of jealousy and desires to wear clothes just as nice and fights with her husband, screaming at him night and day until he purchases what she desires; even though she knows her husband does not have the same means as his fellow, nonetheless, she forces him . . . And because of this her husband is forced to borrow and is unable to repay the loan . . . Some householders have descended into poverty because of their wives . . . And in particular, in our generation, when new fashions for women appear yearly and they reject the previous year's, which are put away, women want to wear the latest fashion, and poor women wish to imitate the rich.[73]

The wealthy elite, with its openness to modernization, also differed from the community at large in its wish to educate daughters as well as sons. In the absence of any Jewish educational framework for girls, many members of this elite sent their daughters to Catholic or Protestant schools.[74] When the Francos appealed to the Alliance to found a school in Aleppo, they wished it also to found a school for girls, so that their daughters would not have to attend Christian institutions. In Damascus, too, it was the wealthy elite that spearheaded the initiative to open a school for girls. Thus, in addition to facilitating the penetration of Syrian Jewry by western Christian education in general and the Alliance Isráelite Universelle in particular, the wealthy, western-oriented, European Jewish families in Damascus and in Aleppo played a crucial role in the

---

[72] Gagin, *Yismaḥ lev*, 34*b*, 'Even ha'ezer', no. 14.

[73] Antebi, *Ḥokhmah umusar*, 31*b*–32*a*, 119*b*. See also Abraham Dayan, *Tuv ta'am*, 199–202.

[74] This phenomenon expanded mainly during the 1860s; it did, however, exist on a smaller scale earlier. On women's education in Ottoman society in general, and among the elites in particular, see Davis, *The Ottoman Lady*, 45–60.

beginnings of improvement in the status of Jewish women in Syria. This influence touched many aspects of women's lives, but its primary effect was in women's education. It is indicative of a changed awareness, and of a willingness to take steps to improve the status of at least a certain sector of the female Syrian Jewish population, that in 1885 a women's committee of Alliance members was established to work alongside the men's committee.[75]

*

This chapter has shown that an apparently homogeneous Syrian Jewish community was in fact a markedly stratified society, divided mainly according to wealth and western or eastern orientation. The next chapter looks at the occupational spheres that formed the backbone of the Jewish economy—on which the class distinctions in Jewish society described in this chapter were in part based—and at the Jewish response to the shifting fortunes of the Syrian economy.

[75] *BAIU*, 2ème sem. 1885–1er sem. 1886, 134. For the influence of the changing economic situation on the status of women in Aleppo, see Meriwether, 'Women and Economic Change'.

THREE

THE JEWS IN THE
LOCAL ECONOMY

T HE Ottoman regime imposed few restrictions on the economic activity of
Jews, who were neither barred from, nor forced to pursue, particular occupations. Where Jews were excluded from a specific sector, this was the result
of the inflexible Ottoman guild system. Syrian Jews engaged in a wide variety
of occupations, ranging from crafts and small workshops to lending on credit
and investment in light industry and agriculture. Before examining this activity in any detail, however, it is necessary to consider its context: the economic
decline of the Ottoman empire.

The Ottoman Empire in Economic Decline

A number of factors were responsible for the economic deterioration of the
Ottoman empire in the mid-nineteenth century. External factors, such as the
transfer of international commercial traffic to the sea routes across the Atlantic
and around Africa, and the opening of the Suez Canal in 1869, were exacerbated by internal factors, above all the inept imperial management of the economy. Huge expenditures on military campaigns, a balance-of-payments deficit,
and the failure to direct funds to economic and technological development in
agriculture and industry had crippling financial effects. The imperial administration's economic difficulties peaked in 1875, when it was forced to declare
bankruptcy. Industrialized, capitalist western Europe was at the centre of the
new nineteenth-century world economic order, and the unindustrialized
Ottoman empire was pushed to the sidelines. For all its efforts to become part
of the new economic order, the Ottoman empire thereafter remained a secondary force in world trade.[1]

---

[1] For studies treating the role of the Ottoman economy in the new world economic order and
its influence on Ottoman development, see e.g. Kasaba, *The Ottoman Empire and the World Economy*; Ilkay Sunar, 'State and Economy in the Ottoman Empire'; Wallerstein et al., 'The Incorporation of the Ottoman Empire into the World-Economy'; Wallerstein and Kasaba,
'Incorporation into the World Economy; Pamuk, *The Ottoman Empire and European Capitalism*.

Syria was badly affected by these trends, impoverished by its loss of importance as a transit point in east–west trade, the decline of trade and crafts, the
dangers of travel, and the absence of public projects, coupled with heavy taxation and monetary instability. Although foreign trade brought some development of commerce and agriculture in its wake, at the same time it destroyed
what remained of local production and industry. Syria was flooded with cheap,
high-quality European goods, which the Syrians purchased in preference to
local products. The sector worst affected by this shift was textile production,
Syria's foremost industry.[2]

Commercial activity, in particular that of local merchants, was impaired by
the capitulation agreements commonly used in the Ottoman empire. Confined
at first to small groups of foreign traders temporarily located in the Middle East,
over time these agreements were transformed into a broad system of immunity
and economic privileges. The advantages they conferred on foreign traders were
enhanced towards the mid-nineteenth century when further commercial agreements extended the privileges they enjoyed, such as exemptions from various
taxes and favourable import/export duties. Local merchants, on the other hand,
continued to pay high taxes and duties, making economic activity on their part
unprofitable and leading to nearly total economic stagnation.[3] Because many
Ottoman Christian and Jewish traders became foreign protégés, they were able
to benefit from the privileges granted to foreign traders. In an effort to stem the
growth of this phenomenon and reassert imperial control over the Ottoman
treasury and the proceeds of the empire's economic activity, in the first half of
the nineteenth century the Ottoman regime granted similar economic privileges to local residents. Notwithstanding the manifold economic advantages
granted to the 'sultan's entrepreneurs', as they were known, whose numbers
included Jews, the success of this measure was limited.[4] The fact that some Jews
and Christians were actually foreign nationals or had purchased foreign citizenship facilitated the concentration of foreign trade in largely non-Muslim
hands, and it was the non-Muslim minorities that flourished economically.

Foreign Trade and Moneylending

Sources providing details of the various facets of Jewish trading and finance
are sparse. Much of this activity was shrouded in secrecy, in part because of the

---

[2] Some studies argue that the textile industry in Aleppo was affected much less, if at all, than is
generally thought. See e.g. Firro, 'The Impact of European Imports'; Quataert, *Ottoman
Manufacturing*, 71–9. On the influence of the European economy on Damascus, see Rafiq, 'The
Damascus Economy' (Arab.); id., 'The Impact of Europe on a Traditional Economy'. See also
Reilly, 'From Workshops to Sweatshops'.

[3] See Chevallier, 'Western Development and Eastern Crisis'.

[4] Masters, 'The Sultan's Entrepreneurs'; Bagis, 'The Impact of Beralti Tuccari'.

Jewish belief that business hidden from the eyes of others will be blessed, in part because a good deal of it was not entirely legitimate. Nonetheless, the extant sources do provide some information regarding the types and estimated scope of Jewish economic activity.

In the early 1840s this was concentrated in foreign trade. Jewish control of the Damascus *wilaya*'s foreign trade was so entrenched that its Jewish merchants were described as the wealthiest group in the district. Contemporary sources mention twenty-four Jewish commercial houses, which traded mainly with Britain, and whose monetary turnover rivalled that of even their leading European counterparts.[5] Jewish traders were also well represented, though not so dominant, in the immense camel caravans that travelled between Damascus and Baghdad and from there to Persia and India.[6] Aleppo's Jewish merchants also participated in the eastward-bound commercial caravans leaving from their home town, but to a lesser extent.[7] However, by the mid-1850s the increased danger of bandit attacks on caravans, coupled with the declining importance of the overland routes in world trade, led many Jewish merchants to abandon trade with the East and to direct their wealth and enterprise towards other pursuits.[8]

The Jewish merchants of Damascus and Aleppo responded differently to the changing economic situation. For most Damascus traders, foreign trade was relegated to second place behind banking and finance. This was not the case for Aleppo's Jewish merchants, the Francos in particular. They continued to concentrate on international trade with the West, dispatching family members to Europe to implement import–export deals, and appointing representatives to open branches in European trading centres, including London, Manchester, Liverpool, and Marseilles.[9] Following the Lebanese civil war of 1860 and the Damascus massacre of Christians in the same year, Europeans in Syria withdrew from the import trade, fearing to do business there, and a significant portion of this trade passed from European traders into the hands of non-Muslim Syrians.[10]

[5] Bowring, *Report on the Commercial Statistics of Syria*, 94. See also al-Hasani, *The Economic History of Syria* (Arab.), 201. In 1842 Jews owned four of seven British commercial houses in Damascus. By 1848 there were five British Jewish commercial houses out of six. See FO 78/872, 'List of British Mercantile Houses established at Damascus, 1842'; 'List of British Mercantile Houses established at Damascus, 1848'. On the development of British trade with Syria, see Issawi, 'British Trade and the Rise of Beirut'.

[6] On a 4,500-camel caravan whose merchandise was owned mainly by Damascene Jewish traders, see Wilson, *The Lands of the Bible*, ii. 364.

[7] See Antebi, *Mor ve'oholot*, 92a, 'Ḥoshen hamishpat', no. 11.

[8] On the plundering of caravans, deaths, and bankruptcies, see FO 78/538, 'Procuration of the Merchants of Damascus to Mess. Piccioto and Taras of Aleppo' 12 June 1843; FO 78/1297, Skene to de Redcliffe, Aleppo, 15 July 1857; FO 78/714, Timony to Cowley, Damascus, 1 Sept. 1847.

[9] Harel, 'The First Jews from Aleppo'. For extensive illustration of this method of trading, see Rozen, 'The Fattoria' (Heb.); FO 78/1934, Skene to Clarendon, Aleppo, 1 Jan. 1866.

[10] Tibawi, *A Modern History of Syria*, 139. The massacre of 1860 is discussed in Ch. 9 below.

Improved methods of transport, in particular the introduction of steamships, made direct contact between commercial houses much easier. In consequence, Syrian commercial houses now preferred to open branches in Europe rather than to rely on European factors in Syria. This both made maintenance of foreign houses in Aleppo unprofitable and at the same time enabled Jewish commercial houses in Aleppo to expand in what was almost a reversal of the conditions that had originally brought the Francos to the city.[11] Whereas at first western traders had sent their representatives to the East, as those pioneering entrepreneurs settled in their new environment and economic conditions changed, they began to send their own representatives from East to West.[12] Thus, from the mid-nineteenth century on, Aleppine Jewish involvement in international trade, especially in the import business from England and America, acquired greater importance. The evidence suggests that more than half of Syrian–English trade was in Jewish hands during this period: in 1857 nine of the sixteen Aleppine merchants possessing foreign nationality who presented a petition to the British consul Henry Skene, asking him to approach the Ottoman authorities with a request to build a pier in the port of Alexandretta (through which most of the Aleppine import–export activity passed), were Jews.[13] Eight years later, twenty-eight of the forty-nine Aleppine import–export agents with Ottoman citizenship who sent a complaint to the same consul, asking him to intervene in the Ottoman plan to move the customs house from Aleppo to Alexandretta, were Jews.[14]

As Syria's importance as a way station in international trade declined, it became an exporter of raw materials and an importer of manufactured goods.[15] But even this level of activity could not survive the opening of the Suez Canal in November 1869, which had a particularly severe effect on Aleppo. Up to that point, the remaining overland trade between the Persian Gulf and the Mediterranean had been channelled via Aleppo and the port of Alexandretta; but now the overland route was almost totally overtaken by the new, swift, safe, and less costly sea route, with the result that Syrian commercial activity dwindled to trade in goods for local consumption and agricultural exports. According to Victor Bertrand, the French consul in Aleppo from 1863 to 1878, the

---

[11] AECCC, Alep, vol. 33, pp. 106–26, Bertrand, 21 Mar. 1865.

[12] See Harel, 'The First Jews from Aleppo'; Halliday, 'The Millet of Manchester'.

[13] FO 78/1297, Skene to Stratford de Redcliffe, Aleppo, 28 July 1857. See also the petition addressed by the merchants Silvera and Picciotto to British Consul Barker on 18 Feb. 1856 in FO 195/416.

[14] FO 78/1877, 'A petition of the Merchants living under the protection of the Imperial Ottoman Government in Aleppo', 16 Nov. 1865.

[15] For examples of such goods, see AECCC, Alep, vol. 31, pp. 287 ff., Jeofroy, 22 Oct. 1853; Ma'oz, *Ottoman Reform*, 177–8; M. Labaton, *Nokhah hashulhan*, 57b, 'Hoshen mishpat', no. 14; 59a, 'Hoshen mishpat', no. 15; I. Dayan, *Zeh ketav yadi*, 238, 'Hoshen mishpat', no. 16; id., *Imrei no'am*, 10b, no. 8.

Aleppine merchants, first and foremost the Jews among them, had failed to foresee the inevitability of a crash and continued to import goods from abroad as in the past, flooding the markets and in consequence having to cut prices to the point of losing any profit on sales or even making a loss. Eventually, a few of the merchants scaled down their commercial activity; however, the majority, including most of the Jewish merchants, stubbornly persisted in buying and selling at any price. Although they succeeded in delaying economic collapse, they could not prevent it indefinitely, and in 1874 catastrophe struck.[16] The first of the commercial houses to be bankrupted was that of the Austrian protégé David Solomon Altaras, hitherto one of the largest and most successful concerns in Aleppo. Its downfall set off a chain reaction among other Aleppine commercial houses and businesses.[17]

Although several Jewish commercial houses failed in the mid-1870s, and most of the important Jewish merchants were hard hit by the economic crisis engendered by the shift away from overland routes in the first half of the decade, this crisis did not lead to the economic collapse of the Jewish collective framework. A number of commercial houses managed to ride out the crisis to some extent and continued to function, albeit with more limited scope.[18] But what gave stability to Aleppo's Jewish communal structure and enabled it to go on functioning through these troubled times was its large middle class, which remained unaffected by the crisis.

In Damascus, on the other hand, the opening of the Suez Canal had little effect on the city's wealthy Jews because they had largely withdrawn from international trade some years earlier. Their concentration on the wealth-generating occupations of banking, finance, and moneylending enabled them to weather, at least for a year or so, the economic crisis sparked by the opening of the canal that affected their co-religionists in Aleppo so profoundly. When the breakdown of Damascene Jewry's economic infrastructure came, it differed both in nature and in severity from that of its Aleppine counterpart.

Although Damascus Jews were involved in granting loans and credit even earlier than the nineteenth century, the decline in foreign trade and other shifts in economic activity in the mid-nineteenth century saw Jewish involvement in these occupations expand.[19] Runaway inflation prevented the Ottoman empire from achieving economic stability, and attempts at monetary reform repeatedly

---

[16] AECCC, Alep, vol. 35, pp. 176–80, Bertrand, 23 Nov. 1874; AAIU, Syrie, III.E., Alep, 21, Behar, 22 Aug. 1870; III.E., Alep, 23, Behor, 24 July 1879.

[17] *Hadiqat al-akhbar*, 853, 17 Dec. 1874, back page (unnumbered); *Ḥavatselet*, 12, 24 Tevet 1874, p. 97. Some of the merchants who had commercial ties with Jews viewed them as scoundrels and cheats. The Altaras house was accused of fraudulent acts that caused the collapse of commercial houses in Aleppo and in Europe. See e.g. Guys, *Voyage en Syrie*, 278–9; AECCC, Alep, vol. 35, pp. 176–80, Bertrand, 23 Nov. 1874. [18] See *BAIU*, 1er sem. 1884, 56.

[19] See al-Qattan, 'The Damascene Jewish Community', 203–4; Cohen, 'Damascus and Jerusalem' (Heb.).

failed.[20] In 1870 at least twenty-five coins of varying values, issued in different countries, were circulating in Damascus. The imperial banking system consistently failed to direct imperial financial activity effectively.[21]

In the absence of banks in Aleppo and Damascus prior to the late nineteenth century, and the failure of the Ottoman Bank, founded in Beirut in 1856, to control the monetary system or to meet the needs of the local economy, Jews filled the gap left by the bank's inability to provide credit on a large scale. The wealthy Jews of Damascus, in particular, took full advantage of the opportunity. Private banks, which ignored the official rate of 8 per cent set in 1851 and charged exorbitant interest rates, entered the picture.[22] Their loan and credit businesses focused on three main areas: loans to the government, loans to commercial companies, and loans to peasant farmers or *fallahin* in rural Syria.[23]

Huge imperial military and administrative expenditures and the balance-of-payments deficit forced the Ottoman authorities to take loans from these private banks. The Damascus regime in particular required funding to finance and protect the *mahmal*—the annual caravan to Mecca—which it obtained from Jewish banks.[24] But its inability to meet the deadlines on loans made against interest-bearing treasury bonds increased the Jewish bankers' reluctance to lend to the regime. For their part, desperate for Jewish loans, on which they were almost totally dependent, the local Ottoman authorities offered high interest rates as an inducement, ultimately increasing their own liabilities.[25]

Faced with Jewish resistance to advancing funds to the *wilaya* treasury, the Damascus authorities took the radical step of imposing an obligatory loan on wealthy Jews. This in turn motivated many Jews to request foreign consular protection in order to avoid harassment by the Ottoman authorities whenever the latter found themselves in need of credit.[26] Thus a breakdown occurred in the traditional relationship between the sovereign authorities and wealthy Jews that had characterized the Ottoman Jewish economy for generations,

[20] See Gerber and Gross, 'Inflation or Deflation'.

[21] See I. Burton, *The Inner Life of Syria*, i. 179. On monetary activity in the empire and in Syria, see Pamuk, *A Monetary History*, 205–22; Ma'oz, *Ottoman Reform*, 170–1. See also Christopher Clay, 'The Origins of Modern Banking', 589–91.   [22] Ma'oz, *Ottoman Reform*, 171–2.

[23] The observation that Jews were barely involved in moneylending at interest in the Ottoman empire does not apply to the nineteenth-century Damascene Jews. See Haim Gerber, 'Jews and Money-Lending'. On Jewish involvement in moneylending, see Schilcher, *Families in Politics*, 83–6.

[24] For a comprehensive treatment of the organization, protection, and financing of the *mahmal* in the eighteenth century, see Rafeq, *The Province of Damascus*, 52–76; id., 'The Syrian Pilgrimage Caravan' (Arab.). For the financial activity of Jewish bankers during the organization of the *mahmal*, see Elmaleh, 'Nouvelles sources' (Heb.), 46.

[25] FO 78/499, Wood to Earl of Aberdeen, Damascus, 12 July 1842.

[26] FO 78/660B, Timoni to Bidwell, Damascus, 6 July 1846. When there was a shortage of currency during the pre-Tanzimat period, the government solved its cashflow problem by imposing heavier taxes on the Jews and Christians. See AECADN, Damas, 01, Cote A/18/54, Beaudin à Regnault, Damas, 22 Mar. 1826; Beaudin à Comte de Guilleminot, Damas, 8 Apr. 1826.

with political as well as economic advantage on both sides. Under this system, government patronage had served as a means of ensuring unfettered economic activity. However, in the new economic circumstances of the nineteenth-century Ottoman empire it was foreign consulates, not the regime, that were providing this security and patronage. Making loans to the Ottoman authorities was now not only economically but also politically unprofitable, as it no longer guaranteed the requisite conditions for flourishing economic activity. Consequently, by the late 1850s direct Jewish loans to the Ottoman authorities were on the downturn.

The second category of Jewish loans—those to commercial houses—also waned with the decline of commercial activity in Damascus as a result of the reduction in overland trade. Indeed, from the late 1850s 'Jewish wealth' had little identifiable influence on commercial development in Damascus.[27]

Loans to rural *fallahin*—who fell into debt because of the need to pay government taxes or to finance their agricultural enterprises—constituted the main thrust of activity by Damascus Jewish bankers. Pushed into the arms of moneylenders at exorbitant interest, the *fallahin* were forced to use their land or their produce as collateral.[28] This branch of loan activity, of limited scope in the early nineteenth century, expanded greatly in the 1840s, and the tremendous profits garnered from these loans quickly transformed Jewish financiers into some of the richest individuals in Syria. In 1848 Raphael Farhi reportedly provided short-term loans for up to four months at a 30 per cent interest rate to 200 villagers; this at a time when the official rate of interest set by the Ottoman authorities stood at 8 per cent.[29] Often unable to repay their loans on time, rural borrowers were forced by these exorbitant interest rates, and harsh collection methods, to take out additional loans. A cycle of ever more oppressive debt, natural disasters, Bedouin incursions, and exploitation by military units led to some villages being abandoned; in other cases, the *fallahin* had no choice but to go on working the land for the benefit of their creditors. On both financial and legal grounds (Ottoman law prohibited Jews from owning land), Jewish moneylenders favoured rolling over the debt to taking land in

[27] On individual loans of this nature, see FO 78/1686, Rogers to Erskine, Damascus, 10 Nov. 1862.

[28] On the underlying causes for the *fallahin*'s need for loans, see Baer, *Introduction to the History of Agrarian Relations* (Heb.), 54–5; Elmaleh, 'Nouvelles sources' (Heb.), 46; Abdul-Karim Rafeq, 'Land Tenure Problems', 383–8. Christian and Muslim financiers also took part in making loans; nonetheless, the Jewish bankers, by dint of their prominence in business dealings relative to their representation in the population, dominated the credit market. See e.g. *Halevanon*, 5, 14 Adar 1866, p. 71; Frankl, *The Jews in the East*, i. 299; Rafeq, 'Land Tenure Problems', 388–9. It is likely that Damascus *shari‘a* court documents can shed additional light on Jewish activity in this realm. See Reilly, 'Shari‘a Court Registers'.

[29] Paton, *The Modern Syrians*, 39–49. For more on Jewish profits in this sphere, see FO 406/12, Burton to Elliot, 21 Nov. 1870; I. Burton, *The Inner Life of Syria*, i. 332–3; Rafeq, 'Land Tenure Problems', 388–9.

lieu of payment. Their status as consular protégés gave them priority over all Ottoman subjects with regard to debt collection and even allowed them to have debtors arrested. The inevitable result was a Jewish lien on hundreds of villages.[30]

Official attempts by the Damascus authorities as early as 1842 to curb the unrestricted activity of Jewish moneylenders, and to limit their profits, met with little success.[31] Twenty years later, in yet another effort to lighten the villagers' burden, the Ottoman authorities appointed a special committee to examine the moneylenders' books and to cut their interest charges back to the accepted rate. Still the large Jewish bankers, such as Isaac Tobi, Jacob Stambouli, and David Harari, all British subjects, remained untouched. Protected by the intervention of the British ambassador to Istanbul, the British consul in Damascus from 1861 to 1868, Edward Thomas Rogers, obtained a firman exempting British citizens and British protégés from this measure.[32] However, in the following years, as officials in Damascus took further steps aimed at lowering interest rates at the behest of the Sublime Porte, the British Foreign Office changed tack to work in support of, rather than against, these attempts. Finding themselves forced to defend the acquisition of immense wealth by Jews —many of whom were British protégés—at the expense of local *fallahin*, and seeing that many Syrians were holding the British largely responsible for the social and economic results of their support for Jewish bankers—namely, the bankruptcy and abandonment of entire villages—they realized that unconditional support of the Jewish bankers was damaging Britain's image in Syria. [33]

In order to maintain a huge cash turnover and at the same time to preserve the value of their money or even turn a profit in the inflationary climate of nineteenth-century Syria, Damascus' Jewish bankers were forced to seek new outlets for investment. One means of preserving monetary value was to link it to the gold standard, but in the 1850s Jews found the tradable, high-interest Ottoman treasury bonds more attractive. In compensation for its inability to meet loan payments on time, the Ottoman treasury offered higher interest rates on future bond redemption. This made Ottoman treasury bonds a widely sought-after investment, as one contemporary observer noted:

We see that everyone, from every nation, state, and kingdom has sold his jewels and his land and gemstones and pearls and everything of value in order to buy these

[30] FO 78/2375A, Green to Elliot, Damascus, 21 July 1872. Nonetheless, after 1849 we find a limited phenomenon of Jewish land purchase in certain rural areas near Damascus, primarily by Jews under foreign protection. See Reilly, 'Status Groups and Propertyholding', 522–7.

[31] AECCC, Damas, vol. 1, p. 078, Ratti-Menton, 4 Mar. 1842.

[32] See the letter by Jewish moneylenders in Damascus, dated 7 Nov. 1862, to Consul Rogers, in FO 78/1686. See also Tibawi, *A Modern History of Syria*, 139.

[33] On the severe socio-economic ramifications of the credit system, see Rafeq, 'Land Tenure Problems', 388–91. See also Gabriel Baer, 'Landlord, Peasant and the Government'.

bonds, thought to be the safest investment, until there is nearly nary a person that has not purchased the above-mentioned bonds. These bonds are like gold and silver and even better.[34]

Ottoman Bankruptcy and its Consequences

On 6 October 1875 the bubble burst. Unable either to acquire new loans or to meet its outstanding obligations, the Ottoman empire declared bankruptcy. Government debt to the Damascus Jewish bankers stood at approximately twenty million French francs, the overwhelming majority of its debt in Syria.[35] The lenders lost their money; many became paupers overnight. Ironically, their transformed circumstances made them worse off than the ordinary poor, who were already used to making do with minimal means: 'The ordinary worker somehow makes a penny for his labour, whereas the [formerly] wealthy person has no means of existence and will therefore be forced to beg or steal if matters continue thus.'[36] The eventual sequel to the economic downfall of the affluent Jews of Damascus—whose generosity was the mainstay of the community—was the collapse of the entire Jewish communal framework of the city.

The Ottoman bankruptcy crisis had a less devastating effect in Aleppo. Not only were the assessment and collection of government taxes more equitable there, they were better organized and more effective. Commercial ventures in Aleppo continued to prosper until the mid-1870s, and *wilaya* revenues therefore generally outstripped expenditures, so that the local administration had no need of the huge loans required by the Damascus regime.[37] Also, the continued focus of Aleppo's wealthy Jews on international trade meant that their stake in lending on credit was relatively limited.[38] It was their choice to invest in commerce, and in tax farming for the government, rather than in Ottoman treasury bonds, that saved them from the catastrophic decline experienced by their co-religionists in Damascus. [39]

[34] Elyashar, *Simḥah le'ish*, 81b, 'Ḥoshen mishpat', no. 4. The bonds issued in Damascus were known as *seragi*. See 'Awad, *Ottoman Administration* (Arab.), 307–8.
[35] For the details of the debt, see AAIU, Syrie, XV.E., Damas, 146, Fresco, 3 Nov. 1880.
[36] AAIU, Syrie, XI.E., Damas, 94, Halfon, 23 Apr. 1877. For additional descriptions of the collapse of Jewish bankers, see FO 195/1113, Jago to Elliot, Damascus, 21 Nov. 1876; Elyashar, *Simḥah le'ish*, 77b, 'Ḥoshen mishpat', no. 4; 78b–79a, 'Ḥoshen mishpat', no. 5; Abulafia, *Penei yitsḥak*, iii. 30a, no. 8; Neumark, *A Journey in the Old Land* (Heb.), 50.
[37] See Ma'oz, *Ottoman Reform*, 72.
[38] In 1870 the British Foreign Office sent Charles Malcolm Kennedy to Syria to investigate the problem of Jewish moneylenders under British protection. Kennedy hints at a similar phenomenon of *fallahin* borrowing money from Jews in Aleppo, but provides no data regarding its extent. See Hyamson (ed.), *The British Consulate in Jerusalem*, ii. 351.
[39] M. Labaton, *Nokhaḥ hashulḥan*, 41a, 'Ḥoshen mishpat', no. 9; 77b, 'Ḥoshen mishpat', no. 24; 112b, 'Ḥoshen mishpat', no. 39.

Jewish Economic Activity beyond the Financial Sector

As noted above, the main difference in social structure between the communities in Aleppo and in Damascus was the presence of a dominant middle class in the former and its absence in the latter; but the lower classes in each community also engaged in different occupations. Until the early 1880s the overwhelming majority of Aleppo's Jewish middle class were small businessmen, moneychangers, and middlemen—a situation that prompted the community's leaders more than once to express their concern that so many Jews should be involved in unproductive commercial negotiation rather than learning crafts.[40] Some sold agricultural products, including butter, wheat and barley, and animals.[41] Among the lower classes, Jewish artisans included jewellers, tailors, shoemakers, bookbinders, bakers, tinsmiths, carpenters, glaziers, painters, and musicians.[42] Jews also worked in light industry: a particular Jewish occupation was the production of sweets and jellies, but Jews also made cheeses, or worked in factories manufacturing pillows and bedding.[43]

The ordinary Jews of Damascus, on the other hand, attracted praise from the Jewish press for engaging in crafts and not in commercial intermediation.[44] Although there were some Jewish moneychangers in Damascus, the majority of its Jewish population earned a living from craft work, especially in textiles: weaving, and silk and cotton dyeing. These were not very profitable occupations, but Jews were excluded from more lucrative sectors by the jealousy of the Muslim guilds, to which Jewish entry was barred.[45] Others in the community served as bakers, butchers, shoemakers, jewellers, copper engravers, and musicians, among other occupations.[46] A fair number of Damascus Jews were pedlars, hawking their wares—soap, pigeons, haberdashery, and used goods—in towns and villages. Jews even engaged in the lowly job of cleaning public toilets. The Jewish contribution to light industry in Damascus was confined to Jewish ownership of the dyeing establishments, and the rental and operation of soap factories.[47]

[40] Antebi, *Ḥokhmah umusar*, 35b–36a.
[41] See Abraham Dayan, *Po'el tsedek*, 59a, no. 7; I. Dayan, *Zeh ketav yadi*, 225, 'Ḥoshen mishpat', no. 14.
[42] See Abraham Dayan, *Vayosef avraham*, 129a, no. 22; M. Labaton, *Nokhaḥ hashulḥan*, 73a, 'Ḥoshen mishpat', no. 20; AAIU, Syrie, II.E., Alep, 11, Altaras, 25 Jan. 1880.
[43] See J. Sutton, *Vayelaket yosef*, 29a–30a; Neumark, *A Journey in the Old Land* (Heb.), 55; Laniado, *For the Sake of the Holy Ones* (Heb.), 165–6.
[44] *Hamagid*, 23, 13 Kislev 1865, pp. 361–2; *Ḥavatselet*, 3, 9 Heshvan 1883, p. 19.
[45] FO 78/579, Wood to Stratford Canning, Damascus, 21 Feb. 1884.
[46] For various lists of Jewish occupations, see Wilson, *The Lands of the Bible*, ii. 336; Neumark, *A Journey in the Old Land* (Heb.), 50–2.
[47] See Abulafia, *Penei yitsḥak*, ii. 26a, 36b–37a, 46b; *Hadiqat al-akhbar*, 126, 31 May 1860, p. 1. For further data on Jewish fields of occupation in Syria, see Zenner, 'Syrian Jews and their Non-Jewish Neighbors', 165–7.

The balance between economic opportunity in the cities and in the outlying towns also shifted as commerce declined from the 1860s onwards. As the towns of 'Ayntab, Urfa, Idlib, and Kilis developed near to Aleppo, there was also a steady decrease in industrial output from the city itself. Whereas the residents of these towns had formerly purchased most of what they needed in Aleppo, now their newly founded factories and workshops produced textiles, soap, and oil of good quality that they could buy more cheaply.[48] Not only did this create new economic opportunities, it also sparked migration from Aleppo to the nearby towns, as well as partnerships between local Jews and those in Aleppo. In the absence of competition from western imports, and with strong government support, for soap production in particular, these industries flourished.[49] Notwithstanding this relative prosperity, poor individuals continued to peddle goods in the surrounding villages.[50]

Syria's economic decline was compounded by natural disasters and other misfortunes. Thus, for example, the few somewhat wealthier individuals who engaged in light commerce in the small community of Antioch, where most Jews were pedlars, lost their possessions, with destructive consequences for the local economy and the lives of the residents, when

in the month of Tamuz 5617 [1857], on Friday night, fire broke out in the marketplace, consuming all the stores. Only a very small number were salvaged. Because of this some of the householders have lost their possessions and are now impoverished, as are some of the Muslims and Christians. Although some of the stores have been rebuilt, nonetheless, they can no longer receive credit.[51]

The opening of new schools in Damascus and Aleppo under the aegis of the Alliance Israélite Universelle had an important impact on an incipient shift in Jewish employment in the larger communities. Alongside the economic factors that motivated a search for new sources of income, the modern education provided by the Alliance schools opened up new fields of economic activity to Jews, in the free professions in particular. In 1868 an Alliance emissary to Damascus suggested that a course in Hebrew calligraphy be added to the ones in Arabic and French, in order to prepare students for jobs with Jewish businessmen, who used this language for their business correspondence.[52] Although the Alliance school in Damascus did not train sufficient graduates with the special skills needed to find jobs as business clerks during its brief existence, an 1884 report mentions some fifty Jews in Aleppo who were earning their living

---

[48] AECCC, Alep, vol. 36, p. 013, Destrée, 25 Feb. 1879.

[49] Ma'oz, *Ottoman Reform*, 180. For partnerships and business dealings between Jews from Kilis, Urfa, 'Ayntab, Idlib, and Aleppo, see the responsa scattered throughout Aaron Dayan's collection *Beit aharon*. See also Azriel, *Kapei aharon*, pt. 1, 111*a*; M. Labaton, *Nokhaḥ hashulḥan*, 73*b*, 'Ḥoshen mishpat', no. 21 and *passim*.

[50] See Abraham Dayan, *Vayosef avraham*, 147*a*, no. 24.   [51] Ibid. 227*a*, no. 37.

[52] AAIU, Syrie, XXI.E., Damas, 222, Weisskopf, 15 Mar. 1868, 27 Nov. 1868.

as 'clerks, and as managers of commercial houses for their co-religionists or for non-Jews, the majority of whom studied at the school founded by the Alliance Israélite Universelle'.[53] By the late 1870s graduates of the Alliance school in Aleppo were engaged in professions such as pharmacology and photography; others held positions in the governmental or consular administrations.[54]

Overview

The picture that emerges from this examination of Jewish economic activity in Syria is one of strong performance up to the mid-1870s, notwithstanding the decline in Syria's economy throughout the nineteenth century with the progressive erosion of its role as an important commercial way station. In Damascus, a small but very wealthy group of individuals, mainly financiers, supported and gave stability to the Jewish communal structure. It was through its Jewish bankers that the Damascus Jewish community was able to maintain its image as supporting and not supported, as a donor and not as a recipient, up to the mid-1870s. The claim that this community was broken economically by the Damascus blood libel of 1840 is unfounded;[55] nor do the sources considered here support the argument that the events of the summer of 1860 mark the turning point that symbolized the destruction and collapse of Damascus' Jewish community.[56] As late as the 1860s the economic position and the concomitant practical political influence of the wealthy Jews of Damascus were so great that they were compared, somewhat hyperbolically, to those of the European Rothschilds.[57]

The profound differences in economic structure between the Jewish communities of Aleppo and Damascus were reflected in the different repercussions for each of the economic crisis. Aleppo was affected somewhat earlier, mainly by the opening of the Suez Canal, whereas Damascus was harder hit by the bankruptcy of the Ottoman empire. These economic crises naturally had an impact on the social structure and leadership of the Jewish communities, just as the economic success of the past had done. My reading of the effect of the economic crisis in each of the two main Jewish centres was that it led to the collapse of the Damascene Jewish community but that the Aleppine community recovered.

Nonetheless, the economic situation was not the sole factor influencing the resilience of the communal leadership and its ability to lead the community

---

[53] *Ḥavatselet*, 36, 17 Av 1884, p. 283. For more detailed reports, including the names of the graduates and their occupations, see AAIU, Syrie, III.E., Alep, 23, Behor, 9 Jan. 1879, 24 July 1879.   [54] *BAIU*, 1er et 2ème sem. 1879, 36.

[55] This argument had already been rejected by Brawer, 'The Jews of Damascus' (Heb.), 83.

[56] See Malachi, 'The Jews in the Druze Revolt' (Heb.), 111.

[57] *Halevanon*, 5, 14 Adar 1866, pp. 71–2; *JC*, 3 Feb. 1865, p. 5; 27 July 1866, p. 6.

during times of crisis. The communal administrative structure, as it developed in the Ottoman context, had a significant influence on the ability of the Jewish communities to overcome the economic crises that threatened them. This administrative context is the subject of the next chapter.

FOUR

LEADERSHIP AND COMMUNAL ADMINISTRATION

For centuries the institutional structure and functioning of the Syrian Jewish community was grounded in enduring worldwide patterns dating back to the talmudic period. By touching upon the structure and leadership of the religious minorities in the Ottoman empire, the Tanzimat altered the traditional autonomy of the non-Muslim communities vis-à-vis the imperial regime. The mid-nineteenth century saw the reorganization and remodelling of the structure of the Syrian Jewish communities under the influence of the Ottoman reforms. The most significant measures related to the institutionalization of the office of chief rabbi (*ḥakham bashi*) and to the establishment of committees whose purpose was to control and to assist in administering the community. Although largely instigated by the Ottoman authorities, these changes also reflected social unrest and criticism of the communal leadership within the Jewish communities, as well as the impact of modernization and secularization.

During the pre-reform era, the inferior status of the Jews under Ottoman law, coupled with their ethnic, religious, and cultural distinctiveness from the surrounding society, promoted the creation and maintenance of an autonomous communal framework. Its function was to protect the community and its individual members and, where possible, to improve their quality of life. The Ottoman system of rule not only enabled but indeed fostered this type of autonomous organization. Each non-Muslim group in the empire was granted the right to maintain its own internal institutions, as well as to regulate the personal status of its members and to follow its religious law. Thus people were defined first and foremost, in administrative and communal terms, by their religious affiliation. Because Ottoman society as a whole was organized on religious lines, each of the various religious communities was held to be subject to the authority of its religious leader. The position of the rabbi as head of the Jewish community was thus recognized officially within the Ottoman administrative system, as well as voluntarily within the Jewish community, which accorded him an authority based above all on his expertise in halakhah, the basis of Jewish daily life.

Syria had no model of regional communal organization; consequently, Jewish leadership there was decentralized. There was no official office of chief rabbi of Syria, and the large Jewish communities—and smaller ones as well—chose or appointed their own chief rabbis, whose formal authority extended only to the members of their community. In the absence of any surviving writs of appointment for chief rabbis in the main communities, with the exception of a single writ from Aleppo concerning Raphael Kassin, the leader of a separatist, reforming faction, the precise extent of their authority and privileges is difficult to determine. From this sole surviving writ, dated 1862, we can perhaps extrapolate to suggest some features likely to be common to other such writs of rabbinic appointment. As this document accords to Rabbi Raphael Kassin nearly unlimited authority, it appears that the chief rabbi in most communities enjoyed relatively broad powers. The signatories of the writ agreed to accept any regulations or compromises by the rabbi on halakhic or commercial matters, with no right of appeal, and granted the rabbi the exclusive right to officiate at all religious ceremonies, particularly those involving personal status, such as marriage or divorce. Moreover, the community committed itself to paying the rabbi an agreed salary and to funding the upkeep of two servants and the rental of an apartment commensurate with the rabbi's status.[1]

This picture of the Jewish public's deference to the chief rabbi's sweeping powers by no means fully represents how the Jewish community functioned. Chosen for centuries by the same method as elsewhere in the Ottoman empire —namely, communal selection without interference by the Ottoman authorities—the rabbis did not have a monopoly on leadership in the Jewish community, but shared that role with its moneyed and hereditary elites. This interdependence frequently gave rise to tension and on occasion even to communal crisis, with repercussions for the chief rabbi's status.[2]

The Chief Rabbinate

In the context of the various administrative reforms instituted by the Ottoman authorities towards the middle of the nineteenth century, the relationship of the empire to its non-Muslim minorities was examined afresh. Under the millet system,[3] minorities organized as autonomous religious entities now received official recognition; however, this recognition brought in its wake increased involvement of the Ottoman authorities in the millets' internal affairs. With regard to the Jews, this involvement reached a peak with the passing of the 1865 Jewish millet decree, which covered how a chief rabbi—*ḥakham bashi*—was to be chosen and his status as the leader of the Jewish millet. It set out the chief

---

[1] See Harel, 'A Spiritual Agitation in the East' (Heb.).
[2] As noted in the case of Rabbi Raphael Solomon Laniado, discussed in Ch. 1 above.
[3] The precise definition of millet has been the subject of many studies. See Levi, 'Changes in the Leadership of the Main Spanish Communities' (Heb.), 266.

rabbi's obligations, establishing his position as the Jewish community's representative to the Ottoman authorities and his responsibility for implementing the Sublime Porte's pronouncements within the Jewish community. The decree also set up an institutionalized communal hierarchy with a defined sphere of authority alongside the chief rabbi, mandating how its members were to be elected and what matters came under its purview.[4] Among the chief rabbi's main public functions were the collection and delivery of taxes from the Jewish community to the Ottoman regime. He was also granted the right to impose new taxes on the Jewish community at his own discretion. These fresh arrangements defining the composition and responsibilities of the Jewish leadership were implemented among the various Jewish communities throughout the empire.

The newly mandated method of choosing a *ḥakham bashi* had some democratic features, such as the secret ballot. Its major innovation, however, was in determining that the candidate so chosen would enjoy the sultan's official recognition; that is, the state, not the community, became the source of the rabbi's authority. In the past, the chief rabbis' authority had been grounded in the Jewish community's voluntary recognition of their qualifications; now, official recognition by the Ottoman authorities was a parallel source of authority —one that could, at times, sustain a leader in whom the community itself had lost faith.[5] Thus the Jewish millet decree transformed a religious authority into the highest governmental official in Jewish society. Because the latter function was not religious, but rather definitively secular and political, the person chosen for this position was usually a scholar selected for his political, over and above his intellectual and spiritual, skills. As we shall see below, although the *ḥakham bashi* was often denoted 'chief rabbi', this was not equivalent to the titles *rosh harabanim* (head of the rabbis) or *rosh haruḥaniyim* (spiritual head), which were reserved under the millet decree for the head of the rabbinic court, the *av beit din* of the community.[6] Occasionally the two posts were held by the same individual, but this was rare.

In practice, the actual involvement of the Ottoman authorities in the selection and work of the chief rabbi was more pronounced in Damascus than in Aleppo. Moreover, during the period in question the chief rabbi continued to be chosen by the long-standing tradition of oligarchic consensus; the more democratic method of election laid down in the millet decree was not implemented in any of the Syrian Jewish communities.[7] In many respects, the story of the succession to the chief rabbinate, in Damascus especially, is the story of

[4] Davison, *Reform in the Ottoman Empire*, 129–31.
[5] In actuality, this recognition was costly. See e.g. ACRI, TR/Is-162a, Damascus notables to Rabbi Moses Halevi, Damascus, 18 Elul 1874.
[6] For a comprehensive discussion, see Harel, *Between Intrigues and Revolution* (Heb.), 20–1.
[7] See Jacob Saul Dweck Hakohen, *She'erit ya'akov*, 31a.

how the oligarchy of wealth influenced the choice of Jewish communal leaders, including its chief rabbis, and of the balance of power between the spiritual and the moneyed leadership. Among the criteria militating for or against
the choice of particular individuals by the communal lay leadership at different times were personal wealth or relative poverty, local or foreign citizenship,
and Torah scholarship or diplomatic skills.

Damascus

Even though, in theory, the community paid the rabbi's salary, as in so many
other spheres of Jewish communal life it was the wealthy members of the Damascus Jewish community who actually contributed most of the money. This led
to massive interference by the wealthy oligarchy in the process of appointing
rabbis. A particular candidate might be chosen, for example, not because he
was 'the most worthy in knowledge and character',[8] but rather because of his
financial weakness, which rendered him dependent on their support. The
moneyed elite sought to create a situation in which the rabbi functioned officially as the community's head but in practice deferred to those who elected
him; by these means they successfully converted economic into political power.
A definitive example comes from the pre-reform period, with the appointment
in 1809 of Rabbi Jacob Antebi to the chief rabbinate of Damascus, although
the other candidate, Rabbi Hayim Nissim Abulafia, was Antebi's senior in age
and his superior in learning and lineage.[9]

From the moment of his appointment to the rabbinate, Jacob Antebi found
himself at the mercy of the communal oligarchy, in particular of the Farhis,
who imposed harsh sanctions whenever they saw that the rabbinic court, which
Antebi headed, was preparing to rule against them. In the late 1830s Antebi
resorted to biblical language to describe his weakness vis-à-vis the Farhis:
'I have no power, for they do not recognize the ordinances [Ps. 147: 20].'[10]
When Antebi did rule against them, the Farhis took the extreme steps of questioning the authority of the rabbinic court, dismissing Antebi from his post,
and bribing Ottoman officials to have him placed under house arrest.[11] Another
prominent Damascus Jewish family, the Hararis, withheld Antebi's salary for
two and a half years because he spoke out against their laxity in religious observance and their refusal to accept his halakhic authority.[12]

In communal matters, as well as legal rulings, the chief rabbis of Damascus
usually bowed to the dictates of the affluent oligarchy. Technically, the wealthy

---

[8] Abulafia, *Penei yitshak*, iii. 39*b*, no. 9.

[9] On Jacob Antebi, see Gaon, *The Jews of the East* (Heb.), ii. 523; al-Halil, 'An Important Document Source' (Heb.), 40–1.

[10] Palagi, *Ḥukot haḥayim*, 7*a*, 'Ḥoshen mishpat', no. 2.   [11] Ibid. 7*b*, no. 2.

[12] See al-Halil, 'An Important Document Source' (Heb.), 42; also Brawer, 'New Material with
Regard to the Damascus Libel' (Heb.), 262.

elite could not enforce its decisions without the rabbinate's official approval, and all regulations had to be mutually agreed. However, the rabbi's power in practice was limited, as may be seen from the example of the indirect tax or *gabilah* on kosher meat promulgated in the late 1860s by Chief Rabbi Jacob Peretz, evidently with the backing of the community's affluent elite. In 1872 one of the leading members of that group wished the tax to be cancelled, but Peretz refused to do so. In order to reduce the price of kosher meat from double that of the meat sold to Christians or Muslims, this individual hired a ritual slaughterer to supply kosher meat to all the Muslim butchers' shops, where it was sold to Jews at its regular price, effectively cancelling the meat tax in the face of Peretz's objections.[13]

When Ottoman rule returned to Syria in late 1840, the leadership of the Damascus Jewish community was in deep crisis in the aftermath of the so-called Damascus affair of that year. Prominent members of the Jewish leadership had been only recently released from gaol, broken physically and emotionally by their experiences while under false charge for the ritual murder of the Capuchin monk Father Thomas.[14] Chief Rabbi Jacob Antebi had been among those arrested, having completed thirty years in this post. In 1842 he realized his wish to resign and spend the rest of his life in Jerusalem.

The striking weakness of the chief rabbi in his role as the Jewish community's representative throughout the Damascus affair led the communal leaders to put new emphasis on the ability of whoever held this post to engage effectively not only with the Ottoman authorities but, above all, with the European consuls; for it was the latter who had protected the Jews. Antebi's local citizenship was seen as detracting from his influence with the regime, and on his retirement the Damascus Jews sought to replace him with a foreign national—Rabbi Hayim Maimon Tobi. This Gibraltar-born British citizen, described as bright, well-educated, and well-mannered, had lived in Damascus since at least 1825, evidently for business purposes. In putting their trust in him to represent the Jewish community to the regime successfully, the communal leadership vested their hopes more in his British citizenship and other qualities than in his Torah scholarship.[15] Tobi's British citizenship did indeed stand him in good stead in his contacts and negotiations with the Ottoman authorities, and even more so in his successful efforts to recruit the British consulate to act vigorously on behalf of the Jews.[16] Yet in internal Jewish communal matters Tobi remained, as Antebi had been, at the mercy of the local notables, especially the

[13] FO 78/2242, Green to Rumbold, Damascus, 15 Apr. 1872.
[14] This episode is discussed in Ch. 9 below.
[15] John Wilson, *The Lands of the Bible*, ii. 330; Woodcock, *Scripture Lands*, 47.
[16] Testimony from as early as 1825 cites Hayim Maimon Tobi as a respected merchant who enjoyed a good relationship with the French consular agent Beaudin and was also known as a friend of the English. See Madox, *Excursions in the Holy Land*, ii. 122–3, 137–8.

Farhis, even though (perhaps because) he declined to become involved in their complicated affairs, particularly the disputed inheritance of the minister Hayim Farhi. Even prior to his appointment as chief rabbi Tobi declined to sign verdicts in cases involving the Farhis, lest this damage his business dealings.[17]

When Rabbi Hayim Maimon Tobi retired from the public leadership in Damascus in 1849, most probably because of his advanced age,[18] he was briefly replaced by the most prominent rabbinic scholar in the city, Rabbi Hayim Romano, the teacher of many later chief rabbis.[19] Romano's retirement from active leadership to concentrate on spiritual and intellectual matters was prompted in some part by poor health; however, once again we cannot discount his shaky relationship with the Jewish notables, exemplified by his denunciation to the Ottoman authorities by the Farhis in 1847.[20] Nonetheless, even after his retirement he continued to enjoy the honour of being the first signatory on letters sent to European Jewish communities, and was invited to serve as head of the rabbinic court when he stayed in Damascus in the intervals between his fundraising travels.[21]

Perhaps because the communal leadership realized that no one person in Damascus combined the necessary qualities of both Torah scholarship and worldly leadership, perhaps because it hesitated to concentrate power in the hands of the *ḥakham bashi*, a new pattern of rabbinical leadership in the Damascus Jewish community emerged in the early 1850s: two chief rabbis. The first, holder of the official title *ḥakham bashi*, was in charge of the community's contacts with the Ottoman authorities; the second, the leader of the scholarly stratum, served as a *dayan* and teacher. The latter's particular concern was the preservation of the communal religious framework, including the rabbinic courts, and his authority was vested less in official Ottoman recognition and more in his Torah scholarship and in communal regard for his status as a supreme halakhic authority. In contrast, the *ḥakham bashi*'s authority derived from both communal appointment and Ottoman approval. The expectation was that official approval and support—and the ability to call upon the Ottoman regime to take action against rivals and opponents—would enhance his standing.

---

[17] M. Labaton, *Nokhaḥ hashulḥan*, 78b, 'Ḥoshen mishpat', no. 25.

[18] See NLIS, DA, V-736/248, Hayim Maimon Tobi to Hayim Nissim Abulafia, Damascus, Iyar 1849. Rabbi Tobi died on 22 Tevet 1857.   [19] Frankl, *The Jews in the East*, i. 297.

[20] See Palagi, *Ḥayim veshalom*, 'Even ha'ezer', no. 28. For his disputes with the Farhis, see NLIS, DA, V-736/99, Hayim Romano to Abraham Hayim Gagin, Beirut, 7 Nisan 1847; V-736/28, Hayim Maimon Tobi to Abraham Hayim Gagin, Damascus, 5 Sivan 1847, Rosh Hodesh Tamuz 1847; V-736/101, Isaac and Abraham Romano to Abraham Hayim Gagin, Damascus, 9 Sivan 1847.

[21] On the attitude of the Damascus and Jerusalem rabbis towards Rabbi Hayim Romano, see e.g. Hazzan, *Nediv lev*, 28b, 'Even ha'ezer', no. 8, 114a, 'Ḥoshen mishpat', no. 63. He was also the first signatory on the approbation for Rabbi Mordecai Galante's book, *Divrei mordekhai*.

The first *ḥakham bashi* whose appointment received official confirmation by the Ottoman authorities was Rabbi Jacob Peretz, whose counterpart in the spiritual leadership was Rabbi Aaron Jacob Binyamin.[22] With Jacob Peretz's appointment as *ḥakham bashi*, formal arrangements were made for the first time to pay his salary and that of the other chief rabbi from communal funds, thus rendering them ostensibly independent of support from litigants.[23] Peretz's prestige in the eyes of both the Jewish community and the wider population of Damascus was enhanced when the sultan granted him a medal of honour in December 1861, alongside other government officials and Christian clerics.[24] Rabbi Aaron Jacob Binyamin, for his part, had undisputed halakhic authority; every ruling by any Damascus rabbi on halakhic matters had a codicil to the effect that it had validity only if approved by him.[25] Nonetheless, the power of the rabbis remained relatively weak in comparison to that of the affluent elite. Although the Ottoman authorities generally refrained from interfering in internal Jewish matters, if this became necessary they would inevitably tend to come down on the side of the moneyed elite, on whose funds they depended, rather than that of the rabbis. In addition, because the salaries of the chief rabbis did not meet their needs, they still had to rely on additional sources of income, perpetuating their dependence on the Jewish notables.[26]

Jacob Peretz and Aaron Jacob Binyamin served together as chief rabbis of Damascus for more than twenty years, during which they co-operated closely. Despite their relative weakness vis-à-vis the affluent class, communal life flowed fairly smoothly and securely under their leadership. Peretz and Binyamin avoided conflict with the affluent elite, despite deficiencies in the latter's religious observance. They also co-operated with the Ottoman authorities—in contrast with some of the Christian minorities, who at times tried to create a common front with the Jews to defend minority rights. Also, in the interests of avoiding conflict with the British consulate, these rabbis did not declare uncompromising war on the Protestant missions, thereby enabling the Jewish community to enjoy the continued protection of the British consul.

The death of these two rabbis in the course of a single year (1873/4) plunged the Damascus Jewish community into internal dissension. It appears that the community now sought to reunite the rabbinic functions in a single post; but, ironically, there were two qualified candidates, Rabbis Isaac Abulafia and Solomon Sukary, and the community found itself unable to reach consensus

---

[22] Frankl, *Jews in the East*, i. 297. For a colourful description of Rabbis Jacob Peretz and Aaron Jacob Binyamin, see Bost, *Souvenirs d'Orient*, 36.

[23] See *Halevanon*, 7, 13 Nisan 1866, p. 102.

[24] *JC*, 4 Apr. 1862, p. 3.

[25] Abulafia, *Penei yitsḥak*, i. 100a, 'Even ha'ezer', no. 16.

[26] See e.g. *Halevanon*, 7, 13 Nisan 1866, p. 102; 17, Rosh Hodesh Elul 1867, p. 269; AAIU, Syrie, XVII.E., Damas, 160, Heymann, 12 Jan. 1866.

on either of them.[27] Having recovered from the Damascus affair, it saw no need for a rabbi with foreign citizenship, and Abulafia's opponents took the view that his French citizenship was a positive drawback, arguing that, according to Ottoman law, a foreign national could not serve as *ḥakham bashi*.[28] When the rival groups found themselves unable to agree on a mutually satisfactory candidate, the community approached the *ḥakham bashi*s in Jerusalem, Rabbi Abraham Ashkenazi, and in Istanbul, Rabbi Moses Halevi, requesting that they choose a suitable candidate. By this means an unknown rabbi by the name of Hayim Isaac Kimhi of Istanbul was chosen for the post. Although his selection received official recognition, the firman of appointment granted him only the status of acting chief rabbi, *kaymakam ḥakham bashi*.[29]

This episode represents a turning point in the history of the Damascus Jewish community, the beginning of a decline to which this internal dissension contributed. Shortly after the rabbi's arrival, the city's affluent Jews were bankrupted, in circumstances described in Chapter 3. Coming on the heels of a long period of prosperity, this economic collapse brought the Damascus community to a new low. In any event, Rabbi Kimhi left no significant mark on the community. Hampered by his lack of a local power base, his inability to speak the local language, and his financial dependence on the soon-to-be bankrupt communal notables, and facing the opposition of conflicting forces in the community fighting for control of its institutions, Kimhi did not remain long in post: he resigned in late 1878, just three years after his arrival.[30] The bitter internecine strife also prevented the selection of a rabbi for the post of spiritual head of the community. In the absence of a single candidate with majority support, Rabbis Isaac Abulafia and Solomon Sukary filled this role jointly until 1880.

As noted above, the Ottoman authorities generally refrained from interfering in the internal affairs of the *dhimmi*s. However, the weakness of the Damascus Jewish community and its inability to choose a new *ḥakham bashi* now led to the direct intervention of the Syrian governor, Midhat Pasha, in the choice of a candidate for the post. In late 1879 he virtually forced Rabbi Ephraim Mercado Alkalai—with whom he was acquainted from his tenure as ruler

---

[27] On Rabbi Solomon Sukary, who was Rabbi Jacob Antebi's son-in-law, see Laniado, *For the Sake of the Holy Ones* (Heb.), pt. 3, 55. See also his approbation of his son Jacob Sukary's book, *Vayikra ya'akov* (Leghorn, 1880), and his son's introduction to his father's book *Ateret shelomoh* (Jerusalem: Ma'arekhet hahashkafah, 1902). See also Jacob Sukary, *Vayeḥi ya'akov* (Leghorn: Ben Amozeg, 1901), 2; id., *Yoru mishpateikha leya'akov* (Calcutta, 1882), 16, 19, 23. On Isaac Abulafia, see, Harel, 'The Influence of the Books' (Heb.), 217–19; id., *Between Intrigues and Revolution* (Heb.), 143–70.

[28] See ACRI, TR/Is-162a, the people of Damascus to Rabbi Moses Halevi, 'Megilat setarim: sod hashem liyerei'av satom veḥatom hadevarim' [Damascus], n.d.; Rabbi Isaac Abulafia to Rabbi Moses Halevi, Damascus, 15 Av 1874.

[29] On the embarrassment in the community, see AAIU, Syrie, XI.E., Damas, 94, Halfon, 19 May 1874; *BAIU*, 1er sem. 1874, 79. [30] See *JC*, 3 Dec. 1880, p. 12.

of the Danube district when Alkalai served as *ḥakham bashi* in Nis (Serbia)—
on the Damascus Jewish community. Although Alkalai was not local, unlike his
predecessor he was independently wealthy and therefore did not depend
on the community for his livelihood. In addition, his enjoyment of full backing by the pasha enabled him to face down his opponents.[31]

Had it not been for the pressure exerted by the pasha and by members of the
community, Alkalai would have preferred to spend his remaining years in
Jerusalem rather than Damascus, where, according to his personal testimony,
the Jewish community was in a poor condition.[32] However, Alkalai's assumption of the post of chief rabbi breathed new life into the beleaguered community. Its institutions were reorganized and co-operation between the *ḥakham
bashi* and the Jewish lay administration was renewed. For as long as Midhat
Pasha continued to serve as governor of Syria, Alkalai enjoyed success in his
tenure as chief rabbi. The crowning achievement of their joint activity on behalf
of the Jewish community was the reopening of the Alliance school in Damascus in 1880. However, when the pasha was forced to step down as governor in
1881, Alkalai's fortunes declined as well. His position undermined by lack of
government support and continued internal strife in the Jewish community,
Alkalai left Damascus in February 1883.[33]

To sum up, the nature of the Damascus chief rabbinate underwent structural
change during the Tanzimat era. However, despite official recognition by the
Ottoman regime, the incumbents—with the exception of Alkalai, who enjoyed
the pasha's support—were still not strong enough to assert their authority over
the moneyed elite.

Aleppo

Like other areas of Jewish life, the nature of the chief rabbinate in Aleppo differed from that in Damascus. In Aleppo the *ḥakham bashi* had no need of
special political skills, mainly because the Jewish consuls belonging to the
Picciotto family constituted the political backbone of the community. Holding itself apart from the communal framework, the Franco elite neither intervened in the election of the chief rabbi nor viewed the *ḥakham bashi* as a
competitor, unlike the wealthy Damascus oligarchy. Nor did the local elite,
whose political activity was limited, regard the *ḥakham bashi* as a rival.

During the period in question the chief rabbinate in Aleppo remained in
the hands of one individual at a time. In his function as the head of the rabbinic
court, the *ḥakham bashi* was in effect recognized as the supreme spiritual

[31] Harel, 'Midhat Pasha and the Jewish Community', 340–1.
[32] ACRI, TR/Is-162a, Rabbi Ephraim Mercado Alkalai to Rabbi Moses Halevi, Damascus, 17
Kislev 1879.
[33] See NLIS, DA, V-736/261, Alkalai to Gagin[?], Damascus, 1883. Rabbi Ephraim Mercado
Alkalai died in Jerusalem on 11 Heshvan 1894.

authority of Aleppo's Jewish community. In the Jewish context, the chief rabbi's title was *rosh al erets* [= *aram tsova*] *rabah* (the head of greater Aleppo), with the title *ḥakham bashi* reserved for official outside contacts.[34] In Aleppo the *ḥakham bashi* normally had an assistant who served as his deputy on the rabbinic court and also represented the community in external matters. An outstanding example of this rabbi–deputy model is the relationship between Chief Rabbi Hayim Mordecai Labaton and his assistant Rabbi Moses Sutton during the 1860s. Sutton was effectively in charge of the community's external affairs from the mid-1850s until his death on 22 Tamuz 1878.[35]

In Aleppo, as in Damascus, only taxpayers could participate in the elections for chief rabbi. However, whereas in Damascus this meant that only a thin stratum of the affluent could vote, in Aleppo there was strong and widespread middle-class participation in the chief rabbi's selection. The fact that the rabbi's salary was paid from the communal treasury, evidently from funds specially earmarked for this purpose, eliminated any dependence on individuals, so influential a factor in the Damascus chief rabbinate's functioning.[36] Moreover, the *ḥakham bashi*'s recognized status as the spiritual head of the community in Aleppo gave him enhanced authority; as a result, the Aleppine chief rabbis generally served out their terms until death, and their successors were generally chosen on the basis of their spiritual qualifications. In Aleppo, then, the process of choosing a chief rabbi proceeded far less turbulently than in Damascus.

In 1840, the year with which this study opens, Rabbi Abraham Antebi had already served as chief rabbi for twenty-three years, with Rabbi Hayim Mordecai Labaton as his deputy.[37] Their joint tenure was marked by stability, and by efforts to strengthen the standing and authority of the rabbinic court, whose status was somewhat reduced by the Ottoman reforms, which left only matters of personal status under its jurisdiction. Their Torah scholarship,[38] the belief in their magic powers to bless or to curse, and the initial confusion of the Jewish public in the wake of the reforms and their implementation, prevented any erosion of the status of the chief rabbis or the maintenance of halakhic rule in the Aleppo community.[39]

In Shevat 1858, shortly after Abraham Antebi's death a month earlier at the age of 93, Rabbi Hayim Labaton was appointed chief rabbi of Aleppo, a position he held for eleven years. Although his tenure saw no radical changes, it was during this period that initial contacts were made with the Alliance Israélite

---

[34] See e.g. Shrem, *Hadar ezer*, introd. to *Ḥakhmei verabanei aram tsova* [Sages and Rabbis of Aleppo].

[35] See Ben-Zvi Institute, MS 3724, *Pinkas rabi mosheh suton*, and his many letters to the Alliance; also AAIU, Syrie, I.B., Alep, 1, 3 Adar II 1875. [36] See Antebi, *Ḥokhmah umusar*, 115*a*.

[37] See id., *Mor ve'oholot*, 54*b*, 'Even ha'ezer', no. 12.

[38] See Benjamin, *Eight Years in Asia and Africa*, 46.

[39] See the folk tales regarding Rabbi Abraham Antebi cited in Antebi, *Mor ve'oholot*, introd. Various legends regarding Rabbi Labaton are found in Yadid Halevi, *Shivḥei moharam*.

Universelle, which opened its first school in Aleppo a few months after Labaton's death on 20 Sivan 1869 at the age of 84.

No clues are available as to why at this point Rabbi Saul Dweck was preferred as the new chief rabbi over Labaton's deputy Rabbi Moses Sutton. Occurring just as severe economic crisis was about to engulf the community, and at a time when the Ottoman reforms had begun to affect various spheres of life and to disrupt traditional patterns, Dweck's election may mark the beginning of internecine strife within the Aleppo Jewish community, which led to disorder and exacerbated economic distress.[40] Dweck was not highly regarded and exercised little influence on communal affairs.[41] This uninspiring rabbi's appointment and his four-year term mark the beginning of a deterioration in the status of the chief rabbinate in Aleppo.

When Dweck died on 4 Shevat 1874 communal controversy broke out as to which local scholar was the most worthy successor. Eventually a decision was reached to recall Rabbi Menashe Sutton, who had left Aleppo four years earlier to serve as the rabbi of Safed. But the attempt to reabsorb Sutton into the troubled community was apparently not a success, and he resigned two years later to accept the Alexandria community's offer to serve in the rabbinate there.[42] The next incumbent was a compromise candidate, Rabbi Aaron Choueka, who evidently found stronger backing among the educated wealthy classes than among many in the scholarly stratum. Saul Somekh, the Alliance emissary in Aleppo, described him as 'praiseworthy' and went on to note: 'He has a liberal awareness, and he protected the school from the attacks of the narrow minded and fanatics.'[43] It was possibly this very attitude that prevented Choueka from acquiring the wholesale support of the scholars, who may have stirred up opposition to him among the Francos, with whom he was engaged in a fierce struggle over whether the Alliance school should be an elitist or a popular institution. Choueka was apparently forced to resign in 1880 when Rabbi Moses Hakohen was appointed *ḥakham bashi* with Rabbi Moses Swed as his deputy.

Moses Hakohen is the first rabbi in Aleppo whom we know definitely to have received official recognition from the Ottoman authorities: this was granted in 1880 in the form of a royal firman and the presentation of a special suit of clothing by the sultan.[44] With this recognition, the formal arrangement by

---

[40] See *BAIU*, 1er sem. 1873, 84–5.

[41] See AAUI, Syrie, III.E., Alep, 21, Behar, 22 Aug. 1870.

[42] See Menasheh Sutton, *Maḥberet pirḥei shoshanim*, introd. by the author's grandson; id., *Mateh menasheh*, introd. Rabbi Menasheh Sutton never reached Alexandria, dying on his way there on 24 Elul 1876.

[43] AAIU, Syrie, X.E., Alep, 83, Somekh, 8 July 1880. He died on 15 Tamuz 1881. See Choueka's signature as *ḥakham bashi* in Aleppo from 24 Tevet 1877 ratifying the 27 Kislev 1876 testimony of the Aleppine sages regarding the British citizenship of the Dweck family, FO 195/1154.

[44] AAIU, Syrie, X.E., Alep, 83, Somekh, 8 July 1880; ACRI, TR/Is-162a, Rabbi Moses Hakohen to Rabbi Moses Halevi, Aleppo, 1880. See also *JC*, 13 Aug. 1880, p. 13.

which the rabbinate was split between two leaders—namely, between the *ḥakham bashi*, who represented the Jewish community before the Ottoman authorities, and the *av beit din*, the spiritual leader of the community—became official in Aleppo as well as in Damascus. In practice, Hakohen continued to serve as head of the rabbinical court and the division between the two functions was implemented only after his death in 1882.[45]

The Satellite Communities

The small Syrian Jewish communities, which did not have many local rabbis, drew upon the pool of scholars in the larger ones, hiring rabbis for set terms. In these more homogeneous, united communities, the rabbis enjoyed greater prestige than in the large urban settings. Rabbis seeking to serve in smaller communities had to be able to perform a broad range of functions, including those of halakhic decisor and communal representative to the Ottoman authorities, as well as to serve in various ritual capacities, such as circumciser, slaughterer, and so on. A document regulating the agreement between the Antioch Jewish community and Rabbi Moses Sasson of Aleppo,[46] signed in 1846, laid out the mutual obligations of the rabbi and the community: the former committed himself to move from Aleppo to Antioch and to serve as a teacher, *dayan*, and *ḥazan* (cantor) for the community, which in turn promised to pay him a salary commensurate with his duties.[47]

Rabbi Abraham Ezra Dweck Hakohen, who next filled the post of chief rabbi in Antioch, widened the scope of his activity beyond the narrowly religious sphere. The support of the Ottoman authorities was very important to him; consequently he made an effort to obtain an official appointment as *ḥakham bashi* and to attain equal status with the heads of the Christian sects in Antioch. His close contact with the Ottoman authorities on behalf of his community emerges from the following description:

There was a scholar who also served as a ritual slaughterer and led the congregation, issuing regulations for the proper running of the congregation. He also taught their sons the words of the sages . . . He has lived in Antioch for the past several years where he serves as their spokesman and leader: most of the congregants are his students and he stands in the breach for them before the authorities. If someone is imprisoned because of financial matters or on libellous charges, he does not rest until he obtains his release.[48]

---

[45] See Harel, 'The Overthrow of the Last Aleppan Chief Rabbi' (Heb.), 113.

[46] Most likely chief scribe in the city. See Laniado, *For the Sake of the Holy Ones* (Heb.), 183.

[47] Benayahu Collection, Ḥet 86 (uncatalogued documents), writ of the contract between Rabbi Moses Sasson of Aleppo and the community of Antioch, signed by Rabbi Moses Sasson and Abraham Shamia, Aleppo, Rosh Hodesh Kislev 1846.

[48] Dweck Hakohen, *Emet me'erets*, 27a–28a, no. 4. See also ACRI, TR/Is-162a, Rabbi Abraham Dweck Hakohen to Rabbi Moses Halevi, Antioch, 22 Nisan 1880, 22 Sivan 1880.

Several of the rabbis serving in the smaller communities were prominent scholars, who agreed to serve in places that were not centres of learning either to earn a livelihood or to enhance their personal status. Among such figures were Rabbi Shalom Chasky, who served as the rabbi of 'Ayntab in the 1840s; Rabbi Mordecai Abadi, who served in Kilis in the 1860s; Rabbis Moses Sasson and Abraham Ezra Dweck Hakohen in Antioch; and Rabbi Aaron Dayan in Urfa.[49]

Notwithstanding the appointment of chief rabbis in some of the satellite communities, these communities continued to rely on the larger ones for certain of their religious needs, for example if they had no *beit din* of their own or needed recourse to halakhic authority. For their part, the spiritual heads of the large communities were aware of their responsibility for the functioning of the smaller nearby communities.[50]

Communal Administration

The Lay Steering Committee

The 1865 Jewish millet decree included a provision calling for organized, regular elections for a lay steering committee to operate alongside the chief rabbi and oversee the administrative needs of the community, including tax collection, supervision of philanthropic bodies, and contacts with government officials. However, although this decree was promulgated in both Damascus and Aleppo, in neither city was it implemented before the late nineteenth century. In the absence of elections, membership of the communal administration and its executive arm was generally determined by wealth, sometimes by distinguished ancestry. The lineage- and wealth-based oligarchies brooked no questioning of their status, and allowed no other elements of the community to take part in its administration. Although membership of the communal administration carried prestige, it also required an outlay of funds; from the point of view of the wider community, therefore, there was advantage in drawing its leadership from the affluent elite. In 1856 the situation in Damascus was described as follows: 'There is not a president of the community; its affairs are managed by the heads of the wealthiest families, along with the Hakham Bashi, recognised by the government.'[51]

[49] On Rabbi Shalom Chasky, see Laniado, *For the Sake of the Holy Ones* (Heb.), 80; Azriel, *Kapei aharon*, pt. 1, 111a, 'Ḥoshen mishpaṭ', no. 3. On Rabbi Mordecai Abadi, see Laniado, *For the Sake of the Holy Ones* (Heb.), 48–50; Mordecai Abadi, *Divrei mordekhai*, author's introd. For Rabbi Abraham Ezra Dweck Hakohen, see Harel, 'The Overthrow of the Last Aleppan Chief Rabbi' (Heb.), 110ff. On Rabbi Aaron Dayan, see Laniado, *For the Sake of the Holy Ones* (Heb.), 10; Schur, *Maḥazot haḥayim*, 17.

[50] See e.g. the recognition by Aleppine rabbis of their responsibility towards the community of Antioch: Benayahu Collection, *Ḥet* 86 (uncatalogued documents), writ of guardianship signed by the rabbinical court of Aleppo, Rabbis Abraham Antebi, Abraham Dayan, and Hayim Mordecai Labaton, Aleppo, Elul 1848.   [51] Frankl, *The Jews in the East*, i. 298.

Even after the initiation of elections in the late nineteenth century, the wealthy and hereditary oligarchies continued to head the communal institutions. According to the Jewish millet decree, it was the function of the lay steering committee to oversee and assist the *ḥakham bashi* in fulfilling his role, yet the absence of an elected, government-recognized body hampered the ability of the lay leadership to discharge this supervisory function. Another measure taken by the Ottoman regime as part of its effort to modernize the municipal governments was the appointment of a *mukhtar* in each urban quarter. The job of the *mukhtar al-yahud* was to keep lists of the male residents, and to oversee relocation, property transfer, and other similar transactions.[52]

The Spiritual Committee and the Rabbinic Court

The lay committee, responsible for the Jewish community's material needs, functioned alongside the spiritual committee, which was responsible for meeting its spiritual requirements; the latter's members also served on the rabbinic court. A spiritual committee formed in the early 1840s in Damascus consisted of ten eminent rabbis who sat on the rabbinic court in rotation with the chief rabbis.[53] In Aleppo, on the other hand, there was no official spiritual committee until the late 1870s, and three judges sat permanently on the rabbinic court.[54]

The Muslim Ottoman authorities had no theological or political objections to Jewish judicial autonomy.[55] Indeed, the existence of a strong communal leadership was in their interest, as social unrest could interfere with the generation of government revenues from taxes. Consequently, the regime gave de facto recognition to the Jewish judicial institutions. Until the mid-nineteenth century the Jewish court enjoyed virtually uncontested authority and its verdicts were almost always obeyed. Contributing to this state of affairs was the fact that, at least outwardly, the majority of the community was observant. There was also considerable pressure against risking the loss of cases or money in the non-Jewish courts, so that, although Jews did in theory have recourse to an alternative in the form of the Ottoman courts, up to the 1860s they generally preferred to conduct their cases in the Jewish court.[56] In Damascus significant legal issues came before a complement of three judges, who sat in the yeshiva operating in the home of Jacob Levy, a prominent member of the elite. Less important matters were arbitrated by one of the judges or by a member of the elite.[57]

Judicial powers of enforcement were partly vested in the judges' moral authority; nonetheless, when necessary, the Ottoman authorities implemented

---

[52] ACRI, TR/Is-162a, Damascus notables to Rabbi Moses Halevi, Damascus, 25 Av 1874. On the creation of the post of *mukhtar*, see Lewis, *The Emergence of Modern Turkey*, 388.
[53] See Wilson, *The Lands of the Bible*, ii. 336; Frankl, *The Jews in the East*, i. 297.
[54] AAIU, Syrie, II.E., Alep, 11, Altaras, 25 Jan. 1880.
[55] See Lazarus-Yafeh, *Muslim Authors on Jews and Judaism* (Heb.), 17.
[56] *Halevanon*, 23, 13 Kislev 1865, p. 362. [57] *Halevanon*, 7, 13 Nisan 1866, p. 103.

the verdicts of the Jewish courts. The Jewish court in Damascus did not hesitate to gaol Jews who departed from religious or social norms.[58] In Aleppo—notwithstanding the ire of the scholarly stratum at this departure from Jewish law—it was customary to bring disputes before a single judge or arbitrator.[59] On occasion, judicial matters were brought before the yeshiva scholars. After discussion by all those present, the rabbi would pronounce a verdict with the scholars' backing.[60] The judges' fees were not fixed but were at the discretion of, and dependent on, the individual litigant's generosity.[61]

It was noted above with regard to Damascus that there was a balance of power between the *ḥakham bashi* and the wealthy elite. The millet decree created a similar balance between the lay and the spiritual committees. Even in Aleppo, where they were less dependent on the affluent class and enjoyed a higher status, the rabbis were aware of the decline in their power and of their need to secure the backing of the lay communal leadership to implement their decisions:

It is the obligation of the scholars to declare prohibitions, and if they declared one and were not heeded, it is then the obligation of the wealthy to back the scholars and to castigate the offenders and to fine them in order to chastise them, as Scripture says: 'Judges and officials you are to provide for yourselves, within all your gates.' [Deut. 16: 18][62]

Despite the situation outlined above, self-discipline and a sense of collective responsibility did not always outweigh litigants' considerations of expediency. Consequently, there were cases in which Jewish men or women preferred to turn to the Ottoman courts. A similar phenomenon is attested for the seventeenth and eighteenth centuries, primarily with regard to the execution of wills and bequests, ratification of endowments (*hekdeshot*), and cases to do with property ownership.[63] As noted above, the widening of the circles of foreign protégés in the latter half of the nineteenth century also brought an increased number of applications to the consular courts. At times, litigants turned to these courts initially; in other instances the litigants sought to appeal against a verdict of the Jewish court. In the long run, this phenomenon played a decisive role in weakening the Jewish judicial system and its jurisdictional scope.[64]

---

[58] *Halevanon*, 23, 13 Kislev 1865, pp. 361–2.

[59] Laniado, *Kiseh shelomoh*, no. 1, 1 ff.; Antebi, *Mor ve'oholot*, 74a, 'Ḥoshen mishpat', no. 2.

[60] Antebi, *Mor ve'oholot*, 58a, 'Even ha'ezer', no. 12.

[61] Benayahu Collection, *Ḥet* 86, *Pesakim*.

[62] J. S. Dweck Hakohen, *She'erit ya'akov*, 54b.

[63] See al-Qattan, 'The Damascene Jewish Community', 205–6; id., '*Dhimmīs* in the Muslim Court'; Establet and Pascual, 'Damascene Probate Inventories'.

[64] See Zohar, *Tradition and Change* (Heb.), 143–95.

Taxation

The local Jewish communal jurisdiction also had the responsibility of over-seeing the payment of communal dues, including both Ottoman and internal taxes. The successful organization of tax collection from the members of the Jewish community relied on each individual's recognition that tax payments were vital to the functioning of the community, together with a fear of heavenly punishment for those who set themselves apart from the community and did not donate their share to the communal coffers. Each individual's contribution was determined by *arikhah*, assessment of his resources.

As with so many aspects of Jewish life, the different ways in which the process of assessment was carried out in the two large communities is linked to their different patterns of socio-economic stratification. In Damascus the burden of financing the community fell mainly upon a small number of families—between ten and twenty, including the Levy-Stambouli, Angel, Lisbona, Farhi, Harari, Tobi, and Hason families—who assessed themselves once every three years in conjunction with the rabbis. On this occasion they split into three groups: each group assessed the share appropriate to its members, and the three assessments were then averaged to arrive at the payment required from each. The level of tax was never higher than 5 per cent, or lower than 0.25 per cent, of a person's assets. This system was cancelled in 1875 when the elite became bankrupt and had no property to assess; no longer could they continue to underwrite the community's needs.[65]

The following description by Rabbi Isaac Abulafia succinctly sums up how internal taxes in Damascus were determined and the purposes for which funds were disbursed:

From the time of its founding . . . it has been the wealthy individuals of our community, may God preserve them, who have provided for the needs of the city from their own pockets and resources, that is, for the ritual slaughterers and the poor, for the scholarly class and the emissaries for the yeshiva in Erets Yisra'el, may it be rebuilt speedily in our day, and for the emissaries themselves, and for needy guests, and for the remaining expenses of the city. They would do an accounting every six months, around the Passover and the Sukkot holidays, in the sum of fifty thousand and more from all the individuals in our city, the assessors and the assessed. From the funds collected they would pay all the expenses and the fixed allotment of the rabbis and *dayanim*; everything was paid from the *arikhah*, for the wealth and profits of the individual townspeople who were the donors, may God preserve them, from their success in trade and in money-lending to non-Jews sufficed to pay the *arikhah* for all the above-named costs and more, with the exception of the taxes and levies such as

[65] See *JC*, 1 June 1854, p. 302; Elyashar, *Yisa ish*, 78a–81b, 'Hoshen mishpat', no. 5; Tarab, *Sha'arei ezra*, 152b.

the *kharaj* [land or produce tax] and *jizya* [the royal poll tax], which each individual paid from his own funds as determined by the officials and communal leaders . . . with the exception of the poor and the scholarly class who were not taxed at all according to the Torah.[66]

This system worked well as long as the crucial few families remained wealthy. However, when the economic crash came in 1875, their personal losses led to the collapse of the Jewish community, which had developed no organizational infrastructure, no fixed budget, and no precise bookkeeping of debits and credits.[67]

This contrasts sharply with the situation in Aleppo, where the number of taxpayers far exceeded that in Damascus. In Aleppo assessors were appointed by the rabbinic court, which instructed them to make an impartial assessment of the members of the community. In cases of a disputed evaluation, communal tradition stated: 'It is the custom of the city that whoever says so must swear to what he possesses on the Aleppo Codex and he then pays according to his oath.'[68] Although Aleppo's budgetary needs were similar to those of Damascus, the burden was divided among more of its members. Moreover, in Aleppo the budget was fixed in advance, and the funds to be disbursed to the various foundations were predetermined. As a result, the Aleppine Jewish community continued to function efficiently even after the commercial crisis of the early 1870s.[69]

In Aleppo and Damascus alike, communal outlay covered three main spheres. First, there were the expenses related to the running of the community as a religious entity: namely, the upkeep of the public synagogues and payment of the officials' salaries. Damascus had seven public synagogues and Aleppo two; in addition, some of the rich maintained private synagogues in their homes. Maintenance of the public synagogues included the provision of oil for lamps and of mats, as well as repairs and renovations. In both communities the funding for synagogue upkeep, which came mainly from donations made upon being called up to the Torah, from private donations, and from charitable foundations, was adequate for these needs.[70] Consequently, synagogue upkeep did not constitute a burdensome item in the budget. The community also paid the salaries of its religious officials—*dayanim*, beadles, prayer leaders, *shofar* blowers, ritual slaughterers, and *kashrut* inspectors—and financed ritual bath and cemetery maintenance.

The second realm was that of philanthropy: namely, assistance to scholars, the poor, orphans, and charitable societies. These needs were generally met by

[66] Elyashar, *Yisa ish*, 78*b*, 'Ḥoshen mishpat', no. 5.
[67] See Elmaleh, *The Jews in Damascus* (Heb.), 17.   [68] Laniado, *Kise shelomoh*, 9*a*, no. 2.
[69] Neumark, *A Journey in the Old Land* (Heb.), 55. See also *Hamagid*, 10, 20 Adar 1880, p. 83.
[70] *Ḥavatselet*, 34, 2 Tamuz 1880, p. 225.

special voluntary bodies; however, in Damascus no properly organized charitable society existed before the 1880s. Although its chief rabbis managed some charitable funds, they were not large enough or generously enough replenished to meet the community's needs, and so the poor depended on the generosity of rich individuals. When necessary, as before Passover, special fundraising campaigns were undertaken. Some wealthy individuals funded soup kitchens for the poor; however, a few personal efforts were not enough to meet the needs of the many.[71] Nor did Damascus have an organization to provide care for the Jewish sick; as a result, on occasion Jews were forced to turn to Christian societies.[72]

In Aleppo, on the other hand, philanthropy was well developed, thanks to the Francos. Exempt from communal taxes, these European Jewish families voluntarily set up charitable funds for the purpose of assisting the poor to achieve a better standard of living. Notwithstanding their originators' elitist background, these foundations helped all sectors of the population without discrimination. Among the societies established as early as the eighteenth century was a *bikur ḥolim* whose aim was to help the sick poor with medicines, doctors' fees, and food. The Franco families took it in turn to administer the fund for a year at a time, and their expertise in taking advantage of investment opportunities increased the capital available to the foundation, as Rabbi Abraham Antebi noted:

How good and pleasant is the ancient practice here in Aleppo, that they created a permanent fund with an immense sum of money, and each of the Jewish notables takes it upon himself in turn to earn money from the capital to devote to the needs of the indigent sick. And if it does not earn well, he provides for their needs from his own pocket. And in the following year a different individual assumes responsibility, according to lot.[73]

Other societies that benefited from Franco funding were the *gemilut ḥasadim* society, which took care of burial needs, and the *malbish arumim* society, which provided winter clothing for the poor, in particular for students in the *talmudei torah*.[74] Yet others distributed flour to the poor, saw to the weekly allocation of bread (and of matzot on Passover), and provided financial aid to the indigent before the Sukkot and Passover holidays. Certain funds were earmarked for the purchase of books for the study houses.[75]

Even after the severe economic crisis in Aleppo, its communal and philanthropic institutions appeared to go on functioning with a considerable degree of success, compared to those of the Damascus community. Nevertheless, the damage to the Francos' enterprises did mean that they could no longer provide

[71] See *Halevanon*, 14, 20 Tamuz 1865, p. 216.   [72] See Frankl, *The Jews in the East*, i. 298.
[73] Antebi, *Ḥokhmah umusar*, 59b. See also *JC*, 10 Aug. 1855, p. 259.
[74] See Antebi, *Ḥokhmah umusar*, 60a. See also AAIU, Syrie, II.E., Alep, 11, Altaras, 25 Jan. 1880.   [75] See AAIU, Syrie, II.E., Alep, 11, Altaras, 25 Jan. 1880.

the same level of support that they had in the past, and over time the charitable funds dwindled. Moreover, from the mid-1870s internal disputes, the ever-increasing poverty of the middle class, the concentration of local businessmen on restoring their businesses, and Franco concern with preserving their elite status in Aleppine society all led to a neglect of communal needs and a steep decline in the ability of the charitable funds to fulfil their function. Although the philanthropic frameworks continued to exist, the Aleppines became indifferent to them, as Saul Somekh, the Alliance emissary to Aleppo, observed: 'There is a perpetual atmosphere of divisive strife; the mutual solidarity and charitableness that usually characterize our people have here given way to apathy and cold selfishness. Self-love is conspicuously active and sentiments of national honour are unknown.'[76]

The third sphere of communal finance involved the provision of funds to emissaries on behalf of the Jews in Erets Yisra'el. Although taken from the communal treasury, donations for this purpose came mainly from families of the affluent elite who hosted the emissaries in their houses and gave them presents from their own pockets.[77]

Paradoxically, the very reforms that aimed to regularize the functioning of the communal leadership in fact weakened the status of the chief rabbis without detracting significantly from the continued influence of the wealthy elites. Eventually, it was economic crisis and decline that fatally undermined the communal institutions, by destroying the ability of those elites to support the Jewish communal infrastructure that had relied on them for so long.

[76] AAIU, Syrie, X.E., Alep, 83, Somekh, 16 Dec. 1879. On the dwindling of the funds, see AAIU, Syrie, II.E., Alep, 11, Altaras, 25 Jan. 1880.

[77] See *Halevanon*, 14, 20 Tamuz 1865, p. 216.

FIVE

EDUCATION— TRADITIONAL AND MODERN

A S IN THE ELECTION of chief rabbis and the communal administration, so in education the wealthy elites, including the Francos, exercised decisive influence within the Jewish communities of Syria. Throughout the period under examination here the majority of Jewish boys continued to study in traditional frameworks; nonetheless, these years also saw a rising number of students enrolling in the modern schools for boys established by the Alliance Israélite Universelle and the foundation of Alliance institutions for girls. The process of introducing modern educational institutions illustrates once again how divisions within the Jewish community affected Jewish life in Syria.

Elementary Education

Kuttabs

In 1840 no signs of modern pedagogy were discernible in the rigid, tradition-bound framework of Jewish education in Syria. As a religious minority, Syrian Jews feared the penetration of external influences that threatened their identity. In seeking to preserve its traditional communal structure, Jewish society placed not the individual but the community at the centre of its educational system. The aim was to provide each child and youth with the ability to function undeviatingly within the traditional communal frameworks, thereby ensuring their preservation and continuity, rather than to encourage a search for potentially hazardous new horizons or revolutionary change.

By and large, the educational system reflected the existing communal social stratification described in earlier chapters. The children of the poor studied in communal institutions and the children of the elites received private education. In the early 1840s Damascus had one communal *talmud torah*, also known by the Arabic term *kuttab*, divided into ten classes. In each class some twenty-five to sixty pupils—ranging in age from 3 to 13—sat on the floor in crowded, unfurnished rooms. Prayer books, the Pentateuch, and talmudic tractates were the only textbooks. At times an entire class shared a single volume, with each pupil approaching the teacher's desk to read a few sentences in turn, or the book being passed from pupil to pupil. Biblical and talmudic passages, studied in the original language only, formed the basis of the curriculum, alongside a focus on prayer and synagogue services, the linchpin of Jewish male social solidarity. Secular studies, including the local Arabic language, had no part in the curriculum. Thus, as compared to the children of the wealthy, whose parents could pay for more advanced private lessons, the children of the poor who generally populated the *kuttab*s remained relatively ignorant.[1] The situation in smaller towns was similar; in the synagogue setting in which most youths studied emphasis was placed on rote learning rather than on reading comprehension.[2]

The teachers in the elementary schools, their already low salaries diminished further by the frequent failure of parents to make their obligatory contributions, often presided over poorly organized, unruly, and noisy classrooms, relying on the whip and stick to impose order and even to beat knowledge into the pupils, as in the following illustrative passage describing a school in Urfa: 'The *melamed*, with his unearthly voice, sits bent over with a staff in his hand and beats the pupils for every little thing . . . the pupil's legs are tied to a stick like a lamb bound for slaughter and the *melamed* beats him unmercifully until his anger recedes.'[3]

In Aleppo, with its less polarized social stratification, the dominant middle class was well aware of the importance of education, and this awareness even filtered down to the lower classes.[4] The high value placed on education, and the consequent establishment of schools in Aleppo, owed a great deal to the Francos. As early as the eighteenth century, the Francos founded two schools for Aleppo's Jewish community, funding them from their own pockets. One was for poor orphans, one for other poor children.[5] The conditions and pedagogical methods in Aleppo differed from those found in Damascus. The 500 students, the same number as in Damascus, were divided among twelve to fifteen different locations rather than being concentrated in a single school, so that the classrooms were less crowded.[6] Moreover, the curriculum was not based solely on rote learning, but included reading comprehension as well. A supervisory body tested students on the previous week's studies each sabbath.[7]

Some graduates of these elementary *kuttab*s went on to the single secondary school in Aleppo.[8] In Aleppo, as in the other Syrian Jewish communities, the

[1] See Wilson, *The Lands of the Bible*, ii. 333–4; FO 78/622, Wood to Canning, Damascus, 31 May 1845; Frankl, *The Jews in the East*, i. 297.   [2] See Schur, *Maḥazot haḥayim*, 14, 17–18.
[3] Ibid. 17–18.   [4] Abraham Dayan, *Zikaron lanefesh*, 45.
[5] AAIU, Syrie, II.E., Alep, 11, Altaras, 25 Jan. 1880.
[6] FO 78/1689, Report of the Consul Skene, Aleppo, 5 June 1862.
[7] See Antebi, *Ḥokhmah umusar*, 7a.   [8] AAIU, Syrie, II.E., Alep, 11, Altaras, 25 Jan. 1880.

purpose of elementary school study was solely to inculcate Jewish tradition. It neither aimed to provide vocational training nor viewed the broadening of knowledge as an end in itself; rather, it disseminated knowledge in order to buttress the Jewish community's continued autonomy. Consequently, graduates of the school system, in both Damascus and Aleppo, had one of two options: either to move on to higher Jewish learning, or, as most did, to end their studies and turn to crafts or commerce.

Yeshivas

For the handful of individuals who chose to continue their education with higher Jewish studies, until the 1860s both of the large Jewish communities boasted many yeshivas. In Aleppo, yeshivas were maintained in the homes of the affluent, and higher rabbinic studies were concentrated in a single central yeshiva. Damascus, on the other hand, had no central yeshiva and advanced rabbinic studies took place only in the private yeshivas in the homes of the rich.[9] In Damascus, the level of Torah learning began to decline from the 1860s; in Aleppo, however, the level of study remained high, as the traveller Wolf (William) Schur noted during his stay there in 1875:

There is a large yeshiva here and many study Talmud and *posekim* [adjudicative literature], but only in Aleppo and in Baghdad, which is Babylon, are there additional individuals who can swim in the depths of the talmudic sea and extract its pearls. Elsewhere in the lands of Syria, Kurdistan, and Arabia, there is no one who can spread a sail on that great sea; neither are the paths of the early *posekim* well paved for them and they simply follow the *Shulḥan arukh*.[10]

The decline of rabbinic study in Damascus is part of a long process of diminution in Damascus' importance as a centre of Torah learning for the surrounding cities and towns. Its proximity to other important Torah centres, such as Tiberias, Safed, and Jerusalem, hastened its dependence on Erets Yisra'el for Torah scholarship and halakhic decisions, and the yeshivas of Aleppo and Baghdad generally filled the needs of communities east of Damascus, such as Mosul. To the west, there was a decline in the Jewish populations of the smaller communities such as Sidon, Deir al-Qamar, Hasbayah, and Tripoli. Beirut, with its nascent Jewish settlement, had a few scholars who met the town's needs, and in cases of great halakhic complexity this community turned to the Jerusalem sages.[11] In Damascus itself, the poverty and relative ignorance of the great majority of the Jewish community did not give rise to much demand for higher rabbinic learning.[12] The bankruptcy in 1875 of the wealthy elite who up to that point had supported the yeshivas and the

---

[9] See Zenner, 'Jews in Late Ottoman Syria'.
[10] Schur, *Maḥazot haḥayim*, 11.
[11] See Neumark, *A Journey in the Old Land* (Heb.), 68.
[12] *Halevanon*, 7, 13 Nisan 1866, p. 102.

scholars was another significant factor in the decline both in the number of scholars and in the level of Torah scholarship in late nineteenth-century Damascus.

In contrast, in the 1880s the scholars of Aleppo continued to exercise an influence on the nearby communities, which depended on them for halakhic guidance. Middle-class participation in Torah learning and the continued existence of the central yeshiva, in which actual and hypothetical halakhic questions were clarified, as well as of yeshivas in private homes, all contributed to the maintenance of a high level of scholarship in Aleppo. The spread of learning beyond a narrowly defined scholarly class stimulated the founding of a Hebrew press in Aleppo in 1865.[13]

Education for Girls

In the Middle East as a whole at this time, not just within Jewish society, education of girls was seen as lacking either value or purpose. Because a woman's work was restricted to her home, she had no need of education beyond the ability to do household work, fulfil her husband's wishes, and care for her children. Women were deemed to have no authority within the family setting, let alone within the communal framework.[14]

Consequently, prior to the second half of the nineteenth century no educational institutions for girls existed in the Syrian Jewish communities, and most Jewish women were illiterate. Ludwig August Frankl described the behaviour of women in the Damascus synagogue when the Torah scroll was removed from the Ark: 'They pressed against the open door of the synagogue, and spread out their arms with fervent devotion toward the thora. Not one of them had a prayer-book, as none of them can read, and this movement and pantomime is the only part which they can take in divine service.'[15] Only some of the wealthy families, primarily among the more open-minded Francos, educated their daughters either privately or in Christian mission schools.

Penetration of Western Education: The Alliance Israélite Universelle in Syria

Changes in the traditional attitude towards education, brought about by the opening of Protestant educational institutions in Syria in the 1850s, intensified with the appearance on the scene of the Paris-based Alliance Israélite Universelle, founded in 1860 with the goal of protecting Jews across the world and in particular establishing a network of schools among the eastern Jewish

[13] For a comprehensive treatment, see Harel, *The Books of Aleppo* (Heb.), 20–5; Yaari, 'Hebrew Printing at Aleppo' (Heb.), 100–5; id., 'Additions to "Hebrew Printing at Aleppo"' (Heb.), 401–2. On the press in Syria, see Cioeta, 'Ottoman Censorship'.

[14] See AECCC, Damas, vol. 7, p. 169, Gillois, 20 Jan. 1893.

[15] Frankl, *The Jews in the East*, i. 295.

communities, in order to provide their children with modern, productive education on the French model. Following the introduction of modern education to Syria through various Christian mission schools, the Alliance introduced similar educational frameworks in Jewish communities, first in Damascus (in 1864) and then in Aleppo (in 1869). Although these schools taught Hebrew, Talmud, and Bible, their curricula focused on French language and culture, acquainting Jewish children with literary works such as La Fontaine's fables and Molière's plays. Additional subjects introduced in the Alliance schools included mathematics, geography, spoken and literary Arabic, and calligraphy.[16]

These years, then, saw both a decline in traditional education and the introduction of modern methods and curricula in a process that was nevertheless slow and beset by difficulties. The prevailing academic viewpoint attributes the uneven progress of the Alliance schools to opposition to modern education on the part of conservative elements within the Jewish population, notably the scholarly class. Indeed, there are those who construe the history of education in Syria from the arrival of the Alliance as a continuous struggle between conservative zealots favouring traditional education and enlightened moderns espousing secular, utilitarian education.[17] Closer examination of the sources dealing with Alliance activity in Syria entirely negates this construction.

Initial support for my alternative argument comes from the absence of any critical note in the following reported dialogue between Alphonse de Rothschild and fifteen Damascene rabbis during the former's visit to Damascus in 1856:

'Why do you not establish schools to impart instruction to your children in such secular branches of knowledge as may promote their future prospects in life?'

'We have not the means, we have to expend so much on the poor.'

'The reason why you have so many poor is, because you do not educate your children; above all, because you are not sufficiently careful to teach them trades.'

'Our children are too weak.'[18]

Nowhere in this exchange do the Damascus rabbis offset modern education against traditional values. It can perhaps be argued that, in their conversation with the wealthy philanthropist, the rabbis deliberately emphasized their poverty rather than any principled opposition to modern education. It is also likely that the rabbis were more concerned with persuading their illustrious visitor to open his heart and his coffers than with revealing their true thoughts.

---

[16] See AAIU, Syrie, III.E., Alep, 21, Behar, 22 Aug. 1870, 19 Jan. 1871. For a comprehensive study of Alliance activity in the Middle Eastern Jewish communities, see Rodrigue, *Images of Sephardi and Eastern Jewries*. See also Antébi, *Les missionnaires juifs de la France*.

[17] See e.g. H. J. Cohen, *The Jews of the Middle East*, 139; Zenner, 'Jews in Late Ottoman Syria', 183; Leven, *Cinquante ans d'histoire*, ii. 59–60.   [18] Frankl, *The Jews in the East*, i. 300–1.

However, their behaviour during, and responses to, events connected with the opening of an Alliance school in their city demonstrate their genuine support for the promotion of modern education in their community.

An elaborate reception awaited the first Alliance emissary to Damascus, Heymann, upon his arrival on 22 January 1865. This included a personal greeting by the *ḥakham bashi* Jacob Peretz, who then hosted the emissary at his home for eight days.[19] Rabbi Isaac Abulafia, who sat on the communal rabbinic court, became a member of the committee formed to oversee the founding of a school in the city.[20] And yet, after a year and a half of efforts to establish a school on solid foundations, Heymann, who was determined to succeed in his task for the sake of the Damascus Jewish community, even, as he said, 'in spite of and without them',[21] was forced to admit failure and to abandon Damascus. This failure, however, was the result not of rabbinic opposition but of unwillingness on the part of the wealthy elite to disburse the promised donations to put the school on a sound and enduring financial footing.[22]

Seligman Weisskopf, Heymann's replacement in Damascus, took steps to ingratiate himself with the rabbis, first and foremost by hiring one of the city's scholars to serve on the school staff. In his reports Weisskopf highlighted the devotion to and concern for the school shown by the chief rabbis, Jacob Peretz and Aaron Jacob Binyamin, who enrolled their children there, joined the Alliance, and did not rest until the community had contributed a building from a *hekdesh* for the school's premises.[23] Weisskopf was forced to leave the school in late 1869, mainly for personal reasons—though again, it was disagreements with the wealthy elite, not with the rabbis, that also played a role in his departure.[24]

Formally, Alliance activity in Damascus now stopped for a decade; however, its spirit was kept alive in Damascus by three of the school's graduates, who founded La Société des jeunes gens à Damas to promote its principles. These young men, who regarded education as a supreme value, founded a library in Damascus with Alliance aid, and began to study Turkish, the official language of the Ottoman administration, on their own. They also sought to send several orphans to study at the Alliance-sponsored Mikveh Israël school in Jaffa.[25]

[19] AAIU, Syrie, XVII.E., Damas, 160, Heymann, 9 Feb. 1865.

[20] Ibid., 21 May 1865.   [21] Ibid., 21 Oct. 1865.

[22] See ibid., 9 Feb. 1865, 31 Apr. 1865, 21 May 1865, 11 July 1865, 21 Oct. 1865.

[23] AAIU, Syrie, XXI.E., Damas, 222, Weisskopf, 29 Aug. 1867, 29 Sept. 1867. See also AECCC, Damas, vol. 4, p. 395, Rousseau, 8 Nov. 1867.

[24] AAIU, Syrie, XXI.E., Damas, 222, Weisskopf, 19 Mar. 1869, 5 Oct. 1869.

[25] See AAIU, Syrie, XI.E., Damas, 94, 'Société de jeunes gens' (Belilios, Reuben, et Halfon), 20 Dec. 1869, 28 Feb. 1870, 18 May 1870, 7 Apr. 1872; I.B., 5, Damas, Halfon, 15 Dec. 1869; *JC*, 25 Feb. 1870, p. 11. See also CZA, J-41, Mikveh Yisra'el Archive, 83, Isaac Halfon to Charles Netter [?], Damascus, 20 June 1871; Halfon, Belilios, and Reuben to Charles Netter [?], Damascus, 20 Dec. 1871.

They worked constantly to spread Alliance ideals among the Damascus Jewish community, disseminating the contents of the *Bulletin de l'Alliance Israélite Universelle* in the city, and continually pressed the Alliance to reopen its school.[26] Through this activity the Damascus Jewish community maintained unbroken ties with the Alliance, and its chief rabbis continued to turn to the Alliance with various requests for aid.[27] Moreover, following the economic collapse of 1875, the entire scholarly class of Damascus appealed to the Alliance for support for them and their families.[28]

In 1880 the chief rabbi, Ephraim Mercado Alkalai, and the governor, Midhat Pasha, made a concerted and successful effort to reopen the Alliance school in Damascus, an initiative backed by the entire scholarly class. Even the scholars who taught in the traditional *kuttab*s, whose livelihood might be threatened by the creation of a modern school, chose not to oppose the Alliance but rather sought to have it take them and the *kuttab*s under its wing.[29] In the following years the spiritual heads of the Damascus Jewish community made it their practice to visit the Alliance school and to test its students' knowledge.[30]

In Aleppo the initiative to enter into contacts with the Alliance and to encourage it to become involved in education there came from the Francos. The main mover on this front was David Solomon Altaras, who as early as 1864 invited the Alliance emissary to Baghdad to stay in his home. Impressed by the society's aims, he started a fundraising drive for the Alliance among other Franco families. In that same year Altaras also founded a local committee, consisting exclusively of Francos, to encourage contributions to the Alliance.[31] Four years later the Francos presented the Alliance with a request to found a school in Aleppo, arguing that the lack of a Jewish *école nationale* was prompting Jews to send their children to Christian schools in order to study French. They urgently requested that the Alliance send a Jewish teacher to teach French to twenty pupils, almost certainly the children of Franco families.[32] The Francos' cultural background, their involvement in international trade, and their positions as consular representatives of European powers heightened their awareness of the need for knowledge of foreign languages: 'Because of the high offices they hold by dint

[26] See AAIU, Syrie, XI.E., Damas, 94, Halfon, 2 Aug. 1872, 7 Jan. 1874; I.B., 5, Damas, Halfon, 8 Jan. 1873, 20 Dec. 1875; Belilios, 1 May 1879.

[27] See e.g. AAIU, Syrie, I.B., 5, Damas, letter of Rabbi Kimhi to the Alliance, late Nisan 1875.

[28] See AAIU, Syrie, I.B., 5, Damas, Heshvan 1879, letter from thirty-one Damascus scholars to the Alliance, with the approbation of the *dayanim* Rabbis Isaac Abulafia and Solomon Sukary.

[29] See AAIU, Syrie, I.B., 5, Damas, 29 June 1880, letter from the Damascus *melamedim* to the Alliance. On Midhat Pasha's initiative, see Harel, 'Midhat Pasha and the Jewish Community'.

[30] See e.g. AAIU, Syrie, XI.E., 96, Aboulafia, 12 Iyar 1881, letter from Rabbis Isaac Abulafia and Solomon Sukary to the Alliance. On the development of secular education in Damascus, see Deguilhem, 'State Civil Education'.

[31] AAIU, Syrie, II.E., Alep, 11, Altaras, 10 Nov. 1864; *BAIU*, dernier trimestre, 1864, p. cxxvi.

[32] See AAIU, Syrie, VIII.E., Alep, 68, I. de Piccioto à Crémieux, 2 Nov. 1868; *BAIU*, 2ème sem. 1868, 82.

of European kings they were forced to let in enlightened education . . . and they
have no hatred for enlightenment . . . and because of their constant business
dealings with Europeans, their opinions have drawn closer to the opinions of
the Europeans.'[33]

For the Francos, the innovative aspect of opening an Alliance school in
Aleppo did not lie in its broad and modern curriculum—after all, they had
already been giving their children such an education through private tutors or
non-Jewish schools—but in the opening of a modern *Jewish* school. Their motivation for founding such a school was not grounded in concern for the younger
generation as a whole, rich and poor, Franco and Mustarib, but rather in their
desire to provide an elitist education for Franco children and for the children
of affluent local families. Accordingly, the school was initially geared towards
the affluent rather than the poor, in contravention of the Alliance's stated principle of supporting the lower, more impoverished strata of Jewish society.[34]

Nonetheless, when the school opened on 30 November 1869 its first intake
did include fifteen children from poor backgrounds, mainly orphans, in addtion
to the sixty-eight students from Franco and other wealthy families.[35] However,
most of the poor students were forced to leave the school after a short time, not
only because of economic constraints, but mainly because of social and class
pressures. This pressure became particularly intense when some of the Francos, headed by Hillel de Picciotto, the American consul in Aleppo, sought to
expel the non-paying, charity pupils. Picciotto directed his considerable
influence to preserving what he saw as the school's intended purpose, namely,
to educate the children of the Francos and other wealthy families. He concealed
his elitist motives by arguing that the principal and sole teacher, Nissim Behar,
could not teach so many pupils simultaneously, a claim he backed by citing the
teacher–pupil ratio of no more than one to ten in Aleppo's Christian schools.
Having failed to persuade Behar to expel the non-paying pupils, Picciotto turned
to his European connections to achieve his goal. With the assistance of the chief
rabbi of Strasbourg he brought a Jewish teacher to Aleppo to head a rival school
that accepted only the children of the well-to-do.[36]

The Alliance did not immediately grasp the social implications of Picciotto's
establishment of a rival school;[37] however, when these became clear, the

---

[33] Schur, *Maḥazot baḥayim*, 9–10.

[34] See Laskier, 'The Alliance Israélite Universelle', pp. lxxi–lxxv; AAIU, Syrie, II.E., Alep, 11,
Altaras, 12 Mar. 1869. Some members of the Muslim elites in Syria also viewed response to change
as the key to retaining their social status, especially in the sphere of modern education. For a comprehensive treatment, see Roded, 'Tradition and Change in Syria'.

[35] AAIU, Syrie, II.E., Alep, 11, Altaras, 12 Mar. 1869, 22 Feb. 1870; III.E., Alep, 21, Behar, 13
Nov. 1869, 21 Jan. 1870.

[36] See AAIU, Syrie, III.E., Alep, 21, Behar, 19 Jan. 1871, 19 Jan. 1872, 11 Nov. 1872.

[37] See CZA, J-41/83, Mikveh Yisra'el Archive, Report on schools in the Orient, sent by the
Alliance to Charles Netter, 18 Mar. 1872.

society made 'opening its gates to the poor' a condition for its continued support of the Alliance school and its reorganization.[38] Nissim Behar took steps
to incorporate poor children into the school, a new supervisory board was
chosen, and in early 1873 some fourteen children from destitute families were
again enrolled. Nonetheless, the hostility on the part of some of the Franco
families continued until Behar retired and left Aleppo on 26 August 1873—at
which point the school was immediately closed.[39]

The reopening of the school six months later, on 16 January 1874, under the
administration of a new principal, Mordecai Behor, initially received the blessing even of opponents to its taking pupils from among the poor. They evidently
imagined that they could persuade the new principal to bow to their dictates.
However, Behor, who immediately grasped the elitist bias of Picciotto and his
supporters, refused to accede to their demands, suggesting to the Alliance that
the school be founded on different operative principles. In order to eliminate
the school's dependence on funding by the wealthy elite, Behor suggested that
it be officially declared a school for the poor and receive full Alliance funding.
His assumption was that, upon seeing the progress the pupils made in their
studies, the affluent would then seek to enrol their children without prior conditions.[40] Thus the school was organized on a new principle of equality between
pupils from the different social strata. Hillel de Picciotto agreed to back down,
especially as he was now invited to head the school's supervisory committee.[41]
However, in June 1876, when the president of the Baghdad Alliance committee, then visiting Aleppo, suggested that an additional fifty poor children be
taken out of the traditional *talmudei torah* and enrolled in the Alliance school,
he was strongly opposed by the Picciotto family. Hillel de Picciotto quickly
announced that he would withdraw his children from the school if they had to
study with the indigent and even threatened to resign his position on the school
board.[42]

Thus the struggle for the character of the Alliance school in Aleppo—elitist or integrative—resumed. Determined to get the better of the Picciottos,
Behor proposed that the Alliance cover the school's expenses, thus lessening
its dependence on the Picciottos, even if they withdrew their children.
Notwithstanding the intensity of the struggle and the risks involved, Behor
was convinced that the Picciottos would not withdraw their children, because
to do so would deprive them of a Jewish educational framework. Behor also
enjoyed the support of the deputy chief rabbi, Aaron Choueka, who, along with
other prominent individuals, including a small number of Francos, campaigned
for more impoverished pupils to be taken into the school. Hillel de Picciotto

[38] *BAIU*, 2ème sem. 1872, 23, 34.
[39] *BAIU*, 2ème sem. 1872, 45; 1er sem. 1873, 65–6; AAIU, Syrie, VIII.E., Alep, 68, Raphael de Picciotto au Président de l'AIU, 23 Sept. 1873.
[40] See AAIU, Syrie, III.E., Alep, 23, Behor, 21 May 1874.
[41] Ibid., 11 Oct. 1875, 9 Mar. 1876.   [42] Ibid., 15 June 1876, 14 Dec. 1876.

and his supporters issued a counter-demand that their numbers not exceed fifteen. In response to Behor's appeal for a decision on the character of the school in Aleppo, the central administration of the Alliance in Paris supported an increase in the number of charity pupils, even making their admission a condition for its increased support. When this policy was implemented, Hillel de Picciotto and his supporters immediately withdrew their children from the school. Nor did they stop there: the Picciottos and other Franco families, such as the Altarases, declared open war on the school, agitating among the parents of the pupils and even offering them money to withdraw their children. As a result the school underwent a transformation: the number of charity pupils rose to fifty, whereas the number of tuition-paying pupils dropped to eighteen, most of them the children of local merchants.[43] A cynical view of this struggle comes from a letter by Nissim Gubbay, a member of the local Aleppo board of the Alliance, to the Alliance committee in Paris: 'Our aristocratic families do not wish to see the children of the poor acquire the same education as their children. They wish to isolate themselves, fearful perhaps that God will not reward them for their generosity towards the locals.'[44]

Behor continued his struggle for free education for the poor and against the Picciottos' snobbery. The latter now set conditions for their children's return to the Alliance school: one was the complete isolation of the paying from the charity pupils, which Behor found totally unacceptable. At this point Moses de Picciotto, the Austrian consul, began to put his weight behind his relative's campaign. Using his authority as head of the school board, Moses found pretexts, such as the school's run-down physical condition, for closing it down. Behor and the Alliance asked the French consul Charles Ferdinand Destrée to try to persuade the Picciottos to soften their position regarding the charity pupils; but even the consul's attempts failed.[45]

Broken by the strain, Behor first resigned, then reconsidered, and finally sent a request to the Alliance that he be allowed to resign after all.[46] Behor regarded himself as a 'martyr', forced to work for six years in a community dominated by the 'selfish and arrogant' Franco families. He attributed their behaviour to the declining status of the Picciottos both in the estimation of the Jewish community and in the eyes of the European powers, which were beginning to cancel the Picciottos' letters of appointment as their consular representatives in Aleppo.[47]

---

[43] AAIU, Syrie, III.E., Alep, 23, Behor, 'Liste nominative des elèves gratuits', 22 Feb. 1877, 'Liste nominative des elèves payants', 26 Mar. 1877, 12 Feb. 1877, 19 Nov. 1877.

[44] Ibid., 19 Nov. 1877.

[45] See AAIU, Syrie, I.E., Alep, 1, Destrée à Crémieux, 2 Apr. 1879; III.E., Alep, 23, Behor, 21 Apr. 1879, 18 May 1879.

[46] AAIU, Syrie, III.E., Alep, 23, Behor, 11 Dec. 1878, 6 Mar. 1879.

[47] See AAIU, Syrie, III.E., Alep, 23, Behor, 19 Nov. 1877, 23 Sept. 1878, 2 June 1879.

Although Behor was replaced as principal in 1879, his achievement in opening the Alliance school to a broad sector of the population outlasted him. Children from different social strata shared the same classroom as equals, and the modern European education that had previously been restricted to the Francos became available to a wider circle of the Aleppine Jewish community from that time on. This exposure to western education, alongside the increasing recognition of the power and efficacy of European consular protection in Syrian cities, played a role in the developing western cultural orientation among Syrian Jews.

Notwithstanding the blatant elitism of the Francos' attitude to education, the creation of a climate favourable to the founding of a modern school in Aleppo is almost certainly attributable to their presence. As early as 1848 the Moldavian traveller Benjamin the Second noted: 'The Jews dwelling at Aleppo distinguish themselves as much by their faithful devotion and fidelity to the great and holy bequest of their fathers—the Jewish Law—as by their profound Jewish-scientific acquirements.'[48] Upon his arrival, the first Alliance emissary to Aleppo, Nissim Behar, reported upon his favourable reception by all classes of Jewish society. When the school opened, Behar boasted that his pupils included the only son of a person he defined as 'the oldest, most respected, holiest, and most important rabbi in the city'.[49] The rabbis Ezra Tawil and Solomon Safdeyé, who later became the spiritual leaders of the community, joined him as members of the school staff.[50] The favourable attitude of the senior rabbis in Aleppo towards Behar and the Alliance showed itself most strikingly in the granting to Behar of permission to photograph the Aleppo Codex, even over some rabbinic objections.[51] Fundraising for the Alliance was undertaken at the celebration of every birth or marriage in the city, activity that could be carried out only with the rabbis' approval. Various rabbis also presented copies of their books to the Alliance as gifts.[52]

The Alliance's philanthropic assistance to the Aleppine community, particularly during the famine of 1880, further enhanced the organization's prestige both among the rabbis and across the wider community. As a way of demonstrating his appreciation for Alliance assistance, Chief Rabbi Moses Hakohen agreed to send his son to the Alliance school, to speak favourably of Alliance philanthropic and educational activity in his sermons, to hold a

---

[48] Benjamin, *Eight Years in Asia and Africa*, 46.

[49] AAIU, Syrie, III.E., Alep, 21, Behar, 21 Jan. 1870. He was apparently referring to Rabbi Shalom Chasky, who returned to Aleppo from 'Ayntab in his old age. Indeed, Chasky's son Eli appears on the list of pupils Behar appended to the above-mentioned letter.

[50] See AAIU, Syrie, III.E., Alep, 21, Behar, 22 Aug. 1870, 19 Jan. 1871. Rabbi Safdeyé's son also appears on the list of pupils mentioned in the preceding note.

[51] See Shamosh, *The 'Keter'* (Heb.), 52 and sources cited there.

[52] See e.g. *BAIU*, 2ème sem. 1873, 67; AAIU, Syrie, I.B., Alep, 1, Rabbi Moses Sutton to the Alliance, 25 Adar 1873.

memorial service for the late president of the Alliance Adolphe Crémieux, and to approach individual members of the community for contributions. He himself set a personal example by donating 10 francs.[53]

Alliance efforts from the 1880s to found a vocational school in Aleppo also struck a chord with Aleppo's rabbis, who frequently preached in favour of vocational study and spoke out against engaging in unproductive commercial intermediation.[54] Prominent among the rabbis who supported Alliance activity was the deputy chief rabbi Aaron Choueka, who chose to demonstrate to the community that secular studies were not opposed to Judaism by transferring his son from the *talmud torah* to the Alliance school, which he further supported by visiting it on Fridays to test the pupils in Jewish subjects.[55] Choueka praised the Alliance school not only because of its religious studies, but also because its heads were willing

to take funds from their own coffers to open schools everywhere to teach Torah and *derekh erets* [secular studies], and languages, and vocations . . . Two scholars teach them Bible with commentaries and Talmud . . . Another important scholar teaches them to write Hebrew, another teaches them to write Arabic, another Turkish, and they are headed by Señor Behor, may God preserve him, who teaches French. And everyone praises them for their present and future accomplishments.[56]

Franco families were also responsible for the initiative to found a Jewish school for girls in Aleppo. The first plan, by which they committed themselves in 1869 to enrol fourteen girls from well-to-do families who would themselves fund the teaching, did not come to fruition. In 1871 the Francos and the local elites stepped up their campaign for the Alliance to open a school for girls, prompted by the intolerable lack of appropriate educational opportunities for their daughters and backing up their request with the argument that Christians gained the advantage when Jews were forced to educate their girls in what were essentially anti-Jewish institutions.[57]

An Alliance school for girls began to operate in March 1872, with a roll of twenty-three pupils. However, at this stage it flourished only briefly. In August the same year the teacher, Melanie Rosenstrauss, left Aleppo for health reasons, along with her husband Nissim Behar, the principal of the boys' school. The girls' school opened and closed at intervals throughout the 1880s; however, it was not until the 1890s that it underwent significant development.[58]

[53] See *Ḥavatselet*, 34, 2 Tamuz 1880, p. 257; AAIU, Syrie, II.E., Alep, 11, Altaras, 3 May 1880, 23 June 1880; X.E., Alep, 83, Somekh, 27 May 1880.
[54] AAIU, Syrie, II.E., Alep, 11, Altaras, 12 July 1880.
[55] See ibid., X.E., Alep, 83, Somekh, 8 July 1880.
[56] Ibid., III.E., Alep, 23, Rabbi Aaron Choueka to the Alliance, 28 Heshvan 1877.
[57] AAIU, Syrie, II.E., Alep, 11, Altaras, 12 Mar. 1869; III.E., Alep, 21, Behar, 25 July 1871; II.E., Alep, 11, Altaras, 15 Aug. 1871, 19 Sept. 1871, 2 Nov. 1871, 24 Nov. 1871.
[58] See ibid., IV.E., Alep, 50, Gubbay, 10 June 1880; II.E., Alep, 11, Altaras, 2 Sept. 1880. See

In Damascus, too, the opening of Christian mission schools aimed at attracting Jewish girls led to acknowledgement of the need to open a Jewish school for girls. As early as 1849, during a visit to Damascus, Moses Montefiore promised to assist in the founding of a Jewish school there; but nothing came of the idea at this time.[59] Greater urgency is evident with the arrival of the Alliance emissary Seligman Weisskopf in Damascus in 1868. Weisskopf reported to his superiors the many appeals to him from parents who sent their daughters to mission schools to open a Jewish school for girls. He also noted the need to eradicate illiteracy among Jewish women and to improve their status. As a first step in this direction the central committee of the Alliance issued a directive to Weisskopf in 1869 to devote two hours a day to instructing girls and to hire a sewing teacher.[60] But it was not until 1883 that a school for girls operated on a regular basis in Damascus. As with the boys' schools, there is no evidence of objections by the rabbis and scholars to the opening of modern Jewish educational institutions for girls in either Aleppo or Damascus. Certainly, for Jewish girls, Alliance institutions were seen as preferable to Christian educational settings.

During the period under consideration the question of founding Alliance schools in the smaller Syrian Jewish communities did not arise in practice. Only for Antioch is there testimony to an incipient attempt. Here, on 12 November 1879, a local Alliance committee was founded for the purpose of founding a modern school in the town. This committee was headed by the local chief rabbi, Rabbi Abraham Dweck Hakohen, originally of Aleppo, who was appointed its honorary president. His efforts were backed by his deputy, Rabbi Isaac Swed, and by the town notables.[61] No school was ever opened in Antioch; however, this episode, in which we see active support for the Alliance's educational work by Rabbi Dweck, who was trained in Aleppo and in 1883 became the city's chief rabbi, provides further proof that the rabbinic class did not oppose Alliance activity in Syria on religious grounds.

This lack of rabbinic opposition to, and even rabbinic co-operation with, the Alliance was grounded in several factors, both ideological and practical. As heirs to the religious humanism characteristic of the Sephardi tradition,[62] which judges general culture according to the sole criterion of whether or not it contests Judaism, the rabbis displayed considerable openness in their encounter with western culture and did not view modern education itself as objectionable.

also CZA, J-41/83, Mikveh Yisra'el Archive, Somekh to Hirsch, 30 Apr. 1885; Schur, *Maḥazot haḥayim*, 85; Leven, *Cinquante ans d'histoire*, ii. 200–1.

[59] Loewe (ed.), *Diaries of Sir Moses and Lady Montefiore*, ii. 14.
[60] See AAIU, Syrie, XXI.E., Damas, 222, Weisskopf, 6 Oct. 1868; *BAIU*, 2ème sem. 1868, 79; 1er sem. 1869, 2, 4.
[61] See AAIU, Syrie, II.E., Alep, 11, Altaras, 21 Nov. 1879; *BAIU*, 2ème sem. 1880, 84, 87.
[62] On this approach, see José Faur, *Rabbi Israel Moses Hazzan* (Heb.), 35–45.

The crucial factor was whether or not the foreign culture's values negated Judaism: if they did not, it could be embraced; if they did, it should be forcefully repudiated. The Syrian rabbis were familiar with the work of their predecessors, both in Spain and throughout the Middle East, who maintained close contact with, and indeed interacted with, the surrounding culture. These sages, who included for example Maimonides, had profound knowledge of both Jewish sources and general culture. In line with this tradition, the Syrian rabbis included scholars who did not restrict themselves to Torah learning but also engaged in secular and scientific studies.[63] In this context, acquisition of broad knowledge was viewed neither as particularly daring nor as a break with traditional norms.[64]

On the practical level, the Alliance was looked up to as a Jewish 'administration' that came to the aid of Jewish communities worldwide. Although the scholars shared this respect, this alone would not have attracted their support, had it not been for the wisdom of the Alliance policy of incorporating Torah study into the curriculum alongside secular studies, and of hiring local scholars to teach the former. The sense that they had influence on, and could oversee, these institutions from within enhanced the scholars' willingness to co-operate with the modern French society and to place the younger generation in its hands.

The relative openness of the scholarly elite was also the result of contacts with the Francos, the 'carriers of western culture' to the Middle East, and with the Franco-influenced consular protégés. These factors virtually extinguished any expressions of religious extremism with regard to secular studies. When extremism did emerge in the Syrian Jewish communities, it remained a relatively weak force, espoused by second-rank scholars who appealed to prejudices grounded in the ignorance of the masses. As a rule, the spiritual leaders of the Syrian Jewish community supported the Alliance and co-operated with the society and its emissaries.

The view that the scholarly stratum of Syrian Jewish society was hostile to the Alliance's activity from the outset is anachronistic.[65] Ultimately, the apparent failure of the Alliance's efforts to entrench its influence on Syrian Jewry can be termed an optical illusion. The claim that the winds of enlightenment did not reach Syrian Jewish communities before the early twentieth century is unfounded.[66] The Alliance's greatest influence inheres in its exposure of young

[63] Rabbi Menasheh Sutton was described as follows: 'Other than his great expertise in Jewish wisdom, in Torah, grammar, and science, he excels in the study of astronomy, engineering, and fractions, and other sciences.' See Menasheh Sutton, *Maḥberet pirḥei shoshanim*, introd. by the author's grandson. See also the author's introduction, fo. 2, and references to Socrates, Solon, Aristotle, Plato, and other philosophers scattered throughout the book.

[64] For a comprehensive study, see Harel, 'From Opening to Closing' (Heb.), 1–58.

[65] On the turning point throughout the Middle East, see ibid.

[66] See Barnai, 'The Jews in the Ottoman Empire' (Heb.), 262.

Syrian Jews to the outside world and in motivating them to build their future outside their homeland. The graduates of Alliance schools drew with them thousands of young people who had not tasted modern education but still sought to emigrate overseas. If the Alliance can be said to have sown the seeds of progress and modernization, the fruits of its efforts were reaped not by the veteran Syrian Jewish communities but by the new communities founded outside Syria. Within Syria's Jewish communities, the weakening of halakhic observance during the period in question cannot be laid at the Alliance's door to more than a very minor degree. The causes of this trend must be sought elsewhere.

The Weakening of Traditional Observance among Syrian Jews

Evidence for the weakening of Jewish traditional observance in Syria during the Tanzimat era comes from the increased composition and dissemination of *musar* (pietistic and ethical) works, particularly in Aleppo during the latter half of the nineteenth century.[67] The denigration of traditional Jewish mores fostered a decline in the status of the rabbinic court and of other Jewish institutions in Syria. Witness Rabbi Abraham Dayan's observations on the mid-nineteenth-century decline in religious observance among Aleppine Jews:

At present the number of servants rebelling against God, their master, has increased. They desire not to fulfil his will and each one constructs an idolatrous platform for himself. In order to fulfil their evil inclination they rush to exercise leniency for themselves and others in all that they do. I know not on whom they rely in so doing.[68]

There are, however, no indications as to the true scope of this lack of respect for tradition. It seems likely that, in berating their congregations, the rabbis exaggerated. Nonetheless, their remarks enable us to identify a number of practices in respect of which this laxity was apparent, including the wearing of *tsitsit* (ritual fringes) and phylacteries, *mezuzah*, and praying with a quorum. The rabbis cite a sharp decline in Torah study; they also note that Jews eat food cooked by non-Jews, gamble, and hold ceremonies raising the spirits of the dead. Other accusations concerned less modest female attire, the mingling of men and women at celebrations, the playing of bawdy songs, and women dancing in front of men. Also observed were cases of young men preening themselves and growing their hair long in order to attract young women, of cheating on weights and measures, and of violating the sabbath.[69]

[67] See Harel, *The Books of Aleppo* (Heb.), index. [68] Abraham Dayan, *Tuv ta'am*, 205.
[69] See Mordecai Abadi, *Divrei mordekhai*, author's introd.; Abraham Dayan, *Tuv ta'am*, 138, 141, 156, 200, 209–10, 218; Antebi, *Ḥokhmah umusar*, 7a–b, 13b–14a, 35a, 96a, 111b–112a, 115b,

Intertwined with this lack of respect for Jewish law was lack of respect for its representatives—the scholarly class—and for their authority. In this sphere as in so many others, the situation in Damascus was different from that in Aleppo. In Damascus this phenomenon had more to do with expediency than with ideology. The first to cross the barrier of non-obedience to the Jewish court were members of the Farhi family; other notables followed in their wake, primarily consular protégés who were not dependent on the Jewish court.[70] The struggle between the city's notables and its rabbis was based not on religious issues, but rather on competition for control of the positions of power in the community. Grounded in ignorance, the belittling of religious observance by the masses did not threaten the status of the spiritual leadership. This leadership continued to command the respect of, and to influence, the masses, who feared the scholars' magical powers. Consequently, the Damascus rabbis were not forced to exercise their full authority; secularization itself did not challenge their status as religious leaders in the community.

In Aleppo, on the other hand, in addition to the disparagement of tradition based on ignorance, we find an ideologically based weakening of adherence to religious observance, similar to the phenomenon of the European Haskalah (Enlightenment) movement. The enlightened stratum, drawn mainly from the upper and middle classes who had enjoyed a private modern education and were in constant contact with Europeans, ceased to believe in the scholars' power and authority, attributing the past faith of the masses in the scholars to their purported magical powers, their ability to excommunicate or curse. As enlightened individuals, they declared that they no longer believed in these powers; nor did they fear excommunication. The *maskilim* placed humans, rather than God, at the centre of the universe.[71] Consequently, in Aleppo we find rabbis being physically threatened, alongside refusal to obey their verdicts not only in monetary matters but also in matters governing personal status, such as the forbidden marriage of a *kohen* and a divorcee.[72] Matters came to a head in 1862 with the return of Rabbi Raphael Kassin to Aleppo after years of travelling. His plan to found a European-style Reform congregation in Aleppo was backed by the group of *maskilim*, who now declared that they no longer recognized the authority of the chief rabbi, Hayim Mordecai Labaton, and

116*b*–118*a*, 125*a*; Abraham Dayan, *Holekh tamim*, 27*a–b*, 54*a–b*, 56*a*; id., *Zikaron lanefesh*, 18, 22, 39; J. Sutton, *Vayelaket yosef*, author's introd.; Mordecai Abadi, *Vikuaḥ na'im*, 7*a*, no. 23; Laniado, *For the Sake of the Holy Ones* (Heb.), 165–6; Frankl, *The Jews in the East*, i. 278–80; Abulafia, *Penei yitsḥak*, ii. 68*a–b*, 76*b*.

[70] See Palagi, *Ḥukot haḥayim*, 7*b*, 'Ḥoshen mishpat', no. 2; id., *Ḥikekei lev*, 174*a*–176*a*, 'Ḥoshen mishpat', no. 53.

[71] Abraham Dayan, *Tuv ta'am*, 206. For more on the hatred of the Aleppine *maskilim* for the rabbinic scholars, see id., *Zikaron lanefesh*, 65; Mordecai Abadi, *Melits na'im*, 32–3, no. 261.

[72] See I. Dayan, *Imrei no'am*, 17*a*, no. 14.

accepted that of Kassin instead. This separatist attempt sparked violent out-bursts and even led to fist-fights in the marketplace. Fearing that the riots would spread—and probably in response to an appeal by conservative forces sup-porting Rabbi Labaton—the Ottoman governor Jawdat Pasha made a rare intervention in an internal Jewish matter and forbade Kassin to continue his preaching of Reform under threat of arrest.[73]

The scholars of Aleppo perceived this attempt to introduce Reform not only as a direct threat to their own status and religious authority, but also as an ideological threat to the foundations of traditional Judaism. They responded by closing ranks among themselves, supervising the community more closely, seeking the support of the wealthy elite, and placing extra emphasis on the unique status of the scholarly class. Herein lie the roots of the image of the Aleppine community as traditional and religiously observant, and of the auth-oritativeness of its rabbis and its rabbinic court.[74] In actuality, the authority of the scholarly class in Aleppo was under constant threat of erosion; hence its unrelenting battle against those who questioned its status.

In their uncompromising struggle against the threat to their authority, the Aleppine rabbis closed the door to any new or different interpretations of Judaism, banning any literature that might reactivate maskilic activity. This opposition climaxed in 1865 with the burning of *Em lamikra*, a commentary on the Pentateuch by Rabbi Elijah Benamozegh of Leghorn which sought to introduce the concept that there was similarity, and perhaps even identity, between the beliefs, customs, and traditions of the ancient peoples. As soon as the book arrived in Aleppo the scholars burned it, thus rekindling the conflict between the *maskilim*, who were captivated by Benamozegh's work, and the scholars.[75] The Damascus scholars hastily followed the example of their coun-terparts in Aleppo and also burned any copies of the book.

This extraordinary opposition to Benamozegh's work was grounded not only in the scholars' intellectual and spiritual world-view, but also in the reality of what was happening within their community, where denigration of the rab-binical leadership was becoming more widespread. When Rabbi Moses Hako-hen was appointed chief rabbi of Aleppo in 1880, one of his first acts was to request special powers from the Ottoman authorities to enable him to impose his will both on those refusing to pay communal taxes and on those breaking with religious tradition. He even appealed to Rabbi Moses Halevi, the *ḥakham bashi* in Istanbul, for a firman endowing him with the power to imprison dis-obedient individuals in the general gaol, a most unusual step.[76] Overall, 'Aleppo

---

[73] For a comprehensive treatment of this episode, see Harel, 'A Spiritual Agitation in the East' (Heb.).   [74] See Zohar, *Tradition and Change* (Heb.), 38, 68–9.
[75] For a full treatment, see Harel, 'The Edict to Destroy *Em lamikra*' (Heb.); Zohar, 'Militant Conservatism' (Heb.), 57–60.
[76] Court verdict, ACRI, TR/Is-162a, Rabbi Moses Hakohen to Rabbi Moses Halevi.

... was not a sacred society in the sense that some nostalgic religious families in Jerusalem today remember it, a community of saints and scholars.'[77]

*

In both Damascus and Aleppo the diminishing communal recognition of the authority of traditional institutions such as the rabbinic court was accompanied by a state attack on their status and jurisdiction in the wake of Ottoman reforms in the government, the judiciary, and the status of the religious minorities. Part III of this book examines the effect of the Tanzimat on the legal status of the Syrian Jewish community.

[77] Zenner, 'Jews in Late Ottoman Syria', 181.

THE LEGAL STATUS
OF THE JEWS

SIX

EQUALITY BEFORE
THE LAW

IN CONSIDERING the impact of the reforms that sought to establish equality before the law for all subjects—Muslim and non-Muslim—in Syrian society, we must first take a brief look at the Islamic social world-view, particularly the principle of inequality before the law which shaped its treatment of religious minorities.

A Tradition of Inequality and the Beginnings of Reform

Islamic society's treatment of non-Muslim minorities was based on a doctrine of inequality between Muslims and the members of the other monotheistic religions. This doctrine was given concrete form in a binding legal code that governed Muslim–Jewish and Muslim–Christian agreements in all areas under Muslim conquest. The status of *ahl al-kitab*—namely the Christians and Jews, whose religions were based on revelation and on Scripture—was necessarily lower than that of the Muslims. Nonetheless, though officially inferior to Muslims, these 'people of the book' were granted toleration and protection in exchange for payment of the *jizya* tax; the legal obligation to protect the religious minorities—the *ahl al-dhimma*—was incumbent on both the Muslim public as a whole and the individual Muslim, on both the regime and its subjects. In the inter-religious struggles between Islam, Christianity, and Judaism, the presence and humiliation of the *dhimmi*s under Muslim rule had significant theological implications for Muslims, essentially serving as proof of Islam's superiority.[1]

Over time, a system of discriminatory laws limiting the rights of *dhimmi*s developed in the context of the *shari'a*, the system of Islamic law. Aimed at highlighting the distinction between *dhimmi*s and Muslims, these laws reached their apex at the beginning of the eighth century with the 'Pact of 'Umar', which prescribed distinctive clothing—different-coloured garments, turbans, and shoes—for each religious minority, outlawed public processions by

---

[1] See Bosworth, 'The Concept of Dhimma in Early Islam'.

non-Muslims, prohibited missionary efforts to convert Muslims, and banned the construction of new synagogues or churches, or of buildings taller than Muslim ones. *Dhimmi*s could not ride horses or mules, possess Muslim slaves, purchase land, wear swords, sell alcoholic drinks, or engage in any activity perceived as detrimental to Islam.[2]

The extent to which these discriminatory laws were applied differed from place to place, and from period to period. A changing, more flexible, social reality, and the need for harmonious daily interaction, often pushed aside strict observance of the draconian laws enacted in the medieval period. However, Islamic societies also saw phases during which deviation from the accepted Islamic tradition with respect to *dhimmi*s led to outbreaks of religious extremism and to renewed enforcement of discriminatory measures.

The institutionalized inferiority of the *dhimmi*s under Islamic rule contributed to a preference on the part of Christian and Jewish communities to organize their communal life in autonomous neighbourhoods on a religious or sectarian basis. This mode of organization, providing the community's members with a protective environment separate from the surrounding discriminatory majority society, was encouraged by the Muslim regime, which preferred to deal with groups rather than with individuals and generally refrained from interfering in internal affairs of the minority communities. Thus *dhimmi* communal and religious institutions enjoyed autonomy and jurisdiction in the internal judicial realm, in taxation, in their choice of leaders, and in their day-to-day operation. When necessary, these institutions received government support.[3] One outcome of this arrangement was that it made the individual dependent on his religious community's institutions for most of his daily needs, obviating the need to turn to the Muslim authorities.

In its treatment of religious minorities, the Ottoman empire was guided by Islamic tradition, modified according to the needs of the regime. Eventually, a combination of external and internal pressures culminated in the mid-nineteenth-century reforms known as the Tanzimat, which had significant repercussions for the regime's relationship to the *dhimmi*s.

A series of overwhelming defeats by Christian powers, beginning in the seventeenth century, reduced the status of the Ottoman empire in the eyes of other powers to 'the sick man of Europe' and forced the Ottoman regime to recognize that it would have to introduce reforms if it was to re-establish Muslim military superiority over the Christian infidels.[4] The status and image of the Ottoman empire were also eroding from within. Frequent revolts in various parts of the empire peaked with the Egyptian takeover of Syria by

---

[2] Hirshberg, 'The Jews under Islam' (Heb.), 270–1.

[3] Ma'oz, 'Changes in the Status of Jews' (Heb.), 11, and extensive bibliography cited there.

[4] The most painful defeats were the ones inflicted by the Russian army. See Lewis, *The Emergence of Modern Turkey*, 36–9.

Muhammad ʿAli, who in October 1831 opened the campaign that ended with the total conquest of Syria in July 1832. The governor of Syria under Egyptian rule was Ibrahim Pasha, Muhammad ʿAli's son, who aspired to reform government and public administration and to inspire local participation in this process. One of his innovative measures was the founding of advisory councils in each of the Syrian cities. Their novelty lies less in their limited administrative and legal prerogatives in the municipal and economic realms, and more in their composition, which included both Muslims and non-Muslims. Grounded in Muhammad ʿAli's policy of toleration for religious minorities, these councils represented new trends, previously unknown in any Muslim state, exemplified by the assumption of administrative responsibility by citizens, the secularization of the legal system, the establishment of venues for appeals, and the mandating of equality for all religions before the law. In return, Ibrahim Pasha expected these minorities to play an important role in reorganizing the public administration and in developing the Syrian economy. From the diplomatic standpoint, the Egyptian regime was aware that showing a positive attitude towards religious minorities would enhance its popularity and win support for its takeover of Syria among the European powers. Accordingly, Ibrahim Pasha took vigorous steps to abolish discriminatory legislation. Jews and Christians were no longer bound by inequitable regulations dictating their attire and forbidding them to ride horses or to carry arms. They were granted freedom of religion and permission to renovate, or to build, churches and synagogues.[5]

Muhammad ʿAli's conquest of Syria struck close to the heart of the Ottoman empire. The Egyptian defeat of the Ottoman forces at Nezib on 24 June 1839 placed the imperial centre at risk, creating an urgent need for European support to guarantee its continued existence. As a means of gaining this support, the young sultan Abdülmecid sought to demonstrate that he too was capable of instituting a modern, liberal administration. On 3 November 1839 a royal decree—the Hatt-i şerif of Gülhane (Noble Rescript of the Rose Chamber) —was promulgated, setting out the key principles on which this new administration was to be founded: preservation of personal security, honour, and property; reform of tax and conscription; justice; and equality between Muslims and non-Muslims.[6] Of these, the one most shocking to Muslim sensibilities was the last, that of equality before the law. Not only did this represent the greatest deviation from accepted Islamic tradition, it was further perceived

---

[5] For a detailed study of Egyptian rule in Syria, see Hofman, 'Muhammed Ali in Syria' (Heb.).

[6] For an English translation, see Inalcik (trans.), 'The Hatt-i Şerif of Gülhane'. Jews were not specifically mentioned in this decree. An official announcement applying the reform decree to Jews is found in a special firman sent by Sultan Abdülmecid to Moses Montefiore in the wake of the Damascus blood libel. For the text, see Maʾoz, 'Changes in the Status of Jews' (Heb.), 27–8 (cited from Loewe [ed.], *Diaries of Sir Moses and Lady Montefiore*, i. 278–9).

as a blasphemous indignity.[7] Nevertheless, with the return of Ottoman rule to Syria in 1840, the measures of the Gülhane decree were implemented in the Syrian region as well.

Although additional reform edicts were issued in the intervening years, 1854 marks the beginning of a new stage of the Tanzimat. Ottoman military weakness, this time in the face of the threat from Russia in the Crimean War, and the resulting renewed urgency in its desire to gain the support of European powers compelled the Ottoman regime to demonstrate more convincingly its reformist intent. In May 1855 the Ottoman government declared its aim of cancelling two outstanding discriminatory measures: the *jizya*, which had been in place continuously since the early days of Islam; and the prohibition on minorities bearing arms, which meant that religious minorities could now be drafted into the armed forces. The official firman announcing these measures, the Hatt-i Hümayun, was issued on 18 February 1856, reiterating the principles of the earlier decree and spelling out the equal rights granted to non-Muslim subjects in greater detail. A third decree, also prompted by external European pressure, issued on 23 December 1876, marks the end of the Tanzimat era. In essence, this final decree introduced the first Ottoman constitution, providing for the establishment of an elected parliament in which all the nationalities in the empire would be represented, based on the principle of equality for all subjects. However, Sultan Abdülhamid II took advantage of the outbreak of war against Russia in 1876 to dismiss the parliament and, from that time on, ignored the constitution entirely.[8]

One of the more intriguing historical questions is to what extent the Ottomans actually intended to fulfil the promises made in the Tanzimat decrees. Any attempt to answer this question must take note of the presence of conservative, anti-Tanzimat forces in Istanbul. The promised political, social, and economic changes threatened various interest groups within Turkish society, and the implementation or abrogation of the reforms across the empire depended on the balance of power between their supporters and opponents not only in the provinces but also in the corridors of power in Istanbul. On more than one occasion, the personality of the *wali* and his affiliation with one or the other of the rival groups in the imperial capital influenced the stance taken by the local Muslim civil service in Syria. Below I examine at length the attempts to implement the anti-discriminatory reform measures in the Damascus and Aleppo provinces, and the reaction to these attempts, paying particular attention to how they played out in Jewish–Muslim interaction.

---

[7] Lewis, *The Emergence of Modern Turkey*, 105–6.

[8] On the various reform decrees and the struggle between conservatives and reformers in Istanbul regarding their implementation, see Lewis, *The Emergence of Modern Turkey*, 101–25, 356–7; Davison, *Reform in the Ottoman Empire*, 3–113.

Cancellation of Discriminatory Measures

The period immediately following the reinstatement of Ottoman rule in Syria was one of total confusion. In the aftermath of the hasty Egyptian retreat, and the lifting of the fear of Ibrahim Pasha's regime, experienced as harsh and cruel by any who opposed him, there were attempts to nullify the Egyptian-granted privileges to Christians and Jews, fuelled by the belief that the return of the sultanate, with the sultan in the role of *amir al-mu'minin*, 'commander of the faithful', marked an opportune moment to overthrow the reforms and return to Islamic tradition. On the evening of 2 January 1841 the *a'yan* (Muslim notables) gathered in Damascus and decided, in direct contravention of the reforms, to enact a decree in the spirit of Islam. Its four measures applicable to Christians and Jews prohibited the wearing of white turbans, the riding of horses, the public sale of wine, and the ownership of Muslim slaves.

But the fanatically anti-*dhimmi* Muslim public was destined to be disappointed in its hopes for a restoration of Islamic law. The acting governor's announcement that the *dhimmi*s were free to wear any headgear, to ride on horseback, and to retain their slaves was accompanied by a guarantee that the authorities would thwart any rabble-rousing attacks on the *dhimmi*s for such acts.[9] Notwithstanding these promises, for fear of reprisals the non-Muslim minorities did not dare to assume Muslim attire. Reports by travellers to Syria in 1841 attest to traditional eastern garb as the prevailing fashion in Damascus: Christian and Jewish turbans were black, blue, or brown, and only Muslims could wear yellow shoes, with the exception of a few privileged Christians, who, as government officials, were granted this right.[10] The missionary John Wilson, who visited Damascus in 1843, claimed that *dhimmi*s had only recently been permitted to wear yellow turbans, the colour worn by the Muslims, and that although this privilege had been formally sanctioned by a firman, few Christians dared to exercise it. According to his account, the long-standing social hierarchy, as reflected by different-coloured turbans, was still in effect at the time of his visit: green was worn by descendants of the prophet Muhammad; yellow by other Muslims; and black by Jews.[11] Five years later Damascus Jews still did not appear in public in light-coloured turbans,[12] and even the affluent ones continued to wear black turbans not only in public but also in their homes.[13] A similar situation prevailed in Aleppo.[14]

The discriminatory features of Jewish attire disappeared only after the 1860

---

[9] AECPC, Turquie, Damas, vol. 1, p. 4, Ratti-Menton, 6 Jan. 1841. For the Muslim reaction, see also Ma'oz, *Ottoman Reform*, 200.

[10] Paton, *The Modern Syrians*, 191; AECPC, Turquie, Damas, vol. 8, p. 206, Hecquard, 4 Aug. 1864.   [11] Wilson, *The Lands of the Bible*, ii. 346.

[12] Woodcock, *Scripture Lands*, 34; M. Margoliouth, *A Pilgrimage to the Land of my Fathers*, ii. 256.   [13] Lynch, *Narrative*, 492.   [14] See Abraham Dayan, *Tuv ta'am*, 216–17.

massacre of Christians in Damascus, with the growing influx of European visitors and the penetration of western modes of dress. The adoption by the Ottoman army of European-style uniforms, and the wearing of European clothes by the upper echelons of the government civil service, and by rich merchants and their wives, served as a model for imitation. In men's dress, the sole eastern feature remained the turban. With the elimination of the final signs of discrimination the turban disappeared from general use, until it was worn only by religious leaders.[15] It is possible that rabbis and scholars continued to adhere to discriminatory elements of attire as an external means of preserving Jewish identity, even after it became permissible to dress like Muslims.[16] During the early 1880s the members of the Syrian Jewish elites wore European clothing when they conducted business, but continued to wear traditional eastern dress at home, in the synagogue, and in the study house. The community's younger members, by contrast, wore European clothing even to the synagogue.[17]

The spiritual heads of the Jewish community did not favour the new fashions in dress. For the preservation of modesty, of women especially, they were prepared to forgo the right to freedom and equality. When Damascus Muslim extremists instituted strict measures during the fast of Ramadan, including a prohibition on women going out unless their faces were completely veiled, the French consul argued that this detracted from the freedom of Jewish and Christian women, who normally appeared in public with only partially covered faces, in their own districts at least.[18] The rabbis, on the other hand, were in complete agreement with the Muslim legislators on this point. In Aleppo and its satellite towns, such as Urfa, it was the long-standing practice among Jewish women to go outside unveiled. This practice aroused the anger of the rabbis, who protested against the loosening of morals and modesty among Jewish women, in contrast to non-Jewish women who kept their faces covered in public. Similarly, the rabbis also decried the introduction of western fashions for women, considering the shorter garments immodest.[19] In this instance, the religious fervour of the '*ulama*' and of the Muslim masses meshed with the rabbis' fear of the encroaching threat to modesty and to Jewish identity. This delayed the implementation of reforms with regard to external signs of discrimination in Syrian Jewish dress.

Another reform measure that was not implemented after the Ottoman return to Syria was that allowing non-Muslims to ride on horseback. Upon reaching

[15] Tibawi, *A Modern History of Syria*, 177.

[16] Thus, even in the early twentieth century we find the Damascus sages wrapping a 'black scarf — in memory of the destruction [of the Temple (!)] — around the turban': see Elmaleh, *The Jews in Damascus* (Heb.), 46.   [17] Neumark, *A Journey in the Old Land* (Heb.), 66.

[18] AECADN, Constantinople, Correspondence avec les Echelles, Damas, 1846–1853, De Ségur au Ministre Plénipotentiaire Envoyé Extraordinaire de France à Constantinople, Damas, 9 July 1851.

[19] See Antebi, *Ḥokhmah umusar*, 116b–117a, 125a; Abraham Dayan, *Holekh tamim*, 55a.

the Damascus city gates, *dhimmi*s had to dismount and walk through the city streets.[20]

For their part, the religious minorities in Syria, the Jews especially, preferred to maintain their distinctive characteristics, to avoid angering the Muslim majority and possibly also in order to maintain communal cohesion. Thus, even when Ottoman law introduced measures intended to improve the conditions of *dhimmi* life, at times the minorities demanded the reinstatement of the old order when this was seen as being to their advantage.

This was the case when the question of reopening taverns arose in Damascus. With the return of Ottoman rule, the notables of the city took steps to prohibit the opening of taverns and of the public sale of alcoholic beverages, fearing that this placed temptation to consume alcohol, forbidden by Islam, in the way of Muslims. This ruling both harmed the livelihood of some of the *dhimmi*s and counteracted their civil freedom to sell wine, which under their religious codes was not prohibited. On the other hand, it did bring about a significant decrease in drunkenness in the city. Its religious zeal notwithstanding, the Damascus *majlis* was forced to agree to the *daftardar*'s decision of 1843 to permit the opening and leasing of taverns, most likely prompted by a desire to refill the treasury's coffers. The *majlis* accepted this decision on two conditions. The first was that wine production be placed in the hands of a supervised monopoly. The second, which called for taverns to be opened only in the Christian and Jewish quarters, impacted more directly on the *dhimmi*s, who feared that this would transform their neighbourhoods into centres of drunkenness and prostitution, making daily life perilous. In the arguments voiced through the agency of the British consul Richard Wood, they mentioned the recent imperial decree calling for the closing of all taverns, as well as the conditions that prevailed in Syria under Egyptian control when taverns operated across the whole city. The innovative aspect of these arguments lies in their reliance on the principle of equality for all subjects. The *dhimmi*s submitted that if it was the *majlis*' intention to act according to the spirit of Islamic law by forbidding alcoholic beverages, then this law should apply equally to all imperial subjects. On this basis, they requested either the total closing of all taverns or, in order to avoid the effects of drunkenness being confined to a single area, their distribution throughout the city. They drew their case to a close with the claim that, according to the Tanzimat, there should be no discrimination between groups.

The city's governor ʿAli Pasha responded favourably to this request, ordering the *majlis* to do everything in its power to preserve the safety of Jews and Christians, and prohibiting the opening of any taverns in addition to the ones already operating in the Jewish and Christian quarters.[21] It soon became

[20] De Saulcy, *Narrative of a Journey*, ii. 520.
[21] FO 78/538, Wood to Earl of Aberdeen, Damascus, 25 May 1843.

apparent that *dhimmi* fears were justified, with disturbances and increased numbers of Muslim drunks in the Jewish and Christian neighbourhoods, and before long the council again ordered the closing, for the time being, of all wine and liquor shops in the city. In the short term this cut off the livelihood of wine and liquor sellers and led to outbursts by Muslim alcoholics, who used threats and physical violence to force the unprotected sellers to supply them with alcohol.[22]

One of the main discriminatory measures embodying the Muslim conception of superiority over non-believers was the prohibition against Jewish or Christian ownership of Muslim slaves. However, under Islamic rule, periods when *dhimmi*s did own Muslim slaves were punctuated by outbreaks of fervent Muslim opposition to the practice. In Syria, where slavery existed until the late nineteenth century, affluent Christians and Jews owned slaves, mostly black Muslim women.[23] Despite declarations of equality, the measures prohibiting minorities to possess Muslim slaves were reinstated during the Tanzimat era; as with many other measures, however, whether or not they were implemented depended largely on the personality of the local *wali*. Thus, in May 1842, citing *dhimmi* ownership of Muslim slaves as demeaning to Islam, the governor of Damascus Najib Pasha called upon the Muslim masses to break into the homes of those *dhimmi*s who refused to release their slaves and forcibly set them free. In this instance, in order to pre-empt violence against them, the Jews and most of the Christian sects acceded to the request of the European consuls and freed their Muslim slaves.[24]

As opposed to Christian Europe, which pushed its Jews into ghettos, the Ottoman empire did not require Jews to live in separate neighbourhoods. The concentration of the non-Muslim minorities in separate areas was a natural consequence of the desire of each group both for the security granted by living in close proximity to co-religionists and for the provision of religious and other communal services. Nonetheless, these quarters were by no means entirely homogeneous, and it was not uncommon for members of one minority either to live or to buy property in another minority's neighbourhood.[25]

[22] AECCC, Damas, vol. 1, p. 199, Devoize, 7 Feb. 1844. On the problems associated with drinking alcohol in Damascus, see Greham, *Everyday Life and Consumer Culture in 18th-Century Damascus*.

[23] There was still a slave market in Damascus in the 1870s, which operated annually under the cover of the *hajj* caravans returning from Mecca. See FO 195/1262, Jago to the Marquis of Salisbury, Damascus, 15 Feb. 1879; Schaff, *Through Bible Lands*, 368–9; Thomson, *In the Holy Land*, 316; and Toledano, *The Ottoman Slave Trade*, 229–30.

[24] AECCC, Damas, vol. 1, p. 104, Beaudin, 3 Aug. 1842; FO 78/499, Wood to Earl of Aberdeen, Damascus, 6 June 1842, 31 July 1842.

[25] On the right of the *dhimmi*s to settle without any restrictions, see Mundy and Saumarez Smith, *Governing Property*. For a discussion of what motivated distinct groups to live in separate neighbourhoods, see Raymond, *The Great Arab Cities*, 58–60; al-Qattan, 'The Damascene Jewish Community', 198.

This trend increased as a result of the reforms, and there were Jewish attempts to leave the confines of the Jewish quarter in Damascus as early as the 1840s.[26] On the whole, however, it appears that social tensions, as well as economic and particularly religious considerations, motivated each minority to remain largely within the confines of its own quarter, near its houses of prayer and communal schools.[27] Thus, in Aleppo, despite legal authorization to live anywhere, the majority of the Jewish community remained in the Jewish quarter, and it was only in the late nineteenth century that Jews began to move out to mixed neighbourhoods in any numbers.[28]

One discriminatory measure that remained in effect for years after its formal nullification was the prohibition on landowning by minorities in Muslim countries, a law that dated back to the days of the early Muslim conquest, when infidel lands were confiscated and their ownership transferred to the Muslim *umma*. In the second half of the nineteenth century there were still some areas in Syria where *dhimmi*s could not purchase land; in others, obstacles were placed in the path of Christians and Jews who attempted to do so. Government directives forbidding Muslims to sell real estate to *dhimmi*s, effective in different places at different times, reinforced this trend.[29]

Freedom of Worship

In the traditional Islamic religious world-view, the fundamental Muslim accusation against Jews and Christians centred on their failure to accept the true religion—Islam. They were further condemned for disseminating false versions of the Old and New Testaments from which references to Muhammad and his mission had been expunged. Nonetheless, acknowledging the essential verity of the sources of the 'religions of the book', the Muslims allowed Jews and Christians to observe their religious commandments, with certain restrictions that touched not upon the rites themselves but rather on the method of their performance: that is, they must be carried out discreetly so as to create no impression of superiority over Islam.[30] The Tanzimat endeavoured to remove those restrictions.

Prohibitions on building new churches, monasteries, or synagogues featured prominently in the Islamic restrictions relating to places of worship. On the other hand, renovation of sites of worship that pre-dated Islamic rule was

---

[26] See Wilson, *The Lands of the Bible*, ii. 334, 343. For further data on mixed neighbourhoods in small cities, see e.g. Saul Dweck Hakohen, *Emet me'erets*, 11*b*, no. 2; I. Dayan, *Imrei no'am*, 17*a*, no. 14.

[27] Frankl, *The Jews in the East*, i. 298–9. For additional testimony on the separate quarters, see I. Burton, *The Inner Life of Syria*, i. 40–3; Porter, *Five Years in Damascus*, i. 147.

[28] Sutton, *Magic Carpet*, 184–5.

[29] Ma'oz, *Ottoman Reform*, 195, and Paton, *The Modern Syrians*, 32.

[30] Ma'oz, *Ottoman Reform*, 12; Bat Ye'or, *The Dhimmi*, 62–3.

permitted, though with certain limitations: for example, the building could not be enlarged or increased in height. Moreover, over the generations the Muslims confiscated synagogues and churches, converting them into mosques. It was to these confiscations and to the law forbidding the erection of new synagogues that the sages of Aleppo attributed the fact that there was only one synagogue in their community.[31] Although it was large enough to hold almost the entire community, worshippers found the simultaneous presence of different prayer quorums disturbing.[32] One method of circumventing the prohibition against building new synagogues was to establish small study houses in the homes of the affluent members of the community, where prayers could be conducted.[33] Thus the Midrash Beit Nasi, constructed in Aleppo in the mid-eighteenth century, served not only as a study house but also as a place of worship.[34]

Reform measures pertaining to the freedom of the non-Muslim minorities to exercise their religion—including the unrestricted right to renovate and build houses of worship, and tax exemptions for study houses and synagogues—had only limited effect in the Syrian Jewish communities. The Jews were more acutely aware than the Christians that the Muslim masses were unhappy about the reforms and not prepared to see the 'inferior' religions raised to terms of equality with Islam. Despite the new legislation, in some instances Muslims blocked the renovation or construction of places of worship by religious minorities. Thus, even in the Greek Orthodox centre of Antioch adherents of this sect were unable to build a church within the city limits and were forced to pray in a chapel some miles distant in the mountains in summer, and to conduct masses in private homes in winter.[35] Given this state of affairs, the Jews of Aleppo decided to make do with the existing synagogue rather than to build new ones. They did, however, take advantage of the opportunity provided by the reforms to enlarge and renovate the synagogue and the Midrash Beit Nasi in 1840 and in 1862.[36] Thus, following the expansion of the existing buildings, Aleppo continued to have, in effect, two public synagogues, and this remained the case until the early 1880s.[37]

[31] Abraham Dayan, *Po'el tsedek*, 'Zikaron divrei erets', 67b. See also al-Ghazzi, *The Golden River* (Arab.), i. 200–1.

[32] Abraham Dayan, *Zikaron lanefesh*, 27. On this problem, see Sasson, *Keneset yisra'el*, 9b; Mordecai Abadi, *Ma'ayan ganim*, 85, 'Oraḥ ḥayim', no. 12. On the central synagogue, see Dothan, 'On the History of the Ancient Synagogue' (Heb.); Cassuto, 'The Ancient Synagogue' (Heb.); al-Ghazzi, *The Golden River* (Arab.), ii. 211–15.

[33] Abraham Dayan, *Vayosef avraham*, 217a, no. 35.

[34] Shneour, *Zikhron yerushalayim*, 18b–19a. Regarding the Midrash Beit Nasi, see Ades, *Derekh erets*, 17–22. See also MC 577, synagogue officials of Midrash Nasi to Montefiore, Aleppo, Av 1849.

[35] Paton, *The Modern Syrians*, 220.

[36] Abraham Dayan, *Vayosef avraham*, 217a; Moses Sutton, *Kehilat mosheh*, 299b.

[37] FO 195/902, Skene, Aleppo, 2 Apr. 1868; *Havatselet*, 34, 2 Tamuz 1880, p. 255. Moses Reischer (*Sha'arei yerushalayim*, 24) claims that there were many synagogues and study houses in Aleppo. This certainly refers to the small private synagogues in the homes of the wealthy elite in which prayer quorums gathered, either daily or on the sabbath and holidays.

According to legend, which apparently contains a kernel of historical truth, Damascus had one large synagogue until the sixteenth century, when a Jewish convert to Islam spitefully donated his seat in the synagogue for the building of a minaret. The Muslims then confiscated the synagogue and its courtyard and converted them into a mosque; at the same time, they granted the Jews permission to build seven synagogues. Eventually the mosque was destroyed, but the seven synagogues remained.[38] Travellers to Damascus in the mid- to late nineteenth century do indeed generally mention seven main synagogues.[39] It appears, then, that, like their co-religionists in Aleppo, the Jews of Damascus did not take the opportunity presented by the reforms to build new synagogues, but did renovate existing ones. In the 1840s and 1850s Christian travellers to Damascus noted the sharp contrast between the run-down condition of the synagogues there and the opulence of the homes of the wealthy Jews they visited. One synagogue is described as an unadorned building, with a clay floor and no furnishings or seats other than a wooden platform.[40] But another observer in the mid-1860s describes the seven Damascus synagogues as 'large, handsome buildings with multicolored marble and alabaster floors, colorfully decorated with gilded blossoms and petals',[41] making it evident that these synagogues had been renovated and redecorated in the intervening years, as was the synagogue in the village of Jobar, near Damascus.[42]

Surprisingly, it was the smaller Jewish communities that took advantage of the permission to build new synagogues. In 1873 the Jews of 'Ayntab began to build a large synagogue to replace the existing one, which was too small.[43] In Alexandretta, which saw the establishment of an organized Jewish community in the 1870s, it was Emil Frank, the Jewish consul for Prussia, Britain, and the United States, who acted on the community's behalf by renting a spacious building to serve as the communal synagogue at his own expense.[44] The fact that new synagogues were constructed in smaller Jewish communities can perhaps be attributed to the late date at which they were built—near the end of the Tanzimat era—and to the involvement of Jewish consuls. It is also possible that closer contacts between Jews and Muslims in these towns may have reduced Jewish fear of Islamic extremism.

As noted above, Islamic law restricted the public performance of *dhimmi* ritual, which was seen as offensive to the Muslim public.[45] Although the

---

[38] On this episode, see Rivlin and Rivlin, 'Chronicles of the Jews in Damascus' (Heb.), 105–10.

[39] FO 78/2242, Green to Granville, Damascus, 29 Feb. 1872; Reischer, *Sha'arei yerushalayim*, 24; Frankl, *The Jews in the East*, i. 292–3; Kestelmann, *Expeditions of the Emissary* (Heb.), 13.

[40] Wilson, *The Lands of the Bible*, ii. 332–3; Anderson, *Wanderings in the Land of Israel*, 155.

[41] Reischer, *Sha'arei yerushalayim*, 24.

[42] See Idelsohn, 'The Jewish Community in Damascus' (Heb.), 102. For a discussion of synagogues in Damascus and Jobar, see Harel, 'The Damascus Jewish Community' (Heb.), 142–7.

[43] AAIU, Syrie, III.E., Alep, 23, Behor, 10 Aug. 1875.   [44] Schur, *Maḥazot haḥayim*, 6.

[45] Ma'oz, 'Changes in the Status of Jews' (Heb.), 13. For the beginnings of public displays of

Hatt-i Hümayun provided for freedom of religion in theory, in practice any public religious displays by the minorities led to agitation among the devoutly Muslim population. This Muslim religious zealotry climaxed in anti-Christian outbreaks in Aleppo in 1850 and in Damascus in 1860, fuelled by public Christian displays of their religious symbols. Although the Jews tried to play down the public aspects of their religious activity, nonetheless there were break-ins to, and robberies from, Jewish holy places in Aleppo, Damascus, and the surrounding areas. For example, Torah scrolls were stolen, apparently for ransom, as were silver synagogue utensils, from the synagogue in Tadef, not far from Aleppo.[46] In Jobar, near Damascus, Muslims attacked Jews who came to pray in its synagogue during the holidays. When a new Torah scroll was installed in the synagogue there, the government dispatched armed gendarmes to accompany the procession from Damascus.[47] However, the regime did not always protect Jewish rites; one Damascus bully used to collect passage money from Jewish funeral processions.[48]

Inter-religious tensions did not affect only relations between Muslims and *dhimmi*s. In Aleppo and 'Ayntab, it was mostly Christians who used to harass the Jews and throw stones at them during Jewish funeral processions; some even desecrated Jewish graves and corpses.[49] This molestation affected the performance of Jewish religious rites; in Aleppo, for example, *sukot* (booths built during the festival of Tabernacles) were generally built outside the city, far from Muslim or Christian passers-by.[50] In Antioch, the ritual bath served as a constant source of friction between the Jews and their neighbours.[51] Certainly, any outward or public demonstration of Jewish religious activity or ceremonial sparked religious zealotry among the Muslim population, which sought to reassert its superiority. A travel account by Benjamin Ze'ev Sapir Halevi, who visited Aleppo in 1877, offers an example:

During Sukkot, on Simhat Torah night, when the entire congregation left the synagogue bearing torches, as was the annual custom, some Muslims passed near the Jewish crowd and snatched the rabbi's turban from his head. Unable to open his mouth or complain, the rabbi covered his head with his shawl and returned to his home with his head bowed. The Jews gathered with ashen faces and remained silent because they were helpless.[52]

Muslim sensitivity to any expression of antagonism towards, or attempt to claim equality with, let alone superiority over, Islam on the part of non-

flags by foreign consulates, see I. Burton, *The Inner Life of Syria*, i. 181; AECPC, Turquie, Damas, vol. 8, p. 210, Hecquard, 4 Aug. 1864.

[46] See e.g. AAIU, Syrie, III.E., Alep, 23, Behor, 28 Jan. 1874; *BAIU*, 1er sem. 1874, 41.
[47] *JC*, 10 Nov. 1854, p. 101.   [48] Frankl, *The Jews in the East*, i. 294.
[49] AAIU, Syrie, III.E., Alep, 23, Behor, 6 Mar. 1879, 17 Apr. 1879, 2 June 1879.
[50] Neale, *Eight Years in Syria*, ii. 96–8.   [51] Abraham Dayan, *Vayosef avraham*, 103*b*, no. 16.
[52] *Halevanon*, 21, 3 Jan. 1877, p. 167.

Muslims was exacerbated by the declaration of reforms endowing equality on the members of all religions. There were instances of Jews and Christians enduring public beatings based upon accusations that they had vilified Muhammad and his religion.[53]

Conversion was another point of contention between Muslims and *dhimmi*s. Although Islam recognizes religious pluralism and the possibility of coexistence with Christians and Jews, and although its legal code prohibits forced conversion of the 'people of the book', the history of Islam is full of episodes in which Jews and Christians were forced to choose Islam or death. Prior to the enactment of the Hatt-i Hümayun in 1856, forced conversion of *dhimmi*s to Islam was common in Syria. On the other hand, a Muslim who wanted to convert from Islam faced the death punishment. The wave of forced conversions was particularly high in the latter half of the 1840s, when Safveti Pasha, who belonged to the opposition conservative party in Istanbul, served as the *wali* of Damascus, where his extreme views amplified further the already marked religious zeal of the city.[54]

On 19 August 1846 a Damascus Muslim persuaded a twelve-year-old Jewish runaway to convert to Islam. Brought before the pasha and the *qadi* after making a statement that he wished to convert, three days later he relented and fled back to his parents. But his father feared to allow his 'Muslim' son to come home without the pasha's explicit permission to return to his former religion; otherwise, he would be liable to the death penalty according to Islamic law. The pasha employed threats and promises in an attempt to persuade the boy to remain Muslim, but two days later, on 24 August, the boy fled again, this time to the British consulate. Safveti's immediate response to the boy's disappearance was to search the Jewish neighbourhood. When the boy was not found, he placed the boy's father and seven other Jews under arrest. Although the British representative Joseph Timoni succeeded in obtaining the prisoners' release, the boy and his parents were forced to leave Damascus that very day for Safed, where they apparently found refuge beyond the fanatical pasha's reach.[55]

In the wake of the Gülhane decree, in the early 1840s Ottoman law mandated that if a *dhimmi* expressed a desire to convert to Islam, he first had to meet with the spiritual heads of the organized religious community with which he was affiliated, to give them a chance to dissuade him from taking such a radical step. If he persisted in converting to Islam, he then had to make a declaration before representatives of his religion and before a high Ottoman official to the effect that he was taking this step uncoerced and in lucid mind.

[53] See e.g. AECPC, Turquie, Damas, vol. 11, pp. 46–8, Guys, 12 Apr. 1876; FO 195/1113, Dickson to Eliot, Damascus, 15 Apr. 1876.
[54] Ma'oz, *Ottoman Reform*, 65, 201. For the general Ottoman policy on this matter, see Deringil, '"There is No Compulsion in Religion"'.
[55] FO 195/226, Timoni to Wellesley, Damascus, 26 Aug. 1846.

Like other reform ordinances, this provision was not consistently implemented in Syria. In April 1847 Timoni, at that point British vice consul in Damascus, reported waves of conversion to Islam among Jewish and Christian youths over a period of a month. According to Timoni, the common denominator in almost all these cases was the enticement, with promises of gifts and money, of poor boys and young men who had troubled relationships with their families. He also testified to Safveti Pasha's intense involvement in encouraging conversion to Islam. To take just one example, when a Christian woman who wanted to divorce her husband expressed a wish to convert to Islam, the *qadi* turned down her request; but the pasha accepted her conversion and married her to a Muslim on the spot. The Greek Orthodox patriarch quickly tendered an official complaint that the execution of her divorce was within his aegis, and that it was his right by law to question the woman as to her motives for converting. Only then, if she held fast to her desire to convert, did it become a personal matter. Safveti Pasha rejected these arguments, arguing that the woman had converted to Islam in his presence and that that alone sufficed to give force to her conversion. He offhandedly sent her embittered husband to complain to the court.

Alarmed by the pasha's assumption of the prerogatives formerly awarded to them by the sultan, and fearing that he would encroach further on their control over their communities, the Greek patriarch, the Catholic bishop, and the chief rabbi of Damascus informed the heads of their millets in Istanbul, who were close to the Sublime Porte, of the potential harm these conversions posed, with particular emphasis on Safveti Pasha's behaviour and the fact that he neglected to invite any of the heads of the minority communities to the *diwan* when *dhimmi*s expressed a desire to convert.[56] For his part, the British vice consul pointed out that Safveti Pasha bestowed much higher sums than the 100 piastres mandated by Turkish law on poor converts. According to Timoni, the pasha's extremism served as a bad example to junior civil servants, who now did not baulk at threatening Christians and Jews with execution at the stake in order to persuade them to convert.[57]

Just a year before the promulgation of the Hatt-i Hümayun, a nine-year-old Jewish girl kidnapped and forcibly converted to Islam in Damascus was returned to her family at the order of the *wali* Namik Pasha. On that occasion the French consul in Damascus, Edmond de Barrère, voiced his hope that legislation would be passed to prevent any more forced conversions and attempts to persuade minors to convert. In his view, the secularizing trend of Ottoman law should encourage further, complementary steps. He called for legislation establishing that conversion carried no civil consequences, in particular that it

[56] FO 78/714, Timoni to Wellesley, Damascus, 28 Apr. 1847.
[57] Ibid., 28 Apr. 1847, 29 May 1847.

would not interfere with parental or familial authority over minors. He also suggested that the legal age at which one could convert be fixed in the law and that clear guidelines be provided for the acceptance of new converts by religious leaders.[58]

These requirements were ostensibly fulfilled with the publication of the Hatt-i Hümayun, which formally established that no person could be forced to convert. In actuality, however, kidnapping and forced conversion of Jewish children continued into the 1870s. At the same time, the Muslim authorities continued to prevent representatives of the non-Muslim minorities from realizing their right to try to dissuade their co-religionists from converting to Islam. The chief rabbis, aware that most of the young Jewish converts came from the lower socio-economic classes, reiterated their demand that these youths at least be allowed to meet with their parents or relatives prior to conversion. On the basis of their experience, the rabbis believed that such meetings opened the eyes of the potential converts and made them relent.[59]

*

In claiming the rights granted by the reform decrees, the Jewish community proceeded with caution, taking care not to arouse Muslim fanaticism, particularly with regard to the discriminatory measures that had for centuries defined such spheres of Jewish life as dress, public religious behaviour, and synagogue construction. The following chapter takes a closer look at the impact of the Tanzimat on the relationship between the Jewish community and the administrative machinery of the Syrian Ottoman regime.

[58] AECPC, Turquie, Damas, vol. 3, pp. 277–8, Edmond de Barrère, 27 May 1855.
[59] FO 195/458, Aron Jacob and Jacob Perez to Misk, Damascus, 15 June 1857. See also Ashkenazi, *Ginzei ḥayim*, 19, 'Oraḥ ḥayim', no. 2. On other, later incidents of conversion, see AECPC, Turquie, Damas, vol. 3, pp. 276–8, Edmond de Barrère, 27 May 1855; *JC*, 26 Sept. 1862, p. 8; FO 78/2282, Green to Granville, Damascus, 29 Oct. 1873; *Hamagid*, 41, 23 Oct. 1862, p. 328.

SEVEN

THE *RA'AYA* AND THE MACHINERY OF THE OTTOMAN STATE

ISLAMIC doctrine mandated that no *dhimmi* could exercise authority over a Muslim. One consequence of this was resistance to the incorporation of infidels—collectively known as the *ra'aya*—in the administrative machinery of the Muslim state. As in other areas, local requirements dictated the extent to which this principle was implemented or ignored; nonetheless, it was enshrined in state law. In this respect, the Ottoman reforms represented fundamental and sweeping political changes for the empire's non-Muslim subjects. They established, for the first time ever in a Muslim state, official equality for all subjects without regard to religion. This required Muslims not only to make legal concessions, but also to forgo the doctrine of Muslim social superiority, which had dictated the discriminatory attitude towards, and lower status of, the non-Muslim minorities.[1]

Representation within Administrative Structures

Several new administrative measures were instituted upon the return of Ottoman rule to Syria, both within the reform context and with the aim of strengthening the power of the central government at the expense of the local *wali*'s authority. As a means of enhancing its direct rule of Syria, the Turkish government acted to implement direct taxation, compulsory conscription, and disarmament of groups and individuals. But the main attempt to limit the *wali*'s authority was made through the provincial council or *majlis idara*. Although originally founded to assist the *wali*, the council enjoyed broad powers that enabled it to block initiatives and to thwart measures that did not meet with its members' approval. Even the more extensive prerogatives granted to the *wali* in late 1852 failed substantially to strengthen his position vis-à-vis the council. In the cities, the reach of the *majlis baladiyya*, the municipal council, extended into the administrative, financial, and judicial spheres: it was empowered to set

---

[1] See Lewis, *The Emergence of Modern Turkey*, 105–6.

tax rates as well as their means of collection, and to approve the appointment of junior officials, set their salaries, and supervise their work. The *majlis idara* oversaw the local municipal councils; in the judicial realm in particular, the local councils did not exercise wide-ranging powers, and important matters came before the *majlis idara*, which also served as a court of appeal for the lower-level courts, including the *mahkama*.[2]

One important reform measure granted non-Muslims representation on the local councils,[3] with the aim of providing them with a voice for their group interests and a role in the provincial administration. These goals were not realized in Syria. With the return of Ottoman rule the *wali* of Damascus, Najib Pasha, swiftly appointed devout Muslims to the *majlis*. At this juncture, it appears that no Jewish representatives were appointed to the council, and the two Christian members, both wealthy individuals, not only lacked political clout but also feared the Muslims. Indeed, one of the *majlis*' first enactments was to reassert the inferior status of the Christian minority, restoring the requirement to wear distinctive *dhimmi* attire when appearing in public. According to an eyewitness account, while this measure was under discussion the Christian representatives sat in fearful silence, not daring to utter a word. Najib Pasha made no secret of his views and publicly announced that he did not want any Christian civil servants in his government. The same traveller further noted that the timidity of the Christian representatives, together with the Muslim threat that they would be thrown into gaol if they so much as voiced any opposition, meant there could be no counterweight to the Muslim majority on the council.[4]

Five years later the British consul in Damascus reported that, when first formed, the *majlis idara* had included Christian and Jewish representatives, but that, subjected to bitter humiliation at the hands of the Muslims—ordered to light the Muslims' pipes and called by derogatory names whenever Jewish or Christian matters came up—they had gradually withdrawn from attendance. In 1845 the last Christian representative was expelled amid curses on the pretext that he had leaked council secrets. For several years thereafter, the council had no Jewish or Christian members.[5] Despite repeated protests by foreign consuls, this state of affairs, in which the Damascus council included no *ra'aya*

---

[2] For further discussion, see Ma'oz, *Ottoman Reform*, 31–6, 89–94, 155.

[3] There was a precedent from the period of Egyptian rule. See Karagila, *The Jewish Community in Palestine* (Heb.), 21.

[4] Paton, *The Modern Syrians*, 33–4.

[5] FO 78/622, Wood to Canning, Damascus, 31 May 1845; Ma'oz, *Ottoman Reform*, 198–9. Elizabeth Thompson argues that the Damascus council should not be viewed as consistently anti-Jewish, anti-Christian, and anti-Tanzimat, but rather as a body that functioned according to majority interests, namely, those of the Muslim public. She criticizes Ma'oz for relying too heavily on the reports by the British consul Wood. See Thompson, 'Ottoman Political Reform', 467–8. For a similar critique of Ma'oz, see al-Qattan, '*Dhimmīs* in the Muslim Court', 436.

representation and was filled mainly with upper-class Muslims, lasted until late 1850.[6] In Aleppo, on the other hand, the local government did not bother to appoint representatives of the *ra'aya* to the local council in the early 1840s, and it was only at a later date that two Christian representatives, but no Jews, were appointed.[7]

In the early 1850s the Turks began to enact measures aimed at strengthening their rule over Syria and at weakening the local power bases, including the *'ulama'* and the *a'yan* in both Aleppo and Damascus. The prevailing membership of the councils in effect discriminated not only against the *ra'aya* but also against the Muslim lower and middle classes, who remained unrepresented. The disproportionate representation of the *'ulama'* and the *a'yan* allowed these elites to protect their narrow interests, even if these ran counter to those of the majority. Although the Ottoman reorganization of the provincial councils saw a reduction in the number of Muslim notables, and the granting of slightly greater representation to the *ra'aya*, nonetheless, when 'Uthman Bey took office as governor in 1850 the Damascus regional council had twelve Muslim members but no minority representatives. He ordered the council dispersed, retaining only four Muslims, including the *mufti* as its president, and requested that the heads of the minority communities, including the Roman Catholics, the Greek Orthodox, and the Jews, send representatives to the new *majlis*. For its representative the Jewish community chose Meir Solomon Farhi, one of the Jews accused during the Damascus affair of 1840.[8] In January 1851 there was a reshuffle in the *majlis baladiyya* as well: the number of Muslim representatives was reduced from sixteen to six, and Christian and Jewish representatives were given places on this municipal council.[9] A more significant step was taken three months later with 'Izzat Pasha's arrival in Damascus. This high official, a member of the reform faction in Istanbul, publicly announced his intention of treating all subjects equally according to the sultan's command, and of revoking any signs of discrimination. To indicate his intent he ordered that the Jewish and Christian members of the *majlis*, hitherto seated on mats at the edge of the hall, take their places among its Muslim members and warned against any attempt to push them to the sidelines, driving his point home by having the names of the non-Muslim representatives engraved on their seats.[10]

[6] FO 78/714, Timoni to Wellesley, Damascus, 29 May 1847; Timoni to Cowley, Damascus, 11 Aug. 1847.   [7] For further detail, see Ma'oz, *Ottoman Reform*, 198.

[8] FO 78/837, Calvert to Palmerston, Damascus, 30 May 1850; Loewe (ed.), *Diaries of Sir Moses and Lady Montefiore*, ii. 21.

[9] FO 78/872, Wood to Palmerston, Damascus, 29 Jan. 1851. For the composition of the council in 1844–5 and reasons for the absence of Jewish and Christian representatives, see Thompson, 'Ottoman Political Reform', 461–8.

[10] FO 78/782, Wood to Palmerston, Damascus, 17 Apr. 1851; 195/368, Wood to Canning, Damascus, 16 Apr. 1851.

There was a Jewish and Christian presence on the various councils through-out most of the 1850s, creating the impression that the Muslims had begun to accept the notion that the *ra'aya* deserved equal privileges.[11] In actuality, the non-Muslim representatives to the councils exercised no influence, for two main reasons. First, these representatives still hesitated to express their opinions freely; and second, the previous imbalance in representation of the various communities was gradually reasserted. As in so many other cases, on these points the proclamation in the 1856 Hatt-i Hümayun that numerical representation on the councils should be fairly apportioned and that all representatives had the right to exercise freedom of thought and speech had little effect.

The rights awarded to the *ra'aya* by the reform decrees simply aroused Muslim anger. Although the minorities were formally granted far-reaching rights, the reality was a reactionary process of limitation of *ra'aya* civil liberties which, encouraged by the *'ulama'*, reached its culmination in July 1860 with the massacre of Christians by the Muslim mob in Damascus. The shameful treatment of the religious minorities by high officials, including Muslim members of the *majlis*, served as a model for the masses, and attacks on defenceless Jews and Christians became commonplace. At the same time, the ever-increasing extremism of the councils' discussions, verdicts, and opinions led to the quashing of the non-Muslim representatives and in many cases to their resignation.[12]

With the restoration of order to Syria in late 1860, the Ottoman authorities again sought to reorganize the various councils. In January 1861 a new Damascus council was chosen, whose members consisted of the *wali*, the *daftardar*, and the mufti; the *qadi*; the administrator of the *waqf*s; and the registrar-general. Together with these officials sat a Jew, a Catholic, and a Greek Orthodox Christian, chosen by their respective millets. But because the *wali* and the *daftardar* were Turks, the meetings were conducted in Turkish, a language understood by neither the Christian nor the Jewish representatives. And even if they could follow the broad outlines of the discussion, the *dhimmi* representatives were still seated on the periphery of the hall, and only rarely dared to offer a comment. These non-Muslim representatives had no influence, not only because of their *dhimmi* status but also because, like the *wali* and the *daftardar*, they refused to take bribes—unlike other members of the council, whose venality is recorded in contemporary testimony.[13]

Jewish representation on the various councils in Damascus was also hindered by the relatively favourable treatment of Christians. Formally, the number of representatives of each group was supposed to be proportional to their numbers

[11] FO 78/961, memorandum of M. Consul Wood's services, Damascus, 28 Mar. 1853.
[12] FO 195/458, Misk to Stratford de Redcliffe, Damascus, 10 June 1857; 195/601, Brant to Esquire, Damascus, 28 Apr. 1858.
[13] FO 406/10, Wrench to Bulwer, Damascus, 1 Feb. 1861. See also Thompson, 'Ottoman Political Reform', 461.

in the population. However, over the course of the 1870s Jewish representatives were consistently pushed out of the various councils and replaced by members of the smaller Maronite Christian millet. Ultimately, this led to a situation in which, by the early 1880s, only one Damascus Jew sat on the *majlis idara*, and Jews had no representation on the councils that dealt with financial, civil, and criminal matters.[14]

In the Aleppo district, despite repeated attempts at reorganization in 1851, the councils did not have a continuous Jewish presence, with the exception perhaps of the *majlis al-ʿadliyya*, the supreme tribunal, on which the spiritual heads of all the millets sat.[15] Isolated references to Jewish representation on the *majlis baladiyya* are available only from the late 1860s. In 1868 the Aleppo city council had a balanced composition, with a Muslim chairman, a Christian vice chairman, and two Muslim, two Christian, and one Jewish representatives.[16] Yet ten years later the British consul, Henry Skene, found the composition and functioning of the Aleppo *majlis* unsatisfactory. Skene remarked on the mistaken impression created by incorporation of minority representatives on the councils, noting their selection not by their communities but by influential Muslims. He also commented on the disproportionate representation of the different communities. In his description of the various councils, including the court of appeals, Skene claimed that the *raʿaya* representatives were ignorant and elderly individuals hand-picked to pose no threat to the opinions and wishes of the councils' Muslim members.[17] In 1879 a committee was convened in Aleppo for the purpose of discussing implementation of the reforms in the *wilaya*. Of its sixty-two members, forty were Muslim, twenty Christian, one a Jew, and one an Armenian. Its Christian members complained that the Muslim majority blocked any attempts on their part to express an opinion, or to suggest ways of implementing the reform measures eliminating inequality. They wished to petition the Sublime Porte for the following, urgently needed reforms in Aleppo: (a) appointment of Christian vice governors to all districts in the region; (b) appointment of Christian vice presidents to the courts; (c) extension of military conscription to members of all religions; and (d) recognition of non-Muslim testimony by the Muslim court. Apparently, aware that these demands ran counter to the wishes of the *majlis'* Muslim members, and even more strongly to those of the Muslim populace, the Jewish representative did not back this petition.[18]

Implementation of the reforms proceeded even more slowly in the smaller towns, where Muslim extremism was at times even greater than in the large

[14] AAIU, Syrie, I.B., 5, Damas, La Communauté de Damas à Crémieux, 23 June 1879.
[15] See Zenner, 'Syrian Jewish Identification', 50.
[16] FO 78/2052, Skene to Elliot, Aleppo, 13 Mar. 1868.
[17] FO 195/1153, Skene to Elliot, Aleppo, 9 Jan. 1877.
[18] AECCC, Alep, vol. 36, pp. 049–051, Destrée, 21 July 1879.

urban centres. Jews had no representation on the administrative councils or courts in the communities of Idlib, 'Ayntab, or Kilis. One exception was Antioch, where the communal rabbi, Abraham Dweck Hakohen, was a permanent member of the Ottoman civil court. He apparently held this position by dint of his personality and his high status in the eyes of both the Ottoman authorities and the local population.[19]

Another significant area in which the Islamic world-view dictated discrimination against the *dhimmi*s was the judicial realm. As part of the reforms, from the 1850s there were courts in Syria that adjudicated cases between foreign residents, and between foreigners and local subjects. Each of these bodies had a different area of responsibility—commercial, criminal, and so on—and each tribunal was composed of an equal number of foreign subjects and local appointees.[20] Although the internal allocation of the local appointees according to the size of each community ostensibly created a Muslim majority, this was the case only with regard to local appointees. The foreigners on the mixed tribunals were mainly Christians and Jews, so that minority representatives outnumbered Muslims. For example, the commercial tribunal founded in Damascus in June 1850 had fourteen members, not including the president of the court. The foreign consulates provided seven merchants: two Europeans, three Jews, and two local Christians who were foreign protégés. For his part, 'Uthman Bey sent seven Ottoman citizens to serve on the court—four Muslims, two Christians, and one Jew. With the presiding judge, who was a Muslim, the Muslim representatives comprised a minority of five out of fifteen.[21] Evidently the Muslim public found this situation intolerable, and over the following years, unable to fulfil its role of promoting commerce because of the rigidity of its Muslim members, who sought to rule according to the *shari'a*, the status of this tribunal declined. This led to threats by its non-Muslim members to resign, apparently effective because they in fact remained on the commercial tribunal.[22] In 1865 a Jew, Raphael Levy, was its chairman. Although he received this appointment by dint of his British citizenship, it is still significant that in the devoutly Muslim city of Damascus a Jew could head an important tribunal before which Muslims appeared.[23]

When it was founded in 1858, the commercial tribunal in Aleppo included

[19] AAIU, Syrie, II.E., Alep, 11, Altaras, Antioche, 21 Nov. 1879. For his tenure in Antioch, see also Franco, *Essai sur l'histoire*, 193, 240.

[20] For additional details, see Ma'oz, *Ottoman Reform*, 155.

[21] FO 78/837, Calvert to Palmerston, Damascus, 30 May 1850, 15 June 1850. The Jewish representatives sent by the foreign consuls were Moses Behar Yehudah, a British citizen; Menahem Rofe, a Prussian citizen; and Zebulun Levy, a Persian citizen. The Jew sent by the Ottoman regime was Tsalaḥ Matalon. See *JC*, 2 Apr. 1852, p. 203.

[22] FO 78/1029, Wood to Earl of Clarendon, Damascus, 26 Sept. 1854; 78/1388, Brant to Bulwer, Damascus, 11 Dec. 1858; 195/458, Misk to Stratford de Redcliffe, Damascus, 10 June 1857.

[23] Regarding Raphael Levy, see *Halevanon*, 14, 20 Tamuz 1865, p. 216.

both foreign and local Jews among its membership, which comprised four Muslims, two Christians, and two local Jews, in addition to three British merchants, two Frenchmen, a Russian, an Austrian, and a Tuscan.[24] Nonetheless, Jewish representation thereafter was not continuous.[25] As in Damascus, having filled the quotas for foreign and local Jews and Christians the Muslim members ignored the new commercial regulations and ruled according to Islamic law. Moreover, even those governors who tried to act in the spirit of the new Ottoman reforms had difficulty imposing their will on the Muslim civil servants, if only because their retention of office depended on the favour of influential Muslims in that city, who could, by turning to the Sublime Porte, have them deposed.[26]

On 8 April 1854 a firman mandating the structure of the criminal tribunal was issued in the Damascus *wilaya*. The Jewish community was given the right to send one representative of its choice, and the Damascus Jewish notables exercised this right by choosing Nisan Farhi.[27] It is unclear whether or not there was continuous Jewish representation on this tribunal; however, it appears likely that, as on other Ottoman councils, there was not, and that such representatives as did take part lacked any real influence.

The Ottoman reforms also opened the civil service to all citizens, regardless of religious affiliation. Jews and Christians had in fact served in the Ottoman administration of Syria even before the Egyptian invasion, but their appointments were made on a personal basis, grounded not in law but in the personal regard of the ruler. When Syria fell to Muhammad ʿAli the upper echelons of the civil service, who were identified with the Ottoman regime—including Jews who held various posts—were replaced by local Christians.[28] With the return of the Ottomans, the Egyptian sympathizers were fired and Ottoman loyalists appointed, or reappointed, in their stead.

The history of the Sasson family of Aleppo illustrates the changing fortunes of Jewish civil servants in the pre-reform and reform periods. This family's rights to collect certain duties, awarded in the eighteenth century, were cancelled by Sultan Mahmud II as early as 1827 in the course of an administrative reorganization aimed at making the central regime the main source of imperial authority. These measures sought to eliminate any intermediary or local posts held by dint of inheritance, tradition, custom, or popular agreement.[29] Despite the cancellation of all writs to tax farmers, including the Sasson family, the Aleppo governor allowed the Sassons to continue collecting duties, which they did, even though the new tax-collection policies diminished their income. In 1832 the

[24] FO 195/595, Skene to Esquire, Aleppo, 20 Feb. 1858.
[25] See Tibawi, *A Modern History of Syria*, 140.
[26] FO 195/1153, Skene to Elliot, Aleppo, 9 Jan. 1877.   [27] *JC*, 26 May 1854, p. 294.
[28] See Philipp, 'The Farhi Family', 42–7. See also al-Dimashqi, *History of Events in Syria* (Arab.), 8 ff.; Mishaqa, *Murder, Mayhem, Pillage, and Plunder*, 49–51, 54–7, 63–70, 105–8.
[29] Lewis, *The Emergence of Modern Turkey*, 88.

Egyptians dismissed the Sassons from their post, most probably replacing them with Christians; then, following the Ottoman reconquest of Aleppo, the new Turkish ruler invited one of the Sassons to assume responsibility for excise taxes, albeit this time as an employee and not an independent tax farmer.[30] The Jew who had served as chief comptroller of the Aleppo *wilaya* before the Egyptian conquest remained in his post as a paid employee, and continued to hold this post when the Ottomans returned.[31]

In Damascus, too, the authorities had need of loyal and experienced Jewish civil servants, first and foremost Raphael Farhi, who had served as the chief *sarraf* (cashier of the treasury) until the Egyptian conquest. In early 1841 a firman was issued safeguarding the status of Jews in the public service; at the same time, Raphael Farhi was restored to his senior position as *sarraf*.[32] According to contemporary accounts Farhi was able to regain his former influence in the Damascus *wilaya*. Not only was he described as having a higher income from trade than any other individual in all of Syria; it was claimed that he also enjoyed profits deriving from his partnership with the pasha, the two men jointly timing the raising and lowering of gold prices to enable themselves to buy low and sell high.[33] Farhi's status as the informal leader of Damascus Jewry enhanced the standing of the Jewish community as a whole. In actual fact, nearly all of the Damascus treasury officials were Christians or Jews.[34]

This dependence on Jewish civil servants from the pre-Egyptian-conquest era did not last long. With the reorganization of the Ottoman regime in Syria and the attempted implementation of reforms came new notions of government that brought significant changes in their wake. Paradoxically, the reformers' aspiration to integrate the *ra'aya* in the institutions of government had the opposite result, actually excluding Jews from positions of power. As on the various councils, minority participation in the civil service was neither continuous nor influential. In aspiring to weaken the governor and to give greater authority to the councils, the reforms destroyed the traditional pattern in which the governors placed their trust in the *dhimmi*s as administrators and financiers. In the past, *dhimmi*s had been preferred over powerful local Muslims for top administrative posts, as the latter posed a greater threat to the governor's status. But the representatives of the *'ulama'* and the *a'yan* on the councils had no need of the *dhimmi*s; thus the Jews and Christians lost their traditional avenue of political influence and their time-honoured dependence on the needs of, and protection by, a single ruler.[35]

[30] See M. Labaton, *Nokhaḥ hashulḥan*, 77b, 'Ḥoshen mishpat', no. 24.

[31] See ibid. 112b, 'Ḥoshen mishpat', no. 39.

[32] Tibawi, *A Modern History of Syria*, 96; Ma'oz, *Ottoman Reform*, 206.

[33] Paton, *The Modern Syrians*, 39–40; AECCC, Damas, vol. 1, p. 078, Ratti-Menton, 4 Mar. 1842.

[34] Paton, *The Modern Syrians*, 39–40. For the enrichment of Damascus Jews because of Farhi's status in the corridors of power, see Mishaqa, *Murder, Mayhem, Pillage, and Plunder*, 65.

[35] For further details, see Philipp, 'The Farhi Family', 47–9.

In addition to establishing various councils, the central regime took other steps aimed at weakening the local *walis*. These measures, aimed at centralization, ultimately weakened Ottoman authority in Syria. Usually appointed only for a year, up to 1852 the *walis* exercised full authority over neither the senior civil servants in their districts nor the troops stationed in the *wilaya*, who were under the command of the *ser'asker*. Nor was the *daftardar*, the senior treasury official, subject to the *wali*. This official's power base was grounded both in the nature of his job and in his independent administrative apparatus, as well as in his relatively long term of office: it was he who determined, for example, government salaries and the budget for expenditures, including military expenses.[36] The arrival of an Ottoman-appointed *daftardar* in each of the Aleppo and Damascus regions further reduced the presence of Jewish officials at the top of the financial administrative pyramid, bringing with it the final dismissal of the Jew who had held the office of chief tax collector until the Egyptian conquest.[37] One Jew did remain in the second rank of officials in the financial administration of the Aleppo district.[38] In Damascus, with the arrival and acclimation of the *daftardar* sent from Istanbul, Raphael Farhi was forced to resign his post as treasurer.[39]

The Sublime Porte finally recognized that its policy of centralization was weakening the *walis* dangerously and, from 28 November 1852, all branches of the local administration were placed under the *wali*'s authority, including the army, the treasury, and the *majlis*. But these measures failed to enhance substantially either the *wali*'s status or his authority. Nor was it possible to turn back the clock and reinstate the old forms of government in which the governor appointed Jews or Christians as district treasurers, as seen from the outcome of the new Damascus *daftardar*'s decision in August 1854 to appoint Meir Farhi to the post of *wilaya* treasurer filled by his father Raphael in the past. Prompted by the shaky condition of the *wilaya* treasury, this appointment had the backing of the *wali*, the municipal council, and various Muslim notables, who hoped that a member of the family that had administered the treasury for many years would be able to improve the Damascus *wilaya*'s precarious financial position. Meir Farhi set to work energetically, hiring many family members as his assistants. However, his imposition of a compulsory treasury loan, on top of his being a Jew, evidently aroused jealousy and hatred within Damascene society. Complaints that Meir might follow in the footsteps of his father, who had been under suspicion for illegal practices and whose running of the *wilaya* treasury had come under attack, were sent to the authorities with demands that he be removed from office. Meir Farhi was forced to resign; but at the same time, in order to discredit his critics, he demanded an investigation

[36] Ma'oz, *Ottoman Reform*, 34–5.
[37] See M. Labaton, *Nokhaḥ hashulḥan*, 112*b*, 'Ḥoshen mishpaṭ', no. 39.   [38] Ibid.
[39] Ma'oz, *Ottoman Reform*, 206.

of his father's conduct in office. Even though the results of this investigation favoured the Farhis, Meir Farhi was not restored to office.[40]

Although denied access to the highest posts, a substantial number of non-Muslims could be found in the lower ranks of the civil service, where their education, talents, and experience were valuable—as was their absolute loyalty to their employers, who did not hesitate to entrust them with management of their finances, including endowments for Muslim religious needs. From 1846, for a period of at least six years, the Jew Moses Lisbona served as treasurer of the Muslim *waqf*s.[41] In both Damascus and Aleppo, Jews (and, to an even greater extent, Christians) were apparently integrated into the financial administration but not into other administrative spheres.[42]

In the wake of the July 1860 massacre of Christians in Damascus and the increased involvement of the European powers in Syria, it again became possible for non-Muslims to enter the civil service. However, they did so only gradually. In the late 1860s a Jew, David Shalom Effendi, was appointed treasurer of the Damascus region. In Aleppo too Jews were employed in managing government finances.[43] But barriers still blocked Jewish entry to the administrative framework. The relationship between the central regime and the local administrations remained uneasy, leading to distrust and bribery. In 1865 the French consul in Aleppo noted that, notwithstanding the Tanzimat, in large measure the defects of the previous system persisted. Local notables still controlled the tax, judicial, and police systems, as they had in the pre-reform period.[44] Moreover, even if all positions had been truly open to the non-Muslim minorities, halakhic issues—the religious prohibition on working on the sabbath and holidays—would have hampered Jewish integration into the system.[45]

'Life, Honour, and Property'

For Jews, the return of Ottoman rule to Syria brought with it an improved sense of physical security compared to the pre-reform period; nonetheless, this still fell short of the situation under the Egyptian regime.[46] The 1839 Hatt-i şerif of Gülhane promised the religious minorities security of 'life, honour, and property'; however, in practice their security under Ottoman rule was influenced by factors including the *wali*'s personality, the size and quality of

[40] *JC*, 29 Sept. 1854, p. 55; 5 Jan. 1855, p. 21.   [41] *JC*, 2 Apr. 1852, p. 203.

[42] See Ma'oz, *Ottoman Reform*, 191–3.

[43] For the appointment of David Shalom, see *JC*, 26 Feb. 1869, p. 6. For Aleppo, see I. Labaton, *Oseh ḥayil*, 189a.

[44] AECCC, Alep, vol. 33, pp. 106–26, Bertrand, 21 Mar. 1865. On the overall difficulty of integrating non-Muslims into the Ottoman bureaucracy, see Carter V. Findley, 'The Acid Test of Ottomanism'; id., *Ottoman Civil Officialdom*, 92–118, 261–81.

[45] *BAIU*, 2ème sem. 1886, p. 64.   [46] Shamir, *A Modern History* (Heb.), 221.

the military and police presence, and the involvement of foreign consuls in safeguarding the community, individuals, and their property.

The early days of the Ottoman return to power in Syria were ones of lawlessness and disorder. A mere two days after the Egyptians' departure and the removal of the feared governor Ibrahim Pasha, the Muslim populace of Damascus avenged itself on those it saw as collaborators with the Egyptian regime, such as tax collectors and conscription officials. Although the temporary ruler, Hasan Bey, threatened to punish the rioters, his power was limited. This episode marks the beginning of a period of calculated Muslim attacks on Christians that was planned to peak with an invasion of the Christian quarter on the night between 31 December 1840 and 1 January 1841, for the express purpose of destroying the churches built under Egyptian rule. This culmination of the violence was only averted by the arrival of the new governor, Sa'id Mehmet Aghat al-Yusuf, at the head of a large armed force on the very day that would have seen the invasion begin.[47]

At times, the very forces that were supposed to protect them posed a danger to the religious minorities. Both the regular armed forces and the irregular militias employed by the *wali* initiated attacks on Christians and Jews.[48] The non-Muslim minorities found the authorities' dependence on the regular forces to quell violence troubling, as these forces, and to an even greater extent the local Muslim police, were known to be hostile to non-Muslims. The weakness and corruption of the Aleppo police encouraged break-ins and robberies, perpetrated in many cases by Muslims against Christians or Jews. From sunset until the gates of the Jewish quarter closed at 8 p.m., robbers roamed the streets looking for easy prey from whom to snatch money and watches. According to one report, Jews hesitated to complain for fear of arousing the resentment of the robber and his relatives, particularly in those cases where they were able to identify the thief; and if they did not recognize the robber, they knew that there was little use in turning to the police in the hope of an arrest. Either way, the person certain to be punished was the Jewish victim of the robbery. Indeed, in some cases in which Jews and Muslims were involved in fights, it was the Jews who were arrested, without any investigation into the cause of the conflict.[49] The situation in Damascus was no better. Jews there were gaoled without investigation in response to any Muslim complaint and cruelly beaten by police officers.[50]

[47] AECPC, Turquie, Damas, vol. 1, pp. 4–7, Ratti-Menton, 6 Jan. 1841. For additional examples of how the governor's personality influenced *dhimmi* security, see FO 78/959, Wood to Stratford de Redcliffe, Damascus, 11 Oct. 1853; AECPC, Turquie, Damas, vol. 11, pp. 46–8, Guys, 12 Apr. 1876.

[48] *JC*, 23 Mar. 1877. On Ottoman military and police forces in Syria until the mid-nineteenth century, see Rafiq, 'Manifestations of Ottoman Military Life' (Arab.).

[49] FO 195/1153, Skene to Elliot, Aleppo, 9 Jan. 1877.

[50] AECPC, Turquie, Damas, vol. 11, pp. 46–8, Guys, 12 Apr. 1876.

The volatile security situation in general, and the view of Jews as despised creatures in particular, created an environment conducive to such acts of robbery and violence, and even of murder. Anti-Jewish acts were justified by the spurious argument, to which no believing Muslim judge or police officer could object, that the assault was in response to Jewish brazenness, a Jewish attack on a Muslim, or a Jew having dared to curse Muhammad or Islam. Underlying this permissive attitude towards anti-Jewish assaults was the notion that the *dhimmi*s owed their existence to Muslim tolerance and protection; consequently, their lives and property were at the believers' disposal. Any *dhimmi* attempt to destroy this balance made them a ready target, providing the Muslims with a legal pretext to kill them and to confiscate their property.[51]

In smaller towns, where extremism and ignorance were even more prevalent and the reach of the central government was restricted, the situation was even worse. A report by the British consul in Aleppo regarding the humiliation of non-Muslims in Kilis illustrates the conditions there: 'Christians and Jews are openly accosted in the streets as accursed infidels, their wives and daughters have their veils violently pulled down, and the Chief Rabbi has had his turban knocked off his head and trampled in the mud.'[52]

Most dangerous of all was travel on the roads. The Ottomans were unable to guarantee safe passage or to maintain security in rural areas. Indeed, Jews considered travel so dangerous that even the completion of a short journey required recitation of the 'blessing of thanksgiving' in the synagogue.[53] The risk of attack was exacerbated by the government's failure to punish those who preyed on travellers, who escaped arrest through bribery or influence, or who avoided punishment because at least until the 1860s no harsh sentences could be enacted without the sultan's approval.[54] Of all sectors of Jewish society, it was those at either extreme who were at most risk: the rich merchants, whose commercial caravans were attacked, and the poor, many of whom were itinerant pedlars. The extremely precarious nature of the Jewish pedlar's life is clear from the fact that nine disappeared in a single year between 1872 and 1873. No effort was made by the local administration either to find them or to find out why they had vanished, and only with the discovery of their corpses did it become clear that they had been murdered by bandits.[55]

---

[51] AECPC, Turquie, Damas, vol. 1, p. 264, extract from a letter addressed to Sir Moses Montefiore Baronet by the principal leaders of the Hebrew community of Damascus, May 1847; p. 194, Devoize, 30 Dec. 1843; vol. 11, pp. 46–8, Guys, 12 Apr. 1876; FO 78/1029, Wood to Earl of Clarendon, Damascus, 26 Sept. 1854; 195/1113, Dickson to Elliot, Damascus, 15 Apr. 1876;

[52] FO 78/2619, Skene to Elliot, Aleppo, 3 Jan. 1877.

[53] See Kestelmann, *Expeditions of the Emissary* (Heb.), 17–18. See also Benjamin, *Eight Years in Asia and Africa*, 44.   [54] Ma'oz, *Ottoman Reform*, 153.

[55] AAIU, Syrie, I.C., Damas, 5, Fuchs à Crémieux, Damas, 9 July 1873, 15 Sept. 1873. See also Abulafia, *Penei yitsḥak*, ii. 26a, no. 1. On similar events in the Aleppo and Antioch regions, see Abraham Dayan, *Vayosef avraham*, 141a, no. 24. On the plundering of caravans, see M. Labaton,

Muslim attacks on the *dhimmi* communities were motivated by contempt for Jews and hatred of Christians. Public ceremonies, such as religious processions and funerals, sparked particular antagonism. In addition, the non-Muslim minorities could even be scapegoated by the Muslim masses over issues which had no direct bearing on the *raʿaya*, such as the constant tension between the Ottoman empire and Russia. When feelings ran high, either because of rumours of approaching war or during wartime itself, Christians and Jews kept to themselves for fear of Muslim fanaticism.[56] Tax hikes also promoted friction, and even ordinary street brawls could mushroom into attacks on minority groups as a whole. In sum, any number of events or disputes could potentially serve as pretexts for Muslims to attack and injure members of the Christian and Jewish minorities.[57] As a result, any change in, or disturbance of, the public order raised levels of anxiety among the *raʿaya*. It would not be overstating the case to say that the Jews lived in the shadow of fear throughout the era of Ottoman reforms intended to establish them on a footing of equality with Muslims.

The Judicial System

Even though the *raʿaya* ostensibly had recourse to the courts to obtain justice, in reality any such attempt was generally doomed to failure by the Islamic principle that litigation between a Muslim and *dhimmi* must be tried before a *shariʿa* court. *Dhimmi* testimony and oaths were generally inadmissible in Muslim courts, the infidel being marked out as a corrupt liar by his refusal to leave his false religion for the true and superior one.[58] In recent years the Damascus *mahkama sharʿiyya* court records from the eighteenth century to 1860, including material on cases involving Jews, have come to light, leading some researchers to conclude that the Muslim courts generally dispensed impartial justice, without respect to religion.[59] To do so, however, is to overlook the pre-existing bias according to which the *shariʿa* court meted out justice. Moreover, even if we accept the claim that the Muslim courts in Syria generally dispensed equal justice to the members of all religions and protected the poor, we can-

Nokhaḥ hashulḥan, 62b–63a, 'Ḥoshen mishpat', no. 17. See also FO 78/1297, Skene to Stratford de Redcliffe, Aleppo, 15 July 1857.

[56] FO 78/959, Wood to Stratford de Redcliffe, Damascus, 13 July 1853; 195/1113, Jago to Elliot, Damascus, 21 Nov. 1876; 195/1154, Jago to Layard, Damascus, 28 July 1877; Jessup, *Fifty-three Years in Syria*, i. 378.

[57] FO 78/1029, Wood to Earl of Clarendon, Damascus, 26 Sept. 1854; 78/579, Wood to Earl of Aberdeen, Damascus, 4 Mar. 1844; AECPC, Turquie, Damas, vol. 11, pp. 66–7, Guys, 18 Sept. 1876; pp. 89–90, Guys, 2 May 1877; AECCC, Alep, vol. 33, pp. 106–26, Bertrand, 21 Mar. 1865.

[58] Ma'oz, 'Changes in the Status of Jews', 12. For the response of the Muslim judiciary in Damascus to Jewish testimony in the eighteenth century and to Jewish litigants, see al-Qattan, 'The Damascene Jewish Community', 206–7.

[59] See al-Qattan, '*Dhimmis* in the Muslim Court', 438–40; id., 'Litigants and Neighbors'.

not extrapolate from the pre-reform to the reform era. During the Tanzimat period, especially up to 1860, many of these courts took a deliberately reactionary stance, motivated by fear that the reform process would be to the detriment of Islam in general and the jurisdiction of the Muslim judges in particular.

It is possible that the Muslim courts ruled fairly when both litigants were non-Muslims, but when one party was a Muslim justice, even in capital cases, was often perverted to favour the Muslim.[60] In general, the Islamic system of law did not allow a Muslim to be executed for a crime against a *dhimmi*. The anti-*ra'aya* bias of the Muslim court system also found expression in court documents, which had particular ways of recording names to identify individuals' religious affiliations. Examination of the Damascus *shari'a* court documents from the late eighteenth century onwards shows the existence of distinctive features identifying Jewish and Christian names. Muslim names were preceded by various honorifics, whereas *dhimmi* names were preceded by the word *al-mad'uw*, 'the so-called'. The identifying words *ibn* (son of) and *al-marhum* (the deceased) were replaced by derogatory terms such as *walad* (child) and *al-halik* (the lost, or destroyed, one). The most obvious marker was the use of the term *al-yahudi* (the Jew). The names of Jewish women were not followed by the phrase *al-mar'a al-kamila al-thabita* (the perfect, steadfast woman), an honorific applied only to Muslim women. In fact, if a court clerk mistakenly appended this honorific to a Jewish woman he would always cross out the phrase; this shows the importance of these linguistic markers in documentation.[61] Another means of distinguishing between Jewish and Muslim names, aimed at emphasizing the *dhimmi* status of the Jews, was the use of a different spelling for names shared by both Jews and Muslims. Names such as Yusuf, Suleyman, and Musa were spelled differently when applied to 'people of the book'.[62]

Prompted by a sincere desire to improve Ottoman administrative jurisdiction and to respond to demands by European powers, the Ottoman reforms reached into the judicial area. With the initiation of reforms in Syria, the councils assumed responsibility for many areas of legal activity that had previously been the province of the traditional courts. In 1847 mixed civil and criminal tribunals were created on which an equal number of European and Ottoman judges sat; these tribunals were supposed to rule according to European norms and to give equal weight to each subject's testimony.

Whereas the first reform decree of 1839, though it promised to preserve the honour of all subjects, did not treat the problem of discrimination between

---

[60] This explains the many cases in which Jews turned to the *shari'a* court rather than to the rabbinic court in cases involving Jews alone: that is, the *shari'a* court dispensed justice when the discriminatory bias against Jews in cases involving Muslims and Jews did not play a role. See A. Cohen, *A World Within*, 16–18.

[61] For further detail, see al-Qattan, 'The Damascene Jewish Community', 204.

[62] Marcus, *The Middle East on the Eve of Modernity*, 40.

subjects in Ottoman administrative and legal documentation, the second
decree, issued in 1856, both mentions this problem and provides explicit
instructions on how it should be dealt with:

Every distinction or designation pending to make any class whatever of the subjects
of my empire inferior to another class, on account of their religion, language, or race,
shall be forever effaced from administrative protocol. The laws shall be put in force
against the use of any injurious or offensive term, either among private individuals
or on the part of the authorities.[63]

Notwithstanding this edict, the discriminatory markers noted above continued to appear in *shari'a* court documents in Syria until the late 1850s, eventually receding only with the creation of alternative tribunals that made Jews less
dependent on Muslim courts and with slow, but consistent penetration of the
new legal norms.

    The application of modern concepts to the Ottoman system of justice trans-
gressed the Muslim religious principle of the divine revelation and derivation
of law, according to which a secular judiciary had no place in the Muslim state
and the *shari'a* was the only, exclusive, and unchanging law. When the Ottoman
reforms officially limited the remit of the *shari'a* courts to issues of personal
status, such as marriage and divorce, transferring jurisdiction over most civil
and criminal matters to courts administering civil, criminal, and commercial
legal codes derived from modern European principles and not from the Qur'an,
the *'ulama'* reacted with fury, considering this an intolerable insult both to
Islam and to their own position as religious leaders. Even worse, in their view,
was the principle of equality before the law for members of all religious minorities, which they perceived as a direct blow to the foundations of the Islamic
state and to their hard-line view of Islamic principles.[64]

    In consequence, the *'ulama'* and extremist local rulers joined forces to repu-
diate the principle of equality before the law.[65] This opposition found expression in their repeated rejection of Christian or Jewish testimony in court, as
well as in their contemptuous and humiliating treatment of *dhimmis*. This discrimination was not always grounded solely in religious principles; contemporary reports attribute the failure of some Muslim members of the mixed
tribunals to fulfil their administrative and judicial duties without bias to corruption.[66] Muslim judges had three tactics at their disposal to avoid accepting
dhimmi testimony. The first was simply to ignore any case brought by a Christian or a Jew against a Muslim. This was rationalized by means of religious

[63] 'Sultan 'Abdülmecid's *Islahat Fermani*'.   [64] Ma'oz, 'The 'Ulamā', 81–5.
[65] See Shaykh 'Umar Effendi al-Ghazzi's words in Ma'oz, *Ottoman Reform*, 87. On the *'ulama*'s
response to the penetration of western influences and their fears for their status, see Roded, 'Tradition and Change in Syria', 184–246. See also Commins, 'Social Criticism and Reformist Ulama
of Damascus'.   [66] FO 78/622, Wood to Canning, Damascus, 4 Dec. 1845.

excuses, as was the refusal to judge according to imperial civil law rather than according to the *shari'a*.[67] A second was to reassign the case to the *shari'a* court, in which *ra'aya* testimony had no force because the court relied on the Qur'an. A third means was employed in the rare cases in which the court was forced to hear *dhimmi* testimony. In such instances, rather than accept such testimony, the Muslim judges preferred to persuade the Muslim to confess to his crime and only then to rule in the *dhimmi*'s favour.[68]

The following case illustrates the workings of the Syrian judiciary during the Tanzimat period. Assisted by two Jewish neighbours, a Damascus Jew from the Romano family intercepted a Muslim thief breaking and entering his house in the middle of the night. The *mukhtar* in charge of the Jewish quarter, responsible for maintaining public order, summoned the guards, who arrested not just the thief but the Jews as well. Before they even had a chance to speak up, one of the guards speculated that the Jews had probably tried to murder the Muslim in order to use his blood for ritual purposes, a suggestion with which the thief hastened to agree. The soldiers proceeded to beat the Jews all the way to the house of the judge, who, on the basis of the thief's declaration that he had narrowly escaped being murdered, ordered one hundred lashes administered to each of the Jews. When Romano claimed Prussian citizenship and tried to insist on his right to contact his consulate before punishment was administered the judge mocked him and doubled the number of lashes, which was doubled again by his enforcers on their own initiative. Beaten severely and thrown into gaol, Romano was bound in chains by his neck. Romano's relatives were not allowed to bring a doctor to see him, or to give him kosher food or medicines. Freed the next day through the intervention of the Prussian consul, despite the best medical treatment Romano died three weeks later.[69]

The new Ottoman tribunals in which *dhimmi* testimony had official force, the first of which were founded in 1847, did not reach Syria until 1854. A year before this the French consul in Damascus had refused to bring the case of one of his protégés before the government tribunal, claiming that it discriminated against Jews and Christians and only endangered any *dhimmi* appearing before it, and declaring that the shamelessness, evil, and fanaticism of the Muslim judges were fully evident from prior cases.[70] In April 1854 the firman relating to the founding of a criminal tribunal in each province, to treat the crimes of Muslims and non-Muslim subjects alike, was read in Damascus and Aleppo. It established two new, central principles. The first was that these courts would give the same weight to Christian and Jewish as to Muslim testimony. The second was that each of the religious minorities would have representation on the

---

[67] Ibid., 31 May 1845.   [68] Ma'oz, *Ottoman Reform*, 196–7.
[69] FO 78/837, Calvert to Canning, Damascus, 28 Aug. 1850.
[70] FO 78/959, translation from the Arabic version of the French Consul's letter to the Pasha of Damascus, 6 Feb. 1853.

court; thus the Jewish community gained the right to send a representative to sit on this tribunal.

Muslims in both Damascus and Aleppo were very reluctant to accept a judicial system that granted Jews and Christians representation on tribunals that were to judge Muslims as well.[71] The earliest testimony to verdicts against Muslims in cases involving either Jews or Christians comes from 1855, from Damascus, and these rulings aroused tremendous opposition.[72] Muslim members of the provincial council, which oversaw the commercial and criminal tribunals, exerted pressure on the tribunals' Muslim members to reject *dhimmi* testimony. Some governors obstructed such intervention; others, more readily swayed by religious zealotry, granted additional powers to the *majlis* as opposed to the secular courts. This naturally had an impact on the Christians and Jews, limiting their freedom of action. Matters worsened when, influenced by the extremism of the provincial council, the Muslim members of the commercial tribunal tried to implement hard-line Muslim measures in the mixed tribunal, which was supposed to judge according to an impartial commercial code, without reference to religious affiliation, for the benefit of trade.[73]

One most exceptional case actually culminated—for the first time in Syrian history—in the execution by hanging of a Muslim for murdering a Jew. This Jew, to whom the Muslim was in debt, was invited to the Muslim's house by subterfuge and murdered there. The Muslim public in Damascus found the death sentence not only astounding but also insulting, indeed impossible, because the Muslims considered themselves 'degraded by being placed on an equal footing even as they say with the Jews'.[74] Naturally, popular anger was directed against the Jews, as if they had secretly conspired to bring about the execution of a Muslim. The fact that the verdict was implemented within twenty-four hours of the murder only compounded the astonishment of Muslims and non-Muslims alike.

Although on the surface this episode appears to demonstrate the progress made by the Ottoman system of justice towards implementation of equality before the law regardless of religion, closer examination reveals two unusual aspects of the case that show this not to be so. First of all, given the chaotic security situation in the Damascus region during the period just preceding the murder, in which a number of killings had given rise to a general mood of fear and uncertainty, the swift execution of justice should be seen as more closely linked to Rashid Pasha's desire to demonstrate publicly that such acts would

---

[71] FO 78/1028, Wood to Earl of Clarendon, Damascus, 14 June 1854.

[72] *JC*, 26 Jan. 1855, p. 45.

[73] FO 78/1029, Wood to Earl of Clarendon, Damascus, 26 Sept. 1854; 78/1388, Brant to Bulwer, Damascus, 11 Dec. 1858.

[74] FO 78/2103, Wood to Elliot, Damascus, 1 Oct. 1869; AECPC, Turquie, Damas, vol. 10, pp. 243–6, Roustan, 28 Sept. 1869.

not be tolerated. More telling was the fact that the murdered Jew had Italian citizenship: thus Rashid Pasha was under pressure to implement the verdict, not because the victim was a Jew, but rather because he was a foreign national whose government might complain to the Sublime Porte if he did not.[75] Neither point made any impression on the Muslim populace, which focused on the unheard-of circumstance of a Muslim being executed for murdering a Jew in a Muslim land. But this outcome was not repeated. In subsequent cases of Muslims murdering Jews no death sentences were handed down and ways were found to exchange execution for a fine or several years' hard labour.[76] Further evidence for the singularity of this case comes from the late 1870s, when the French consul noted the failure to implement death sentences for Muslims convicted of murdering non-Muslims.[77]

The situation in Aleppo was no different. The non-Muslim representatives to the various tribunals were effectively neutralized because their Muslim members, who comprised a majority in the mixed tribunals, insisted on ruling according to the Qur'an. In further refusing to accept circumstantial evidence from *dhimmi*s, apparently under the influence of the Muslim court that did not recognize Christian or Jewish testimony, they simply reflected the majority opinion of Aleppo's Muslim population.[78]

Taxation and Conscription

One part of the Hatt-i şerif of Gülhane decree was concerned with the establishment of 'a regular system of assessing taxes'.[79] The system initiated by the Egyptian regime in Syria as a means of eradicating the feudal system of tax farming had strengthened local leaders and impoverished the rural population. The new system introduced by the returning Ottomans—whose main shortcoming was that it was not progressive—bore heavily on the Muslim middle class in general and especially on the urban lower classes, as the wealthier classes managed to avoid payment either by exercising political influence or by dint of their membership on the councils.[80] The non-Muslim minorities were particularly hard hit, as the *dhimmi*s continued to pay the *jizya* as required by the law of the Muslim state, in addition to the other taxes imposed on its subjects.

One of the taxes levied on the Syrian population under the Egyptian regime was the *ferde*—a personal poll tax required of all subjects, including

[75] FO 78/2103, Wood to Elliot, Damascus, 1 Oct. 1869.
[76] AECPC, Turquie, Damas, vol. 11, pp. 87–8, Guys, 13 July 1877; FO 195/1153, Jago to [?], Damascus, 14 Apr. 1877.
[77] AECCC, Damas, vol. 6, p. 9, Rousseau, 17 Mar. 1878.
[78] FO 195/1153, Skene to Elliot, Aleppo, 9 Jan. 1877; and AECCC, Alep, vol. 36, pp. 49–50, Destrée, 21 July 1879.
[79] Inalcik (trans.), 'The Hatt-i Şerif of Gülhane', 270.
[80] For a more extensive treatment, see Ma'oz, *Ottoman Reform*, 75–81, 182–3.

non-Muslims.[81] Initially, the Ottomans promised to abolish this non-progressive tax, and to replace it with a 10 per cent property tax; however, this promise was not fulfilled. In Damascus, a combination of administrative difficulties and a desire to win popular support prompted the restored Ottoman regime to waive payment of the *ferde* until 1843. When it was reinstated, on the orders of the *majlis* the tax was distributed inequitably among the Muslim, Jewish, and Christian sectors, with the *dhimmi* communities charged sums out of all proportion to their numbers in relation to the Muslim population. Under Egyptian rule the religious minorities were required to pay up to one-quarter of the total tax imposed on the Damascus taxpayers. After the Ottoman return, the division of the tax among the various sectors was discussed by the *majlis* only after its Muslim members had expelled the Christian representative from the room. The sum imposed on Damascus came to one million piastres, which the *majlis* decided to distribute according to a ratio of 6,000 Muslims to 2,000 Christians and Jews; as the actual population of the city stood at approximately 95,000 Muslims to 25,000 Jews and Christians, this allocation of the tax burden was patently unfair.[82]

From 1844 the *ra'aya* tried to get this injustice redressed. The steps taken indicate that neither Christians nor Jews believed in the sincerity of the Ottoman regime's intentions regarding, or its ability to implement, reforms. Their initial move, the employment of the time-honoured method of bribery in an attempt to change the decision of the Muslim members of the *majlis*, met with no success. Evidently the *majlis* feared that, if it agreed to lower *ra'aya* taxation, the resulting deficit would have to be covered by increased taxes for Muslims, which would in turn antagonize the population. At the suggestion of the European consuls, the *ra'aya* then tried to work through legal channels with the local government. Although their appeal to the *majlis* met with an expression of willingness to lower their taxes, no practical measures ensued. A petition presented to the *wali* 'Ali Pasha in early 1844 went unanswered. The main *ra'aya* demand was that the tax rate be determined according to class-related criteria, such as occupation, income, and property ownership, rather than on the basis of religious or communal affiliation, seeking by these means to promote relative equality with the Muslims. Because such a system would transfer a larger share of the burden to the affluent, the Muslim lower classes also favoured a progressive tax.

---

[81] Antebi, *Mor ve'oholot*, 94*b*, 'Ḥoshen mishpat', no. 13. See also Saul Dweck Hakohen, *Emet me'erets*, 11*b*, no. 2. On the *ferde* tax under the Egyptian regime, see Abu 'Izz al-Din, *Ibrahim Basha in Syria* (Arab.), 145.

[82] AECCC, Damas, vol. 1, p. 207, Devoize, 7 Feb. 1844, 6 Mar. 1844; FO 78/538, Wood to Earl of Aberdeen, Damascus, 27 Dec. 1843; 78/579, Wood to Stratford Canning, Damascus, 21 Feb. 1844. See also an undated letter of the Damascus Jewish community to Montefiore regarding this matter, MC 577.

The Damascus authorities' attempts to collect the tax, including making chalk marks on the doors of many Muslim, Christian, and Jewish homes, only led to increased unrest in the city. Wealthier individuals began secretly to transfer their belongings to safety.[83] The *ra'aya* now presented petitions to the Sublime Porte via the heads of their religious communities in Istanbul; these appeals also went unanswered.[84] Resistance to payment by Damascus residents on the one hand, and a desperate need for funds, in particular for military activity, on the other, forced the local Damascus regime to resort to violence to collect the *ferde*. This was directed first and foremost at the weaker elements in Damascene society, namely, Christians and Jews. Soldiers and policemen arrested Christians and Jews in the bazaars or made unannounced visits to their homes at night, beating the men, humiliating the women, and plundering their belongings. *Ra'aya* -owned stores in the bazaars were robbed in broad daylight, causing the bazaars to close for long periods because the shopkeepers had gone into hiding. The desperation felt by the *ra'aya* is exemplified by a suggestion made by one *dhimmi* that he would meet the tax payment by selling his son into slavery.[85] Even when the local regime temporarily lightened the *ra'aya* tax burden it soon reinstated the full payment, and sometimes also compelled the *ra'aya* to pay the difference for the years when they had enjoyed a discount.[86] The steps taken to enhance tax collection from the *ra'aya* even extended to arresting the leaders of the *dhimmi* communities. This policy of harassing the *ra'aya* rather than demanding that the Muslims pay a fairer share of the tax burden continued in Damascus until the early 1850s.[87]

In Aleppo the distribution of the tax burden was equally distorted, and served as the excuse for a large-scale Muslim rebellion in 1850. Its main demand was that the *ferde* be changed from a poll tax to a property tax in line with the Tanzimat measure implemented elsewhere in the empire.[88] In Damascus the major property owners were the members of the *majlis*, the *a'yan*, and the *'ulama'*. They consistently obstructed any attempt to change the *ferde* to a property tax, the *vergi*, arguing that, because the Christians and Jews did not own substantial property, the burden would then fall mainly on the

[83] FO 195/226, Wood to Canning, Damascus 21 Feb. 1844; AECPC, Turquie, Damas, vol. 1, p. 200, Devoize, 7 Feb. 1844; FO 78/579, Wood to Earl of Aberdeen, Damascus, 4 Mar. 1844.

[84] AECCC, Damas, vol. 1, p. 220, Devoize, 6 Mar. 1844; FO 78/579, Wood to Canning, Damascus, 21 Feb. 1844.

[85] AECPC, Turquie, Damas, vol. 1, pp. 214–17, Devoize, 8 May 1844; FO 78/379, Wood to Earl of Aberdeen, Damascus, 8 May 1844.

[86] For a description of the tax burden, see NLIS, DA, V-736/28, Hayim Maimon Tobi to Abraham Hayim Gagin, Damascus, 5 Sivan 1847.

[87] FO 78/714, Timoni to Cowley, Damascus, 1 Sept. 1847; Timoni to Palmerston, Damascus, 8 Sept. 1847; 195/291, Wood to Canning, Damascus, 25 July 1849; 78/660A, Wood to Earl of Aberdeen, Damascus, 9 Mar. 1846.

[88] M. Labaton, *Nokhah hashulhan*, 27b–28a, 'Even ha'ezer', no. 16.

Muslim population.[89] Likewise, in Aleppo these upper echelons of Muslim society were in the vanguard of opposition to changing the tax. Here, too, a third group, comprising the Jewish consuls to Aleppo—the Picciottos—and their coterie, joined forces with the *'ulama'* and the wealthy property owners, for they too would be affected by any changes: the property tax was applicable to foreign residents, and as long-time residents of Syria these consuls had amassed a great deal of property. Their stance contrasted sharply with that of the other European consuls, who owned no local property and therefore sought to benefit the locals through the substitution of the *vergi* for the *ferde*.

The Jewish consuls tried in a number of ways to avoid paying the *vergi*, including questioning the validity of the measure requiring foreign nationals to pay imperial taxes, and obscuring the true extent and nature of their holdings. The local British consul testified that, in concert with the *'ulama'* and the *a'yan*, the Jewish consuls placed every possible obstacle—using threats, interference, and coarse language—in the path of the officials appointed to assess Aleppo's subjects. The Austrian consul, Elijah de Picciotto, ordered all Austrian protégés under his protection not to remit their property assessment tax.[90] In this case the Jewish consuls were acting against the interests of the local population, and even those of the entire Jewish community.

Despite vocal opposition from the elites, in April 1852 the Sublime Porte ordered the *ferde* changed to a property tax in Damascus. Contemporary reports testify to spontaneous celebrations in response to this announcement, in the non-Muslim quarters in particular.[91] A similar step was implemented a year later in Aleppo. In both cities assessment committees were formed to assess the property—houses and land—of all subjects, regardless of ethnic or religious affiliation.[92] However, the corruption permeating all matters linked to distribution of the tax burden in Muslim society led in many instances to the *a'yan* and the *'ulama'* avoiding full payment, either through bribery or because of family ties with officials serving on the assessment council. Naturally, this increased the burden on the other, mainly Muslim, strata of the population and heightened the socio-economic divisions in Muslim society.[93] Even if the *dhimmi*s continued to pay more than their real share, the transformation of the *ferde* into a property tax did somewhat lighten their heavy tax burden.

The main component of this heavy tax burden was the *jizya*. A personal tax, it was collected from each individual and not from the community as a representative body. In Muslim eyes, by paying this tax the *dhimmi*s gave expression

[89] FO 78/910, Wood to Canning, Damascus, 27 Apr. 1852.

[90] FO 78/910, Werry to Canning, Aleppo, 29 May 1852; Werry to Stratford de Redcliffe, Aleppo, 5 June 1852; Werry to Malmesbury, Aleppo, 10 June 1852.

[91] FO 78/910, Wood to Canning, Damascus, 27 Apr. 1852.

[92] See M. Labaton, *Nokhaḥ hashulḥan*, 28a, 'Even ha'ezer', no. 16.

[93] See Ma'oz, *Ottoman Reform*, 184.

to their subjugation, their recognition of their lower status, and their dependence upon their Muslim rulers. The manner in which the *jizya* was collected further contributed to their degradation, as government tax collectors had no qualms about humiliating or striking taxpayers.[94] Lobbying by the European powers to abolish this discriminatory tax met with no response in the first reform edict, the Hatt-i şerif; nonetheless, continued pressure for steps in this direction was accompanied by a demand that, as a preliminary measure, no oppressive procedures be used for its collection. It was not until the early 1850s that these efforts bore fruit. On his arrival in Damascus, ʿIzzat Pasha implemented measures changing the *jizya* from a personal to a communal tax. The heads of the non-Muslim millets were empowered to determine the distribution of the tax burden within their communities, to undertake collection of the tax, and then to forward the funds to the *wilaya* treasury through a special agent.[95] With hindsight, this actually constituted the first step towards abolition of the *jizya*. European pressure continued until the promulgation on 7 May 1855 of a firman cancelling the *jizya* throughout the empire. The second reform decree, the Hatt-i Hümayun of 1856, included clauses treating equitable and organized tax collection.

Complementing the cancellation of the *jizya* was the abolition of the discriminatory law forbidding non-Muslims to bear arms. Essentially, the abolition of the *jizya* meant that the *dhimmi*s had the right to self-defence and were no longer dependent on Muslim protection and toleration. On the other hand, it also meant that *dhimmi*s could be conscripted into the Muslim Ottoman army, an innovation suspect in both Muslim and *dhimmi* eyes.

Within Syrian Muslim society itself there was resistance to conscription. Muslims feared the draft and, despite the employment of both persuasive and coercive measures, refused to serve in the Ottoman forces, compelling the sultan to postpone recruitment here: only in 1850 was a general draft carried out in Syria, following a population census. This was a major contributory factor in an uprising in Aleppo that October, in consequence of which there was no further general conscription there until 1861.[96] For their part, by dint of residing in one of the four holy cities—the other three being Mecca, Medina, and Jerusalem—Damascus' Muslim citizens were exempt from army service. Therefore, in Damascus the Ottoman regime was able to draft recruits only from the criminal or the lower classes. Determination of who was subject to conscription lay entirely with the local notables, who used their position to ensure exemptions for their own children. It was not until after the July 1860

---

[94] FO 195/291, Wood to Canning, Damascus, 25 July 1849. On the humiliating features of the *jizya*, see Lewis, *The Jews of Islam*, 14–16.

[95] FO 78/872, Wood to Palmerston, Damascus, 29 Mar. 1851; 195/368, Wood to Canning, Damascus, 16 Apr. 1851.

[96] For a more detailed treatment, see Ma'oz, *Ottoman Reform*, 81–4.

massacre of Christians in Damascus that Fu'ad Pasha, sent by the Sublime Porte to restore order in Syria, took advantage of his sweeping powers to break the tradition of non-conscription in Damascus. The compulsory draft of Muslim youths imposed by this governor in the Damascus district conscripted some 20,000 men within a three-month period, all of whom were deployed outside Syria.[97]

Against this background of general Muslim resistance to conscription, it is not surprising that Syrian Jews saw the draft as a burden rather than a benefit. For their part, the Muslims found the idea of fighting alongside Christians and Jews difficult to accept. This differed from the European attitude. The supporters of awarding Jews citizenship in Europe saw Jewish conscription to the army and Jews' willingness to die for their countries as a key element in their civil emancipation, and as proof of their loyalty to, and identification with, the state. The very granting of the right to be conscripted was seen as representing the state's disposition towards recognition of Jews as equal citizens. This was not the case in Syria. When rumours spread in Aleppo regarding the forthcoming conscription of non-Muslims in 1855, the city's rabbis hastily posted letters to influential European Jews begging their co-religionists to lobby for the abolition of this law. Jewish opposition to the draft was grounded in the fear that Jews would be forced to violate Jewish laws such as sabbath observance and *kashrut* during army service, and that it would also result in increased assimilation.[98] These specifically Jewish fears added an additional layer to the existing general hostility to conscription in Syria, which was also shared by Christians.

A combination of factors—Muslim opposition to *dhimmi*s having equal obligations and to serving alongside *dhimmi*s, coupled with the Ottoman regime's inability to deal with the difficulties that *dhimmi* conscription would entail—led to a search for a new solution to this problem. It emerged in the form of a commutation tax to be paid by the non-Muslim minorities in exchange for exemption from the army. Known as the *bedel-i 'askeri*, this tax was collected in the same fashion as the *jizya*; in essence, only the name of the tax was changed and, like the *jizya*, it was perceived as a discriminatory tax. Although Muslims could also obtain exemption from army service through payment, the amount exacted from them was larger and only wealthy Muslims could escape the draft by this means. On the other hand, as members of religious minorities, the *ra'aya* had no choice but to pay, and thus the tax perpetuated their inferior status.[99]

On 28 July 1856 the firman concerning conscription of Jews and Christians into the Ottoman army, read in the *seray* (government building) in Aleppo, set

---

[97] Ma'oz, *Ottoman Reform*, 81–4; Jessup, *Fifty-three Years in Syria*, i. 207.

[98] Ben-Zvi Institute, MS 3724, *Pinkas rabi mosheh suton*: Moses Sutton [?] to Abraham [Albert] Cohn, Aleppo, 1855. See also Abulafia, *Penei yitshak*, i. 83a, no. 13; Elyashar, *Simhah le'ish*, 37a, 'Even ha'ezer', no. 7.   [99] For further detail, see Ma'oz, *Ottoman Reform*, 195.

the quota for these communities at forty-eight conscripts, translated into a monetary payment of 240,000 piastres, namely, 5,000 piastres per soldier. This sum was remarkably close to the amount of *jizya*—230,000 piastres—paid by the *dhimmi* communities in the past. In addition, these communities were asked to make good the debt for their non-payment of *jizya* in the years preceding its abolition.[100] The Jews raised no objections, but the Christians, who viewed the new demand as merely the *jizya* in a different guise, refused to pay and expressed their willingness to enter the army instead. Threatened with incarceration, the Christian community finally agreed to pay the tax, on condition that it be collected only when there was a general draft among the Muslim population. The Muslims accepted this compromise, and so a deferment was agreed which benefited Aleppo's Jews as well.[101]

In the event this delay lasted for nearly six years, but whether this was a result of administrative incompetence or of the regime's giving way to Christian objections is not entirely clear. Either way, it was not until March 1862 that the Aleppo governor invited the bishops and the *ḥakham bashi* to a meeting at which he demanded that the *raʿaya* pay the *bedel-i ʿaskeri*, set for that year at 240,000 piastres. In addition, the *wali* demanded payment for the previous six years, in the amount of 1,400,040 piastres. Once they recovered from their initial shock, the Jewish representatives requested, and received, permission to spread the payments over a period of three to four years. The Christians, however, were unhappy about being required to pay at all. They backed their objections with a reminder that the terms of the agreement stipulated that the tax would be collected only when a general draft took place among the Muslims, noting that there had been no such draft during the past six years. Moreover, because the sultan had promulgated this tax in response to pressure from the European powers—as a measure intended to prove his goodwill towards his Christian subjects to the participants at the Congress of Paris, held in 1856—the Christians argued that the present demand for payment distorted the sultan's intentions. They further pointed out that when the *jizya* was still in effect the sum required of Jews and Christians did not surpass 100,000 piastres, whereas now more than double that sum was being demanded in addition to the new property tax, the *vergi*. On this occasion the Christians lost the argument, and both they and the Jews were forced to hand their tax payments over to the *wilaya* treasury.[102]

In Damascus, the *wali* Muhammad Pasha invited the leaders of the non-Muslim minorities to a meeting at which he revealed the contents of a similar firman on conscription even prior to its public reading in that city. He maintained that the *raʿaya* should recognize the commutation of the draft for monetary payment as a measure in their favour; for their part, the minority leaders

[100] FO 78/1220, Barker to Stratford de Redcliffe, Aleppo, 29 July 1856.
[101] Ma'oz, *Ottoman Reform*, 204.   [102] FO 78/1688, Skene to Bulwer, Aleppo, 29 Mar. 1862.

preferred not to respond until the public proclamation.[103] When this came about, a week later, the quota announced for the *dhimmi* communities stood at thirty-five soldiers, and the *bedel-i 'askeri* tax was set at 175,000 piastres—again, 5,000 piastres a head. The Christian and Jewish leadership were outraged at this demand and, in an unprecedented move, met at the Greek patriarch's home in order to plan a joint response. All agreed that this was an arbitrary measure which, because it essentially renewed the *jizya* in a different form, negated the principles of the Hatt-i Hümayun. They decided to inform the *wali* that the *ra'aya* were willing to fill their quota of conscripts but that poverty rendered them unable to offer monetary payment in exchange. However, following a heated initial discussion, the representative of the Jewish community, the *hakham bashi* Jacob Peretz, announced his intention of accepting the principle of payment in lieu of conscription, while reserving the right to object to the amount: 51,000 piastres for ten soldiers, the Damascus Jewish community's quota. Outside observers interpreted this stance as based on the religious barriers to Jews serving with non-Jews, but also pointed out that the Jewish community in the city was enormously wealthy and could well afford to meet the necessary payments.[104]

The Christian argument that the *bedel-i 'askeri* tax was too high, that it negated the principle of equality, and that unless the *ra'aya* had the option of being conscripted without being required to make monetary payment in lieu of service it was merely a renewal of the *jizya* under another name, was not entirely accurate. Certainly, the *bedel-i 'askeri* was higher than the *jizya*, but unlike the latter it was not a personal tax on each individual adult but rather a tax imposed on the community, which the community in question could distribute among its members as it saw fit. It is also true that, despite their demands to be eligible for military service, the Christians privately hoped that the regime, which did not really want them in its armies, would also forgo payment. From their point of view, the option of payment for exemption from army service still remained a possibility, as it did for any Muslim who sought to free himself from service.[105] Christian objections to the *bedel-i 'askeri* continued until 1860; indeed, the Christian refusal to pay this tax, perceived as an act of rebellion against the sultan, the commander of the faithful, can be seen as implicated in the massacre that struck their community in that year. With the abolition of the *jizya* Christians had lost their right to Muslim protection and acquired the status of condemned men in the eyes of the Muslim populace.[106]

[103] FO 78/1220, Misk to Clarendon, Damascus, 27 Aug. 1856.
[104] Ibid.; AECPC, Turquie, Damas, vol. 4, pp. 79–86, Outrey, 16 Aug. 1856; FO 195/458, [Misk] to Stratford de Redcliffe, Damascus, 27 Aug. 1856.
[105] See Ma'oz, *Ottoman Reform*, 233; Tibawi, *A Modern History of Syria*, 118.
[106] On the massacre in Damascus and on the conflict between Muslims and Christians in Lebanon, see Fawaz, *An Occasion for War*, and p. 174 below.

In the years following the massacre of the Christians the main taxes on the *ra'aya* continued to be a residence tax and the *bedel-i 'askeri*.[107] Notwithstanding the *ra'aya*'s exemption from military service, from time to time the regime made attempts to involve its members in local army or police activity. In 1877, during the Russo-Turkish wars, the withdrawal of regular troops from Damascus reduced the garrison to a mere 200 soldiers and, in order to maintain safety and security in Damascus, the authorities ordered the formation of a national civil guard. For the first time, Jews and Christians were ordered to join. The Muslims, impoverished by a conflict no longer regarded as a holy war against the infidel, refused, announcing publicly that they would contribute no more men or funds to the war effort. By way of bringing home their point they plundered the arms warehouse. The Christians and Jews also made some complaints, though these were kept low-key lest they attract accusations of collaboration with the enemy or inflame popular hostility. In effect, the *ra'aya* relied on what appears to have been the Muslim population's success in preventing the formation of a civil guard.[108] But a wholesale exemption with nothing given in return was not an option, and the Jews and Christians were pressed into paying a 'voluntary war tax' that had also been imposed on the Muslims. In the final event, the non-Muslims paid an enormous sum. In doing so, the Christians and Jews highlighted their contribution to the war effort and their loyalty to the empire.[109]

Jews and Christians continued to pay the *bedel-i 'askeri* tax, which was imposed on the entire community without reference to the actual number of potential conscripts, until the early 1880s. Once they realized that the population statistics on which they had based the quota for each community had been falsely lowered as a means of reducing the tax liability, the Ottomans began to hold their own censuses upon which they based the quota for each community. Thus the tax became a personal tax, although the leaders of the *ra'aya* retained the right to distribute the burden as they saw fit.[110] It was not until August 1909 that the *bedel-i 'askeri*, the last remaining symbol of Jewish and Christian civil inequality, was abolished with the promulgation of a law making conscription obligatory for non-Muslims as well as Muslims.

---

[107] For a description of the various taxes, see the letter of the leaders of the Damascus Jewish community to Moses Montefiore, published in *Hamagid*, 31, 8 Aug. 1861, pp. 194–5. Montefiore responded by turning to the British consul in Damascus for an explanation of the tax structure in Syria. This letter is housed in the CAHJP, INV 521D, Rogers to Montefiore, 19 Aug. 1861. A copy is located in BofD, ACC/3121/A/9, 10 Oct. 1861.

[108] AECCC, Damas, vol. 5, p. 223, Rousseau, 28 Dec. 1877; FO 195/1154, Jago to Layard, Damascus, 26 Dec. 1877.

[109] FO 78/2850, Jago to Earl of Derby, Damascus, 24 Mar. 1878.

[110] On tax collection in Urfa, see Aaron Dayan, *Beit aharon*, 16b, 'Ḥoshen mishpat', no. 23.

The *Ra'aya*'s Relationship with the Regime

The Ottoman regime's success or failure in implementing reforms in Syria in general, and with regard to the *ra'aya* in particular, was largely dependent on the personality of the district *wali*. The extent of his Islamic fervour and the balance of power between *wali* and *majlis* strongly influenced *wilaya* policy towards the non-Muslim minorities. Moreover, if the central regime in Istanbul did not always take a favourable view of equality between Muslims and the *ra'aya*, a principle largely forced upon it by the European powers, it is not surprising that there was even less enthusiasm for it in distant provinces. Pressure from conservative elements in Istanbul and in Syria itself caused even relatively liberal governors who assisted the *ra'aya* in Syria to devote greater attention to the areas of security, standard of living, and religious freedom than to full political and legal equality. Governors could even be removed if they showed excessive pro- *ra'aya* tendencies. The devout Muslim public, whose support governors hoped to win, also influenced whether and how reforms were implemented. Muslim history has known periods in which hard-line rulers set out to correct what they saw as mistaken leniency on the part of their sinful predecessors. Some local rulers in Syria exercised a strict policy of unyielding orthodoxy, co-operating with the *'ulama'*, who preached the need to return to pure Islam and to reject the innovative reforms that countered Islamic tradition and law. The sole guarantee of implementation of the Tanzimat reforms was a strong ruler able to tackle conservative forces.[111]

With the return of Ottoman rule to Syria, Hajj 'Ali Pasha was appointed governor of Damascus. Upon 'Ali's appointment shortly thereafter as ruler of Mecca and Medina, he was replaced by Najib Pasha, the first governor to address the problem of the non-Muslim minorities. Although his administrative abilities and contribution to Damascus' development are indisputable, with respect to the *ra'aya* Najib pursued a consistently discriminatory policy, particularly towards the end of his tenure, even actively stirring up hostility towards non-Muslims. This is surprising, because in the early part of his term as governor he acted in the spirit of the Hatt-i şerif. One of his first measures was to reactivate the *majlis* and to make each and every member swear on his holy scriptures not to take bribes.[112] But immediately thereafter he announced his hatred for Christians and his opposition to a Christian civil service. Similarly, before leaving Damascus he incited the devout Muslim populace to attack those Jews and Christians who continued to hold Muslim slaves. The foreign consuls attributed this change to Najib's desire to curry favour with the Mus-

---

[111] Tibawi, *A Modern History of Syria*, 96; Ma'oz, *Ottoman Reform*, 221–2. On the reformers' efforts to implement reforms throughout the empire, see Davison, 'Turkish Attitudes'.

[112] Tibawi, *A Modern History of Syria*, 96.

lim population of Damascus and a calculated decision to play the part of a devout Muslim even though in fact he was an educated, secular individual.[113]

So seminal was the role of the *wali* to the safety, security, and dignity of the *ra'aya* that a change in incumbent elicited either elation or trepidation, depending on the personalities of the outgoing and incoming governors. Thus, for example, in 1845 Jews and Christians openly expressed their sadness over the sudden death of a senior official in Damascus, known for his toleration and protection of the *ra'aya*.[114] In Aleppo, on the other hand, Jews and Christians feared the appointment as governor of 'Uthman Pasha, believed to be a fanatical Muslim; and these fears were heightened when the leaders of the non-Muslim minorities, having come to congratulate him on his appointment, were ignored while he granted every one of the Muslims a gracious personal reception.[115] At times, the *ra'aya* and the European powers viewed those governors favourably predisposed to the Tanzimat spirit as representative of the progress that had penetrated the empire and Syria. Thus, for example, at the cornerstone-laying ceremony for the Alliance school in Damascus, the French consul remarked on the city's reception of the ceremony and, more particularly, on the presence of the *wali*, Rushdi Pasha, which 'once again represented the equality of all religions in Turkey'.[116] However, as noted above, the question of equality before the law was ultimately in large part dependent on the *wali*'s personality and not on the supposed 'winds of progress', which had not yet truly penetrated the empire. This is apparent from the joy expressed within the *ra'aya* at the transfer in 1877 of Zia Pasha, a governor of Damascus who was particularly hostile to the non-Muslim minorities and had used the official *wali* mouthpiece, the provincial newspaper of which he was the chief editor, to publish inflammatory articles against them. Before leaving his post, Zia used his authority to cancel all outstanding debts and mortgages to Jews and Christians, transferring the income to the *wali* treasury.[117]

One measure of a *wali*'s partiality, or hostility, towards Jews was his attitude towards the activity of the Alliance Israélite Universelle in his realm. Notwithstanding its overt concern with the Jewish community, the Alliance's French origins usually ensured it at least an initially favourable reception. Thus, upon his arrival in Aleppo in 1869 to serve as principal of the Alliance school there, Nissim Behar was met by the governor. A senior official accompanying the *wali* by the name of Isma'il, who was in charge of the *wilaya*'s foreign affairs, openly proclaimed his positive attitude towards the school and praised the Alliance

[113] Basili, *Memories from Lebanon* (Heb.), 191. On the troubled relationship and power struggle between Najib Pasha and British representatives in Syria, see Farah, 'Necip Paşa and the British'.

[114] FO 195/226, Wood to Canning, Damascus, 3 Nov. 1845.

[115] AECPC, Turquie, Alep, vol. 1, pp. 223–4, Guys, 3 Apr. 1845.

[116] AECPC, Turquie, Damas, vol. 8, pp. 206–10, Hecquard, 4 Aug. 1864.

[117] AECPC, Turquie, Damas, vol. 11, pp. 117–20, Guys, 20 June 1877.

for setting it up. He also enrolled his son as the first Muslim pupil in the Jewish school, prompting Behar to wonder whether to open the school to further Muslim and Christian enrolment. Given the fact that Isma'il had spent several years in Paris, his attitude is not surprising. He was undoubtedly influenced by European culture and therefore welcomed the penetration of European education into Aleppo, as well as the opportunity to give his son a European education outside the framework of a religious Christian setting.[118]

As noted in Chapter 5, Midhat Pasha played a seminal role in the renewal of Alliance activity in Damascus in 1880. This talented individual, one of the chief reformers in the Istanbul corridors of power, was posted to Syria because of court intrigues. On arriving in Damascus, Midhat initiated an intensive reorganization of the *wilaya*, devoting special attention to education.[119] This activity was not restricted to the Muslim public but extended to the entire population. Midhat's modus operandi was to draft donations from the wealthy residents of the city for the establishment of schools. Upon seeing that the Jewish community, impoverished by the crash of 1875, did not have sufficient funds to found a modern school of its own, he turned on his own initiative to prominent European Jews—such as Count Camondo in Paris, and Baron Henry de Worms and Sir Albert Sassoon in London—for aid. In a letter dated 8 December 1879 the pasha noted his astonishment at the contrast between the Beirut and the Damascus Jewish communities. Whereas the Beirut community had made giant strides towards modernization, the Damascus community had regressed; in the absence of even a single elementary school, its children remained ignoramuses. Drawing upon his knowledge of Jewish feelings of responsibility for their co-religionists, he called upon these wealthy European Jews for swift assistance in founding of a school through the agency of the Alliance. This appeal was received favourably and in due course the school reopened.[120]

It must be noted that this unusual degree of involvement in the affairs of the Jewish community was unmatched by either Midhat's predecessors or his successors. Indeed, as described in Chapter 4, because he recognized the weakness of the Damascus Jewish community, Midhat even took a hand in choosing Ephraim Mercado Alkalai as its chief rabbi. He understood that, in order to realize his goal of advancing the community, educationally in particular, he needed to find an intelligent spiritual leader, a rabbi endowed with leadership ability and personal integrity, who would co-operate with him and thereby lead the community in the right direction. A chance meeting with Alkalai, who was

---

[118] AAIU, Syrie, III.E., Alep, 21, Behar, 13 Nov. 1869.

[119] For comprehensive treatments of Midhat Pasha's activity in Syria, see Shamir, 'The Modernization of Syria'; Saliba, 'The Achievements of Midhat Pasha'; Abu-Manneh, 'The Genesis of Midhat Pasha's Governorship'.

[120] For further detail, see FO 195/1514, Dickson, Damascus, 12 Nov. 1885; *JC*, 16 Jan. 1880, p. 7, 26 Mar. 1880, p. 8, 10 Sept. 1880, p. 13.

on a business trip to Damascus, set his appointment as the city's chief rabbi in motion.[121]

The relationship of the minorities to the Ottoman regime was not restricted to local governors, but also extended to the broader context of the empire and its monarch, the sultan. A major source of Muslim–Christian friction centred on Muslim suspicions of Syrian Christian collaboration with the European Christian powers to bring the Ottoman empire down from within. Although Jews were not under similar suspicion, nonetheless the Jewish community did everything in its power to demonstrate its loyalty to the Muslim empire.

During wartime, the need for such proofs of loyalty by the non-Muslim minorities became more pressing. Because Jews could not enter active service in the army, they had to find alternative ways to show their support for the empire. In late 1853 the leaders of the non-Muslim communities in Damascus, including the chief rabbi, were invited to the reading of the firman announcing the opening of a campaign against Russia, subsequently known as the Crimean War. Somewhat later, public prayers for the victory of the sultan's army were recited in all the synagogues. In November that year a rumour spread that the Turkish forces had crossed the Danube. The city, including its Jewish quarter, lit up spontaneously in celebration. Contemporary reports suggest that Jewish hopes for a crushing Turkish victory were grounded in their fears of being on the receiving end of Muslim wrath in the case of defeat, even though enlightened Muslims were well aware that the Jews had no reason to back Russia.[122] Evidently, such fears motivated the Jewish community's decision to make a patriotic donation of 20,000 piastres to the government for war needs. When the Ottoman regime found itself in need of additional finance, which it raised by taking loans from Damascus residents, wealthy Damascus Jews provided the lion's share of the loan capital.[123]

A similar situation is attested for Aleppo during the Russo-Turkish wars. When the Muslim population seemed to be threatening Jews and Christians in 1877, the Jewish response was to hold a festive prayer service in the Al Safra synagogue on 29 April for the safety of the sultan and the imperial army. An eyewitness account reports that this ceremony, reportedly attended by about half of the Jewish community, and also by Muslim notables, had a calming effect on the city's residents, particularly after the *wali* ʿUmar Pasha sent warm thanks to the acting *ḥakham bashi* and the *dayanim*, and after an Arabic translation of the Jewish prayer for the government appeared in the local government newsletter.[124]

---

[121] For a contemporary report, see *Shaʾarei tsiyon*, 7, 27 Tevet 1880, p. 10. See also Harel, 'Midhat Pasha and the Jewish Community'.   [122] *JC*, 20 Jan. 1854, p. 142.

[123] FO 78/1028, Wood to Stratford de Redcliffe, Damascus, 12 Apr. 1854.

[124] AAIU, Syrie, III.E., Alep, 23, Behor, 3 May 1877. On the situation in Damascus, see AECPC, Turquie, Damas, vol. 11, pp. 89–90, Guys, 2 May 1877; FO 195/1153, Jago to Earl of Derby, Damascus, 29 Apr. 1877.

The Ottoman authorities and Syrian Jews also, of course, had a financial relationship. As noted in earlier chapters, the imperial authorities were greatly in need of Jewish credit. To recall, Syria's importance to the Muslim world—and therefore the sultan's desire to rule Syria—was vested in Damascus' importance as the starting and ending point for the *hajj* caravans. Responsibility for the caravans' organization and safety, and their exit from and entry into Damascus, which called for huge expenditures, lay with the Damascus ruler.[125] Forced to take out loans to fund and protect the caravans, the *wali* relied on credit extended by the affluent Damascus Jews.[126] Jewish bankers in both Aleppo and Damascus purchased the treasury bonds issued by the local governments, thus providing funds for both the maintenance of the regular army brigades in Syria and the expenses of government. Given the precarious financial situation of the *wilaya* treasuries, the purchase of these bonds was not without risk; but the Jews viewed their loans to the government not in purely economic terms but also as a way of demonstrating their loyalty to the regime and promoting a good relationship with the governor and his senior officials.[127] These were by no means bribes, however; the lenders did not advance money without intending to be repaid.

These expressions of Jewish loyalty were positively received by the Ottoman authorities on both the local and the imperial levels. Wealthy Jews who extended financial support to the government were often honoured in their lifetimes and even after their deaths, conferring honour on the Jewish community as a whole. Witness the following description of the funeral of Shemaiah Angel, a leading wealthy Damascus Jew:

All the scholars and rabbis in the city, and the notables of the Jewish community walked before his coffin carrying lit wax candles in their hands. After them came all the pupils in the *talmud torah* and the schools, accompanied by their teachers and melamdim, singing psalms. The great prince—the *wali*, the ruler of the district of Syria—and all the senior officials and European consuls, heads of the Christian churches, and the city notables walked behind his coffin, dressed in black. Two hundred armed soldiers surrounded his coffin with the rifle butts pointing down as a sign of mourning.[128]

Clearly, only a chosen few were so honoured by the regime, even among the Muslim population. The holding of such a grand funeral for a Jew in a devoutly Muslim city like Damascus was certainly unusual, and undoubtedly temporarily elevated Jewish status in the eyes of the non-Jewish public.

[125] For a description of the departure of the caravan as seen through Jewish eyes, see Benjamin, *Eight Years in Asia and Africa*, 43.

[126] See Curtis, *The Howadji in Syria*, 264; *JC*, 18 Aug. 1854, p. 12.

[127] FO 78/499, Wood to Earl of Aberdeen, Damascus, 12 July 1842; 78/1389, Skene to Bulwer, Aleppo, 4 Sept. 1858.

[128] *Ḥavatselet*, 36, 18 Tamuz 1874, pp. 273–4. For further detail on Shemaiah Angel, see Harel, 'The Influence of the Books' (Heb.), 219–22.

But wealth was not the sole source of prestige. Even the chief rabbis received medals—*majidi*—from the sultan. Those recognized in this way included the chief rabbis of Damascus, Jacob Peretz (1862), and of Antioch, Abraham Dweck Hakohen (1867).[129] Even the chief rabbi of Aleppo, Moses Hakohen, received an imperial medal in 1880, along with the title *muwali*, until then reserved for Muslim judges. This was even more remarkable as no Christian religious leader had previously received this accolade.[130]

The Jewish Response to the Tanzimat

The response of Jewish society—and in particular of its religious leadership —to the Ottoman reforms must be examined against the background of the Tanzimat's reception in wider Syrian society and especially by its Muslim elites. As noted above, there was a wide gap between public imperial declarations and their implementation in the provinces, including Syria. Even if their motivation was sincere and impartial, the instigators and partisans of reform in Istanbul remained a minority. European pressure encouraged acceptance of their opinions among the elites, but did not have much influence over the Muslim masses. In marked contrast to the popularly generated European revolutions, the legal and political reforms in the Ottoman empire were perceived by the majority of the population not only as being imposed against its will, but also as contravening the fundamental tenets of Islam and the foundations of the Muslim state. Most scholars agree that the *'ulama'*—who, in addition to their role as religious leaders, also held key positions in the Ottoman establishment —did not initially raise objections to the Tanzimat reforms because they hoped to enhance their own power through the process of change. Later, realizing that the Tanzimat would have a direct impact on the Muslim nature of the state, and in fact weaken their status, the *'ulama'* became opponents of westernization and modernization. 'In sum, the *'ulama'* in Syria managed to become part of the process of modernization in all that involved institutions and administration of government, much to their own advantage. At the same time, they did all in their power to halt Westernization and the secularization of Syrian society, and in this they succeeded.'[131]

With regard to the Jewish response to the reforms, evident mainly in rabbinic literature, several questions must be addressed. Did Jews see themselves as equal citizens in the changing Ottoman empire? Did emancipation become an actively sought goal, based on a desire to become equal and useful citizens? Or was emancipation viewed passively, only as a means of

---

[129] See Franco, *Essai sur l'histoire*, 193, 240.

[130] AAIU, Syrie, II.E., Alep, 11, Altaras, 23 June 1880; *JC*, 13 Aug. 1880, p. 13.

[131] Ma'oz, 'The 'Ulamā'', 88. For more on the Syrian Muslim reaction to the Ottoman reforms up to 1860, see Max L. Gross, 'Ottoman Rule in the Province of Damascus', 20–30.

release from the oppression and discrimination characteristic of life in the Diaspora?

Interestingly, nowhere in the diverse Syrian Jewish rabbinic literature do we find direct discussion of the Ottoman reforms. The sources are silent, expressing neither approval nor disapproval, with the exception of Rabbi Abraham Dayan's remark in the context of permission granted to renovate synagogues that, since 1840, 'restrictions have been lightened'.[132] Discussion of the Tanzimat is found only in the context of legal issues, in cases in which the law of the land and Jewish law came into conflict; and in these instances the rabbis sought to strengthen the legitimacy of the Jewish judicial system.[133] It seems likely that, in a similar fashion to the *'ulama'*, the rabbinic leadership had reservations regarding many aspects of the reforms; however, unlike the Muslim leaders, their objections could find expression only in halakhic, not in public, contexts.

As distinct from the European revolutions, in which a small number of Jews actively participated, or the fight for equal rights or recognition as citizens in western states, in Syria Jews did not participate in the struggle for emancipation. If the reforms were alien to the world-view of the Muslim public, their message went far beyond any emancipatory hopes on the part of the Jewish community. Certainly, the Jewish community sought the abolition of all signs of discrimination and humiliation, and of restrictions on religious worship. But it did not even begin to conceive an aspiration to become an organic part of the broader population on an equal basis, even after centuries of co-existence with devout Muslims.

There is no doubt that the rabbinic leadership's initial response to the Tanzimat was favourable, particularly with regard to the regulations mandating freedom of religion and cancellation of humiliating measures. But somewhat later, recognizing that the reforms could pose a challenge to Jewish autonomy, the rabbinic leadership began to voice reservations about some of the state-sponsored innovations. For one thing, the founding of a secular judicial system undermined a central feature of Jewish autonomy, its independent court system, which had played a central role in communal life. Once many judicial prerogatives had been stripped from the Jewish courts, as they were from the *shari'a* courts—restricting the purview of the religious courts mainly to matters of personal status—Jews pursued most of their litigation in the secular courts. Although Jews had turned to the Muslim courts for adjudication of disputes in the past, this was rare, and was usually done with the permission of the Jewish court, generally in cases in which one of the parties had to be forced to accept the verdict.[134] These cases generally involved wealthy and influential

---

[132] Abraham Dayan, *Vayosef avraham*, 217a, no. 35.

[133] For a comprehensive treatment, see Zohar, *Tradition and Change* (Heb.), 150–95.

[134] See e.g. M. Labaton, *Nokhah hashulhan*, 78b, 'Hoshen mishpat', no. 26.

individuals, who feared that if their cases were judged according to Jewish law the verdict would not go in their favour.[135]

In contrast to the Jewish secular elite, the rabbis continued to avoid turning to the non-Jewish courts, preferring to apply other persuasive means to settle disputes even in cases in which the court's verdict was rejected. Their distress at the rabbinic courts' loss of authority, and their disinclination to turn to the secular courts, emerges clearly from a letter by the chief rabbi of Damascus, Hayim Maimon Tobi, to the Rishon Letsion (the title of the chief rabbi in Erets Yisra'el in this period, literally meaning 'First in Zion') in Jerusalem, Rabbi Abraham Hayim Gagin, in response to the latter's request that Tobi help a Jew named Solomon Hamway collect money owed to him by Damascus Jews. Tobi replied: 'Let me add that the only way he can collect his debts is through the agency of non-Jews and by having them arrested. I have never done so regarding any Jew in matters that touch me, and I will certainly not do so for an outsider.'[136] In Aleppo, too, an increasing number of Jews turned to the Muslim courts in cases involving other Jews; however, the process seems to have been slower there than in Damascus.

With the religious courts weakened in scope and authority, and with individual Jews able to turn to state rather than to communal institutions to resolve their disputes, the status of the spiritual heads of the Jewish community declined. This trend was aptly encapsulated in Rabbi Isaac Abulafia's description of those who disobey the rabbinic authorities: 'Because of the freedom granted them, we have no power to restrain them.'[137] As their status declined, the rabbis and scholars became more vocal in their opposition to Jews linking themselves to the state institutions, and they sought to dissuade Jews from joining the secular administration and judiciary.[138] Their hostility to the regime may also have been influenced by the paragraph in the Hatt-i Hümayun regulating—in actuality reducing—their salaries.[139]

The winds of change accompanying the Tanzimat, which promoted the opening of both Christian mission schools and Alliance schools in Syria, threatened the traditional educational framework and further weakened the religious community's influence over its individual members. As we saw in Chapter 5, there was at first no rabbinic opposition to modern education; nonetheless, as members of the community sent their children to these schools for a modern secular education, rather than giving them only traditional Jewish schooling,

[135] For that reason, the disputants in the case of Hayim Farhi's inheritance avoided the Jewish court. See NLIS, DA, V-736/218, announcement by the Damascus scholars and rabbis, 14 Adar 1847.
[136] NLIS, DA, V-736/28, Hayim Maimon Tobi to Abraham Hayim Gagin, Damascus, 5 Sivan 1847.   [137] Abulafia, *Penei yitshak*, ii. 76b.
[138] For a summary of the differences between the approaches of the Damascene scholars and those of Aleppine scholars and Egyptian rabbis, see Zohar, *Tradition and Change* (Heb.), 193–5.
[139] See Tibawi, *A Modern History of Syria*, 118.

this indirectly led to laxity in observance of Jewish law and to a decline in deference to the scholarly class. The rabbis also expressed concern that the Tanzimat would indirectly lead to assimilation by encouraging too much interaction between Jews and non-Jews.[140] This concern was particularly acute in respect of the possibility that Jews would be subject to military conscription.

Ultimately, the opposition of the Muslim masses, coupled with that of the *'ulama'* and conservative governors, and reservations on the part of the *dhimmi* religious leadership, hindered and delayed implementation of the reforms. It can be argued, as Moshe Ma'oz does, that the very fact of Jewish participation in the governmental, administrative, and judicial systems, even if not particularly influential, marks a positive change in their legal and political standing. He acknowledges, however, that the Ottoman empire, including Syria, did not become a modern secular state in the nineteenth century, but rather remained a Muslim state in which true equality between *dhimmi* and Muslim could not become a reality.[141] Nevertheless, although proceeding only slowly, change occurred perceptibly enough to make the more enlightened members of the Jewish community aware of the advantages of the Tanzimat. If the Jews were at first passive with regard to the reforms and their implementation, towards the 1880s we find appeals by communal leaders, including rabbis, to the Ottoman authorities and to outside forces, asking them to act in pursuit of equality for Jews in the various Syrian frameworks.

In March 1869 the Jewish community in Aleppo took vigorous steps, through the agency of the Alliance and of the British consul in Aleppo, to put pressure on the *wali* to implement the reforms that touched upon the Jews, who still suffered discrimination and inequality, and to treat them like other Ottoman subjects.[142] A decade later the Damascus Jewish community sent a complaint to the Alliance that the Ottoman quota for Jewish representation on the various councils was not being filled, and that the community suffered discrimination and inequality.[143] In another letter to the central committee of the Alliance in Paris the heads of the Jewish community gave forthright expression to the lack of reform in practice, to their awareness of worldwide developments in emancipation, and to the need to execute the reforms:

In all the cities of the kingdom, may it be exalted, equality is being established between all the subjects, known as *islahat* in Arabic, except for here in our city, and for our Israelite nation, which still suffers from an inferior status and has not been made equal to other subjects. No Jew serves on the state court in our city, whereas representatives of all the other sectors have a prominent place in the ranks of the [Ottoman] courts. And why should we Jews not be among them, as is the practice in

---

[140] See e.g. J. Sutton, *Vayelaket yosef*, which deals with the prohibition against eating food prepared by non-Jews.   [141] Ma'oz, 'Changes in the Status of Jews' (Heb.), 19.
[142] AAIU, Syrie, II.E. Alep, 11, Altaras, 12 Mar. 1869, 12 July 1869.
[143] Ibid., I.B., 5, Damas, 23 June 1879.

other places according to state law? And this has brought suffering to the holy Jewish community, the people of Israel, may God preserve them, who live here and we request that your honour speak in our favour before the authorities, may they be exalted, that they grant us rights equal to those granted to other subjects.[144]

This type of activism, apparent only in the late 1870s, was still exercised cautiously for fear of angering the Muslim population. In this the Jews differed radically from the Christians, who emphasized and publicly demanded their rights. As we shall see, Jewish political reticence apparently saved them from the fate that twice befell the Christians at the hands of the Muslim mob, in Aleppo in 1850 and in Damascus in 1860.

---

[144] Ibid., letter of the heads of the Damascus Jewish community to the Alliance central committee, Heshvan 1879.

PART IV

MUSLIMS
CHRISTIANS
JEWS

EIGHT

MAJORITY–MINORITY RELATIONS

WITHIN the Ottoman empire's vast kaleidoscope of national, ethnic, and religious groups, Syria was itself a smaller mosaic. The majority of its Muslim population was Sunni, but other religious streams including Shi'ites, 'Alawites, and Druze were also represented. The Syrian Christian population was similarly divided, consisting of Latins, Maronites, Greek Orthodox, eastern sects, and, in the period under study, Protestants as well. The Syrian Jewish population, by contrast, displayed much greater homogeneity than either the Muslims or the Christians, especially after the disappearance of the Damascus Karaite community in the late eighteenth century.[1] While relationships between different groups of Muslims—and, indeed, different groups of Christians—were not always harmonious, the divisions between Muslims and Christians, and between Muslims and Jews, were even more pronounced.[2]

Jewish–Muslim Relations

An interesting feature of the relationship between the Muslim majority and the Jewish minority in Syria, and indeed elsewhere in the Ottoman empire, is the scarcity of references to Jews in Arabic works and in the expanding nineteenth-century range of Arabic newspapers.[3] While this would not be surprising if the Jewish community had played only a marginal or insignificant role in Ottoman society, this was certainly not the case for Syrian Jewry. Until 1875 a thin stratum of wealthy Jews comprised the economic backbone of the local regime, profoundly influencing the economy through its involvement in banking, the setting of exchange rates, and the value of government bonds.

---

[1] See Basili, *Memories from Lebanon* (Heb.), 332; Frankl, *The Jews in the East*, i. 291–2. On the division of Jews into Orthodox, Karaites, and Samaritans in Middle East research, see Hourani, *Minorities in the Arab World*, 10.

[2] For a more comprehensive treatment of intra-Muslim relationships, see Ma'oz, 'Society and State in Modern Syria' (Heb.), 36–8.

[3] This phenomenon is surveyed from the early days of Islam by Hirschberg, 'The Jews under Islam' (Heb.), 274–5. In recent years there has been an awakening of interest in the history of Jews in Islamic countries. See e.g. Kiwan, *The Jews in the Middle East* (Arab.), 48–9.

The significant attention paid by foreign sources—such as Christian accounts of travels in the East—to the Jewish community in general, and their amazement at the enormous wealth and local economic power of some Jewish families, stand in stark contrast to the silence of the Arabic sources.

One scholarly viewpoint attributes this phenomenon to Muslim animosity towards their Jewish neighbours. From this perspective, nothing but hatred and jealousy could possibly explain the overlooking of the Farhi family 'in all the Arabic and Turkish literature of the period'.[4] But this argument, grounded in a limited number of sources that exhibit narrow-mindedness, bitterness, and envy of the Jewish bankers' success and status, is inadequate. If hatred were indeed the explanation, we would rather expect the contemporary Arabic literature to be replete with similar anti-Jewish outbursts. As this is not the case, therefore, it is the sources cited in support of this argument that must be regarded as exceptional. As we shall see, before the late nineteenth century profound hatred was not the prevailing tone of Muslim–Jewish relations in Syria.[5]

A more satisfactory explanation for the silence of Arabic sources with regard to Jews attributes it to the separatism and autonomy of the religious minorities under Ottoman rule. From this perspective, the absence of references to Jews in Arabic literature is seen not as deliberate, but as a natural consequence of a Muslim lack of interest in Jewish society. Backing for this explanation comes from a parallel phenomenon in local Jewish literature, which makes little mention—positive or negative—of the Muslim or Christian populations, except where relevant to halakhic or ethical matters. For Ottoman subjects, the primary social bonds were those of blood relation, origin, and religious and ethnic affinity.[6] For reasons of safety, among others, Jews tried to underplay their presence in Syrian society; at the same time, the Muslims did not seek to highlight it. We may term this trend, manifested in the preservation of separate neighbourhoods, and in the limiting of social contacts purely to business contexts, compartmentalization.

Compartmentalization had far-reaching social consequences.[7] By and large, contacts between Jews and the surrounding Syrian society were formal and functional in nature; nonetheless, from the late 1850s it is possible to point to some interaction between the different religious communities, mainly in the upper echelons of society and usually at social gatherings under the aegis of a foreign power or local office-holder. Thus, in 1858, the chief rabbi of Damascus was invited, along with foreign consuls, leading Christian clerics, and Franciscan monks, to celebrate the marriage of the daughter of the mufti

---

[4] Elmaleh, 'Nouvelles sources' (Heb.) 40–1.

[5] The immediate prompt for Elmaleh's article was an article published by the contemporary Arab historian Muhammad al-Maghribi, 'The Jews of Syria in the Last Hundred Years' (Arab.). Perhaps Elmaleh's analysis was coloured by the extreme Arab animosity towards Jews that was current during the late 1940s.   [6] See Ma'oz, *Modern Syria* (Heb.), 18–20.

[7] Landau and Ma'oz, 'Jews and Non-Jews' (Heb.), 10–11. For the ethnocentric focus of Muslim historians on their civilization and immediate forebears, see also Lewis, *Islam in History*, 115–28.

Abu Saʿid Effendi, a member of one of the most conservative Damascus Muslim families.[8]

Some scholars attribute the phenomenon of compartmentalization in part to nineteenth-century Syria's late emergence from the medieval period, in which compartmentalization on the basis of religion was the norm. This religious framework discouraged excessive interaction, let alone integration, between members of different religions. Like the Christians, the Jews on the one hand wished to enjoy equality with the Muslims but on the other were unwilling to be absorbed by Muslim society. Although Jews undoubtedly desired to improve their social condition and status, they were in no hurry to break out of the communal framework. Also conducive to this social compartmentalization were European patronage, which lessened the various groups' dependence on other, local sectors of society,[9] and the respective religions' separate educational systems. These socio-cultural and socio-religious divisions inhibited the growth of dialogue either between Muslims and the minorities, or between one minority and another, on the basis of shared interests.

Nonetheless, closer examination of compartmentalization in Syrian society reveals that it was by no means rigid. There were various degrees of interaction in social, cultural, economic, and religious contexts. In conditions that forced the minorities to enter into economic relations with the Muslim majority, there is abundant evidence of Muslim influence on everyday aspects of Jewish life. In Damascus, and to some extent even in Aleppo, not to mention the smaller towns of Antioch, Kilis, Idlib, and ʿAyntab, a deep process of popular acculturation is apparent, in which Jews adopted local customs and dress, making them almost indistinguishable from their neighbours.

This acculturation did not fully encompass the linguistic sphere, in which differences constrained interaction between Jews and non-Jews. Although Syrian Jews spoke Arabic, their unique dialect incorporated words from Hebrew and from Judaeo-Spanish, a relic of the language spoken by the exiles who settled in Syria after their expulsion from Spain. At times, because it enabled Muslims to identify them as Jews by their speech, this distinctive language was an impediment. Only the more educated, for example those serving in the civil service or engaged in joint business enterprises with Muslim or Christian colleagues, were fully fluent in Arabic and used it for their accounts and record-keeping.[10] Internal Jewish correspondence was carried out in Hebrew or in Judaeo-Arabic, which was written in Hebrew characters.[11] Some individuals, mostly immigrants, were proficient in Judaeo-Spanish and in Italian, but very few made use of these languages.[12]

---

[8] *JC*, 3 Sept. 1858, p. 303.   [9] Landau and Ma'oz, 'Jews and Non-Jews', (Heb.), 10–11.
[10] See Abulafia, *Penei yitshak*, 167*a*, no. 23; Benjamin, *Eight Years in Asia and Africa*, 48.
[11] John Wilson, *The Lands of the Bible*, ii. 336.
[12] Landau and Ma'oz, 'Jews and Non-Jews' (Heb.), 11.

Although their language remained somewhat distinctive, in their outward appearance Syrian Jews attracted no special interest. By and large, as Jewish travellers noted, '[Jewish] clothing resembles that of the Arabs and there is almost no noticeable difference between Jews and non-Jews'.[13] In the past, the colour of the turban had been the most prominent sign of an individual's religion; with the slow implementation of the Ottoman reforms, which cancelled the law requiring non-Muslims to wear distinctively coloured turbans, even this difference gradually faded.

Jewish men in Syria not only dressed like Muslims, but aspired, if only for reasons of physical safety, to appear non-Jewish in other respects, as the following description from Damascus illustrates:

Jews do not have sideburns, because they remove them, almost to the root . . . leaving a bit of hair, so as to resemble the Muslims in everything . . . and for safety when they travel so that they will not be identifiable as Jews, because the Muslims shave their heads, including the sideburns up to the beard, for their religion is lenient regarding this precept.[14]

Jewish women in Syria also dressed like their Muslim counterparts, in public at least. There was a difference, however, between general practice in the two main centres: in Damascus, Jewish women partially veiled their faces in public, whereas in Aleppo they did not.[15] Another aspect of acculturation during this period regards the adoption of personal names. Although Jews in the various diasporas, including Syria, continued to use typically Jewish Hebrew names, or translations of these names into the local languages—perhaps as a means of retaining their unique Jewish identity and for ritual purposes—during the period under study here Syrian Jews came to resemble their Muslim neighbours in their use of pure Arabic names. This was true of men and women alike. Though the practice was more widespread in Damascus, we also find Jews in Aleppo using Arabic names, such as Jamil for men, and Salha and Jamila for women.[16]

Poetry and music comprise yet another sphere that reflects the impact of popular Muslim culture on Syrian Jews. Arabic songs penetrated not only the parties and balls of the Jewish elite but the community's daily life as well. Many Syrian Jews adopted secular tunes, including the love songs of the surrounding

---

[13] Kestelmann, *Expeditions of the Emissary* (Heb.), 19.

[14] Ibid. 19. Jewish pedlars murdered on the road were identified by the *tsitsiyot* (ritual fringes) that they wore on their undergarments. See Abulafia, *Penei yitsḥak*, ii. 26a, no. 1.

[15] Antebi, *Ḥokhmah umusar* 116b–117; Abraham Dayan, *Holekh tamim*, 54a; Schur, *Maḥazot haḥayim*, 18. See also AECADN, Constantinople, Correspondance avec les Echelles, Damas, 1846–1853, De Ségur au Ministre Plénipotentiaire Envoyé Extraordinaire de France à Constantinople, Damas, 9 July 1851.

[16] J. J. Rivlin, 'First Names' (Heb.), 6; Elmaleh, *The Jews in Damascus* (Heb.), 18; al-Qattan, 'The Damascene Jewish Community', 204.

Muslim society, and secular melodies found their way into synagogue liturgy and religious ceremonies, at times raising halakhic issues.[17] In an era before radio and recorded sound, Jews would hear these songs in public places such as the coffee houses and markets. Jewish musicians performed in non-Jewish homes, and female Jewish singers appeared before Jewish and non-Jewish audiences.[18] In addition, the Jewish elite evidently invited Muslim singers and entertainers to perform in their homes.[19] Given the class differences between the singers and other performers, who belonged to the lower classes, and those they entertained, these contacts cannot be viewed as social intermingling; nonetheless, musicians and entertainers did serve as carriers of the local Arab culture into Jewish homes and the Jewish world.

Further indication of an incipient, though not widespread or consistent, trend of intersocietal interaction comes from the breaking of the traditional pattern of separate neighbourhoods, in the East usually defined (not necessarily exclusively) by religious and ethnic criteria.[20] The trend was for Muslims to move into the Jewish quarter, rather than for Jews to move into non-Jewish quarters. Nonetheless, in the early 1840s we do find Jewish families renting houses on the periphery of the Christian and Muslim areas in both Damascus and, to a lesser extent, Aleppo.[21]

Notwithstanding halakhic restrictions on contacts between Jews and non-Jews in social or religious settings, the necessary daily interaction in economic matters indirectly fostered the creation of links between Jews and non-Jews outside the strictly commercial sphere. As a minority group, Jews depended on the surrounding non-Jewish society for many of their daily needs, such as food products that could be purchased only from their Muslim neighbours. Although Muslims do not have the problematic status in Jewish law of idol-worshippers, whose food Jews are forbidden to consume, nevertheless the purchase of food items from Muslims required a significant degree of trust. Conversely, Muslims who wished to profit by selling to Jews had to merit that trust by adhering to the Jewish dietary laws in their food preparation. Jews in Aleppo purchased butter from Muslims and also, even more surprisingly, meat,

---

[17] See M. Abadi, *Ma'ayan ganim*, 92, 'Oraḥ ḥayim', no. 12; id., *Divrei mordekhai*, author's introd. On the introduction of Arab musical traditions into the sacred liturgy, see Seroussi, 'On the Origin of the Custom' (Heb.), 112.

[18] On music and dances in coffee houses, see Marino, 'Cafés et cafetiers de Damas'. On visits of Jews to coffee houses, see Abulafia, *Penei yitsḥak*, 68a. On musicians and female singers, see ibid. 76b. [19] Al-Halil, 'An Important Document Source' (Heb.), 37.

[20] See al-Qattan, 'The Damascene Jewish Community', 198. See also Schroeter, 'Jewish Quarters', 291.

[21] Wilson, *The Lands of the Bible*, ii. 334, 343; Bocquet, 'Un example de minorité au Levant'. See also al-Qattan, 'Litigants and Neighbors'. On the Jewish quarters in Aleppo, see al-Asadi, *Districts and Markets of Aleppo* (Arab.), 43, 127. The phenomenon of living in mixed quarters was more prominent among Muslims and Christians than among Jews. See e.g. Rafeq, 'The Social and Economic Structure'.

as Aleppo had no Jewish butcher's shop. Meat slaughtered by Jewish butchers was stamped with the communal kosher seal and sold to a non-Jewish butcher, who marketed it to Jews. Likewise, the grinding of wheat for the Passover matzot was performed by non-Jews under Jewish supervision.[22]

Peddling, a significant strand in the Syrian Jewish economy, also brought increased social contacts with Muslim society. Wandering between villages where no Jews resided, the pedlars of necessity conducted all their daily contacts, business and personal, including finding accommodation, with and among non-Jews.[23]

One area of the Syrian economy where strict separation between Muslims and non-Muslims was maintained was the guild system. Although guilds were usually defined by profession, in actuality there was also a religious identification, with members of the different religions typically concentrated in certain professions. Each professional union or commercial branch was headed by a *shaykh*.[24] A letter from Rabbi Moses Sutton of Aleppo to Abraham Camondo in Istanbul refers to this rigid division: 'Some months ago I wrote to his honour . . . about the art of silver- and gold-working, in Christian hands for years . . . And they stand fast against the Jews and do not allow them to pursue this profession, and without their permission no one can practise this craft.'[25] The most prestigious guilds in Damascus, such as the tanners' and leatherworkers' guild, and the immensely wealthy gluemakers' guild, barred non-Muslims from their ranks.[26] Even in cases where members of different religions or groups shared the same profession, divisions within the guild were reflected in distinctive religious and ethnic markers: for example, within the shoemakers' guild Muslim shoemakers made one type of shoes, Christian shoemakers another, and Jews yet a third.[27] There were, however, exceptions, of which the most outstanding was that Jewish butchers belonged to the general butchers' guild,[28] as the following comment indicates: 'Reuben, Simeon . . . are butchers . . . in one slaughterhouse for all the butchers in the city, Jewish and non-Jewish.'[29] It is inconceivable that Muslim butchers would have allowed their Jewish counter-

---

[22] On the purchase of butter, see Abraham Dayan, *Po'el tsedek*, 39*b*, no. 6; 59*a*, no. 7; Y. Abadi, *Kol rinah viyeshuah* , 'Kuntres sha'arei yeshuah', 106*a*. On the purchase of meat, see Abraham Dayan, *Zikaron lanefesh*, 56; M. Abadi, *Ma'ayan ganim*, 108, 'Yoreh de'ah', no. 1; FO 78/2242, Green to Rambold, Damascus, 15 Apr. 1872. For wheat grinding, see M. Abadi, *Ma'ayan ganim*, 107, 'Orah hayim', no. 12.   [23] Abulafia, *Penei yitshak*, 26*a*, 36*b*–37*a*, 46*a*.

[24] Paton, *The Modern Syrians*, 200. On the appointment of the *shaykh* and the scope of his authority, see Marcus, *The Middle East on the Eve of Modernity*, 173, 175. See also Rafiq, 'Manifestations of the Military System' (Arab.), 32–3.

[25] Ben-Zvi Institute, MS 3724, *Pinkas rabi mosheh suton*, 157.

[26] Paton, *The Modern Syrians*, 201; FO 78/579, Wood to Stratford de Redcliffe, Damascus, 21 Feb. 1844.   [27] Zenner, 'Syrian Jewish Identification', 57.

[28] On the Jewish butchers' guild and the conditions under which it was incorporated into the Muslim butchers' guild, see also Rafiq, 'Manifestations of the Military System' (Arab.), 43.

[29] Abulafia, *Penei yitshak*, ii. 7*a*, no. 2.

parts to purvey meat to Muslim butchers' shops unless they were members of the same guild.

There were also occasional Jewish–Muslim or Jewish–Christian business partnerships,[30] as well as more ad hoc joint activity by members of the different religions on a basis of shared interests. Thus, when stolen goods from the commercial caravan to Baghdad appeared in the Aleppo markets, the major Damascus traders from all the religious denominations banded together in an attempt to locate the stolen property and return it to its rightful owners, even appointing members of the Aleppo Picciotto and Altaras families as their representatives.[31]

Of all the spheres of the Syrian economy, it was the bazaar, perhaps the institution that most strongly epitomized the Muslim city, that most effectively lowered social barriers. Merchants, stand owners, porters, errand boys, and customers—all with different religious affiliations—mingled freely in the hubbub of the markets. Here, members of the different religions spent most of their time in a single urban environment. Direct interreligious contacts also came about through the employment of many Jews as workers or apprentices in non-Jewish workshops. This had problematic aspects, as it could at times lead to infringement of Jewish regulations, for example through eating food prepared by non-Jews.[32]

In more extreme cases, socio-economic interaction could assume religious overtones, taking the form of pressure to convert. Indeed, until the 1850s there was in Syria a trend fostering Christian and Jewish conversion to Islam, the intensity of which depended largely on the *wali*'s personality and religious zeal. A governor strongly influenced by the *'ulama'*, or by religious rituals such as the *hajj*, often encouraged the Muslim civil and religious administration to seek converts, or even to promote forced conversion.

Notwithstanding the conservative and observant image of Syrian Jewry, in each of the communities there were some (though not many) who converted to Islam. From the sparse statistical data available for this period it is impossible to determine either the number of Jews who converted or their proportion in Jewish society. Nonetheless, it appears that this phenomenon was more extensive than the known cases and sources suggest.[33] Conversion clearly existed, and disturbed the Jewish community, but never in any way constituted a threat to its existence.

What motivated Jews to convert to Islam, given the fact that, like their counterparts in other Middle Eastern Muslim societies, the Syrian Jewish communities neither idealized, nor aspired to be integrated into, the surrounding

[30] Ibid. 4a, no. 1; I. Dayan, *Imrei no'am*, 9a, no. 7.
[31] FO 78/538, Procuration of the Merchants of Damascus to Mess. Picciotto and Taras of Aleppo, Damascus, 12 June 1843.
[32] See also J. Sutton, *Vayelaket yosef*, 30a. On the Jews in the Aleppine bazaars, see al-Asadi, *Districts and Markets of Aleppo* (Arab.), 37.   [33] Antebi, *Hokhmah umusar*, 36a.

society?[34] Not grounded in religious conviction, namely by belief in Allah and his prophet Muhammad, Jewish conversion to Islam was motivated either by external factors (monetary inducements, threats, and coercion) or by internal factors (as a desperate means of escape from troubled parent–child or marital relationships, or as a way of exerting pressure on the Jewish community and its institutions).[35] Even if the impulse was instigated by other factors, the promise of payment was the main inducement. Rabbi Abraham Antebi noted the tendency of Jewish youths apprenticed to Muslim artisans to convert: 'They convert due to greed. Every day their instructor incites them with money, and they fulfil the wishes of their master and instructor.'[36] In addition to the grant promised to converts under Turkish law, the convert often received many other presents.[37] Also, devout Muslims were not averse to forcing individuals to convert.[38]

Jewish converts to Islam who believed that their choice would give them improved social status were likely to be disappointed. The reception afforded to the new convert was often degrading and unfriendly; converts remained on the periphery of Muslim society, unable to penetrate its upper echelons, especially the ranks of the *'ulama'*.[39] For its part, Jewish society certainly despised the convert to Islam.[40]

Looking from the opposite direction, we know of no Muslim converts to Judaism in Syria. Indeed, because conversion to another religion was a capital offence in Islam, it is virtually certain that no such acts took place. Nor is there any evidence for Christian converts to Judaism—with the exception of a single case, which further attests to the rarity of this phenomenon. The contemporary Jewish press carried reports of a Christian youth from a village near Beirut pleading with the heads of the Damascus Jewish community in late 1874 to allow him to convert.[41] At a loss faced with this hitherto unknown situation, and fearing the reaction of the Damascus Christian public to this news, the Jewish communal leaders and rabbis sent the youth in question to Jerusalem to convert.[42] Similarly, there is sparse evidence for mixed marriages; apparently rare, they did not undermine Jewish communal existence.

[34] See M. Abitbol's remarks from the discussion chapter in Nini, *Western Cultural Assimilation* (Heb.), 34–5.

[35] FO 78/714, Timoni to Wellesley, Damascus, 28 Apr. 1847; 195/458, Aaron Jacob and Jacob Perez to Misk, Damascus, 15 June 1857.   [36] Antebi, *Ḥokhmah umusar*, 36a.

[37] FO 78/714, Timoni to Wellesley, Damascus, 28 Apr. 1847; 78/2282, Green to Granville, Damascus, 29 Oct. 1878.

[38] FO 78/714, Timoni to Wellesley, Damascus, 18 Apr. 1847; NLIS, DA, V-736/39, Rabbi Hayim Maimon Tobi to Rabbi Abraham Hayim Gagin, Damascus, 5 Sivan 1847.

[39] Paton, *The Modern Syrians*, 261–2.

[40] Abraham Dayan, *Tuv ta'am*, 216; Abulafia, *Penei yitsḥak*, 73a, no. 13. One measure taken against converts was to cut them out of wills. See Jessup, *Fifty-three Years in Syria*, ii. 424.

[41] *JC*, 25 June 1875, p. 213.

[42] NLIS, DA, V-736/272, Solomon Sukary to Shalom Moses Hai Gagin, 8 Kislev 1874. On Christian converts to Islam, see Levtzion, 'Conversion to Islam'.

What emerges from this review of the evidence is that, with regard to many spheres of daily life, the 'compartmentalization' of the religious communities in Syria was far from complete. This state of affairs, and the importance of Jews to the Syrian economy, returns attention to the surprising absence of Jews from Muslim literature, the question with which this chapter opened. Clearly, even if partially responsible for this phenomenon, 'compartmentalization' alone cannot explain the silence of the sources. The missing explanatory feature is Jewish political unobtrusiveness. Coupled with its social counterpart, this 'political compartmentalization' more fully explains the lack of interest Muslim sources displayed in Jews.

Muslim–Christian Relations

In marked contrast to the Jewish preference for keeping out of the political spotlight, the Christian minority in Syria had an appetite for political activism which played a crucial role in its relations with the Muslim majority. For Syrian Christians, the period of Egyptian rule was seen as a 'golden age'.[43] The enhanced rights and freedom of worship enjoyed by Christians under Muhammad 'Ali are essential to an understanding of the Muslim attitude towards Christians under renewed Ottoman rule. Accustomed to subjecting the *ahl al-kitab* to humiliation—assaulting, robbing, and even murdering them in the context of religious agitation or simply as criminal acts—Muslims found the rights granted to the minorities under Egyptian rule offensive. Muslim antipathy towards non-Muslims was further aggravated by the limitations placed on the authority of Muslim clerics under Egyptian rule. Notwithstanding Muhammad 'Ali's desire to endow equality on the members of all religions, the Muslims continued to regard Christians and Jews as contemptible slaves.[44] Only the iron rule of Ibrahim Pasha prevented angry outbursts against the religious minorities.[45]

Adding to this injury to Muslim religious sensibilities was the insult to their patriotic feelings for the Ottoman empire and the sultan. Muhammad 'Ali's takeover was perceived as rebellion against the largest Muslim empire of all time and against the *amir al-mu'minin* who stood at its head.[46] To a large extent, the Egyptian regime was seen as maintaining its hold by virtue of European backing, and as granting excessive rights to the non-Muslim minorities— Christians in particular—in order to curry favour in European eyes. This in turn fostered a profound Muslim hatred of the Christians in their midst, whose past image of a tolerated religious minority was transmuted into that of a political foe.

[43] Paton, *The Modern Syrians*, 33.
[44] AECADN, Damas, 01, Cote A/18/54, Beaudin, Damas, 26 Aug. 1835.
[45] See Ma'oz, *Ottoman Reform*, 187.   [46] Shamir, *A Modern History*, 223.

One element in the Muslim welcome for the Ottoman reconquest of Syria was the hope that the lenient Egyptian treatment of religious minorities would be reversed.[47] The disappointment of this hope with the promulgation of the Hatt-i şerif and the Hatt-i Hümayun only increased anti-Christian animosity among the Muslim public, fuelled by suspicions of a potential Christian political takeover of Syria and indeed of the whole Ottoman empire, with the aid of the European powers. This represents a new development in Muslim anti-Christian feelings: no longer simply religious and economic as in the past, they were now also grounded in a view of Christians as a political and security risk to the Muslim empire.[48] For their part, Christians made no attempt to counter these impressions, rather doing everything in their power to outwardly demonstrate their new-found equality with Muslims: ringing church bells, carrying crosses in public religious processions, riding horses, and dressing in apparel previously reserved for Muslims. The increased interference of the European powers in internal Ottoman affairs and their support and protection of the Christian population further heightened Muslim hostility.[49]

The Christians openly flouted all previous ground rules governing relations between Muslim and *dhimmi*. If, in the past, *dhimmi*s sought proximity to Muslim governors in order to exercise influence and power in the Muslim state, it now appeared that the Christians had opted to rely on the Christian European powers instead.[50] The opening of foreign consulates, which sought to fly flags with crosses, and their growing intervention in the empire's internal affairs, fuelled Muslim animosity towards both local and foreign Christians. As early as the 1840s it was reported that the hitherto Jewish-oriented Muslim fanaticism in Damascus was now directed at Christians, even going so far as to call for their expulsion from Syria.[51] Local Christians complained to their foreign co-religionists that dogs fared better in Damascus than they did, and begged: 'Pray for us, brother; we Christians here sit on a barrel of gunpowder.'[52] Mark Twain, who visited Syria in 1867, provides the following description of the Syrian attitude towards European Christians: 'in Damascus they so hate the very sight of a foreign Christian that they want no intercourse whatever with him; only a year or two ago, his person was not always safe in Damascus streets. It is the most fanatical Mohammedan purgatory out of Arabia.'[53]

Antipathy towards foreign Christians, who were seen as representatives of hostile powers, exacerbated Muslim ill-will towards local Christians. Nor did the opening of mission schools contribute to Muslim–Christian harmony, to

[47] AECPC, Turquie, Damas, vol. 1, p. 4, Ratti-Menton, 6 Jan. 1841.

[48] Ma'oz, 'Changes in the Status of Jews' (Heb.), 20.

[49] See Ma'oz, *Ottoman Reform*, 190–219; id., 'Intercommunal Relations'.

[50] For further detail, see Philipp, 'The Farhi Family', 48–9.

[51] *Voice of Jacob*, 16, 29 Apr. 1842, p. 126.   [52] Thomson, *In the Holy Land*, 318.

[53] Twain, *The Innocents Abroad*, 346. For a more comprehensive treatment, see Yoram Shalit, 'European Foreigners in Damascus and Aleppo'.

say the least. These foreign institutions, which quickly became part of the local Christian scene, were a thorn in the side of the *'ulama'*, who preached day and night against the ever-increasing power of Christianity.[54]

The Muslim–Jewish–Christian Triangle

The Christians' political activism and the public parading of their equal status with Muslims culminated in anti-Christian riots and massacres. For their part, Jews escaped Muslim wrath but not Muslim contempt. The Muslim attitude towards Jews remained grounded in the religious sensibilities and Qur'anic commandments that mandated humiliation, but not hatred, of the Jews. In essence, Jews were deeply scorned, seen as the lowest creatures in Muslim society.[55] But this anti-Jewish hostility was generally founded on a religious, not a political, basis, as the missionary William Graham noted: 'An old Muslim cursed them in my house, and said they had no religion; they had perverted the religion of Moses; they put Jesus to death; Muhammad could make nothing of them; they, too, killed seventy of their prophets in one day; God had given them up, and man could not use them too vilely.'[56] Another missionary depicted the low status and image of the Jews in Syria by ranking the curses in the East. The most humiliating insult was to call someone not ass, dog, or swine, but Jew.[57]

The explanation for this differential attitude—profound contempt for Jews but fathomless hatred for Christians—lies in the fact that, in contrast to the Christians, the Jews demonstrated no elation at the institution of the Egyptian, and subsequently Ottoman, reforms.[58] In 1859 the Jewish traveller Yehiel Kestelmann testified that not only was there no Muslim hatred for Jews, but 'to the contrary, they love each other, but the Muslims hate the Christians, and when they call someone a Christian, this is to shame them'.[59] The explanation provided by Joseph Elias, secretary to the Austrian consul in Damascus, to the traveller Ludwig August Frankl in 1855 singled out the political factor: 'The Turks here are more hostile to the Christians than to the Jews, or rather

---

[54] Ma'oz, *Ottoman Reform*, 211.   [55] I. Burton, *The Inner Life of Syria*, i. 105–6.

[56] Wilson, *The Lands of the Bible*, ii. 347.

[57] Jessup, *Fifty-three Years in Syria*, ii. 424. James Brant, the British consul in Damascus from 1855–60, used 'Jew' as an insulting, derogatory name for Christians or Muslims. See Burton, *The Jew, the Gypsy and el Islam*, 39.

[58] With the exception of Abraham Dayan, *Vayosef avraham*, 217a, no. 35. There is discussion of halakhic problems fostered by the Tanzimat, but not of the reforms as a whole, good or bad. On the Syrian rabbinic response to these problems, see Zohar, *Tradition and Change* (Heb.), 143–95.

[59] Kestelmann, *Expeditions of the Emissary* (Heb.), 19. There is certainly a considerable degree of hyperbole here, which can be explained by the timing of his visit. In 1859, when Kestelmann was in Syria, anti-Christian feeling in Damascus was approaching boiling point, reaching a climax in the massacre of the following year. This perhaps made him equate the lack of anti-Jewish hatred with love.

the latter are less hated than the former, because they do not aim at political influence or superiority.'[60]

Even if the Syrian Jewish communities did not wholeheartedly embrace the Ottoman reforms, perhaps for fear that the changes would detract from Jewish autonomy or rabbinic authority, their lack of expressed enthusiasm for the implementation of their rights is attributable primarily to their wariness of arousing Muslim hostility. Outwardly, at least, the Jews deliberately continued to live as a second-class religious minority, making no public statements of political ambition or of aspirations to equality.[61] The wisdom of this policy was proven when the Jews emerged unscathed from the anti-Christian riots in Aleppo in 1850, and in Damascus in 1860.

The different reactions of the Christian and Jewish communities to the requirement to pay the *bedel-i 'askeri* tax in lieu of military service in August 1856 are illustrative of their respective approaches to living within a Muslim state. As noted in Chapter 7, whereas the heads of the Christian denominations vociferously objected to paying the huge tax, Rabbi Jacob Peretz announced that the Jewish community was prepared to accept the concept of payment in principle. By so doing, the rabbi isolated the Jewish community from the Christian stance, perceived by the population and administration of Damascus as anti-Muslim.[62] Indeed, this step was typical of the Jewish communal modus operandi in Syria, which may be typified as moderate action aimed at avoiding drawing attention to itself and thereby deflecting Muslim hostility. The Christian refusal to pay the *bedel-i 'askeri* was unquestionably a prime contributory factor to the massacre in Damascus four years later.[63]

Additional evidence for the low political and legal profile maintained by Syrian Jews, and their decision not to stand up for their rights, is provided by the case described in Chapter 7, in which a Muslim was executed for murdering a Jew. Seeking to maintain good relations with the Muslims, the Jews lobbied actively, but unsuccessfully, for the transmutation of this death sentence. Clearly perceiving that religious humiliation sparked Muslim anger, the Jews did everything in their power not to incense the Muslim populace, even if they had the backing of the law.

Jewish willingness to compromise and to maintain a low profile, as opposed to Christian provocativeness, also came to the fore in the issue of ownership of Muslim slaves.[64] The leaders of the Jewish community acceded to the request of the British consul Richard Wood that they free their Muslim slaves voluntarily, and by so doing defused Muslim animosity and averted the immediate

[60] Frankl, *The Jews in the East*, i. 291.   [61] Ma'oz, *Ottoman Reform*, 209.
[62] AECPC, Turquie, Damas, vol. 4, pp. 79–86, Outrey, 16 Aug. 1856; FO 78/1220, Misk to Clarendon, Damascus, 27 Aug. 1856.   [63] Ibid.
[64] AECCC, Damas, vol. 1, p. 104, Beaudin, 3 Aug. 1842. The issue of slave ownership is discussed in Ch. 6 above.

danger of persecution and assault.[65] For their part, the refusal of the Greek Catholics to perform a similar gesture incited the hatred of the Muslim masses.[66]

It is by no means the case that Jews never attempted to assert their rights. Yet attempts to do so were rare, generally originating in Aleppo, and had two defining characteristics: they often involved Jews who were consular protégés, and therefore had external support and protection; and they usually ended with a retraction of Jewish claims for fear of inciting Muslim riots. The extreme example of the disputed ownership of a warehouse in Aleppo exemplifies both features. The *'ulama'* tendered a claim before the court that a warehouse owned by one Ezra Belilio, an Austrian protégé, had formerly been used as a mosque. After the court ruled in the *'ulama'*'s favour, Belilio protested, arguing that the case had been tried without his knowledge or presence, and further submitting that the court had perverted the principle of possession upon which its verdict had been based.[67] Nonetheless, in preparation for its use as a mosque the *'ulama'* went ahead and restored the *mihrab*. After the Muslims ignored his demand that the prayer niche be removed, Belilio's next move was to destroy the *mihrab* on the night of 9 April 1860. When news of this act came to light the next morning, a Muslim mob surrounded the home of the Austrian consul Moses de Picciotto, demanding Belilio's arrest. Fearing riots, de Picciotto advised Belilio to flee to Beirut; at the same time, the Jews proffered an explanation of insanity for Belilio's hasty act. With the assistance of the military chief of the Aleppo *wilaya*, 'Umar Pasha, the mob was scattered, calm was restored, and ownership of the warehouse was transferred to the *'ulama'*.[68] This frontal confrontation with the *'ulama'* focused Muslim agitation on the Jews, and some feared that it would also be turned against the Christians.[69] This hatred merged with the general animosity towards European consuls, most of whom in Aleppo were Jews, who flaunted their status by parading in public on holidays, dressed in the official garb of office and feathered headdresses, and accompanied by bodyguards holding silver-headed staffs.[70] Indeed, some claimed that the Picciottos' standing with the governor made the Jews of Aleppo generally arrogant, as opposed to their co-religionists elsewhere in the Ottoman realm.[71] On the contrary, in pursuit of a peaceful life those Jews in Aleppo who were

---

[65] *Voice of Jacob*, 22, 22 July 1842, p. 174; ibid., 40, 17 Feb. 1843, p. 118.

[66] AECCC, Damas, vol. 1, p. 104, Beaudin, 3 Aug. 1842; FO 78/499, Wood to Earl of Aberdeen, Damascus, 6 June 1842; Ma'oz, 'Communal Conflict in Ottoman Syria', ii. 99.

[67] Jewish newspapers of the day issued erroneous reports that the court actually recognized Belilio's ownership of the warehouse. See *Hamagid*, 29, 25 July 1860, p. 114; *JC*, 13 July 1860, p. 6. The consular reports are more reliable.

[68] FO 78/1538, Skene to Bulwer, Aleppo, 14 Apr. 1860; AECPC, Turquie, Alep, vol. 3, pp. 140–2, de Lafosse, 12 Apr. 1860.   [69] *JC*, 13 July 1860, p. 6.

[70] Neale, *Eight Years in Syria*, ii. 105–6.

[71] AECPC, Turquie, Alep, vol. 3, pp. 140–2, de Lafosse, 12 Apr. 1860.

Ottoman subjects maintained a low profile and did not actively assert their rights. Even when victims of robbery, Jews preferred to absorb financial loss rather than face the hostility associated with making an official complaint, viewing monetary loss and silence as the lesser evil.[72] It was this attitude that saved them from the anti-Christian riots in Aleppo in October 1850.

On Wednesday evening, 17 October 1850, at the height of the Muslim holiday *ʿid al-adha*, riots broke out in Aleppo. The Muslim mob targeted two Christian neighbourhoods, injuring and killing many Christians and plundering homes and churches. The riots lasted two full days, dying down only on the Friday. The mob that had taken control of the city presented a list of demands to the regime, relating to conscription, taxes, and intercommunal relations, fulfilment of which was a precondition for restoration of order. The riots originated in protests against the regime, specifically the *wali*'s demand that the janissaries and the *ashraf* pay the tax on the revenues from their land leases, accompanied by a threat that failure to pay would prompt their arrest, compulsory conscription, and the collection of the *ferde* tax; but the violence itself was directed against the Christians for their arrogant behaviour. From the time of Egyptian rule the *ashraf* had been intensely opposed to the very idea of Christian–Muslim equality, which they viewed as a profound insult to the community of the faithful. The combination of incitement and the desire for booty diverted the anger of the masses from the regime to the Christians, on whom they took the opportunity to visit their hatred.

Once the riots had died down, the *wali*, Mustafa Zarif Pasha, pretended to accede to the rebels' demands and even made some concessions aimed at restoring order. At the same time, he requested military reinforcements from Istanbul. When they arrived he took harsh punitive measures against the rebels, and reinstated full authority over the city.

The immediate trigger for the outbreak of violence had been the grand entrance to the city of the Greek Catholic patriarch, at the head of a cross-carrying and bell-ringing procession.[73] A Jewish eyewitness gloatingly described the course of events:

And it came to pass in our time in Aram Tsova, may the Lord grant it His protection, in the year 5611 to the Creation, Wednesday evening, the 11th of the month of Heshvan [17 October 1850]. The Muslims rose up in fury and anger and rage against the homes of the uncircumcised [Christians], and looted their possessions and killed

---

[72] FO 195/1153, Skene to Elliot, Aleppo, 9 Jan. 1877.

[73] For a description of the events, see the diary of Naʿʿum Bakhkhash in al-Yashuʿi, *Historical Documents about Aleppo* (Arab.), iii. 140–2; al-Ghazzi, *The Golden River* (Arab.), iii. 366–82; Qarali, *The Most Important Events* (Arab.), 79ff.; and al-Tabbakh, *Eminent Nobles in the History of Aleppo* (Arab.), iii. 438–40. See also HHSTA, PA, XXXVIII/93, Gödel für von Schwarzenberg, Beirut, 29 Oct. 1850; XIII/3 (Constantinople), E. de Picciotto, Aleppo, 19 and 23 Oct. 1850; Türkei, PA, XII/42, E. de Picciotto für von Klezl, Aleppo, 29 and 31 Oct. 1850.

some of them and raped their women and seized all their treasures; in the morning they returned again and the entire day they burned their churches and shattered their icons and then [the Christians] escaped from them to the orchards, the rooftops and the fields, and hid in caves so they would not be seen. On Friday they escaped and came to the Khanat [the European quarter] and into the city, and a proclamation was issued not to harm them any more. And some two hundred houses and courtyards were pillaged; may God protect His people, the children of Israel, and may they never again know hardship from now until eternity. And on Tuesday, Rosh Hodesh Kislev [5 November] the governor of Aram Tsova rose up against the Muslims and waged war on them and killed some 2,000 men and destroyed their homes and courtyards and mansions and their stores and burned down their dwellings, and thank God that the Jewish people were spared . . . And all that befell the uncircumcised took place because they gave offence to the Muslims in their garments and their speech and spoke to the Muslims disrespectfully, and mocked them with the wicked Mutran [patriarch] who came to them holding a statue of idolatry and displayed it in a procession through the marketplaces and the streets before the Muslims to taunt them. His fate was terrible and bitter, though we know not what became of him . . . thus it is written: 'The swords shall pierce their own hearts, and their bows shall be broken' [Ps. 37: 15] . . . May it be well with Israel [Ps. 125: 5; 128: 6].[74]

In addition to their demands related to conscription and taxes, the rebels sought to prohibit the ringing of church bells, public processions in which crosses were carried, and the employment of Muslim slaves in Christian households. The nature of these demands indicates the significant role played by Christian behaviour in arousing the anger of the rebellious Muslim mob.[75] Nonetheless, Jews too certainly feared for their lives and took active steps to turn the rebels away from the Jewish quarter, paying them the huge sum of £2,000.[76]

Friction between Jews and Muslims centred on the Jewish occupation of moneylending. As has become clear in previous chapters, Jews played a significant role in extending credit throughout Syria. Despite repeated rabbinic cautions against 'extorting non-Jews',[77] some Jewish moneylenders charged high interest rates and employed such measures as arrest and foreclosure

---

[74] British Library, Gaster Collection, Or. 10709, 933, Solomon ben Yom Tov Sutton [copyist?]: Prayer and *piyutim*, 39v. For additional *piyutim* written in the wake of the Jewish rescue from these events, see Aboud, *Habakashot leshabat*, 440–1; JTSL, Mic. 3102, Diwan, arranged according to tunes, fo. 154.

[75] For a comprehensive treatment, see Harel, 'Jewish–Christian Relations in Aleppo'. For a different explanation, see Masters, 'The 1850 Events in Aleppo'.

[76] FO 195/1153, Skene to Elliot, Aleppo, 9 Jan. 1877. At a later date the Christians in Aleppo also adopted this system of purchasing protection. See FO 78/1538, Skene to Bulwer, Aleppo, 30 June 1860. In the later period we find the French consul encouraging the Jews to divert some of the Alliance donations intended for poor Jews to impoverished Muslims who had been hard hit by the famine. See AAIU, Syrie, X.E., Alep, 83, Somekh, 3 May 1880, 1 July 1880; I.E., Alep, 1, 18 June 1880.   [77] See e.g. Abraham Dayan, *Zikaron lanefesh*, 41.

against creditors who failed to repay their loans. Travellers and European diplomats noted the growing unrest among villagers who were deep in debt to Jews. One such observer warned the Damascus Jewish community that it would pay for the sins of the moneylenders: 'When the time comes, and it will come, the trampled worm will turn. The Moslem will rise not really against the Christian—he will only be the excuse—but against you. Your quarter will be the one to be burnt down; your people to be exterminated, and your innocent tribe will suffer for the few guilty.'[78]

But there were also Muslim moneylenders, and even European observers admitted that it was preferable to take loans from Jews than from them. According to these observers, Jewish moneylenders did not foreclose on all the debtor's property if there was hope that he might make an economic recovery; indeed, they would even support him until he recouped his losses.[79]

In order to avoid attracting Muslim envy and greed, the Jews took care not to display their great wealth publicly, though the affluence of some Jewish individuals was no secret. As noted in earlier chapters, many European travellers voiced their astonishment at the immense gap between the nondescript facades of Jewish homes in Damascus and the opulence of their interiors.[80]

Jewish political reserve, especially as contrasted to Christian boldness, tended to draw them closer to the Muslims. Time and again, Muslim members of the *majlis* sided with Jews in cases of Christian–Jewish litigation. Thus, in the wake of a refuted blood libel in Aleppo started by the Christians, the Muslims came out strongly in support of the Jews and were even prepared to testify in their favour, as a contemporary Jewish observer notes.[81] At times, Jewish appointees to official positions were preferred over Christian candidates, simply because Jews belonged to a minority without political ambitions.[82]

Another sphere in which Muslims favoured Jews over Christians pertained to inheritance. Having once interfered in estates involving either Christian or Jewish minors, from 1849 the *shar'ia* court intervened only in cases involving Christians, to the extent that in 1854 the latter complained that the *qadi* had sealed homes, warehouses, and stores of deceased persons until receiving what he saw as adequate payment from the heirs. As these dues mushroomed

[78] I. Burton, *The Inner Life of Syria*, i. 343.

[79] *Halevanon*, 5, 14 Adar 1866, p. 71. See also Hyamson (ed.), *The British Consulate in Jerusalem*, ii. 350.

[80] There was a contrast between nondescript exteriors and internal beauty with regard to non-Jewish homes as well, grounded in their residents' desire to lower their tax burden by hiding the extent of their wealth from the authorities, and to prevent robberies during periods of upheaval and looting. See e.g. Lynch, *Narrative*, 493; Wilson, *The Lands of the Bible*, ii. 334; I. Burton, *The Inner Life of Syria*, i. 41; Woodcock, *Scripture Lands*, 38; de Saulcy, *Narrative of a Journey*, ii. 523; Porter, *Five Years in Damascus*, i. 34; Bell, *The Desert and the Sown*, 146; Tilt, *The Boat and the Caravan*, 409–10.   [81] Ben-Zvi Institute, MS 3724, *Pinkas rabi mosheh suton*, 20.

[82] Landau and Ma'oz, 'Jews and Non-Jews' (Heb.), 5.

the Christians refused to pay, complaining that Jews were not subject to this law. The response of the Sublime Porte to the Christian refusal to pay was to send instructions requiring both Jews and Christians to accept the *qadi*'s authority and intervention.[83] Only in 1861 was this measure cancelled, in the wake of European-backed Jewish and Christian petitions submitted to the Sublime Porte. In the present context, the description of the *qadi*'s behaviour supports the claim that his failure to enforce the law in cases of Jewish inheritance was not fortuitous and constituted some type of reward for their behaviour.[84]

In 'Ayntab, where Muslims, Christians, and Jews paid equal shares of the *ferde* tax under Egyptian rule, with the return of the Ottomans the Muslims attempted to place the burden mainly on the Christian population, gaining relief for themselves and, indirectly, for the Jews. The outcome was Christian isolation in opposition to Muslim–Jewish co-operation.[85]

The episodes described here make it clear why Syrian Jews opted to maintain a low profile, not necessarily socially, but politically. Their doing so enabled them to avoid arousing Muslim animosity, so that while Jews continued to be treated with the traditional humiliation prescribed by Islamic doctrine, they were never seen as a threat or even a nuisance to the Arab Muslim society. This understanding provides a fuller explanation for the mystery of why Muslim writers ignored the Jews. Social compartmentalization, still largely intact even if cracked, coupled with political reserve and avoidance of any direct provocation of the Muslim masses—sensitive to any insult to their religion or to their superior status over the infidels—kept Jews out of the limelight, out of trouble, and out of the literature. Far removed from issues of government and, as we shall see below, from ideological organization for a national Syrian identity, the Jewish question did not attract the attention of Muslim writers. Also almost totally ignored was Jewish economic activity, which played a dominant role in funding the regime and development in Syria until the bankruptcy crisis of the mid-1870s. This may perhaps be explained by a reluctance on the part of Muslim writers to acknowledge the Islamic regime's dependence on Jewish credit.[86]

It must be noted in closing this chapter that the relative lack of overt hostility on the part of the Muslims towards the Jews must be seen in contrast to the deep Muslim antipathy for Christians. However intermittent and however

---

[83] FO 195/458, Brant to Redcliffe, Damascus, 18 Nov. 1857.

[84] See Ma'oz, *Ottoman Reform*, 195–6.

[85] Saul Dweck Hakohen, *Emet me'erets*, 11b–12a, no. 2.

[86] Leading to Jewish perceptions of the Muslims as ungrateful. See M. Margoliouth, *A Pilgrimage to the Land of my Fathers*, ii. 249. On the attitude of the late-nineteenth-century Muslim press in general towards Jews, see Malul, 'The Arabic Press' (Heb.), 445. For Syria especially, see ibid. 367–74.

limited, this Muslim preference for the Jewish minority was one factor aggravating Christian jealousy, and hatred, of the Jews, which found its sharpest expression in repeated blood libel accusations. The complex Jewish relationship with both the Catholic and the Protestant denominations is examined in the next chapter.

NINE

INTERMINORITY
RELATIONS

T HE PREVIOUS chapter explored the interaction, interdependence, and rivalry between the Muslim and *dhimmi* communities in Syria. The focus now shifts to relations between the Syrian Jewish community and the two main Christian denominations, the Catholics and the Protestants. Although each is treated more or less as a unitary whole, we must bear in mind that both broad Christian denominations were further subdivided into smaller groups.

For the most part, Jewish–Catholic relations were dominated by a long-standing animosity, which found an extreme outlet in a series of ritual murder accusations. In contrast, Protestant–Jewish relations were initially friendlier, up to the point at which the Jewish community recognized the strength of Protestant missionary aims. Ultimately, despite increased contacts with the Christian minorities, the Jews remained outside both Christian and Muslim society.

Jewish–Catholic Tensions

Grounded in historical and religious circumstances, and in competition for economic and commercial advantage, tension and conflict between Jews and Catholics in Syria date back to antiquity. In more recent times, the quest for favour with the regime, which frequently drew its civil servants from the minorities, also promoted friction between the two groups. Underlying the regime's preference for placing *dhimmi*s in high administrative and financial posts was their lack of an independent power base; this in turn made *dhimmi* appointees dependent on the ruler, as their retention of, or removal from, office was entirely at his disposition. Nonetheless, *dhimmi* officials were not entirely without power: for example, a governor's reliance on the civil servants in charge of routine tax collection could effectively neutralize his ability to fire these administrators; they in turn were able to accumulate power and influence, which could be channelled to their co-religionists' benefit.[1]

---

[1] Philipp, 'The Farhi Family', 37–8.

Each of the minority groups, seeking support from the various sectors of the ruling Muslim majority—the regime, the elites, and even the masses—in order to overcome rival minorities in the economic, administrative, or public spheres, from time to time attempted to incite the Muslims against its competitors.[2] Muslim antipathy towards Christians, and relative partiality for Jews, triggered complaints by Damascus Christians to the European consuls. Requests for assistance to counter abuse by Muslim *qadis* were backed by the claim that Jews received preferential treatment.[3]

Heightened Muslim hatred for Christians towards the end of Muhammad 'Ali's regime in Syria, and Christians' fears that the return of Ottoman rule would be accompanied by an outburst of Muslim violence against them, motivated them to seek ways to divert Muslim antipathy to the Jews. In this, they found allies in European monks belonging to Catholic orders, including the Franciscans and the Capuchins. These bearers of western Catholicism to the East brought with them not only a religious and cultural message but also the outdated medieval notion that the Passover rites required human blood. It was this belief that fuelled the Damascus blood libel, and any other causes must be viewed as secondary. When it became apparent that such charges had the ability to inflame the Christian masses and even the Muslim public against the Jews, the Syrian Christians used accusations of ritual murder as a tool to their political and economic advantage at the expense of the Jews. In Syria, in any event, until the 1860s at least, blood libel accusations had nothing to do with so-called modern antisemitism. These were ritual murder libels in the medieval mould, which found fertile soil among the ignorant Christian and Muslim populace.[4]

Of these blood libels in Syria, the most famous was the February 1840 Damascus affair.[5] Nearly all Jewish historians stress its significance as a catalyst strengthening Jewish identity and fostering renewed contact between the Jewish communities of the East and the West. Missing from the discussion hitherto is any consideration of the impact of the affair on Syrian Jews and on the fabric of intercommunal relations in Syria over the subsequent decades.[6]

---

[2] Ma'oz, *Modern Syria* (Heb.), 40; Landau and Ma'oz, 'Jews and Non-Jews' (Heb.), 6.

[3] *JC*, 7 Mar. 1856, p. 509, 10 Oct. 1856, p. 755.

[4] Jacob Barnai, '"Blood Libels" in the Ottoman Empire', 191–3. For descriptions of the ignorance, corruption, and degeneration of the local Christians, see I. Burton, *The Inner Life of Syria*, i. 354–5; Jessup, *Fifty-three Years in Syria*, ii. 424–5.

[5] Scores of papers and books treat the Damascus affair. The most comprehensive study is Frankel, *The Damascus Affair*. See also Florence, *Blood Libel*. Two other seminal studies merit mention. One is Mishaqa, *Murder, Mayhem, Pillage, and Plunder*, originally written in Arabic (*Al-jawab 'ala iqtirah al-ahbab*), which contains the author's eyewitness testimony. The second is the memoirs of an anonymous author, a high official in Muhammad 'Ali's regime in Syria, who participated in the investigation of the affair: al-Mukhallisi (ed.), *Historical Memoirs* (Arab.). For the protocols of the investigation, see Rustum, *Arab Roots of Syrian History* (Arab.), vol. v, document 501, pp. 1–41.

[6] See Dinaburg, 'The Political Nature of the Damascus Libel' (Heb.), 518, and his response

On 5 February 1840 a Capuchin monk named Thomas and his servant disappeared in Damascus. Shortly thereafter rumours that they had last been sighted in the Jewish quarter were accompanied by a claim that the two had been murdered to obtain their blood for the Passover rites. Damascus Jewish leaders were arrested and tortured in order to coerce them to confess. The investigation was headed by the French consul in the city from 1839 to 1842, Benoît Ulysse-Laurent-François, Count de Ratti-Menton, the self-styled protector of the Catholics, who sided with the libel's instigators.[7] Some of the Jews arrested broke down and 'confessed', others died under torture, and one chose to escape his tormentors by converting to Islam. Their release was eventually secured, following intense diplomatic activity, through the intercession of Moses Montefiore and Adolphe Crémieux, who headed a Jewish delegation to Egypt to meet Muhammad ʿAli.[8]

When the release order arrived in Damascus in early September, the prisoners were freed but no due process was observed. The victory celebrations by Jews of the Diaspora and within Damascus overlooked the fact that the general population failed to share their joy at the eventual triumph of justice. Furthermore, because this release order did not carry the force of a legal verdict in favour of the Jews, in coming years it constituted a stumbling block in relations between Syrian Jews on the one hand and Syrian Muslims and Christians on the other. The Damascus population, including its Muslim sector, held fast to the belief that the Jews were murderers who had escaped punishment by dint of their European co-religionists' wealth and influence.[9] In Damascus and throughout Syria during the following years there were repeated outbursts of anti-Jewish agitation grounded in accusations of atrocities carried out in connection with Jewish ritual. In effect, the Damascus affair lasted another twenty years, until the 1860 massacre of Christians in the city.

Between 1841 and 1860 at least thirteen public blood libel accusations are documented for Syria: ten for Damascus, and three for Aleppo.[10] There may well have been others, as Christians employed the threat of a blood libel as an

to Graetz there. See also Leven, *Cinquante ans d'histoire*, ii. 57. This topic was treated briefly by Brawer in 'The Jews of Damascus' (Heb.) and id., 'Notes on the Damascus Blood-Accusation' (Heb.)'.

  [7] See Harel, 'Le Consul de France'.
  [8] For the text of the release order, see Laurent, *Relation historique des affaires de Syrie*, ii. 254–5.
  [9] Kiwan, *The Jews in the Middle East* (Arab.), 46; Brawer, 'The Jews of Damascus' (Heb.), 85.
  [10] FO 78/1751, Harari to Montefiore, Damascus, 24 May 1841; 78/622, Wood to Earl of Aberdeen, Damascus, 2 Mar. 1845; 78/714, Timoni to Wellesley, Damascus, 28 Apr. 1847, 19 May 1847; 78/761, Wood to Palmerston, Damascus, 7 Apr. 1848; 78/1220, Misk to Earl of Clarendon, Damascus, 31 July 1856; AAIU, Syrie, I.C., Damas, 5, Weisskopf, 20 Feb. 1868; *JC*, 19 Aug. 1853, p. 365, 24 Oct. 1856, p. 770, 18 June 1875, p. 197; Baron, 'The Jews and the Syrian Massacres', 6; AAIU, Syrie, III.E., Alep, 23, Behor, 7 June 1875; BAIU, 2ème sem. 1875, 13; *Ḥavatselet*, 29, 16 Iyar 1875, p. 234; Yadid Halevi, *Shivḥei moharam*, 9, no. 17; Ben-Zvi Institute, MS 3724, *Pinkas rabi mosheh suton*, 18–20.

extortionary tactic. Indeed, these blood libels were almost an annual event, usually started just before the Passover holiday. The Jews were forced to pay large sums, mainly to the Greek Orthodox and the Roman Catholics, in order to prevent them inciting the mob with libellous accusations of the ritual murder of a Christian or Muslim child.[11] This provocation generated one of the more intriguing phenomena characteristic of Syria at this time, namely, the appearance of Muslim blood libels as not only Catholics but Muslims began to link the disappearance of a boy or girl to the Jews, either to exact revenge for an individual dispute or to extort money. A typical Damascus Muslim blood libel took place in May 1847. In the course of an argument with a Muslim in the marketplace, a Jewish dealer in old clothes was beaten. His complaint to the local guard resulted in two soldiers accompanying him in order to place the Muslim responsible under arrest. Upon seeing the soldiers, the Muslim began brokenheartedly shouting that he had hit the Jew because the latter had kidnapped a two-year-old Muslim child, a claim verified by the Muslim's relatives, standing nearby. All the way to the *seray* the Muslims continued to accuse the Jew vociferously, assaulting and humiliating Jewish passers-by as well. The riot spread to target the entire Jewish community. Joined by Christians, the Muslim mob turned towards the Jewish quarter, demanding the death sentence for all Jews. Twenty-three Jews were injured in the riots and the entire community feared for its existence. Eventually the libel was repudiated through the intervention of the acting British consul.[12]

The uproar in Damascus was further inflamed by Christian allegations concerning the kidnapping of a Christian boy from the town of Baalbek by Jews just a few weeks earlier.[13] The chief accuser in this case was the French consular agent Jean-Baptiste Beaudin, also a key player in the 1840 Damascus libel. As their letter to Moses Montefiore seeking help reflects, Damascus Jews clearly recognized that the Christians were engaged in a deliberate, concerted effort to divert Muslim antipathy to themselves in the direction of Jews, to which end they had created a demonic image of Jews as vicious murderers, for ritual purposes, not only of Christians but of Muslims as well: 'The Christians, in particular, endeavoured to persuade the Mahomedans that the Jews were actually murderers; so that all the Mahomedans, men, women and children believed that the Jews did kill the Mahomedans for the purpose of taking their

[11] Jessup, *Fifty-three Years in Syria*, ii. 424.

[12] NLIS, DA, V-736/28, Hayim Maimon Tobi to Abraham Hayim Gagin, Damascus, 4 Sivan 1847. For a description of this event, see FO 78/714, Timoni to Wellesley, Damascus, 19 and 29 May 1847; Timoni to Palmerston, Damascus, 7 Aug. 1847. For additional Muslim accusations of ritual murder by Jews in Damascus and Aleppo, see *JC*, 14 Oct. 1856; FO 78/1220, Misk to Earl of Clarendon, Damascus, 31 July 1856; 195/458, Misk to Stratford de Redcliffe, Damascus, 29 July 1856; 78/837, Calvert to Canning, Damascus, 28 Aug. 1850.

[13] FO 78/714, Timoni to Wellesley, Damascus, 28 Apr. 1847, 19 May 1847.

blood for the making of the passover cakes, and great hatred against us was thus instilled into their hearts.'[14]

During the two decades following the Damascus affair and other blood libels, Catholics found it easy to incite anti-Jewish feeling, in large part because the belief that the Jews had indeed murdered Father Thomas and his servant had taken firm root. The Catholics also deliberately perpetuated the libel, notably by having an inscription placed on the tomb, in Italian and Arabic, which read: 'Here rest the bones of Father Thomas of Sardinia, apostolic Capuchin missionary, murdered by the Jews on 5 February 1840.'[15] Almost every Christian tourist to Damascus stopped at the Capuchin monastery, where he was treated to an exposition of the details of the affair while standing opposite the epitaph. The missionary John Wilson noted that even in 1847 the residents in the Damascus monasteries mentioned the subject of Father Thomas's murder to every visiting traveller.[16] Undoubtedly, by keeping the memory of the blood libel accusation alive, the epitaph contributed to anti-Jewish agitation.

In early 1845, in what was purportedly a humanitarian gesture but in reality a response to consular pressure, the Jews freed their black, Muslim house slaves. One of the freed female slaves, who had worked for Isaac Harari, divulged to a local physician that she was in possession of a terrible secret that gave her no rest. She reported that Father Thomas's murder had taken place in her master's home, further claiming that although her master had locked her and another slave in a nearby room before doing the deed, she had managed to see what transpired. This story spread rapidly throughout Damascus, and the doctor was invited to the French consulate to make an official statement regarding the slave's testimony, which was eventually shown to be baseless.[17]

The intermittent renewal of the blood libel placed the Jews at constant risk. In their distress, the heads of the Jewish community turned to the European consuls and to leading European Jews, requesting that they press for the removal of the epitaph, which, they claimed, filled its viewers with hatred and loathing for the entire Jewish people.[18] The Damascus Jewish community worked tirelessly to have the inscription deleted, lobbying every influential European visitor, Jews in particular, on the matter. This itself heightened Jewish–Catholic tension. Fearing that Jewish efforts would be successful, the Catholics took steps to protect the epitaph. Even though they had abandoned the monastery after forty years of activity, renting it to the Armenian Catholics

[14] AECPC, Turquie, Damas, vol. 1, p. 264, extract of a letter addressed to Sir Moses Montefiore Baronet by the principal leaders of the Hebrew community of Damascus, May 1847.

[15] Translation of epitaph cited from Frankel, *The Damascus Affair*, 379. See also AECPC, Turquie, Damas, vol. 2, pp. 95–6/A; pp. 132–5, de Ségur, 12 Dec. 1850.

[16] Wilson, *The Lands of the Bible*, ii. 342; Stewart, *The Tent and the Khan*, 489–90; Belgiojoso-Trivulzio, *Asie Mineure et Syrie*, 302; AECPC, Turquie, Damas, vol. 4, pp. 44–6, Outrey, 20 Apr. 1856. [17] FO 78/622, Wood to Earl of Aberdeen, 27 Mar. 1845.

[18] Loewe (ed.), *Diaries of Sir Moses and Lady Montefiore*, ii. 11–13.

in 1848,[19] two years later the Capuchins dispatched a monk to serve specifically as caretaker of the tomb.

Intercommunal tension peaked during Baron Gustave de Rothschild's 1850 visit to Damascus. When Rothschild attempted to purchase cloth from a Christian factory, its owner, suspecting that this was simply a cover for Rothschild's real mission of using his influence to bring about the removal of the tomb inscription, found pretexts not to make the sale.[20] Nonetheless, neither local Jewish efforts nor those of their supporters met with any success. The tomb, and its epitaph, remained standing until demolished in the course of the July 1860 massacre of Christians. Then a new libel began to be spun, one that sought to defame the entire Jewish community and brand its members as murderers.

Thousands of Christians lost their lives in the 1860 massacre; women were kidnapped and raped, and children forced to convert to Islam. Nearly all Christian homes, churches, and monasteries were looted, destroyed, or burned down. This massacre marks the apex of Muslim–Christian antagonism, sparked by the beginning of the Tanzimat and exacerbated by the 1856 Hatt-i Hümayun.[21] Several factors coalesced to bring it about. Of these, arrogant Christian behaviour throughout Syria in asserting the equal rights granted under the Ottoman reforms has already been noted. Because Damascus was an important Islamic centre, the city's Muslim residents were ultra-sensitive to any injury to its traditional nature or status, and anti-Christian feelings ran particularly high there. The Muslims took a particularly jaundiced view of the public exercise of Christian religious privileges.[22] They also resented the Christians' economic success and their prominence in foreign trade and the government administration, and feared for the unity of the Muslim state, suspecting the Christians of taking part in a European conspiracy against it. The Christian refusal to pay the *bedel-i 'askeri* tax further heightened Muslim fears.[23] In June 1860 reports reached Damascus of the government-supported Druze massacre of Christians in Lebanon. The governor, Ahmad Pasha, took no steps to impose calm in a stormy atmosphere, and Christians in Damascus were publicly beaten and humiliated without any governmental interference.

---

[19] AECCC, Alep, vol. 32, p. 17, Bentivoglio, 17 June 1858; AECPC, Turquie, Damas, vol. 2, pp. 132–5, de Ségur, 12 Dec. 1850.

[20] AECPC, Turquie, Damas, vol. 2, pp. 132–5, de Ségur, 12 Dec. 1850. On Gustave de Rothschild's trip in the region, see also de Saulcy, *Narrative of a Journey*, ii. 533.

[21] Ma'oz, *Ottoman Reform*, 231.

[22] Fawaz, *An Occasion for War*, 100. Fawaz argues that the main factor underlying the riots was the ever-increasing gap between increasingly wealthy Christians and impoverished Muslims. This argument is correct regarding Lebanon, but not Damascus. Contemporary reports note that the motivation for the attacks in Damascus differed from that in Lebanon, citing the openly demonstrative, public display of their rights by Christians as the basis for the Damascus outburst. See Mishaqa, *Murder, Mayhem, Pillage, and Plunder*, 244.

[23] Fawaz, *An Occasion for War*, 79.

The immediate cause for the outbreak of the 1860 riots can be identified as public humiliation of Muslims. On 9 July, seeking to insult Christians, Muslim youths drew chalk crosses on the paving stones of the Christian quarter, which forced every passer-by to step on them, and on Christian homes; they also tied crosses to dogs' necks or tails. Some of the youths responsible were arrested, placed in shackles, and forced to sweep the streets of the Christian quarter. Finding this punishment intolerable, the Muslim mob forcibly released the prisoners and directed its rage at the Christians. Over the next five days the violence continued unhindered: the Christian population of Damascus was decimated, suffering a blow from which it took years to recover.[24]

The reaction of the European powers and their citizens was fierce. France, which viewed itself as the protector of Christians in the Levant, demanded immediate military intervention on their behalf. For fear that France would either take over the area, or at the very least declare it a French protectorate, the Sublime Porte sought to prevent such intervention, with British support. Although the Turkish sultan Abdülmecid made a written commitment to the French emperor Napoleon III to restrain, and punish, the anti-Christian rioters, nonetheless the French continued to insist on the need to send a task force to impose order. Eventually, the European powers reached general agreement that French intervention would lead neither to a takeover nor to annexation of the region. The force that landed in Syria in mid-August under General Beaufort d'Hautpoul's command was composed entirely of French soldiers. But by the time the French force arrived order had already been restored, not by any alacrity on the part of the local regime but by the Sublime Porte's swift intervention.[25] The sultan's response—designed to prevent European intrusion—was to appoint a special commissioner, Fu'ad Pasha, and to dispatch him to Syria immediately at the head of military reinforcements. Fu'ad made full use of the unrestricted powers granted him by the sultan. He executed hundreds of soldiers and officers by firing squad, hanged many civilian participants, exiled several notables, and imposed a collective tax on the city. Most of the able-bodied men in Damascus were conscripted into the army, and some of the booty stolen from the Christians was returned. A committee was formed to determine the extent of, and reparations for, the damage.[26]

[24] Reports of the massacre appear in many local works and travel accounts. See e.g. Mishaqa, *Murder, Mayhem, Pillage, and Plunder*, 249–62; Porter, *The Giant Cities of Bashan*, i. 344–9, 357–64; D. S. Margoliouth, *Cairo, Jerusalem and Damascus*, 275–85; Salibi, 'The 1860 Upheaval in Damascus'. For an impressive list of sources describing the massacre, see Fawaz, *An Occasion for War*. See also Ma'oz, *Ottoman Reform*, 231 ff.

[25] Tibawi, *A Modern History of Syria*, 129–30; Schwarzfuchs, 'Jews, Druzes, Muslims and Christians' (Heb.), 431.

[26] Mishaqa, *Murder, Mayhem, Pillage, and Plunder*, 263–70; Gross, 'Ottoman Rule in the Province of Damascus', 35–51. Many documents on events in Damascus during the riots and after Fu'ad Pasha's arrival, and protocols of the compensation committee, are housed in HHSTA,

Like the events in Aleppo a decade earlier, the rage of the Damascus mob focused on the Christians and was not directed at the Jews. This 'wondrous' fact did not escape Christian eyes. Envious that the Jews had been spared, they sought to attribute this to Jewish–Muslim co-operation. One Christian claim was that, had the sole goal of the Muslims and the Turkish troops been booty, they could have found far greater riches in Jewish homes.[27] Nor could the amazed Jews ignore this fact in their attempt to explain why they were over-looked by the fanatical mob. Damascus Jewish leaders proffered the following explanation in a letter to James de Rothschild in Paris dated 18 Elul 1860:

We have seen and have heard the powerful Christian hatred for, and jealousy of, the people of Israel, their saying, 'Why did the Muslims not kill, or loot, or burn the homes of the Jews?' And these words reflect their hatred, and jealousy, and compet-itiveness, and they question the divine will that made the looters show mercy to the Jews, leaving them and their property unharmed.[28]

In fact, Jews were in various degrees of danger during the course of, and after, the riots. The active stage of the rioting posed the most extreme peril, pre-senting a real threat to Jewish lives and property. Early communications, writ-ten before the true picture had become clear, contain reports of the burning of Jewish homes and of Jews seeking hiding places.[29] This direct danger passed, only to be replaced by an indirect one: allegations that Jews had taken part in the massacre, including premeditated murder of Christians. This accusation

Türkei, PA, XII/70, XII/71; PA, XXXVIII/134, XXVIII/139. On the reconstruction of the Christian quarter, see Bocquet, 'Un example de minorité au Levant'.

[27] See e.g. Mishaqa, *Eye-witness Account* (Arab.), 179.

[28] *Hamagid*, 39, 5 Oct. 1860, pp. 154–5.

[29] Reports of attacks on Jewish property that appeared in the Jewish press were exaggerated and inaccurate from the start. For example, the *Jewish Chronicle* (3 Aug. 1860, p. 5) reported that the Jewish quarter of Damascus, which adjoined the Christian quarter, had burned down. See also two letters written shortly after the riots ended (15 July 1860), published in a special section appended to the İzmir newspaper *L'Impartial, Supplément au numéro 1065 de L'Impartial*, 21 July 1860. Baron ('The Jews and the Syrian Massacres', 5) cites a report that 850 Jewish and Muslim homes had burned down in the riots. This information, drawn from the contemporary press, is misleading and incorrect. In letters to European Jewish communities written somewhat later, the Jews of Damascus emphasized that their quarter had remained unharmed. Indeed, there is but a single complaint regarding the torching of a Jewish home, which highlights its exceptionality. In a letter, Albert Cohn of Paris requested that the committee in charge of reparations formed in Beirut also treat the matter of David Picciotto, whose house had burned down, 'for fear that they will not intercede in this matter, because Senor David's house, may God preserve him, is alone among the houses of the Christians, he is the only one'. See Benayahu, 'The Jews of Damascus and the Galilee' (Heb.), 97, 101. This also answers Baron's query ('The Jews and the Syrian Massacres', 14) as to why the Damascus Jews entered no claims for compensation to the funds providing assistance to those injured during the riots. Because the Jews were not directly harmed, they had—with the exception of Picciotto—no grounds for demanding compensation. On the fact that the Jews were in danger, see the testimony of the Prussian consul in Damascus, Dr Wetzstein, in a letter to Albert Cohn, cited in *JC*, 23 Nov. 1860, p. 50.

of direct involvement in murder was then toned down into one of Jews having encouraged the Muslims, greeting them with joy and cold drinking water. Further blame accrued to the Jews for using the massacre as a way to make quick profits by buying cheaply and selling dear property plundered from the persecuted Christians.[30] As a result of this claim the Jews were required to contribute to the monetary levy imposed on the non-Christian residents of Damascus for the purpose of rehabilitating the Christians.[31]

As in Aleppo a decade earlier, it was the low political, religious, and social profile maintained by the Jews that saved them from being targeted by the Muslim mob. However, whereas in Aleppo this rational explanation was acknowledged, in Damascus most of the extant Hebrew sources gave their escape a miraculous tinge.[32] In the above-mentioned letter to James de Rothschild, the heads of the Jewish community asserted: 'And a great, awesome miracle took place, almost overshadowing the miracles of the Exodus from Egypt.'[33] The traveller Moses Reischer described this 'miracle' as follows:

The following proclamation was made, saying that the Jews have been our brothers since antiquity, and anyone who harms them, who takes so much as a thread or a sandal-strap will die. Only, command the Jews to open the doors to their houses and to put out water to slake the heat of the murderers and to clean their swords. They should also mark the houses in which they dwell with the *tsitsit* [ritual fringes] that they wear on the corner of their clothes, so that the Destroyer will not enter and smite you. They further announced that any Jew in whose premises a Christian was found hiding would be put to death along with him [the Christian], and the Jews did so out of fear. The Christians imitated the Jews, borrowing prayer shawls with *tsitsit*. When this became known to the Muslims, they said, 'Let circumcision be the sign.' Coming upon one [a Christian], he said, 'I am a Jew.' They immediately demanded to see the sign of circumcision, the covenant with our father Abraham . . . and the Jews experienced a great miracle. And the miracle was even greater, for the Muslims relate that an elderly Muslim *shaykh* appeared and spread the word among them, warning them harshly not to speak to the Jews for either good or bad, that failure to do so would give them cause for regret. And until the present, they are unable to determine who it was. They saw this as well and were astonished, how the Muslims had a change of heart, how great love for the Jews entered them, which had not been the case from yesterday and the day before.[34]

---

[30] See Mishaqa, *Murder, Mayhem, Pillage, and Plunder*, 253, 263; id., *Eye-Witness Account* (Arab.), 179.   [31] Baron, 'Great Britain and Damascus Jewry', 181.

[32] The sole rational–political explanation found in the Hebrew press of the day for the Jewish escape was Jehiel Brill's report to *Hamagid*, 35, 5 Sept. 1860, p. 138: 'Because the Jews in Muslim lands do not raise their heads, therefore the sword of Muslim revenge did not touch the Jews.'

[33] *Hamagid*, 39, 5 Oct. 1860, pp. 154–5.

[34] Reischer, *Sha'arei yerushalayim*, 47. See also Benayahu, 'The Jews of Damascus and the Galilee' (Heb.), 92–3.

Another description further highlights the motif of the miraculous salvation of the Jews. According to an anonymous traveller, after wreaking its anger on the Christians the mob then intended to turn on the Jews and their property. A prestigious *shaykh* who was a friend of the Jews called upon the mob not to harm them, and succeeded in delaying the attack for two days. On the third day, when calls to attack the Jews intensified, the *shaykh* sought to demonstrate to the masses through miraculous means that this opposed Allah's will. He asked that they fire a gun, with the sought-after sign being that it fail to shoot. This 'miracle' occurred, deflecting the crowd from its plan to massacre the Jews.[35]

These accounts, which emphasize the exercise of God's will through a Muslim holy man, made it possible for the Jews to elicit Muslim sympathy and turn aside the rapidly spreading Christian accusations, in European cities as well as in Syria, that Jews had taken part in the massacre, or had at least aided the Muslims in carrying it out. It was necessary to draw Muslim public opinion to the Jewish side, because the Muslim population, which paid dearly for the massacre in lives and property, had begun to exhibit signs of jealousy of the Jews, who had escaped unscathed both from the massacre and from the punishment meted out to the residents of Damascus in its wake.

At first vague, these accusations gained in clarity when an accusatory finger was pointed at specific Jewish individuals. According to the extant sources, the sultan's commissioner protected the Jews so that the Christians could not arrest any of them while Fu'ad Pasha remained in the city. On the other hand, it is also possible that Fu'ad was so preoccupied with the rioters and with the restoration of public order that he simply had no time to deal with complaints against Jews. In any event, the turning point in the attitude of the Damascus regime towards the Jews came with Fu'ad's departure for the Beirut region. For fear of censorship, the Damascus Jews smuggled out a letter to London, in which they described the situation in the wake of Fu'ad's departure:

Christians and Muslims banded together to bear witness that our unfortunate brethren had a hand in the massacre, and the judges lent credence to this claim. Many of our brethren were imprisoned. For naught does a Jew bring witnesses to his innocence, for the judges are unreceptive. Any Christian or Muslim youth who comes before the judge and says that he saw a Jew kill a Christian, is believed, as when someone consults the *urim* [oracular objects], and Jewish testimony is inadmissible. Moreover, even if a Christian testifies that a Jew hid him from the murderers while the massacre was taking place, no credence is lent him . . . Yesterday they arrested the esteemed rabbi Jacob Abulafia [son of the chief rabbi of Jerusalem] and brought him before the court, testifying that they saw him . . . murder two Christians that day. To no avail did he bring reliable witnesses to testify as to his whereabouts on that day; they ignored their testimony and threw him into prison.[36]

[35] *JC*, 2 Nov. 1860, p. 5.
[36] *Hamagid*, 44, 14 Nov. 1860, p. 176. See also the letter from the heads of the Damascus

One hundred and twenty-five prominent members of the Jewish community were arrested in the wake of these accusations; of these, twenty-five were sentenced to death.[37] The Jews now faced a new problem in the judicial process set in place by Fu'ad Pasha to sentence the rioters: the special court established precisely for that purpose. The haste with which sentences were passed, and the clear preference for Christian testimony—even over and above that of Muslim notables—aroused the Jewish leadership's fears that the falsely accused Jews would be to put to death even before they had had a chance to stand trial. Jewish lobbying therefore focused on persuading the regime to allow the Jewish defendants to follow ordinary judicial procedure rather than to appear before the special court; that is, on creating a distinction between trials of Muslims and of Jews.[38]

By including the Jews in the tax imposed on the Damascus population to recompense the Christians, Fu'ad Pasha indirectly legitimized claims of active Jewish involvement in the riots, which also lent some credence to the notion that Jews had participated in looting Christian homes. Thus, the Jewish desire to nullify the fine was impelled not only by the immense financial burden, but also by a desire to exonerate the community from blame.

In their attempt to achieve these goals, the Jews appealed to almost every potential advocate they could think of, including the British consul and Moses Montefiore, and through their agency to the British government and Queen Victoria. At the same time, they approached Albert Cohn, James de Rothschild, and the French consul, and through them, the French government. Appeals were also forwarded to the Prussian consul; to the Jewish Austrian vice consul, Joseph Elias; to Abraham Camondo, head of the Istanbul Jewish community; and to Fu'ad Pasha himself.[39]

This time the lobbying was successful. The imprisoned Jews were released and the Jewish community freed from the tax payment. However, the non-Jewish population of Damascus continued to believe that the Jews had taken part in the riots, and that, as in the Father Thomas affair, they had once again escaped punishment because of their European brethren's economic and political influence; this despite the substantial contribution the Jewish protégés of foreign consulates had voluntarily agreed to make to the regime treasury.[40] Some ten years later, the British consul Richard Burton gave succinct expression

---

Jewish community to Montefiore, 7 Tishrei 1860, found in FO 406/10, Montefiore to Russell, Ramsgate, 16 Oct. 1860.

[37] *Hamagid*, 6, 6 Feb. 1861, p. 21. A list of four Jewish arrestees appeared in *Hadiqat al-akhbar*, 8 Nov. 1860, p. 2.

[38] Baron, 'Great Britain and Damascus Jewry', 191.

[39] Loewe (ed.), *Diaries of Sir Moses and Lady Montefiore*, ii. 117–19; Baron, 'The Jews and the Syrian Massacres', 22–3; FO 406/10, Brant to Fuad Pasha, Beirut, 26 Nov. 1860; Franco, *Essai sur l'histoire*, 209.   [40] On this contribution, see Fawaz, *An Occasion for War*, 159.

to these feelings. After accusing the Damascus Jews of assisting the Muslims and of participating in the looting, he angrily commented: 'Unfortunately they escaped punishment by the influence of their supporters in England. There is no one in Damascus who does not know this fact.'[41]

Thus the Jewish community remained the sole sector left unharmed, both physically and economically, by the 1860 riots. It was but a short step to accuse it of robbery. This new allegation, that the Jews had amassed great wealth in benefiting from the disaster that befell the Christians, circulated in Damascus for many years, creating an image of a Christian-hating Jew, who, whenever he sees Muslims spilling Christian blood, follows them 'as the jackals follow the lion and waxing rich on their cruelties'.[42] It was the Christians themselves who spread rumours of Jewish participation in the massacre and looting. Various readers, mainly anti-Jewish Christians, sent similar reports to European newspapers. The antisemitic press, in Russia in particular, used these reports as a pretext for Jew-baiting, giving prominence to reports of Jewish involvement in the massacre.[43] The allegations were spearheaded by the Greek Orthodox, but other denominations followed in its wake.[44]

The Prussian consul Johann Gottfried Wetzstein cited four factors to explain the imputation of blame to the Jews. The first was the fathomless Christian antipathy towards the Jews, especially among the Greek Orthodox. Second was Muslim anger that many of their co-religionists had been executed in the wake of the anti-Christian outbreak, whereas the Jews had remained untouched. The third was Jewish fear, itself encouraging attacks by their enemies. But the fourth and, in Wetzstein's view, the most significant reason was simple greed: the opportunity to extort money from the Jews. Indeed, there is abundant evidence of Christian officials, and even ordinary individuals, taking advantage of the opportunity to enrich themselves by threatening to point the finger at Jews and allege their participation in the massacre.[45]

The question then arises whether these charges were completely false to begin with or whether they contained a kernel of truth—which, in the antagonistic intercommunal atmosphere in Syria, would be enough to attract harsh accusations against the entire Jewish community. Scholars are divided on this question. At one end of the spectrum there is the opinion that the Jews who were arrested were guilty of murdering Christians;[46] at the other, we find the categorical statement that 'Jews did not participate in plunder and did not attack

[41] FO 78/2260, Burton to Granville, Damascus, 28 Nov. 1870.

[42] François Lénormant, *Une persecution du Christianisme en 1860* (Paris, 1860), 140, cited in Baron, 'The Jews and the Syrian Massacres', 8–9.

[43] Baron, 'The Jews and the Syrian Massacres', 8.

[44] This may explain why the Greek consul Spartali sided with those who blamed the Jews. See Baron, 'The Jews and the Syrian Massacres', 7; *JC*, 23 Nov. 1860, p. 5.

[45] FO 406/10, Brant to Russell, Beirut, 8 Nov. 1860; *JC*, 21 Dec. 1860, p. 5.

[46] Fawaz, *An Occasion for War*, 159.

with swords. Perhaps they purchased booty when the situation calmed down.'[47]
The confidence displayed by the latter statement is perhaps justified with
regard to acts of actual murder, but it is likely that a considerable portion of
the Jewish community saw the massacre as retribution for the ongoing blood
libel accusations over the years, and took the opportunity to settle the score.
That Damascus Jews certainly gloated over the downfall of the hated Christians emerges from the following poem by Rabbi Shalom Mahadib, which
thanks God for their rescue:

> Sing praises to God
> for the deliverance of the Jews
> when the Christian seed fell
> in the hands of Ishmael . . .
>
> They killed many
> and took their children captive
> carrying out atrocities against their women and children in God's eye . . .
>
> The exalted, everlasting one on high/ remembered the libel of Thomas[48]
> Exact vengeance on them
> the vengeance of the people of Israel . . .
>
> Their idols were burned
> their priests cursed
> they fainted in the streets
> under the banner of Ishmael . . .
>
> Their blood was spilled out on the ground
> their foreskins severed
> in his mouth they placed
> the [severed] foreskin of the chieftain of Magdiel [Gen. 36: 43; a reference to
>   an important Christian] . . .
>
> God is my strength and my stronghold [Jer. 16: 19], a refuge to the children
>   of Israel [Joel 4: 16].[49]

Such a sensibility could well prompt individual Jews to assist the Muslim attack
on Christians, whether by hinting at Christian hiding places or by cleaning the

---

[47] Brawer, 'The Jews of Damascus' (Heb.), 103.

[48] The 1840 ritual murder accusation regarding Father Thomas in Damascus. Ma'oz, in
'Changes in the Status of Jews' (Heb.), 22, noted the role of revenge for blood libels in Jewish–
Christian relations. Thus, for example, we find reports of Christians being beaten by Jews in
reprisal for the 1840 Damascus affair during the Egyptian withdrawal from Syria. See Brawer,
'The Jews of Damascus' (Heb.), 87; also Harel, 'The Status and Image of the Piccioto Family'
(Heb.), 185.

[49] The poem was first published in full in *Sefer mishmeret beḥadash* (Safed, 1863). On this poem
and the transformation of the day on which the riots started (20 Tamuz) into a day marked by the
Damascus community, see Harel, 'The Damascus Jewish Community' (Heb.), 141.

Muslims' swords and offering drinking water, as described above. There were even allegations that the Jews took advantage of this opportunity to destroy Father Thomas's tomb in the Capuchin monastery.[50]

There is no doubt that Jews took part in trading in the looted property. Compelling testimony comes from the strongly worded injunction issued by the Damascus rabbis to the Jewish community: 'Under the threat of excommunication let no Jew, man or woman, buy any artefact or precious gems or pearls from the Muslims or the Druze, not even one hundred for a penny, lest this ruin be under their care [Isa. 3: 6].'[51] This clearly demonstrates that Jews dealt in plunder and that this in turn gave rise to allegations of Jewish participation in the riots. For fear of being caught with Christian property, the Muslims unloaded the goods at bargain prices or even threw them in the street, thereby creating a situation in which Jews were able to purchase valuable merchandise at ridiculously low prices. According to an eyewitness account, because the surviving Christians were still afraid to go out in public they experienced severe losses, whereas Jews made significant profits.[52] Even the head of the French task force, Beaufort, who exonerated the Jewish community of any collaboration with the Muslims, did note the possibility that there were cases in which individual Jews from the poorer classes had helped themselves to booty.[53] Other testimony identifies a member of the affluent Jewish elite as assisting the Muslims, including the governor Ahmad Pasha, to hide booty.[54] Careful reading of these remarks makes it impossible to rule out the likelihood that at least some individual Jews were involved in trading in stolen goods, which sufficed to cast a shadow over the entire Jewish community at that time. The Christian exaggeration of the extent of Jewish involvement in plundering and in the subsequent sale of the loot was grounded in the new reality in which only the Jews remained physically and economically untouched by the riots. It was a simple matter to blame them for taking advantage simultaneously of Christian ruin and of Muslim impoverishment to enrich themselves.[55]

Jewish efforts to prove that they had taken no part in either the massacre or the looting—neither as a community nor as collaborators with the Muslims—

[50] FO 195/965, Burton to Elliot, Damascus, 1 Sept. 1870. The Jewish sources attribute the smashing of the epitaph to Muslims. See *Hamagid*, 44, 14 Nov. 1860, p. 176. On the destruction of the Capuchin monastery in Damascus during the riots, see Poujoulat, *La vérité sur la Syrie*, 160–1.   [51] Reischer, *Sha'arei yerushalayim*, 47.

[52] Mishaqa, *Murder, Mayhem, Pillage, and Plunder*, 263; id., *Eye-Witness Account* (Arab.), 188.

[53] FO 406/10, Bulwer to Russell, Constantinople, 26 Oct. 1860.

[54] FO 406/10, Brant to Russell, Beirut, 8 Nov. 1860.

[55] With regard to their economic impact on the Jewish community, the riots certainly had some immediate effect both on the lower artisan class, who found themselves temporarily without work, and on the upper-class moneylenders, who were now forced to write off many loans because of Muslim and Christian inability to pay. However, contrary to Malachi, 'The Jews in the Druze Revolt' (Heb.), 111, I think that the long-term economic effects were not great, as Brawer, 'The Jews of Damascus' (Heb.), 83, has already noted.

were supported by many prominent figures in Damascus, including foreign consuls, the French commander Beaufort, and the exiled Algerian emir 'Abd al-Qadir.[56] Nonetheless, similar assertions continued to seethe beneath the surface of Jewish–Christian relations throughout the coming years, and were again disseminated, both in Damascus and in the British press, in late November 1870. The allegations pinpointed supposed profits from dealing in looted Christian goods as the source of the wealthy Jews' enormous economic power.[57] In actuality, the Jews did benefit greatly in the aftermath of the riots: paradoxically, not through profits from booty, but through Christian dependence on Jewish wealth. On the one hand, the reparations committee established that the compensatory treasury bonds awarded to the Christians could not be redeemed before their due date. At the same time, the committee allowed the bonds to be traded on the free market. Individuals in desperate need of cash sold the bonds to Jewish bankers for 70 per cent of their value. Then, when the money from the special tax imposed on the Muslims was directed to other purposes, delaying payment of reparations and redemption of the bonds, the immediate upshot was the devaluation of the bonds and their holders' desire to unload them at any price, for fear that the Ottoman authorities would not redeem them at all. The Jewish bankers took advantage of this state of affairs to purchase the bonds at half their face value. European traders, believing that the European powers would force the Ottoman government to fulfil its guarantee to redeem the bonds, also sought to purchase these bonds, leading to a steep rise in their value and greatly enriching the Jewish bankers. Another source of Jewish profits was the Muslim need for cash to pay the fine that had been imposed on them, which forced them to borrow money from Jewish moneylenders at an extortionate interest rate of 35 per cent.[58] The impoverishment of the Christian merchants with whom they had formerly had to compete also gave the Jews absolute control of certain sectors of the Damascus markets.

The widespread view in Damascus was that Jewish wealth had increased at Christian and Muslim expense. Fuelling this belief were long-standing hostility, the Jewish escape from the massacre unscathed, minor Jewish dealing in the booty, and major Jewish involvement in trading in the compensatory treasury bonds. It was only in the late nineteenth century, when the Jewish community had lost its economic prominence, and the wealth of its elites no longer aroused Christian jealousy, that the accusation that the Jews had benefited from the calamity of others died down.[59]

---

[56] *Hamagid*, 42, 31 Oct. 1860, p. 275, 28 Nov. 1860, p. 183.

[57] Loewe (ed.), *Diaries of Sir Moses and Lady Montefiore*, ii. 233–5; Hyamson (ed.), *The British Consulate in Jerusalem*, ii. 352.

[58] AECPC, Turquie, Damas, vol. 7, pp. 256–8, Hecquard, 21 Jan. 1863; Mishaqa, *Eye-Witness Account* (Arab.), 188, 191; id., *Murder, Mayhem, Pillage, and Plunder*, 266–7.

[59] Mishaqa, *Eye-Witness Account* (Arab.), 188.

Another consequence of the weakening of the Damascus Christians' political and economic power was the cessation of blood libels. Although many continued to believe that Jews required Christian blood for ritual purposes, they no longer had the power to whip up hostility by making public accusations. Syrian Christian dependence on the Christian European powers—which no longer supported such blood libels—was one factor in silencing them; another was the action of the Ottoman authorities, who in accord with the firman granted by the sultan to Moses Montefiore blocked nearly every Christian attempt to start a blood libel. Thus from 1860 to the end of the century ritual murder accusations were rare.[60]

Christian hostility to Jews was also apparent in Aleppo, where the main Christian denominations were the Armenians and the Greek Orthodox. The members of the large Christian community in Aleppo had strong religious sensibilities and self-confidence. Overall, Christian–Jewish tension in Aleppo appears to have been grounded more in religious hostility than in economic factors.[61] The belief that Jews engaged in ritual murder, which remained alive in the minds of Aleppo Christians until the late nineteenth century, strongly influenced their attitude towards the Jews, as the French consul Victor Bertrand notes:

Les juifs d'Alep appartiennent à une secte farouche, dont la doctrine est secrète, à laquelle on attribue de barbares superstitions et des pratiques sanguinaires. C'est cette secte qu'on accuse d'avoir substitué au sacrifice d'un agneau prescrit lors de la Pâque par la loi de Moïse, le mélange de sang humain à la pâte des *Azymes*. De là l'horreur qu'ont ici les chrétiens des Israélites, et la haine qu'en retour ceux-ci leur manifestent en toute occasion.[62]

[The Aleppine Jews belong to a cruel sect, with secret doctrines, to which barbaric superstitions and ritual murder are attributed. This same sect is accused of utilizing human blood to knead the matzot, instead of sacrificing a lamb for the paschal sacrifice, as the Law of Moses commands. This is the source of Christian fear of Jews, and of the antagonistic response displayed by the latter at every opportunity.]

Against this background of loathing it is not surprising that blood libels circulated and that the performance of Jewish rituals, such as funerals, was frequently interfered with. For their part, the Muslim police did not put much effort into protecting the Jewish minority.[63] On rare occasions, Jewish antipathy towards Christians found an outlet in assaults. For example, on one

---

[60] Kean, *Among the Holy Places*, 334. On the firman granted to Montefiore, see Kushnir, 'The Firman of the Ottoman Sultan' (Heb.).

[61] On the religious fanaticism of Aleppine Christians, see AAIU, Syrie, III.E., Alep, 21, Behar, 22 Aug. 1870.

[62] AECCC, Alep, vol. 33, pp. 106–26, Bertrand, 21 Mar. 1865; emphasis in original.

[63] *Hamagid*, 9, 25 Feb. 1880, p. 76; for examples of Christian harassment, see AAIU, Syrie, III.E., Alep, 23, Behor, 6 Mar. 1879, 17 Apr. 1879, 2 June 1879.

occasion Jewish youths beat and humiliated a Capuchin monk, most probably in retribution for accusations that Jews had murdered Father Thomas in Damascus.[64] For the most part, the Jewish response to Christian hatred in Aleppo was indirect, taking the form of gloating over Christian troubles and inciting the Muslim mob against them. The joy displayed at the Christian downfall in the riots of 1850 provides a definitive example.

Among the main sources of Jewish–Christian friction in Aleppo were the many disagreements between the Picciotto family and various Catholic orders, including the Capuchins and the monks of the Terra Sancta monastery. On the surface, these disagreements were purely economic. Capuchin activity in the East began in 1626, with Aleppo as its first outpost. Later on it raised funds by renting shops to the Picciottos. The eighteenth century saw the beginning of a rent dispute between the parties, which later developed into a disagreement regarding the ownership of the shops. To outside observers, this dispute had religious overtones, with Jews taking on a Christian order. The French consul Philip Bentivoglio, who intervened in this dispute in 1858, described the means he used to persuade and even threaten the Picciottos, reporting that it was he who made the point that the general public would certainly view their hostility towards the Capuchins as a manifestation of religious hatred.[65] A year later, when the Picciottos prevented members of the Terra Sancta monastery from using a water source near their residence, they were accused of exacerbating Christian antagonism towards Jews and heightening interreligious tension.[66] These disputes climaxed in 1865. Even though primarily grounded in economic factors, in the public eye they were seen as a religious quarrel, and greed and profit-seeking were portrayed as innate Jewish characteristics.[67]

On the other hand, the Picciottos offered help to endangered Christians during the November 1850 upheaval, and assisted their rehabilitation after the riots. Some 200 Christians found refuge in the home of Raphael de Picciotto, the Russian and Prussian consul in Aleppo. Others hid in the home of the Austrian consul, Elijah de Picciotto.[68] The provision of refuge was indeed part and parcel of the Picciottos' consular obligation as representatives of Christian powers. In every contact between Picciottos and Christians, whether helpful or harmful, the Aleppine public had difficulty in severing the religious factor from ordinary, everyday relations; consequently they did not distinguish the fact that the Picciottos were merchants holding diplomatic posts from the fact that they were Jews.

[64] AECCC, Alep, vol. 30, p. 208, Guys, 10 May 1841.
[65] Ibid., vol. 32, p. 17, Bentivoglio, 17 June 1858.
[66] AECPC, Turquie, Alep, vol. 3, pp. 104–9, de Lafosse, 18 June 1859.
[67] Ibid., vol. 4, p. 157, Bertrand, 2 Aug. 1865; pp. 131–9, Bertrand, 12 July 1865.
[68] *JC*, 29 Nov. 1850, p. 63. On co-operation between the Jewish and the French and British consuls to punish the Muslim rioters, see FO 78/836, Werry to Rose, Aleppo, 24 Oct. 1850.

Jews between Catholics and Protestants

If Jewish–Catholic relations in nineteenth-century Syria, coloured by enmity
dating back for generations, were characterized by bitter animosity, this was
not true of the initial Jewish response to the Protestants, newcomers to the
Syrian arena. During the nineteenth century, a belief that the Jews' return to
their original land was imminent crystallized among millenarian groups affiliated with the evangelical movement in England. These groups, and their supporters, sought to hasten the End of Days by founding missionary societies
and dispatching emissaries around the world to spread the message of Christianity, devoting special attention to the Jews, and to oriental Jews in particular.[69] Underlying Protestant activity among oriental Jews was the notion
that the second messianic coming depended on the Jewish return to their land
and on their conversion to Christianity. Damascus and Aleppo were chosen
to house permanent Protestant missions not only because of their Jewish communities, but because they were way stations for caravans that travelled to Jewish settlements in Baghdad, Mosul, Persia, and Kurdistan several times yearly.
These far-flung communities suffered from a lack of sacred books, which they
ordered from Syria via commercial caravans, thereby creating an increased
demand for these books in Damascus and Aleppo. The basic Protestant missionary approach was to focus on the Syrian Jewish communities, and to use
their members as purveyors of translated missionary material to the more distant Jewish communities.[70] The missionaries were further attracted by Damascus' close connection to the cradle of Christianity and to Scripture, and by
the presence in Damascus and Aleppo of British consuls under whose aegis
they could operate.

When the first British Protestant missionaries arrived in Damascus in the
1820s, Jews and Catholics stonewalled their efforts to distribute missionary
tracts.[71] Against this background, the hospitality extended by the Syrian Jewish communities to the Protestant missionaries a couple of decades later, and
their toleration of efforts to convert them, in Damascus in particular, is striking. In describing the hospitality and generosity of the Aleppo Jews towards
European visitors, the traveller Israel Joseph Benjamin noted: 'But not only to
the members of his tribe and faith, but to every Christian traveler is the Jewish home open.'[72] Missionaries sent by the Scottish church who were active in
the region in 1839 testify that the Jews of Damascus, notwithstanding their

[69] See e.g. Kedem, 'Mid-Nineteenth-Century Anglican Eschatology' (Heb.); Vereté, 'The
Restoration of the Jews'. See also Harel, 'Latakia' (Heb.).

[70] Missionary literature is replete with examples of this approach. See, among others, Bonar
and M'Cheyne, Narrative of a Mission of Inquiry; Gidney, The History of the London Society, 256.

[71] AECADN, Damas, 01, Cote A/18/54, Damas, 31 July 1824.

[72] Benjamin, Eight Years in Asia and Africa, 48.

anti-Christian prejudices, greet the missionaries graciously, visit them, and 'willingly receive' their gospels and tracts.[73]

In 1843, the first Protestants to reach Damascus with an eye to encouraging Jews to convert to Christianity were the Reverend John Wilson of the United Presbyterian Mission of the Church of Scotland and the Reverend William Graham of the Irish Presbyterian Church. They recorded that they were warmly received by Chief Rabbi Hayim Maimon Tobi—who openly expressed enthusiasm for Graham's plan to settle and work in Damascus—and by the rabbi's wife, who reportedly graciously declared: 'our houses shall be one'.[74] The missionaries pledged to give the rabbi's young son a Hebrew Bible, and the rabbi, for his part, undertook to give them a tour of the Jewish quarter and of the *talmudei torah* for children, showing them two synagogues and biblical codices as well.[75]

Evidently the rabbi and his wife were unaware of the missionaries' intention to convert Jews to Christianity, both because the missionaries failed to make this clear, claiming to be primarily interested in scriptural study, and because the rabbi was above all pleased that Jew-loving Protestants were settling in Damascus, where hitherto the only Christians had been Jew-hating Catholics. Five years later, Rabbi Tobi favoured the apostate missionary Moses Margoliouth and his associate William Woodcock with a similar reception. They were his guests and, although they debated theological issues, they did so without rancour.[76] Other witnesses indicate that the chief rabbi was not alone in his friendly attitude towards the missionaries. During their visit, Graham and Wilson were welcomed by Rabbi Jacob Peretz, who later served as the *ḥakham bashi* in Damascus. A welcoming committee of four important Damascus rabbis, accompanied by the communal leaders, awaited the two missionaries in the Farhi household.[77] Protestant missionaries preached the 'Gospel' to a Jewish rabbi in the Jobar synagogue near Damascus and in the homes of the leading Damascus Jews.[78] In Aleppo, missionaries visited the great synagogue. The chief rabbi even summoned one missionary to meet him, albeit only to inform him graciously that he would find it difficult to fulfil his mission to convert the Jews.[79]

[73] Bonar and M'Cheyne, *Narrative of a Mission of Inquiry*, 527.

[74] Wilson, *The Lands of the Bible*, ii. 332.

[75] Ibid. 332–3. This intriguing phenomenon of the displaying of Jewish 'treasures' to missionaries recurs throughout the nineteenth century. The aspiration to see biblical codices was evidently linked to the scientific–theological study of the Bible by Protestant ministers. This phenomenon reached its height with the exhibiting of the Aleppo Codex and the granting of photographic rights to the converted missionary Joseph Segall. See Segall, *Travels through Northern Syria*, 95–8. See also Shamosh, *The 'Keter'* (Heb.), 53–5. On the various biblical codices in Damascus, see Harkavy, *New and Old* (Heb.), 102–6; Yellin, 'About the Biblical Codices' (Heb.); Harel, 'The Damascus Jewish Community' (Heb.), 145–6.   [76] Woodcock, *Scripture Lands*, 47.

[77] Wilson, *The Lands of the Bible*, ii. 334–5.

[78] M. Margoliouth, *A Pilgrimage to the Land of my Fathers*, ii. 249, 257.

[79] Gidney, *The History of the London Society*, 256–7.

By and large, it is the Protestant missionaries themselves who attest to this warm reception. But, even allowing for the fact that they may have exaggerated their success with an eye to gaining increased support for their efforts to convert the Jews, there is no doubt that the initial encounters between Jews and Protestants were friendly. In the early 1840s Jewish gratitude for Protestant assistance to the Jewish community, first and foremost by George Wildon Pieritz—who took a public stand in their favour during the 1840 Damascus affair and even published a manifesto in Europe defending the Jews—fuelled this favourable attitude.[80] References to this appreciation, accompanied by expressions of joy that the missionaries had founded a permanent mission in Damascus, appear in reports of nearly every meeting between Protestant missionaries and the heads of the Damascus Jewish community.[81] The perception of Protestants as Jew-loving Christians, in contrast to the local Catholics, was heightened among the Jews of Aleppo in June 1853, when a Protestant convert rescued the Jews from the consequences of the Greek Catholic patriarch's accusation that they had kidnapped a Christian youth, a jeweller's apprentice, for ritual purposes. The Protestant jeweller revealed to the Jews that the Catholics had hidden the boy in order to make these false charges.[82]

Another factor in the missionaries' favour was the fact that most of them were British, as Britain had been the primary protector of the Jews before, during, and after the Damascus affair. Furthermore, the Jewish scholars in particular admired the missionaries' expertise in Scripture and their knowledge of Hebrew, for their Catholic neighbours showed no particular interest in the Old Testament.[83] Now, for the first time, Syrian Jewish scholars had the opportunity to engage in dialogue with intellectuals from outside the Jewish community on the basis of a shared interest in the Jewish Scriptures, a dialogue facilitated by the fact that many of the missionaries were converts from Judaism and so shared a language with Syrian Jews. Jews also made use of the missionaries to replenish the small stock of Hebrew Bibles in Syria, which in turn gave the missionaries the opportunity to distribute prayer books, and Hebrew Bibles bound together with the New Testament—books that, because they were in Hebrew, at first aroused no suspicion.[84] Perhaps Jews also felt flattered to be the targets of missionary activity, seen at first as enlightened interest rather than fanatical pressure.[85]

---

[80] See Salomons, *An Account of the Recent Persecution*.

[81] See e.g. Wilson, *The Lands of the Bible*, ii. 332; M. Margoliouth, *Pilgrimage*, ii. 249; Gidney, *The History of the London Society*, 254. Following the Damascus affair there was increased interest among European Protestant societies and press in the fate of the Jews in the East and of Damascus Jews in particular. See e.g. *Jewish Intelligence*, 6 (1840), 200, 253, 255, 283, 287.

[82] *JC*, 19 Aug. 1853, p. 365.   [83] See e.g. Wilson, *The Lands of the Bible*, ii. 333–5.

[84] Gidney, *The History of the London Society*, 255; Tilt, *The Boat and the Caravan*, 413.

[85] AECADN, Damas, 5, Cote A/18/19, Devoize au Baron du Bourquency, Damas, 10 Oct. 1843; Wilson, *The Lands of the Bible*, ii. 330.

Jews and Protestants were also drawn together by their common experience of Catholic persecution in the East. The first Protestant missionaries to reach Syria were publicly denounced by the monks of the Terra Sancta monastery in Damascus, and Catholic subjects of the Sublime Porte were forbidden to rent them houses, to send their children to their schools, or even to accept Bibles from them. The Catholic orders also attempted to persuade other Christian denominations to follow their lead. It is possible that, beyond the theologically based enmity between the two Christian sects, local Catholics feared disruption of the delicate communal balance in Syria, anticipating that when the Muslims learned of the Protestants' missionary aims they would respond with new outbreaks of anti-Christian violence.[86] The Protestants certainly made use of their common cause with the Jews as targets of Catholic hostility to win Jewish trust and gain access to their houses and what they considered their greatest treasures—their biblical codices.[87]

When the Jews realized that the Protestants' amiability was aimed primarily at conversion, their attitude towards the newcomers altered. Paradoxically, these 'friends' posed a greater danger than the Catholics, who tended to remain completely apart from the Jews and engaged in virtually no missionary activity. Although Catholic-sponsored schools were open to Jews, their overwhelming concern was with the existing Christian population. Thus, for example, in 1841, only seven places in the Capuchin-run college in Aleppo were reserved for Jews, and six for Muslims.[88] Twenty years later there are reports of a small number of Jewish and Muslim students in the Franciscan college in Aleppo,[89] and in the first half of the 1850s six Jewish students were enrolled in the Lazarist school in Damascus. Ludwig August Frankl, who visited Damascus in the latter half of the decade, notes: 'Jews and Mohammedans sometimes send their children to the schools taught by the French missionaries of the order of St. Lazare, so that they may be instructed in languages and other important branches of education. The Rabbis do not object to their attendance.'[90] Nonetheless, it is clear that the activity of the Catholic orders among the Jews was marginal compared to that of the Protestants, who saw the bringing of the gospel to the Jews of the East as their main objective.

Protestant missionary activity proceeded by direct means—handing out Bibles, holding meetings and joint prayer sessions[91]—and also by indirect

---

[86] FO 78/538, Wood to Earl of Aberdeen, Damascus, 6 Oct. 1843. On Catholic animosity towards Protestants in Syria, see also Churchill, *Mount Lebanon*, i. 187–8.

[87] See M. Margoliouth, *Pilgrimage*, ii. 253.

[88] AECCC, Alep, vol. 30, p. 208, Guys, 10 May 1841; AECPC, Turquie, Alep, vol. 1, pp. 109–12, Guys, 24 May 1843; AECCC, Alep, vol. 33, pp. 106–26, Bertrand, 21 Mar. 1865.

[89] FO 78/1538, Skene to Bulwer, Alep, 4 Aug. 1860.

[90] Frankl, *The Jews in the East*, i. 297. For Christian schools in general, see Somel, 'Christian Community Schools'. For Austrian Catholic missionary activity in Aleppo and Lebanon from 1833 to 1860, see HHSTA, Adm. Reg., F60/25.　　[91] Tilt, *The Boat and the Caravan*, 413.

means, such as the founding of hospitals and other welfare institutions.[92] Schools were founded for girls, targeted especially at poor families. In 1854 some forty Jewish girls were enrolled in the Protestant school.[93] Christian travellers applauded the very fact that Christian and Jewish children not only studied together but played together like sisters.[94] In 1854, however, the rabbis in Aleppo issued a ban on any contact with Protestants.

The turning point, at which the Protestant missions were openly declared a danger to the Jewish communities, took place in summer 1854. In May that year the Protestant sect was awarded recognition as a millet, entitled to the same privileges and status as other Christian sects. This step aroused jealousy and concern among the Catholic communities, which took rapid action aimed at halting the spread of Protestantism in Syria. For fear that many Catholics would be tempted to send their children to study in the schools of the rival denomination, which offered free tuition, the thrust of their campaign focused on Protestant schools, whose student body came primarily from the lower classes, including Jews. As official recognition of the Protestants by the Ottoman authorities barred a frontal attack, the Catholics persuaded the rabbis to declare an official ban on those visiting or sending their children to Protestant schools.[95] Although the ban was soon lifted, under pressure from the British consul (as described in Chapter 10 below), it marks a crossroads in the Jewish attitude towards Protestantism, to the extent of joining their sworn enemies, the local Catholics, in a joint front to counter Protestant inroads.

Education lay at the heart of the battle. The flight of the members of the Catholic orders from Damascus as a result of the July 1860 riots created a shortage of schools.[96] When the riots ended and the refugees returned to Damascus, this state of affairs, along with the greater attention of European powers to the intersectarian struggle in Syria, brought about a surge in Catholic and Protestant missionary activity, with a primary emphasis on education. Schools were founded at various levels, stimulating cultural life in Syria and even contributing to the rebirth of the Arabic language.[97] This turn of events had a marked impact on the Jewish community's attitude towards Christian educational institutions. Now Jewish children were enrolled in these schools not only because they offered tuition free of charge, but also because they recognized the importance of modern education for their young people. In 1875 the

[92] Gidney, *The History of the London Society*, 256–7.
[93] Porter, *Five Years in Damascus*, i. 146.   [94] *JC*, 11 Jan. 1856, p. 443.
[95] FO 78/1029, Wood to Earl of Clarendon, Damascus, 2 Sept. 1854.
[96] AECPC, Turquie, Damas, vol. 8, pp. 150–3, Hecquard, 20 Feb. 1864. The nuns engaged mainly in education and in humanitarian medical aid. Thus, in Nov.–Dec. 1854, of the 6,696 patients treated, 5,361 were Muslim, 1,019 Christian, and 316 Jewish (189 women and 127 men). See AECCC, Damas, vol. 3, p. 306, Edmond de Barrère, 25 Jan. 1855. On the school founded by the nuns, see FO 78/1118, Wood to Earl of Clarendon, Damascus, 5 Jan. 1855.
[97] Ma'oz, *Ottoman Reform*, 242. See also Tibawi, *American Interests in Syria*, 152–5.

Jewish traveller Wolf (William) Schur noted that many of Aleppo's Jews were sending their children to the Alliance school or to Christian-run institutions for this reason.[98] A few years earlier, the growth in the number of Jewish children from affluent families in the British Syrian School in Damascus had forced the principal to expand the school in order to provide enough places for poor and orphaned Jewish children.[99]

Protestant missionaries also penetrated the Jewish community via its lack of educational facilities for girls, even among the upper echelons of Jewish society. Scores of Jewish girls, in both Aleppo and Damascus, enrolled in Christian schools after visits by female missionaries, who enticed Jewish families to send their daughters to these institutions to study 'language, and literature, and womanly household crafts', in addition to paying one and a half francs for each girl coming under their wing.[100] The wealthy stratum of the Jewish community, in Aleppo in particular, used the threat of enrolling their children in these Christian institutions as a tactic in its conflict with the principals of the Alliance schools.[101] Nonetheless, there is also evidence that Muslims and Christians sent their children to the Alliance school, which they valued for its academic prowess and the access it provided to French culture.[102] One Alliance principal in Aleppo, motivated by ideals of universalist education and religious tolerance, even arranged meetings between his pupils and pupils from the Terra Sancta school.[103]

Alongside their educational activity, the Protestants continued to try to convert Jews directly. This endeavour was led by the London Society for Promoting Christianity amongst the Jews. Although it had no permanent mission in Damascus until 1870, the society's Jerusalem-based missionaries began to make annual visits to the Damascus Jewish community from 1863, even renting a room in the Jewish quarter where Jews could obtain books and medicines.[104] In September 1870 the missionary E. B. Frankel, a convert from Judaism, took up permanent residence in Damascus. As well as distributing books, he preached in public and printed a weekly sermon in Hebrew, which he pasted on the walls of the Jewish quarter every Saturday. He also founded

---

[98] Schur, *Maḥazot haḥayim*, 10. It is possible that the founding of Alliance schools in the Middle East was in response to, and imitated, the model of missionary educational activity, particularly with regard to the teachers' devotion to their task of spreading their socio-cultural message. In this context, see Zohar, 'Quelques réflexions' (Heb.), 31–5.

[99] FO 78/2051, Elizabeth Maria Thompson to Rogers, Damascus, 8 June 1868.

[100] AAIU, Syrie, XXI.E. Damas, 222, Weisskopf, 6 Oct. 1868; II.E., Alep, 11, Altaras, 12 July 1869, 19 Sept. 1871, 2 Sept. 1880; III.E., Alep, 21, Behar, 1 Sept. 1871; IV.E., Alep, 50, Gubbay, 10 June 1880.

[101] Ibid., XVII.E., Damas, 160, Heymann, 21 May 1865; VIII.E., Alep, 68, Moïse de Piccioto, 29 June 1879.

[102] Ibid., III.E., Alep, 21, Behar, 13 Nov. 1869, 22 Feb. 1870; *BAIU*, 2ème sem. 1871–1er sem. 1872, 128.   [103] AAIU, Syrie, III.E., Alep, 23, Behor, 24 July 1879.

[104] Gidney, *The History of the London Society*, 380–1. On the London Society, see also Perry, *British Mission to the Jews*.

an evening school, where, in order to attract Jews, he appointed a Hebrew teacher from the Jewish community. Apparently, unlike his predecessors, Frankel enjoyed some limited success in persuading Jews to be baptized as Christians. This aroused antagonism among the rabbis, who again declared a ban on any Jewish contact with the Protestants. As a result, the Hebrew teacher resigned his post and Jews stopped attending Frankel's sermons. The mission's response differed, however, from the usual pattern of retreat and recovery: this time the Protestants blamed the Jews for hampering missionary activity, taking their claim that they aimed only to spread education and culture, not to contradict Judaism and its institutions, to the British consul.[105] Tension peaked when members of the London Society threatened that if the ban were not withdrawn they would publicize allegations of Jewish extremism in Europe and incite the Muslims against the Jews, renewing accusations of ritual murder.[106] As in 1854, under pressure from the British consul the ban was withdrawn.

Although they attracted some Jews to their educational and medical institutions, with the exception of the few baptisms performed by Frankel the Protestant missionaries did not enjoy much success in their main objective. The chroniclers of missionary activity in Syria, and zealous Christian travellers, could not hide their disappointment at the failure of Damascus Jews to convert.[107] This lack of success is attributable to the absence of social incentive to espouse Christianity in Syria, where Jewish converts to Christianity would have remained *dhimmis*, without any improvement in their social standing. For the same reason, education in mission schools was not perceived as particularly threatening to Jewish existence in the Middle Eastern Jewish communities. It is likely that studying with Christian children fostered, to some extent at least, the removal of barriers and the weaving of broader social relationships. In the late 1840s Jewish girls in Damascus visited their friends from upper-class Christian families, and girls from both denominations participated jointly in various social functions. A significant indication of the close relations created by these contacts is the boycott by Christian girls, as a sign of identification with their Jewish friends, of a dinner given by the British vice consul for the wife of the French consul, viewed with hostility by Jews since the Damascus affair.[108] These relationships also promoted business partnerships between Jews and Christians, and preserved the basically positive attitude of the rabbis towards educated Christians who were experts in Scripture, as long as the latter did not engage in missionary activity.[109] Yet this growing closeness failed to gain momentum, or

---

[105] FO 78/2242, Green to Granville, Damascus, 29 Feb. 1872.

[106] *JC*, 14 Mar. 1873, p. 730, 21 Mar. 1873, p. 750.

[107] I. Burton, *The Inner Life of Syria*, i. 136; Gidney, *The History of the London Society*, 459; Jessup, *Fifty-three Years in Syria*, i. 231.   [108] Martineau, *Eastern Life*, 462–3.

[109] On such a business partnership, see Abulafia, *Penei yitsḥak*, ii. 4*a*, no. 1. For evidence of Rabbi Isaac Abulafia's friendly attitude towards Christians, see Weld, *Sacred Palmlands*, 281.

to develop into wider social contacts; and this was mainly because the Christians were engaged in moving closer to the Muslims during the period of the building of a Syrian national identity, a process of which Jews did not feel a part.

Political Cooperation: Syrian Nationalism

The 1840s and 1850s saw the development of limited but important moves within Syria by some who sought to split off from the Turkish-administered Ottoman empire and to join a new framework: an Arab state under the leadership of the *sharif* of Mecca. A separate development began to take shape after the 1860 riots in Damascus. Notwithstanding its religious nature, mission education, which gained momentum in the wake of the massacre, contributed to the creation of an important cultural movement. In essence, the 1870s saw the beginning of the formation of a 'neutral society', in which Syrian Muslim and Christian intellectuals could meet and co-operate without regard to religious affiliation. Uniting the members of the different religions was an idea of 'Syrian patriotism', grounded in the shared Arabic language, the Syrian homeland and its culture, and the principle of secularism. Some see these principles as an outgrowth of the 1860 massacre, which instilled in a small group of Syrian Christians who witnessed the suffering of their co-religionists the understanding that religious loyalty constituted a dangerous foundation for collective political life. This recognition, coupled with the influence of European ideas that they sought to inculcate in Syria, sparked a search for a common secular basis for the founding of a new Syrian society.

Thus we must distinguish between two intellectual movements, one resting on an Arab Muslim identity and loyalty, the other on a secular Syrian Arab identity. Ideologically, the latter movement shared its goals with the Ottoman reform movement; but it was in the minority. The greater part of Muslim society found these ideas unacceptable, viewing their proponents as rivals seeking to transform state and society. The Muslim population's primary loyalty was to a religious state with a political structure determined by Islamic doctrine. Political change based on any other principles aroused Muslim fears of loss of dominance. It was only in the late nineteenth century that these two opposing trends—an Arab Muslim movement seeking to separate from the empire but opposing the spirit of the Tanzimat, and a secular and patriotic Christian–Muslim movement that supported the reforms—united to become a single national movement.[110]

This analysis raises the question of whether Syrian Jews could have found a place in either of these movements, eventually becoming part of the Syrian

[110] For a comprehensive treatment, see Ma'oz, *Ottoman Reform*, 242–8. See also Commins, 'Religious Reformers and Arabists in Damascus'; Rogan, 'Sectarianism and Social Conflict in Damascus'; Philipp, 'Identities and Loyalties in Bilad al-Sham'.

national movement, as Jews in Europe were incorporated into, and even became leaders of, various national movements. For Syrian Jews, this was impossible. Jews had no shared cultural or political base with these movements, nor did Jewish intellectuals in Damascus and Aleppo have a common language with their Arab counterparts. Graduates of Alliance schools had a western, not an eastern, orientation. No Jewish encounter or dialogue took place with their intellectual counterparts among Christians or Muslims because as yet there was no joint cultural base or even curiosity that could lead either to mutual understanding or to the breaking of centuries-old patterns of interreligious relations.

Overall, then, the relationship between Jews and their neighbours in Syria continued to be one generally of separation. If there was greater communication between Jews and non-Jews, this took place on the everyday level and not on any higher cultural plane. We have no evidence for any interest on the part of Jewish intellectuals in Arabic writings, and they certainly did not participate in local Arab cultural activity, as their counterparts did in Iraq, for example.[111] The Syrian Jewish communal leadership restricted itself to administering its own affairs and did not seek incorporation into the general political framework.[112] It must also be noted that the ideas of Syrian nationalism not only were absent from the Jewish intellectual repertoire but had no purchase on the majority of the Syrian population, remaining restricted to narrow social circles. The social referents of most of the population remained, as they had been for centuries, the more restricted frameworks of family and religion. The religious zealotry and enmity that had permeated Syrian society, and continued to do so, did not encourage any attempt to breach these established frameworks.[113] Consequently, Syrian Jews did not view the surrounding society as an environment they might enter, and did not seek to share its culture, problems, or dreams; nor did enlightened Muslims and Christians show any interest in Jewish problems or aspirations during this period. Concern with Jewish national longing, and pressure to identify with the Syrian nation, came to the fore only when Zionist aims clashed with Arab Syrian nationalism.[114]

Strong communal ties, and the inability to disengage from these except through conversion, bound Jews within the established frameworks. Because the Arab Muslim movement demanded religious identification, and the patriotic movement called for secularism and an Arab identity, by their very nature

[111] In Beirut, Jewish intellectuals engaged actively with questions also of interest to Arab intellectuals, both Muslim and Christian. See Moreh and Sadgrove, *Jewish Contributions to Nineteenth-Century Arabic Theatre*, 74.

[112] Khoury, *Urban Notables and Arab Nationalism*, 45–6. For a valuable discussion of the integration of Jews in the Ottoman empire's Arab districts in the various political and ideological streams, see Masters, *Christians and Jews*, 174–5.

[113] For a more extensive treatment, see Ma'oz, *Modern Syria*, 47–8.

[114] See Harel, "'Great Progress'" (Heb.), 83–91.

the emerging movements and frameworks could not encompass Jews. The closer ties with, and dependence on, Jewish communities in Europe fostered by the Damascus affair, alongside the founding of Alliance schools in Syria, strengthened Jewish identity—on a religious basis with nationalistic elements —and prevented the formation of a Syrian national, or all-Ottoman, identity. This separatist tendency, coupled with the decline in Jewish importance to, and influence on, the local Syrian economy, pushed the Syrian Jewish communities to the periphery of Syrian society. In this respect, the Alliance doctrine calling for 'assimilation'—as the proper way for modern Jews to remain Jewish, yet be fully integrated in the national societies in which they lived— failed.[115]

The lack of Jewish participation in any political activity, and their loss of status in Syrian society, stood out in the first general elections held throughout the Ottoman empire in early 1877. One hundred and twenty representatives from the various imperial districts, Muslim and non-Muslim, were elected to the Istanbul parliament. Although the representatives were chosen under official pressure, and there was widespread indifference to the elections throughout the empire, Jews were elected from other districts, but not from Syria.[116]

✳

The reforms of the Tanzimat fostered neither a sense of Syrian belonging nor an Ottoman or Syrian identity among Syrian Jewry. The Jews continued to perceive themselves as strangers in their homeland, subject to a fate different from that of their fellow Syrians. A prime factor in this state of affairs was the opening of a window on to the different world and culture of the West.

[115] See Schwarzfuchs (ed.), *L' 'Alliance' dans les communautés du bassin méditerranéen*, 4 (Hebrew section), IV (French section).

[116] Given the separatist tendencies of the Jews it is not surprising that no Jew appears in Zachs, *The Making of a Syrian Identity*. On the elections to the Ottoman parliament and the participation of non-Muslims in its activity, see Lewis, *The Emergence of Modern Turkey*, 164–5; Karal, 'Non-Muslim Representatives'; and Kayali, 'Jewish Representation'.

PART V

TURNING TO
THE WEST

TEN

'SHIPS OF FIRE'

Western influences began to penetrate the Middle East as early as the eighteenth century, manifested in the adoption of western dress, western-style military and administrative structures, and technological and economic developments. European ideas also infiltrated the East, transmitted by Muslim travellers and diplomats in Europe and by western visitors to the East, including teachers, missionaries, expert advisers, tourists, and European consuls. More specifically significant in the case of Syria, however, is Muhammad 'Ali's takeover of this region, which saw the opening of his regime to the West, politically, economically, and educationally. Egyptian rule brought the official inauguration of the first foreign consulates in Syria, whose presence fostered contacts between representatives of European Christian powers and the local Damascus population. With the return of Ottoman rule, western influence continued to intensify.

The most fundamental single contributory factor to the process of change was the launching in 1825 of a regular steamship service, which 'shrank' the Mediterranean, leading to a sharp rise in the number of travellers to and from Syria. As these vessels, referred to in rabbinic sources as 'ships of fire', plied their way between Europe and the Levant, the effects of the new traffic were described by Rabbi Isaac Abulafia, a member of the Damascus rabbinic court: 'From the cities of Ashkenaz [Europe] there are convoys by ship and many from there [Europe] come here [Syria] and many more go from here to there.'[1]

Other innovations affected daily life in Syria. These included faster and more comfortable land travel from the 1860s, with the paving of roads to carry stage-coaches, and improved communications, with the introduction of the telegraph to the large centres.[2] The forging of closer economic ties with Europe flooded local markets with European goods. Great advances in health and sanitation services significantly lowered the incidence of epidemics in Syria. Western schools, mostly missionary institutions, comprised another significant agent of change, as already noted in previous chapters.

---

[1] Abulafia, *Penei yitshak*, ii. 36a.
[2] On the introduction of the stagecoach service to Damascus, see Tibawi, *A Modern History of Syria*; Ma'oz, *Ottoman Reform*, 167–9.

   The prevailing picture of the Syrian Jewish communities at the end of the
nineteenth century as backward perhaps conveys the misleading impression
that only a small degree of modernization reached Aleppo and Damascus, and
that even less penetrated the consciousness of their Jewish communities, with
the exception of the students in Alliance schools.[3] Given that western penetration was evident in every aspect of daily life during the period under consideration, impacting, directly and indirectly, on every single Ottoman
city-dweller, it is hard to accept that the Jewish communities were simply
unaware of it. Rather, the causes of isolation and insularity from westernization lie elsewhere. Undoubtedly, the infiltration of the East by western culture
challenged the traditional communities' attempt to preserve their way of life.
Even as Syrian Jews continued to adhere to Jewish and oriental tradition by
choice, they were profoundly influenced by European culture.[4]
   Western innovations made their way most rapidly into the homes of the
affluent elites and passed into the public sphere through their example. Contacts with western culture among the more affluent strata of the Jewish community were relatively broad and often unmediated, as for example when
European travellers to Damascus made the prescribed visits to the palatial
homes of the city's wealthy Jews, considered a not-to-be-missed tourist attraction.[5] In Aleppo, the western habits and practices of the Jewish elite—mainly
Francos who preserved their European ways—served as a model for the local
nouveau riche.[6] Commercial ties between the Jews of Aleppo and Damascus
and leading European mercantile centres also promoted the penetration of
European goods and manners into the homes of Jewish merchants. Dress styles
became more westernized, and even table manners underwent a change. As
early as 1856, Dr Ludwig August Frankl described a meal honouring Alphonse
de Rothschild at the home of a wealthy Damascus Jew: 'It is worthy of remark,
that we sat on four-legged chairs, and ate with knives and forks. This must be
regarded as a step in advance, and as a corruption introduced from Europe,
which has replaced the naïve process of eating with the fingers.'[7] Even in the
small community of Urfa the wealthy Jews had western table utensils, leading
one traveller to comment in 1875, 'At long last! The customs of the Jews here
will soon resemble European ones.'[8]

---

   [3] A claim was even made that 'life was carried on almost entirely in the same manner as in . . .
Baghdad . . . in the ninth century.' See J. A. D. Sutton, *Magic Carpet*, 177.
   [4] See Zenner, 'Jews in Late Ottoman Syria', 184.
   [5] See e.g. M. Margoliouth, *A Pilgrimage to the Land of my Fathers*, ii. 258–60; Woodcock, *Scripture Lands*, 44–6; John Wilson, *The Lands of the Bible*, ii. 330, 337; Benjamin, *Eight Years in Asia
and Africa*, 48.
   [6] See AAIU, Syrie, III.E., Alep, 21, Behar, 13 Nov. 1869; Neale, *Eight Years in Syria*, ii. 105;
Tibawi, *A Modern History of Syria*, 177.
   [7] Frankl, *The Jews in the East*, i. 277. On attire and household utensils, see Neumark, *A Journey in the Old Land* (Heb.), 66.   [8] Schur, *Maḥazot haḥayim*, 18.

Western ideas were also spread by the expanding Jewish press in many languages, which as a result of improved communications with Europe and the beginnings of Alliance activity in Syria began to infiltrate the wealthy and educated strata of the Syrian Jewish communities in the 1840s. By the late 1870s, as Rabbi Isaac Abulafia observed, it was widely known that 'newspapers and journals and periodicals constantly arrive from the cities of Ashkenaz'.[9]

Members of Syrian Jewish high society also had direct contact with European consular personnel at joint social gatherings, combining western etiquette with oriental cultural programmes, held in Jewish homes or in the homes of consular representatives.[10] Western travellers testify to the initial appearance of signs of westernization in the homes of the elites: 'Only in the homes of the wealthy in Damascus and Aleppo is there a European atmosphere.'[11] Thus a new bourgeois stratum emerged in Syrian Jewish society that identified with the West and its values. However, although awareness of change spread more widely through the Jewish community, most of its members continued to adhere to their traditional ways, either by choice or through lack of financial or social means to change.

Western Political Influence

Even the strata of Syrian society less influenced by direct contacts with European and western culture benefited from European political engagement in the affairs of the Ottoman empire as a whole and of Syria in particular. Historically, European involvement in the internal affairs of Syria began with the capitulation agreements of the seventeenth century. As the Ottoman empire began to crumble, this involvement expanded from the economic sphere to encompass promotion of political interests. One outcome of this broader role was the extension of protection to religious minorities and the application of pressure on the Ottoman authorities to improve their lot.[12]

In this struggle for influence, Britain and France were the main players in the region. Britain's Syrian interests stemmed from its long-standing ties with India. In line with its policy of preserving Ottoman territorial integrity against the constant threat from Russian attempts to weaken the empire and thereby gain access to the Mediterranean, Britain took steps to shore up the Ottoman regime and to counter Russian-incited agitation among the Slavic religious

[9] Abulafia, *Penei yitshak*, ii. 36a. On subscriptions to European periodicals, such as *L'Univers Israélite* and Alliance publications, see e.g. AAIU, Syrie, II.E., Alep, 11, Altaras, 10 Nov. 1864; III.E., Alep, 23, Behor, 11 May 1877; XI.E., Damas, 94, Halfon, 7 Apr. 1872; I.B., 5, Damas, Belilios, 20 Dec. 1875, 1 May 1879.

[10] I. Burton, *The Inner Life of Syria*, i. 143; Martineau, *Eastern Life*, 463.

[11] Neumark, *A Journey in the Old Land* (Heb.), 65. On the role of Jews and Christians as carriers of westernization, see Davison, 'The *Millets* as Agents of Change'.

[12] Friedman, 'The System of Capitulations', 281–3; Schlicht, 'The Role of Foreign Powers'.

minorities under its rule, such as the Greek Orthodox. France's affinity with Syria was rooted both in a centuries-long tradition of maintaining trading posts and consuls in the Levant and in its role as the recognized representative of European Catholic interests in the Ottoman empire, including the Christian holy places in the Middle East. Austria was concerned less with the Levant and more with its shared borders with the Ottoman empire, and with protecting its trade and religious interests.[13] Prussia had no direct interests in the empire during the period in question and adjusted its policy in accord with the shifting European balance of power.[14]

With the broadening of the capitulation agreements and the granting of consular protection to local individuals came more direct European interference in the empire's internal affairs. Each country granted protection to a different sector: Russia to the Slavs, the Greek Orthodox, and the Armenians; Catholic France and Austria to the Catholics; and Britain to the Jews. Lacking as yet any Protestant congregations in the empire requiring its protection, Britain sought to gain a stake in the local Ottoman regimes by taking the eastern Jewish communities under its wing. Through its Jewish protégés, Britain could lay claim to a role similar to that exercised by France and Russia.[15] Alongside these political considerations ran a profound British attachment to the Holy Land and its environs, which peaked with the messianic expectation of the Second Coming.[16]

On 12 April 1841 the Foreign Secretary, Lord Palmerston, directed all the British consuls in the Ottoman empire to guarantee Jewish rights under the Tanzimat, namely the protection of their lives, their property, their freedom of worship, and their honour. The sultan had promised the British ambassador in Istanbul that the regime would address every complaint involving injustice to, or abuse of, Jews; the consuls were instructed to observe the implementation of Jewish rights in their jurisdictions and to report any infringements to the embassy in the capital. It should be noted that Foreign Office directives limited British consular involvement to reporting such abuses to the Istanbul embassy;[17] any commitment to the welfare of Jews above and beyond this minimum requirement was at the individual consul's discretion, and the

---

[13] In some places Austria attempted to assume France's traditional role as protector of the Catholics. See e.g. HHSTA, Türkei, PA, XII/51/11D, Copie d'une phrase de la lettre du Consul de Pays Bas à Alep du 14 Janvier 1854.

[14] Duparc, *Turquie*, pp. xxvi–xxix; Goren and Ben-Arieh, 'Catholic Austria and Jerusalem'; Baron, 'Great Britain and Damascus Jewry', 179–80; Kedourie, *England and the Middle East*, 9–28; Churchill, *Mount Lebanon*, pp. v–xvi.

[15] Eliav, *The Land of Israel and its Jewish Settlement* (Heb.), 50. At the same time the British strengthened their ties with the Druze population. See Saleh, *History of the Druzes* (Heb.), 101–6.

[16] For a more extended treatment, see Jaffe, *A Portrait of The Land of Israel* (Heb.), 134–8; see also Baron, 'The Jews and the Syrian Massacres', 21.

[17] Hyamson (ed.), *The British Consulate in Jerusalem*, i. 35–41; FO 78/448, Werry to Palmerston, Aleppo, 28 July 1841.

consul's personal disposition would turn out to be critical in determining the extent of his involvement with, and protection of, the Jews in his jurisdiction.

Foreign intervention in the Damascus affair brought home to the city's Jews the advantages of consular protection. Given the pro-Catholic stance of the French, the chief accusers of the Jews, the outcome could have been very different if the Austrian and British representatives had not given their assistance.[18] This understanding is reflected in the appointment soon after the affair of Rabbi Hayim Maimon Tobi as the community's chief rabbi. Tobi, who held British citizenship, would thereby carry greater status both with the local regime and with the Damascus consular corps.

In the period before the Damascus affair only a limited number of Jews enjoyed foreign protection, and most of them were Tuscan, Austrian, Prussian, or Persian protégés, undoubtedly because Jews served as the consular representatives of these nations in both Damascus and Aleppo.[19] Thus, for example, a Picciotto served as Prussian consul in Damascus until 1846. Outstanding among these consular representatives was Joseph Elias, a Jew from Corfu, who served as Austrian consular secretary in Damascus from 1839, and as its official agent from May 1847. Highly educated, with a command of eight languages, and a successful merchant, Elias became a sought-after mediator in disputes between Muslims and Christians, and often stood in for the Austrian consul to the Damascus district.[20] However, in the years after the Damascus affair, and after the return of Ottoman rule to Syria, the leading consuls were those of Britain and France; the remainder, being for the most part local merchants, exercised little real influence. The British consul in Damascus from 1841 to 1855, Richard Wood, noted the lack of qualifications of the consular agents of Prussia, Greece, and the United States, describing, by way of example, the consular agent for Prussia, a Jew from the Picciotto family, as a twice-bankrupted

---

[18] Frankel, 'A Historiographical Oversight'; Eliav and Haider, *Österreich und das Heilige Land*, 40–1. See also HHSTA, Türkei, VI/74/403, Stürmen, Constantinople, 13 May 1840; Laurin, Alexandrie, 6 May 1840. For the recognition by Damascus Jews of Caspar Merlato's role in sparking international intervention for their release, see MC, 576: a song of praise to Montefiore by Shalom Mahadib Shakshouk.

[19] On Jews from Leghorn who lived in Damascus under Tuscan protection until its cancellation, see MC, 576, Leah de Farhi to Judith Montefiore, Damascus, 4 Tamuz 1849. For the complaints by the few Jews, mainly immigrants from Bukhara, Persia, and Afghanistan, regarding the Persian consul in Damascus, see MC, 576, Zebulun Baba Halevi and other merchants to Montefiore [Damascus, 1849].

[20] FO 195/226, Wood to Canning, Damascus, 18 May 1844. Elias served in the Austrian consulate until his death on 7 Iyar [8 May] 1870. For a sample of his reports, see HHSTA, PA, XXXVIII/98, Gödel-Lannoy für Schauenstein, Beirut, 25 Nov. 1853 (appendix). For a complete description of the services rendered by Elias and his son—a dragoman—to the Austrian consulate, see HHSTA, Adm. Reg., F4/82, Elias Moise au Ministère Imp. et Royal des affaires étrangères à Vienne, Damas, 28 Aug. 1900. On the founding of the Austrian consulate in Damascus and its consular representation, see the copy of d'Adelburg's report of 27 Aug. 1836 in HHSTA, Adm. Reg., F8/6.

merchant whose businesses were again on the verge of collapse at the time of his report.[21] Until the 1880s the British and French consuls in Damascus and Aleppo were the only ones to hold salaried positions as *consules missi*, whereas the others, representatives of weaker nations or of economic interests alone, received the honorific *consules electi*.[22]

Thus, with the Ottoman return to Syria, the struggle for spheres of influence in the region was reduced to two main players: Britain and France. Until 1860 almost no administrative sphere of government, from the treasury, to the judiciary, to purely political matters—including the protection of religious minorities—remained untouched by the consuls of these two nations.[23]

At the time Ottoman rule was re-established in Syria, France had a much lower status than Britain in Syrian eyes. In the complex international negotiations regarding the Ottoman empire's continued existence or dissolution, particularly with respect to the power struggle between the sultan and Muhammad 'Ali, France stood alone in supporting the Egyptian ruler, whereas Britain, Austria, Russia, and Prussia questioned the legality of the latter's takeover of Syria. The dispatching of a European fleet to Syrian shores in July 1840 accelerated the Egyptian withdrawal from Syria. Muhammad 'Ali discovered that France was not prepared to defend its policy via force, leaving him open to attack by the other powers. This French weakness did not go unnoticed in Syria, devaluing French protection, whereas Britain, which had proven itself a decisive, strong power, rose in Syrian estimation. Another mortal blow to French prestige in Damascus public opinion was dealt by the outcome of the Damascus affair, when the release of the Jews who had been accused of the ritual murder of Father Thomas betrayed the weakness of France's position as protector of Catholics.

Nevertheless, instructions issued by the French ambassador to Istanbul, Charles Edouard comte de Pontois, to the consul Ratti-Menton after the Damascus affair emphasized the need to protect Catholic subjects under similar circumstances in the future.[24] Accordingly, when the Damascus and European Jewish communities began to lobby for removal of the epitaph asserting Jewish guilt for Father Thomas's murder, France sided with the Catholics, perhaps hoping thereby to regain their trust. British backing for the Jews, and French backing for the Catholics, turned a dispute grounded in local antagonism between non-Muslim groups in Damascus into part of a broader power

[21] See FO 195/226, Wood to Canning, Damascus, 18 May 1844; 78/660B, Wood to Bidwell, Damascus, 7 Mar. 1846. Wood was evidently referring to Hillel de Picciotto, the nephew of Elijah de Picciotto, the Austrian consul in Aleppo. See HHSTA, Adm. Reg., F8/6, Metternich für Kübeck, Wien, 7 Feb. 1845, 28 Mar. 1845, 26 Apr. 1845.

[22] For a more detailed treatment, see Ma'oz, *Ottoman Reform*, 210–20.

[23] HHSTA, Adm. Reg., F8/38, Weckbecker für von Mensdorff-Pouilly, Wien, 23 Feb. 1865; Guys, *Voyage en Syrie*, 254.

[24] AECADN, Damas, 66, Pontois, Constantinople, 1 Mar. 1841.

struggle for influence in Syria. Nevertheless, although political considerations ensured the French foreign ministry's support of its representatives in Damascus, every new French consul posted to the city was convinced that the Jews were guilty of ritual murder, attributing their escape from punishment to the exertions of their European co-religionists and of the British government on their behalf, which in turn further weakened French status in Syria. From this perspective French suspicions regarding the British motivation for granting protection to the Harari brothers, who had been accused of criminal involvement in Father Thomas's murder, are understandable.[25]

When the French consul Anthony Devoize arrived in Damascus in February 1843, like every incoming office-holder he received courtesy visits from the heads of the communities and their notables; etiquette demanded that he visit their homes in turn. The heads of the Jewish community were among those who came to greet him, evidently hoping to open a fresh phase in their relationship with the French consulate following Ratti-Menton's transfer. Among those attending the reception were the Harari brothers, but the fact that they had been accused in the Damascus affair was made known to Devoize only after their departure. In his report to the French foreign ministry Devoize stated his intention to omit the Hararis from the return courtesy visits to the homes of Jewish notables, feeling that such a step would win the affection and understanding of all Catholics in Damascus.[26]

For their part, the heads of the Jewish community left this meeting encouraged by their gracious reception and with hopes for an improved relationship with the French consulate.[27] But these aspirations were disappointed: the French continued to grasp at every opportunity to assert Jewish guilt. In March 1845, when a freed slave from a Harari household 'confessed' to her physician that she had witnessed Father Thomas's murder in her master's home, the French consulate hastened to take an official deposition of her testimony from the doctor.[28] Two years later, the French consular agent Jean-Baptiste Beaudin was chief among those calling upon the governor to order a search of Jewish homes for a missing Christian child.[29] In his report to the foreign ministry, the new French consul, Victor de Bourville, backed Beaudin's action: 'Il a évidemment agi sous l'influence d'une prévention malheureusement trop fondée

---

[25] AECCC, Damas, vol. 1, p. 117, Devoize, 8 Mar. 1843. On the granting of British protection to the Harari brothers, see FO 78/447, Wood to Bidwell, Damascus, 29 Sept. 1841.

[26] AECCC, Damas, vol. 1, p. 117, Devoize, 8 Mar. 1843. See also Belgiojoso-Trivulzio, *Asie Mineure et Syrie*, 302.   [27] See *Voice of Jacob*, II, no. 48, 9 June 1843, p. 183.

[28] As described in Chapter 9, the claim was subsequently shown to be groundless.

[29] AECPC, Turquie, Damas, vol. 1, p. 265, copy of a letter addressed to His Highness Sefata Pasha by Monsieur Beaudin, Damascus, 22 Apr. 1847. The letter is also found as an appendix in FO 78/714, Timoni to Wellesley, Damascus, 19 May 1847. A copy is also housed in BofD, ACC/3121/A/6, pp. 69–70. See also Loewe (ed.), *Diaries of Sir Moses and Lady Montefiore*, ii. 3 ff.; *JC*, 17 Sept. 1847, p. 242.

depuis le lamentable événement du Père Thomas.' (He evidently acted under
the influence of an unfortunately well-founded suspicion, after the lamentable Father Thomas affair.)[30] Bourville's radical anti-Jewish position took
the extreme form of refusal to receive even French Jewish citizens or French
Jewish consular protégés. Beaudin was even heard to declare that Bourville
intended to withdraw French protection from all Jews.[31] This attitude aroused
fresh Jewish anger against the French, who were now considered the sworn
enemies of the Jews.

It must be noted, however, that the French foreign ministry in Paris did
not always see eye-to-eye with its representatives in Damascus regarding the
latters' anti-Jewish activity. Even though forced by larger political concerns to
support the Damascus consular staff, the foreign minister Guizot in particular found their actions objectionable. In response to complaints by Moses
Montefiore and the British ambassador to Paris, Guizot stressed that Beaudin
was not acting as an official French representative and that the anti-Jewish
activity in Damascus did not reflect the French disposition towards the Jewish
people. Instructions calling upon the French representatives in Syria not simply to discourage, but to fight, blood libels, succeeded to some extent in
restraining anti-Jewish activity by the Damascus consulate's Jew-hating staff.[32]

Notwithstanding Guizot's protestations, Palmerston continued to attribute
the rekindling of the blood libel and of anti-Jewish feelings in Damascus generally to the representatives of France in the East, and instructed British representatives there to back the Jews. The epitaph on Father Thomas's tomb
became a major political issue in the British–French struggle for influence in
Damascus and for primacy in Syrian public opinion. Successive French consuls were united in their opinion that open British support for the Jewish
request was aimed at showing French influence and goals in a negative light,
and that the ultimate goal of British consular activity was to increase its already
considerable influence over the Jews. In response to repeated British requests
to remove the epitaph, Pierre Duperron de Ségur, French consul in 1849–50,
replied:

cette démarche du gouvernement anglais ne pouvait avoir qu'un but: celui d'éten-
dre l'influence que l'Angleterre exerce déjà sur un grand nombre d'Israélites de cette
ville; sans cela, en effet, quel intérêt pourrait avoir la Grand Bretagne, pays et gouvernement chrétien, à la disparition d'une inscription de cette espèce, existant dans
une ville qu'on visite peu, et dans une église que les étrangers ne visitent pas.[33]

[This step by the English government has but one objective: to extend the influence
that England already exercises over a large number of Israelites in this city; without

---

[30] AECPC, Turquie, Damas, vol. 1, p. 272, Bourville, 28 Sept. 1847.
[31] FO 195/291, Timoni to Cowley, Damascus, 1 Sept. 1847.   [32] Ibid.
[33] AECPC, Turquie, Damas, vol. 2, p. 132, de Ségur, 12 Dec. 1850.

there being, in effect, any interest on Great Britain's part, a Christian government and country, in the removal of an inscription of this nature, found in a little-visited city, in a church unvisited by foreigners.]

De Ségur feared that to accede to Britain's demand would not only increase British influence over the Jews but also decrease French influence over Syrian Christians. He declared the question of the epitaph to be a complex matter, one to be addressed carefully with the Jews without alienating the Christians. Any other path would, in his opinion, reward Britain with victory.

From de Ségur's remarks it is clear that the French consuls found themselves in a 'catch-22' situation: in the context of the campaign to remove the epitaph, France was perceived as consistently taking the Christian side, pushing the Jews into British arms; however, if France were to reverse its policy, this might be interpreted as surrender to Britain, which would further encourage Jews to seek the stronger British protection, and would also disappoint the Christians, who would themselves turn to other protectors.

In the event, the French adhered to their policy of unconditional backing for the Christians. De Ségur's successor, Maxim Outrey (consul from 1855 to 1861), unequivocally believed in Jewish responsibility for Father Thomas's death, and testified that the murder, which he said had placed a mark of Cain on the Jewish community, was in 1856 still alive in Damascus' popular memory. He asserted that all Syrians, even children, knew of this episode's circumstances and could identify the murderers, who were still respected, wealthy Damascus citizens. In his opinion, Jews should realize that their stubborn insistence on the epitaph's removal simply heightened Christian suspicions, and that time alone could erase the memory of the past. His remarks make it apparent that responsibility for erecting the stone bearing the epitaph on Father Thomas's grave lay with the French consulate. Even if it had been carried out in conjunction with the Capuchin order, as Outrey contends, this by no means diminishes French responsibility for deepening the roots of anti-Jewish hatred and for propagating a 'tradition' of ritual murder accusations in Damascus.

British efforts to have the epitaph removed, including direct intervention by Palmerston, failed to achieve the desired result. Only during the July 1860 massacre of Christians were the tomb and epitaph destroyed, along with the Capuchin monastery.[34] Nonetheless, the Damascus Jews were grateful for British activity on their behalf, especially in repudiating the accusations of ritual murder.[35]

The events of 1860 mark a watershed in the relationship between the Damascus Jewish community and the French consulate. Although England

---

[34] The epitaph was restored at a later date and the gravestone reset. See AAIU, Syrie, XVI.E., Damas, 151c, Loupo, 27 June 1919.

[35] FO 195/291, Timoni to Cowley, Damascus, 1 Sept. 1847.

remained the chief protector of the Jews, several factors brought about note-worthy improvement in Jewish–French relations: the depleted Christian con-gregations in the wake of the massacre; the arrival of a new French consul personally well disposed towards the Jews; and the beginning of activity in Damascus by the Alliance Israélite Universelle, the bearer of French culture to the Jewish communities of the East. Weakened economically by the mas-sacre, notwithstanding promised compensation and European assistance funds, and numerically by the flight of many Christians from Damascus, the remain-ing Christian community had lost much of its political power, making it more dependent on European powers.[36] The French representatives, for their part, now less fearful of a hostile Christian reaction to any signs of French assistance to Jews, felt able to shift their stance. Even Outrey, late in his tenure, obeyed strict orders from the French foreign minister to protect Jews from harm after the massacre, though he made no special efforts to assist them.[37] The Damas-cus Jews immediately sensed this improvement in Outrey's attitude, as they stated in a letter to Albert Cohn in Paris:

When our master's [Cohn's] letters reached all the consuls, the French consul in par-ticular, all of the officials softened their views, and the attribute of mercy triumphed ... especially the letter to the French consul, may he be exalted, for all the Christian notables who falsely accuse Israel gather under his aegis, and when they saw that the consul had softened and no longer sought the destruction of Israel ... they too returned from their evil ways and were silent and issued no more false accusations.[38]

Relations between the Jewish community and the French consulate in Dam-ascus under Outrey continued to thaw, and the Jews began to regard the French with less suspicion than formerly. This relationship progressed to the extent that the Jews expressed sorrow upon Outrey's departure from Damascus.[39]

Outrey's successor Hyacinthe Hecquard, consul from 1862 to 1866, per-sonifies the transformation in the French consulate's attitude towards the Jews of Damascus, on whose behalf he worked tirelessly. As he read the situation, if France could take credit for the waning of religious fanaticism in Damascus, and attract greater confidence on the part of both Europeans and the non-Muslim minorities, this would redound to the benefit of French influence in Syria.[40] Certainly, the landing of French forces on the Syrian shore to come to the rescue of the Christians in 1860, in marked contrast to French inaction in 1840, advanced France's standing in the eyes of the Syrian population.

[36] On the economic damage and on the assistance funds, some of which were founded at the initiative of European Jews—notable among them Adolphe Crémieux and Moses Montefiore—see Leven, *Cinquante ans d'histoire*, ii. 395–6.
[37] See *JC*, 30 Nov. 1860, p. 6; FO 406/10, Brant to Russell, Beirut, 8 Nov. 1860.
[38] *Hamagid*, 46, 28 Nov. 1860, p. 183.
[39] AECCC, Damas, vol. 4, p. 84, Lanusse, 24 Jan. 1862.
[40] AECPC, Turquie, Damas, vol. 8, pp. 208–10, Hecquard, 4 Aug. 1864.

Hecquard was the first to understand that drawing in the Jews as well was essential to widening French influence. To his mind, this could be achieved by demonstrating religious toleration and by encouraging the widespread introduction of the French language and culture to the Syrian population.[41]

Hecquard's approach found a responsive audience in the Paris-based Alliance Israélite Universelle.[42] Close examination reveals that the first Alliance school in Damascus was founded at Hecquard's initiative.[43] Proceeding on two planes simultaneously, Hecquard both lobbied the Alliance to found a school in Damascus and at the same time promoted this initiative locally, encouraging the Jewish community to help fund the project by promising to provide any assistance necessary. His efforts met with success and plans commenced to construct a school.[44]

Although this French activity within the Jewish community certainly aroused British concern, the British consulate was unable to offer similar assistance, though it hoped to outstrip the French by persuading Moses Montefiore to contribute towards the construction of the school during his projected trip to Damascus. As the initial preparations were proceeding apace, the French remained confident that the building would be completed before Montefiore's expected arrival. In the event, Montefiore did not visit Damascus at that time, and the Jewish community's appreciation went largely to the French consul.[45] With the arrival of Albert Cohn to represent the Alliance at the cornerstone-laying ceremony for the school on 29 July 1864, the French consulate's status soared in Syrian Jewish eyes. The consulate was the starting point for the procession to the site, and it was here that all the invited notables, including the governor Mehmet Rashid Pasha and the British, Austrian, and Russian consuls, were to assemble.

Two days before the ceremony the British consul, Thomas Rogers, sent his regrets that he would be unable to attend owing to prior obligations that required him to travel to Baalbek. The participation of the entire European consular community and the head of the Damascus administration made his absence even more conspicuous. It is certainly possible that Rogers, who had an excellent personal rapport with the Jewish community, could not afford politically to be present at a ceremony in which France, not Britain, would take centre stage. Indeed, Albert Cohn's speech, delivered in French, not only

[41] Ibid., pp. 150–3, Hecquard, 20 Feb. 1864.

[42] On the influence of the interface between Alliance cultural activity and French interests in the Ottoman empire, see Rodrigue, *French Jews, Turkish Jews*, 145–57.

[43] See Leven, *Cinquante ans d'histoire*, ii. 15; *JC*, 5 Feb. 1864, p. 8. See also AAIU, Syrie, XI.E., Damas, 94, Hecquard au Président de l'AIU, 27 Feb. 1863.

[44] See Hecquard's correspondence in AAIU, Syrie, XI.E. Damas, 94, 27 Feb. 1863, 27 May 1864, 30 Dec. 1864, 5 Apr. 1866; extrait d'une lettre de Mr Hecquard Consul de France à Damas, 13 Nov. 1863. See also *BAIU*, Oct. 1864, p. 5.

[45] AECPC, Turquie, Damas, vol. 8, pp. 150–3, Hecquard, 20 Feb. 1864.

stressed France's central role in the founding of the school, but also highlighted France's pioneering emancipation of its Jews and showered extravagant praise on Emperor Napoleon III for assisting the Jews. The emperor's signature was engraved on the cornerstone, and a gold ring inscribed with the name of the sultan, 'Abd al-'Aziz, was placed inside it. At the ceremony's conclusion, the chief rabbi recited prayers for the welfare of the Ottoman sultan, the French emperor, the Russian tsar, and the Austrian emperor. Britain, hitherto the great protector of the Jews, received no mention.[46]

Hecquard consistently demonstrated his affection for the Jews and continued to work towards the opening of the school. When the first teacher dispatched by the Alliance arrived in Damascus, Hecquard dispatched a kavass from the consulate along with the chief rabbi, Jacob Peretz, to greet and accompany him.

However, despite this encouraging start, the school's construction ground to a halt as a result of a dispute among the Jewish notables who had agreed to fund it. The first to withdraw their support for the school were British protégés, followed by those of Austria and Prussia, which is suggestive of an indirect link to the British–French struggle for influence. After the project had been at a standstill for a year, Hecquard asked Rogers to compel the British subjects who had promised to fund the school at least to pay the schoolteacher Heymann's salary, so that he could return home.[47] At this stage neither the French consulate nor the Alliance was prepared to admit defeat, and a new teacher was dispatched eight months later. This teacher received the unconditional support of the new French consul, Alphonse Rousseau, who viewed the founding of a French Jewish school in Damascus as a worthy philanthropic project with the potential to spread the ideas of progress and civilization and also to strengthen French influence in the region.[48]

The French Jewish school in Damascus did not become an enduring reality for many more years: closed again in 1869, it did not reopen until 1880. Nonetheless, the French consulate's support and encouragement for the school, and the consuls' changed attitude towards the Jews, undoubtedly strengthened French influence within the Syrian Jewish community. More and more Jews sought to become French subjects—including Joseph Elias, the Austrian consular secretary who had hitherto held British citizenship.[49] Nevertheless,

[46] AECPC, Turquie, Damas, vol. 8, pp. 206–10, Hecquard, 4 Aug. 1864; *JC*, 2 Sept. 1864, p. 5.
[47] AECADN, Damas, 27, Cote A/18/42, Hecquard à Rogers, 23 Dec. 1865; AAIU, Syrie, XI.E., Damas, 94, Hecquard au Président de l'AIU, 5 Apr. 1866.
[48] AECCC, Damas, vol. 4, p. 395, Rousseau, 8 Nov. 1867; AAIU, Syrie, XI.E., Damas, 94, Rousseau au Secrétaire de Comité Central de l'AIU, 18 Oct. 1867.
[49] For additional data on Elias' British citizenship, see FO 78/579, Wood to Bidwell, Damascus, 26 June 1844; 78/660B, British merchants to Timoni, Damascus, 24 July 1846; FO 195/291, list of British subjects, Damascus, 1848. On the handling of his request for French citizenship, see AECCC, Damas, vol. 4, p. 250, Elias, 24 June 1864; AECADN, Damas, 27, Cote A/18/42,

Britain maintained its position as the prime protector of the Jewish community, and in the 1860s boasted the largest number of Jewish protégés, replacing Austria. Although growing French influence encroached on Britain's primacy among the Jews, as we shall see, greater damage was done to British interests by the hostility of some British consuls towards Jews, in contradiction to the directives of Her Majesty's Government.

Incentives for Seeking Consular Protection

Having seen the political advantages to European powers, Britain and France especially, of providing protection to the religious minorities in Syria, it remains to look at this phenomenon from the perspective of the Syrian Jews. Before the Damascus affair Jews sought consular protection mainly for its concomitant economic or mercantile advantages;[50] thereafter, the prime incentive was protection against the background of new ritual murder accusations. Britain, which emerged as the main protector of the Jews in the wake of the Damascus affair, inaugurated its protection of the Jews in this era with an impressive public act: the recall of the British consul Nathaniel W. Werry, who backed the accusers of the Jews. Werry's recall, and the posting in his stead of the more positively inclined Richard Wood, encouraged Jews wishing to become British protégés.[51] The first to approach the British with this request were the three Harari brothers who had been under suspicion in the Damascus affair. In their application they submitted that despite the restoration of their freedom, their return to their families, and their more secure day-to-day existence, yet

nevertheless we are still exposed to the momentary caprice of those who, tho' they succeeded not in their vile designs against us, have not ceased to be our enemies. Even now if by accident an individual is absent from his usual place of abode or resort, and his absence is unaccounted for by those around him, suspicion is immediately awakened against us and we are unhesitatingly accused of the crime of assassination.[52]

The wording of this request was suggested by a British colonel, Charles Henry Churchill, who was in Damascus at the time and advised the Harari brothers to place themselves beyond their enemies' reach by obtaining British

---

Hecquard au Vice-Consul de Grèce à Damas, 16 Dec. 1865; Hecquard à J. Elias Vice-Consul d'Autriche à Damas, 16 Dec. 1865.

[50] See Rozen, *In the Mediterranean Routes* (Heb.), 54. On related struggles, see Harel, 'The Status and Image of the Piccioto Family' (Heb.), 179.

[51] See Brawer, 'The Jews of Damascus' (Heb.), 92; Hyamson, 'The Damascus Affair', 47–52; Frankel, 'A Historiographical Oversight', 287.

[52] FO 78/1751, a copy of the letter from the Brothers Harari to Sir Moses Montefiore, Damascus, 24 May 1841.

passports and official British protection.[53] However, their arguments were deemed insufficient to justify the granting of protection, and the Hararis were asked to prove that one of their ancestors had held British citizenship. Upon their doing so, the Foreign Office then ratified their British citizenship.[54]

This success sparked requests for British citizenship by other branches of the Harari family. Although they were received favourably by Wood, he was unable to grant protection on his own initiative and requested instructions from the Foreign Office. Seeking to avoid conflict with the Ottomans on the grounds of too readily and unjustifiably granting protection to characters of unproven reputation, the current British policy was to discourage broad expansion of the circle of consular protégés and to accept as such only those individuals whose special status, or British employment, warranted it. Accordingly, the Foreign Office instructed Wood to deny the request for protection by other branches of the Harari family, at the same time clarifying that the protection granted to the three brothers—Isaac, Aaron, and David—was restricted to them and to their employees.[55] Thus in 1843 only a handful of Damascus Jewish families held British passports, including Joseph Elias and his family; Chief Rabbi Hayim Maimon Tobi, a native of Gibraltar, and his family; and the three Harari brothers and their families.[56]

Britain's high status, its favourable attitude towards Jews, and the commercial advantages accruing from its protection, brought additional requests from Jewish merchants and financiers to become British protégés. In 1848, of six British commercial houses in Damascus, five were Jewish-owned. A decade later, of the fourteen merchants with British citizenship or protection in Damascus, ten were Jews. By the late 1870s most of the British protégés and citizens in Damascus were Jews.[57]

In the 1840s, with the exception of a number of Algerian Jewish families that had migrated to Damascus, few Jewish families were under the protection of

[53] Ibid. On Colonel Churchill and his favourable attitude towards Jews, see Brawer, 'The Jews of Damascus' (Heb.), 88.

[54] FO 78/447, Bidwell to Wood, Foreign Office, 11 Aug. 1841; Wood to Bidwell, Damascus, 29 Sept. 1841. See also a copy of Wood's letter to the Harari brothers from 26 Sept. 1841 in BofD, Minute Book, ACC/3121/A/5/4, pp. 71–3.

[55] FO 78/498, Wood to Bidwell, Damascus, 28 May 1842; 78/499, Wood to Bidwell, Damascus, 24 Aug. 1842. On the granting of British protection to the Hararis in the coming years, see FO 372/1933, memorandum respecting the nationality of Mr Solomon Harari, E. Hertslet, 15 Mar. 1886.

[56] See Wilson, *The Lands of the Bible*, ii. 331; Belgiojoso-Trivulzio, *Asie Mineure et Syrie*, 292. For appeals by other members of the Harari family to Moses Montefiore for assistance in acquiring British protection, see MC, 576, Moses Harari and Najim Harari to Montefiore, undated [1849].

[57] FO 78/802, list of British mercantile houses established at Damascus, 1848; 78/1388, British and Prussian merchants to Brant, Damascus, 11 Dec. 1858; 195/1153, Jago to Layard, Damascus, 10 June 1877. For additional data for the 1850s, 1860s, and 1870s, see FO 78/873, Wood to Bidwell, Damascus, 31 Dec. 1851; 78/912, Wood to Malmesbury, Damascus, 31 Dec. 1852; 78/2260, Burton to Granville, Damascus, 28 Nov. 1870; Hyamson (ed.), *The British Consulate in Jerusalem*, ii. 353–8.

the French consulate. The status of Algerian-born individuals in the Ottoman territories was a contested issue: it was not clear whether the French conquest automatically entitled them to French citizenship or whether, because the Ottomans had ruled Algeria prior to the French conquest, they remained Ottoman subjects. Seeking to retain the allegiance of those former Algerians who had not completely severed their ties with their homeland, the French foreign ministry began to address this problem intensively in 1834. Nonetheless, hoping at the same time to rid itself of troublemakers and rebels and to prevent exploitation of this background to obtain French protection, France subjected any claims of Algerian origin to careful scrutiny.[58] In the early 1840s the French consulate looked after the affairs of some ten Algerian Jewish families, who, together with Algerian Muslims, were targeted by a hostile Ottoman regime which refused to recognize them as French citizens.[59]

Over time, the desire to obtain economic advantages and to escape payment of Ottoman taxes became prime incentives for Jews to seek the protection of European powers. Isaac Hayim Farhi's 1846 petition to the British Foreign Office for citizenship, which submitted that, because all the other affluent Jews already enjoyed some sort of consular protection, he alone was harassed for loans by the Ottoman authorities, is illustrative.[60] The Foreign Office having rejected this argument, Farhi then obtained a post as dragoman for the French consulate, liaising with the Algerian Jews who were still arriving in Damascus. By this means he became a French protégé. His relatives David and Nathaniel Farhi followed his lead: David became a Turkish-language clerk for the French consulate, and Nathaniel served as a treasurer.[61]

There were also cases in which an individual lost his protected status. In such instances, efforts were made to exchange it for protection by another country, as when, for example, in 1849 the Ottoman regime refused to recognize Tuscan protection. Several Jews with Tuscan citizenship turned to the French consulate with a request to be taken under its wing.[62]

[58] For more extensive treatments, see Bardin, *Algériens et Tunisiens*, 27–39; Buzpinar, 'The Question of Citizenship'. See also Schwarzfuchs, 'The Jews of Algeria' (Heb.).
[59] AECCC, Damas, vol. 1, pp. 019–023, Ratti-Menton, 21 Dec. 1839; p. 072, Ratti-Menton, 22 Feb. 1842; p. 117, Devoize, 8 Mar. 1843; AAIU, Syrie, XI.E., Damas, 94, Halfon au Comité Central de l'AIU, 23 Apr. 1877; Harel, 'The Citizenship of the Algerian-Jewish Immigrants'.
[60] FO 78/660B, Timoni to Bidwell, Damascus, 6 July 1846.
[61] AECADN, Constantinople, Correspondance avec les Echelles, Damas, 1846–53, tableau des protégés du Consulat de France à Damas, 1 Apr. 1849; AECCC, Damas, vol. 2, note des protégés actuels du Consulat de France à Damas, 1847; FO 406/10, Brant to Russell, Beirut, 8 Nov. 1860. On the growth in the number of Algerian Jews under French consular protection in Damascus, see AECCC, Damas, vol. 2, p. 146, tableau des protégés qui se sont présentés à la Chancellerie du Consulat de France à Damas pour y faire connaître leur titres, 1 Sept. 1847; AECPC, Turquie, Damas, vol. 2, pp. 23–30, Bourville, 2 Mar. 1848.
[62] Two factors determined the Jewish rapprochement with the French consulate in that year: (a) the growth in the number of Algerian Jews under French protection, which perhaps induced

In the 1840s some of the most respected and affluent Jewish families in Damascus, such as the Angel, Farhi, Lisbona, and Picciotto families, were Austrian protégés, a status they apparently achieved prior to the Egyptian conquest of Syria. Three families enjoyed Prussian protection: the Romano, Rofe (Hakhim), and Matalon households.[63] At times the Austrian consul took the Prussian protégés under his wing, and vice versa. The extension of protection at different stages by these two countries in particular was probably the result of service by the Picciottos, and later Joseph Elias, as their representatives in Damascus and Aleppo. In 1865, of twenty-two Austrian consular protégés in Damascus, twenty were extremely wealthy Jews defined as the backbone of the city's commerce.[64] In that year the Austrian foreign ministry sought to appoint a full-time vice consul in Damascus, a post temporarily filled by the consular secretary, Joseph Elias, from 4 December 1862. All of the candidates for the post were Jews: Joseph Elias himself, Hillel de Picciotto, and Shemaiah Angel, the preferred candidate.

One concern felt by the Austrian foreign ministry was whether a Jew could effectively discharge his duty as protector of the local Catholic population. However, as the Austrian consulate in Damascus provided no special protection for Catholic rites there, a role largely assumed by France and Spain, the Austrian consul general in Beirut, Peter Ritter von Weckbecker, did not see this as an impediment. Weckbecker was convinced that should occasion arise in which a Jewish consul was required to protect the Catholic population, he would faithfully follow his employers' instructions. Moreover, Weckbecker argued that in the Damascus context Angel's Jewish faith did not constitute a stumbling block because most of the Austrian citizens in Damascus were Jews, and that his appointment to this post would only enhance Angel's status in their eyes. In the final analysis, a dispute regarding what the Austrians saw as his excessive demands for payment apparently prevented Angel from receiving the appointment.[65]

---

warmer feelings towards the French among local Jews; and (b) the death on 23 July 1848 of the French consular agent Jean-Baptiste Beaudin, the sworn enemy of the Damascus Jews. See AECADN, Constantinople, Correspondance avec les Echelles, Damas, 1846–53, Combes à l'Ambassadeur à Constantinople, 31 July 1848; Nisim Farhi au Consul de France à Damas, 4 Apr. 1849; Levi à Garnier, Damas, 4 Apr. 1849.

[63] AECADN, Damas, 27, Cote A/18/42, Hecquard à Rogers, 23 Dec. 1865; Wilson, *The Lands of the Bible*, ii. 331. No data are available for the initiation of Prussian protection for Jewish subjects, or for why it was granted to these families in particular. Note the intriguing point that Damascus Jews believed the Prussian royal family to be Jewish. For a description of the Damascus Jews' enthusiastic reception of, and gestures of affection for, the Prussian prince Adalbert, see Poujade, *Le Liban et la Syrie*, 213–14. On the other hand, there are data for Prussian Jewish subjects in Damascus for later periods. See e.g. their letter to the Alliance, AAIU, Syrie, I.C., Damas, 5, 11 Aug. 1881. See also FO 78/837, Calvert to Canning, Damascus, 28 Aug. 1850.

[64] HHSTA, Adm. Reg., F8/38, Weckbecker, Wien, 23 Feb. 1865.

[65] HHSTA, Adm. Reg., F8/38, Weckbecker, Beirut, 7 Aug. 1864; Wien, 23 Feb. 1865; Prokesch, 18 Aug. 1864, 11 Oct. 1864; Angel, Damascus, 6 Apr. 1863.

Joseph Elias continued to serve as consular secretary and to stand in for the consul during his absences from Damascus.

Smaller countries like Denmark and Portugal copied the Austrian pattern, preferring to appoint eminent, independently wealthy, Jewish merchants as their consular representatives to Damascus, and even to Beirut. Thus in 1874 Solomon Stambouli was appointed Danish vice consul in Damascus.[66]

Throughout the period under consideration the Ottoman authorities, including the local councils in each *wilaya*, looked askance at the ever-increasing involvement of foreign consuls in every sphere of life. Their disapproval was directed particularly at the Christian powers' protection of the non-Muslim minorities, which placed these minorities beyond the reach of the Ottoman judiciary, and an extended struggle ensued between the Ottoman regime and the foreign consulates. In 1857 the Damascus *majlis* passed a resolution that foreign representatives had no right to interfere in matters concerning the religious minorities, and that the *raʿaya* communities had to declare officially whether or not their members were Ottoman or foreign subjects.[67] At first, seeking to preserve their status, the consulates strongly fought any steps intended to narrow the protection they could offer. However, when the various consuls discovered that some individuals had acquired protection by deceitful means, they themselves began a process of winnowing out their protégés.

It was not until the 1870s that Britain began to reassess the necessity for granting protection to Jews, in the wake of mounting complaints about Jewish commercial activity. The allegation was that corrupt acts committed under its protection and in its name, by moneylenders in particular, harmed England. A special envoy dispatched in 1871 found that the primary rationale underlying British protection—namely, the need to protect the Jews from persecution—was no longer valid. Endowed with wealth and honour, Syrian Jews were no more exposed to the risk of danger or torture than their compatriots elsewhere in the Ottoman empire.[68] This marks the inception of British efforts, in co-operation with the Ottoman authorities, to reduce the scope of British protection, motivated perhaps not only by the desire to solve a local problem but also by a broader overview of the Ottoman imperial situation. Britain now expressed its willingness to assist the empire in the restoration of its sovereignty over the majority of its subjects, many of whom had for years enjoyed foreign protection on dubious grounds. Notwithstanding this intensive British activity, the available data indicate that, up to the early 1880s, not a single Jew was deprived of his status as a British protégé.[69]

[66] *Hadiqat al-akhbar*, 853, 17 Dec. 1874, back page. See also Wood, *An Eastern Afterglow*, 482. [67] Ma'oz, *Ottoman Reform*, 215. See also Schilcher, *Families in Politics*, 82.
[68] For further detail, see Hyamson (ed.), *The British Consulate in Jerusalem*, ii. 349.
[69] See documents ibid. ii. 391 ff. Prussia too implemented a policy of limiting protection. On the policy of von Wildenbruch, the Prussian consul general in Syria, see Eliav, *Die Juden Palästinas*, doc. 4.

The Consuls as Defenders of the Jews

As a rule, the attitude of a particular foreign consulate towards Syrian Jews was largely governed by the consul's personal attitude and preconceptions. In more than one instance there was disparity between official policy—set by the foreign ministries in the European capitals—and the policy actually exercised by their local Syrian branches. Because of the western consulates' crucial contribution to the quality of Jewish life in defending their rights, life, property, and honour, shifts in local consular personnel were always a cause of anxiety mixed with hope among Jews. A hostile consul's departure could be accompanied by demonstrations of joy, and a new consul's arrival could bring fresh prospects of improvement.

Foreign consuls dispatched to Syria found it no easy task to pick their way through the tangled and delicate web of intercommunal relations. In order to appease all parties and to win their trust, the consul had first and foremost to avoid angering the Ottoman authorities, who were sensitive to any hint of interference in the empire's internal affairs; at the same time, he had to demonstrate to his protégés and to the various minority communities his capacity to stand up to Turkish injustice. This complex set of demands required that, in addition to complying with the general directives from his foreign ministry, every consul develop a local policy and modus operandi. The British consul Richard Wood gave pertinent expression to this juggling of different needs in relation to the unfair *ferde* tax imposed on the population of Damascus:

The confidence, which the Authorities and the native Mussulmen, Christians and Jews seem to repose in Her Majesty's Consulate, having led them severally, either to ask for advice, represent their real or imaginary grievances or seek assistance, I have exerted myself in engaging the former, on the one hand, to a greater display of firmness and energy, whilst I have, on the other, endeavoured to convince the latter of the certain and inevitable dangers they would be incurring by a fruitless and illegal attempt at resistance to the will of their Sovereign; or of the necessity of submitting, in proper time, their grievances to the consideration of those, who only had it in their power to redress them. Thus, without having assumed the appearance of opposing any party I hope to have succeeded, in some degree, in bringing both the Authorities and their Subjects to a better sense of their duty to each other.[70]

Nevertheless, consuls rarely turned down a request for intervention by the religious minorities, and generally attempted to assist them—when this harmonized with their interests. Below I examine events related to implementation of the reforms in which consular involvement played a major role in determining *ra'aya* strategy and, ultimately, quality of life.

[70] FO 78/538, Wood to Earl of Aberdeen, Damascus, 27 Dec. 1843. See also 195/226, Wood to Canning, Damascus, 27 Dec. 1843; 78/579, Wood to Canning, Damascus, 21 Feb. 1844.

One objective of the European consuls was the introduction of European cultural concepts—freedom, humanism, and love of humankind—into the Ottoman arena. Humanitarian principles, specifically the abolition of slavery, guided consular activity in 1842 when Najib Pasha incited Damascus' Muslim population to attack the Jews and Christians if they did not free their Muslim slaves. After negotiations among themselves, all the foreign consuls decided to announce to their protégés that they should manumit their slaves. Although the principles of equality established in the Hatt-i şerif did not bar non-Muslims from holding Muslim slaves and Najib Pasha's demand was based solely on Qur'anic law, the demand to free the slaves was in harmony with the European powers' humanitarian principles. In suggesting to Christian and Jewish leaders that they pre-empt Muslim anger by promptly freeing their slaves, Wood noted this act's humane and philanthropic aspects.[71] Not surprisingly, given its dependence on the British consul for its safety and security, the Jewish community was the first to respond to his plea. After informing Wood of the Jewish notables' willingness to comply, the chief rabbi continued: 'We have deemed it proper to convey the foregoing to you Sir, and may we always continue to have similar proofs of your love and friendship from which we experience such great advantages.'[72]

Foreign consuls often served as the watchdogs of equality before the law, safeguarding, above all, their subjects' and protégés' rights and honour. Any infringement of these rights was perceived as a potential affront to the consulate and to the power it represented. Such considerations prompted the French consulate's response to an incident relating to the temporary closure of all the Damascus taverns. In the course of implementing this decision, prompted by outbreaks of disorderly conduct, the police broke into the home of an Algerian Jewish tavern-keeper under French protection, evicted the family, and locked the premises, having given no advance notice to the French consulate. Shortly after the French consul's intervention effected this family's return to its home, some Muslims illicitly demanded that the wife of the Jew sell them wine. When she refused, the Muslims created a disturbance and broke into the storeroom. Not satisfied with detaining the rioters, the policeman summoned to the scene also placed the Jewish owner and his elderly father under arrest, and the local authorities not only punished the brawlers but

[71] FO 78/499, 'Translation of a Private Note addressed by Mr Wood to the Heads of the Christians and Jew Communities in Damascus, as per Margin, under date of 11th of May 1842'.

[72] FO 78/499, 'Translation of the Chief Rabbin Yacoub Meshaï's reply to Mr Wood under date Damascus 14th May 1842'. No rabbi by this name is known in Damascus. Perhaps this is a corruption of Jacob Boka'i, who filled in as chief rabbi for a number of weeks during the interval after Rabbi Jacob Antebi's resignation and before Rabbi Hayim Maimon Tobi's assumption of office. See also ibid., Wood to Earl of Aberdeen, Damascus, 6 June 1842, 31 July 1842; AECCC, Damas, vol. 1, p. 104, Beaudin, 3 Aug. 1842; *Voice of Jacob*, 22, 22 July 1842, p. 174.

whipped the Jew as well. The argument submitted by the police chief in defence of his actions illustrates both the extent to which the use of real or pretended foreign protection to avoid Ottoman jurisdiction had spread and the Ottoman regime's impotence in the face of this phenomenon. The police chief claimed that he beat the Jew because, from the moment of their arrest, many lower-class members of the *ra'aya* would declare themselves foreign citizens or protégés as a way of buying time to bribe civil servants or to invoke foreign consular involvement. In this case the police chief was dismissed at the request of the French consul Devoize, and the Jew was awarded substantial compensation.[73]

The various consuls adhered to this pattern of robustly assisting their protégés, even if this meant a head-on confrontation with the Ottoman authorities in defending their protégés' rights and honour through the agency of the newly founded tribunals, in which the representatives of the *ra'aya* and of the foreign consulates had numerical superiority. In 1854, shortly after the founding of the new criminal tribunal in Damascus, a Muslim beat a Jewish craftsman for failing to perform his job to his satisfaction during the month of Ramadan, a time when Muslim outbursts of fanaticism were especially frequent. When Moses Behar Yehudah, a Jewish merchant with British citizenship who witnessed the incident, took the Muslim to task, the latter turned on him and insulted him too. When the details of this episode came to Wood's attention, he demanded that the *wali* hand the Muslim over to the new tri-bunal, which would undoubtedly find him guilty. Following appeals by Muslim notables for arbitration, Wood agreed to withdraw the complaint on condition that the Muslim make a public apology in the bazaar for having insulted Jews. The Muslim having agreed to these conditions, the complaint was then withdrawn.[74]

Wood showed no reticence about intervening in the day-to-day functioning of the various Ottoman courts in cases of what he viewed as injustice towards the *ra'aya*. When the British consulate's representative to the commercial tribunal founded in Damascus, the same Jewish merchant Moses Behar Yehudah, resigned in June 1851 because of the chief justice's use of such disparaging epithets as 'pig' and 'infidel' for Jewish bankers appearing before him, Wood sent a sharp letter to the governor condemning the chief justice's behaviour and the perversion of justice by the tribunal under his leadership. This complaint led to the chief justice's dismissal, and the *wali* allowed the merchants themselves to choose a new chief justice, bringing relief to the Jewish traders, the main target of the previous incumbent's abuse.[75]

Consular influence in achieving justice for their protégés peaked with the Italian consul's success in September 1869 in compelling the regime to execute a Muslim for murdering a Jew—in this instance, a Jew with Italian citizenship.

[73] AECCC, Damas, vol. 1, p. 199, Devoize, 7 Feb. 1844.   [74] *JC*, 28 July 1854, pp. 368–9.
[75] FO 78/872, Wood to Palmerston, Damascus, 27 June 1851.

As noted earlier, this case was an exceptional one and by no means represents a transformation of the Ottoman system of justice in Syria.[76]

Another sphere that saw extensive consular intervention on behalf of the religious minorities was taxation, particularly the inequitable distribution of the *ferde* tax. When first petitioned by the Jews and Christians on this matter in late 1843, the British and French consuls seemed in no hurry to intervene, and advised minority leaders first to explore their options within the Ottoman system. Contributing to the consuls' caution was their fear that, should they fail in this case, this would detract from their capacity to intervene effectively on other matters.[77] But the Ottoman regime's attempt to apply the *ferde* to foreign property-holders in Syria forced the consuls into a campaign against the local authorities, which they pursued with only intermittent success.[78]

The humiliating treatment of the minorities by the tax collectors constituted another 'red flag' for the consuls, and one to which they readily responded. To his superiors, Wood justified his intervention on behalf of Jews who had been subjected to degrading treatment by tax collectors in 1844 as follows:

Sentiments of humanity no less than the spirit of the Instruction of Her Majesty's Government to Her Majesty's Consuls in Turkey with regard to the degree of protection that may be granted by them to Israëlites, induced me to send a verbal and respectful message to the Authorities to beg they would mitigate their proceedings against them, which had the desired effect and procured them some relief.[79]

Requests for assistance on taxation continued until April 1852, when the *ferde* was replaced by the *vergi*, a property tax. In nearly every appeal on this matter the Jews took the opportunity to remind the British consul of Foreign Office instructions to assist the Jews whenever they found themselves under duress.[80]

Consuls also intervened to protect freedom of religion. In the latter half of the 1840s, a period that saw intense attempts to entice or to force Jews and Christians to convert to Islam, the British and the other consulates engaged in a combined effort to combat this trend. On more than one occasion, young Jewish and Christian converts to Islam who changed their minds took refuge from Muslim fanaticism in the British consulate.[81] Local efforts alone having

---

[76] AECPC, Turquie, Damas, vol. 10, pp. 243–6, Roustan, 28 Sept. 1869; AECCC, Damas, vol. 6, p. 09, Rousseau, 17 Mar. 1878.

[77] AECCC, Damas, vol. 1, p. 207, Devoize, 7 Feb. 1844; p. 220, Devoize, 6 Mar. 1844; AECPC, Turquie, Damas, vol. 1, p. 200, Devoize, 7 Feb. 1844; FO 195/226, Wood to Canning, Damascus, 27 Dec. 1843, 21 Feb. 1844; 78/538, Wood to Earl of Aberdeen, Damascus, 27 Dec. 1843.

[78] FO 78/660A, Wood to Canning, Damascus, 8 Apr. 1846.

[79] FO 78/579, Wood to Earl of Aberdeen, Damascus, 8 May 1844.

[80] FO 78/714, Timoni to Cowley, Damascus, 1 Sept. 1847; 78/910, 'Translation of a Petition addressed by the Israelites of Damascus to Mr Consul Wood under date the 19th April 1852'.

[81] For further details, see FO 195/226, Timoni to Wellesley, Damascus, 26 Aug. 1846; FO 78/714, Timoni to Wellesley, Damascus, 28 Apr. 1847.

proven ineffective, at the height of this Muslim campaign the British consul solicited the assistance of the British ambassador to Istanbul concerning the problem of forced conversion.[82] This request produced British threats in May 1847 to have the Damascus governor Safveti Pasha, who encouraged forced conversion to Islam, dismissed from his post, which proved effective in reducing pressure on individual Jews to convert. Nonetheless, attempts at forced conversion of Jewish children were still being made in the late 1850s. Once again, the Jewish community's response was to appeal to the British consul for assistance in restoring the converts to their families and to Judaism. The following letter reflects Jewish gratitude for the swift and effective action of one British consular staff member, named Misk, in returning the young girl Simha to her family:

We beg to express our deepest gratitude to this British Consulate presently under your direction for having delivered the girl Simha . . . from being compelled to embrace islamism. This being not the first instance of such a favour being granted to our coreligionists by your Consulate . . . and we have no other support but your mighty Government for whom we unceasingly beseech the Divine blessings.[83]

Consuls were concerned not only with relations between the minorities and the Ottoman regime but also with intercommunal relations. In instances of Catholic–Jewish conflicts, as noted above, the British consulate usually sided with the Jews, particularly in cases involving accusations of ritual murder, over which it was prepared to confront the French consulate. In response to the blood libel accusation of April 1847, the British acting consul Timoni spoke out forcefully against the French consular agent Beaudin for setting out 'to bring discredit upon the Jewish nation without any proof of their guilt'.[84] When, barely a month later, a Jewish dealer in old clothes was accused of kidnapping a Muslim child, occasioning assaults on Jews and raising the danger of attacks on the Jewish quarter by a Muslim and Catholic mob, the Jews turned to Timoni, asking him to use his influence to protect them from the mob. Timoni immediately dispatched the consular dragoman to the pasha, demanding restoration of order, protection of the Jews, and punishment for the rioters. Dragoman Misk's pertinacity in not simply delivering these demands but waiting at the pasha's residence until they had been implemented ensured harsh punishment for the false accusers and the issuing of a warning to the residents of Damascus that similar treatment awaited anyone harming, or making false accusations against, Jews. The governor also dispatched a police detachment

[82] NLIS, DA, V-736/28, Rabbi Hayim Maimon Tobi to Rabbi Hayim Gagin, Damascus, 5 Sivan 1847. See also FO 78/714, Timoni to Wellesley, Damascus, 29 May 1847.
[83] FO 195/458, 'Translation of a letter addressed to the Chief Rabbis of the Jewish Communities of Damascus to Mr Acting Consul Misk', Damascus, 15 June 1857.
[84] FO 78/714, Timoni to Wellesley, Damascus, 19 May 1847.

to guard the Jewish quarter and prevent the Damascus mob from attacking Jews with impunity.[85]

At times, recognizing the Ottoman regime's impotence in investigating crimes against Jews and Christians, the foreign consuls conducted their own independent investigations of incidents in which religious minorities were victimized, bringing the results to the attention of the Ottoman authorities so that the latter could take the necessary measures. Against the background of yet another ritual murder accusation, this one around Passover 1848, under the pretence of searching for a missing child Christians broke into the homes of Damascus Jews in the middle of the night and assaulted members of the Jewish community. Even after the child was found safe and sound with a Catholic monk, the Jews feared that, unless emphatic steps were taken to demonstrate the falsity of the blood libel, they would continue to be accused on every such disappearance. Not only did Consul Wood back the Jewish demand for an investigation, he had it carried out by the consular staff. Following presentation of its findings to the Ottoman authorities, the Christian perpetrators who had beaten Jews were punished.[86]

After the change in the French consulate's attitude towards the Jews following the events of 1860, described above, the French consuls too took steps to prevent the spread of ritual murder accusations. On 9 February 1868 a rumour spread in Damascus that an attempt had been made in the Farhi home to murder Dr Nicora, a physician in the French consulate's employ, resulting in attacks on Jewish workers passing through the Christian quarter. Investigation of the physician himself by Seligman Weisskopf, the Alliance representative to Damascus, showed the entire affair to be based on a misunderstanding, and Nicora immediately apprised French consul Rousseau of the truth. This step further incensed the already inflamed mob—convinced of Jewish guilt—which accused the doctor of accepting a bribe to testify on the Jews' behalf. The leaders of the Jewish community, along with the chief rabbis and Weisskopf, now turned to the French consul, requesting that he exert his influence to pacify the Christian public. Receiving the delegation courteously, Rousseau promised that he would confer with the Christian leaders and act to restore calm to the Christian quarter. This he did, and his timely intervention restored order and averted the danger of an attack on the Jewish quarter.[87]

In the context of intercommunal relations, foreign consular assistance to Jews peaked in July 1860, when most of the consuls stood by the Jews who faced accusations of participating in the rioting and in the Muslim massacre of Christians in Damascus. They also attempted to free the Jews from the heavy fine

[85] Ibid., 19 and 29 May 1847; Timoni to Palmerston, Damascus, 7 Aug. 1847. A similar event took place in 1856. See FO 78/1220, Misk to Earl of Clarendon, Damascus, 31 July 1856.

[86] FO 78/761, Wood to Palmerston, Damascus, 7 Apr. 1848.

[87] See AAIU, Syrie, I.C., Damas, 5, Weisskopf, 20 Feb. 1868.

imposed on Damascus' non-Muslim residents in compensation for the harm inflicted on the Christians.[88]

The British consul bore responsibility not only for protecting the Jews, but also for managing relations between Jews and Protestants, for he was the patron of the nascent Protestant congregations in the East.[89] Protestant missionary activity among Jews, and the friction that began to emerge between them in the 1850s, as described in Chapter 9, forced the British consul to mediate between two groups that both viewed him as friend and protector. Ultimately, because the issue revolved around education, one of the foundations of Jewish communal life, Jews were willing to pay what might be considered a stiff price in exchange for continued British protection. As noted earlier, in 1854 the rabbis issued an official ban excommunicating any Jew attending, enrolling his son in, or accepting material assistance from, Protestant educational institutions. When parental complaints regarding the ban reached the consul, probably at the missionaries' prompting, he hastened to invite the rabbis to a meeting. Wood repudiated rabbinic claims that the missionaries enticed students to convert, arguing that the Protestant schools had been founded in order to provide the members of all the sects in Damascus, particularly their poor, with the opportunity to receive a modern education, namely, to acquire knowledge of the sciences, arts, and culture. He further argued that these schools deliberately avoided subjects offensive to the religious sensibilities of particular groups. Having concluded his educational arguments, Wood saw fit to remind the Jews that warfare against the Protestants meant rebuffing their friends and benefactors: 'The Jews throughout the world, and particularly those in Damascus, are greatly indebted to Protestant England, America and Prussia for the universal discontinuance of the persecution with which they were weighed down and oppressed; and they consequently owe to their sympathy and good offices the liberty and protection they now happily enjoy.'[90]

Wood, then, perceived the Jewish hostility towards Protestants as ingratitude, particularly in the light of the surprising Jewish–Catholic cooperation on this matter. In his view this approach had the potential to turn public opinion in Britain and America, two nations that had greatly benefited the Jews, against them. Given the extent to which British representatives had assisted and protected the Damascus Jewish community under difficult circumstances, he was most aggrieved by the anti-Protestant stance of the city's rabbis and

[88] For a profound consideration of the involvement of the various consuls in this affair, see Baron, 'The Jews and the Syrian Massacres'; id., 'Great Britain and Damascus Jewry'. See also Farah, *The Politics of Interventionism*, 618–19.

[89] On the relationship between the Protestant penetration of Syria and British diplomacy there in the early 1840s, see Farah, 'Protestantism and British Diplomacy in Syria'; id., 'Protestantism and Politics'.

[90] FO 78/1029, Wood to the reverend, the rabbis, and the elders of the Hebrew community in Damascus, 15 July 1854.

scholars. Pointing out that British intervention alone guaranteed the same rights for Jews as for other subjects of the Sublime Porte, Wood advised the Jewish leaders to cancel the ban on Jewish co-operation with the Protestants. Moreover, recognizing the extent of Jewish dependence on British protection, Wood inserted a threatening note into his remarks. He reminded Jewish leaders how, during his tenure, the British consulate had always willingly and determinedly come to the aid of the Jews, calling to their attention how

it [the Consulate] is no less determined on the other hand, should its offer be rejected to cease its relation with your community with a view to avoid their unjust and unmerited hostility. The adoption of such a course would be attended with much regret because it would seriously injure the position of the poorer classes whom you can neither protect nor assist, to whose children you cannot give an education such as would enable them to improve their social condition and thereby afford them better means for obtaining their livelihood; and indeed it would destroy at one blow all that has been hitherto effected with so much care and trouble in behalf of your co-religionists. But if by your Excommunication you are the first to manifest publicly your desire that the relations and intercourse hitherto maintained between us should cease, I have no other alternative left me but to yield to your wishes, however injurious the future may show it to be to your nation; for it is impossible to foresee what circumstances may yet arise to render the protection of this Consulate both necessary and valuable to you.[91]

A true champion of the Jews throughout his extended tenure as consul in Damascus, responding to every call for assistance from high and low alike, Wood may well have honestly found the Jewish community's steps against Protestant education, which was aimed mainly at the children of the poor, not just extreme but also misguided. The sharp tone of this letter was the result neither of hostility nor of his own Christian faith; it should rather be viewed as the remonstrance of a close friend, as demonstrated by his efforts to remove any obstacles that could serve as a pretext for excommunication. First, Wood was truly convinced that the Protestant schools imparted nothing inimical to the Jewish faith; second, at his request the school principals agreed to transfer the responsibility for scholarships for poor Jewish pupils to the rabbis.

Upon receiving Wood's letter, the rabbis immediately convened to consider their dilemma and their response. Eventually, recognizing the value of British protection and Wood's regard, the Jewish community backed down regarding its opposition to sending children to mission schools. Notices cancelling the ban were immediately posted in all the synagogues, and the British consulate was so informed. In explanation for their previous actions the rabbis cited a misunderstanding cleared up by Wood's missive. The rabbis' letter heaped praises on Her Majesty's government for its assistance to Damascus

[91] Ibid.

Jewry and for the fact that British protection alone undeniably enabled the Jews of Damascus and elsewhere to live in peace and security. They stressed that British aid, during Wood's tenure in particular, fostered their sense of obligation to accept Wood's proposals with regard to Protestant education, and they further submitted that they had misjudged the damage caused by the ban. Their letter concluded with prayers for continued British protection: 'May the Almighty preserve that Prosperous Government and your own life; and we hope we may continue to be favoured with that good will which you have already evinced towards us.'[92]

But this was not the sole instance of consular mediation of Jewish–Protestant tension. Although in line with Foreign Office directives British consuls refrained from direct association with any Protestant conversionary missionary activity,[93] nonetheless, in their role as protectors they did come to the Protestants' aid, even in cases of attempted conversion. Following declaration of a ban in the Damascus synagogues on 24 February 1872 on anyone co-operating with the Protestant minister Frankel, the latter turned to the British consul Kirby Green to exert pressure for its withdrawal. Despite standing instructions against assisting missionary activity, Green decided to intervene. At a meeting with the *ḥakham bashi* Jacob Peretz, Green protested against this attack on the Jewish community's part, in his view not only unwarranted but also unwise in so religiously fractured a region as Syria.

Like his predecessor Wood, Green 'spoke softly and carried a big stick'. While portraying himself as a friend of the Jews, always prepared to come to their assistance, at the same time Green made the point that, as the chief official at the British consulate, he was aggrieved by the hostile treatment of British Protestants at the hands of the Damascus Jewish community and by the exclusion of Catholic institutions from the ban. He took care to remind the chief rabbi of the many occasions on which British affection, and British policy, had proven themselves the Jews' best friends in Syria and elsewhere in the East, where unfounded prejudice sparked their persecution. He also warned the Jewish community that reports of Jewish hatred for Protestants had the potential to provoke renewed allegations in the British press regarding Jewish involvement in the July 1860 massacre in Damascus.[94] Finally, aware of the close ties between Jews in Britain and Damascus, and the influence of the former on the latter, Green suggested that Jews in London would find the attack on the Protestants disturbing. Accordingly, he requested that Rabbi Jacob Peretz withdraw the ban.[95]

[92] FO 78/1029, 'Translation of the Reply of the Rabbis and Jewish Elders of Damascus to Mr Wood', 24 Aug. 1854.   [93] See Hyamson (ed.), *The British Consulate in Jerusalem*, i. 46.
[94] Loewe (ed.), *The Diaries of Sir Moses and Lady Montefiore*, ii. 233.
[95] FO 78/2242, Green to Granville, Damascus, 29 Feb. 1872; AAIU, Syrie, XI.E., Damas, 94, Halfon au Comité Central de l'AIU, 7 Apr. 1872.

This veteran *ḥakham bashi*, who had also served as chief rabbi eighteen years earlier during the exchange with Wood in similar circumstances, immediately acknowledged the justice of Green's arguments and reported that the ban had been published without his approval; it was an independent initiative by rabbis resentful of the ever-increasing number of Jewish children enrolling in Frankel's school, and motivated by a desire to underscore the Jewish community's commitment to its traditional ways. Rabbi Peretz expressed confidence in his ability to persuade the rabbis to cancel the ban. Green summed up the affair as follows: 'Rabbi Jacob Perez carried out most fully his promises to me by causing an order to be published in all the Synagogues to the effect that the Excommunication in question is null and void, that the Protestants have ever been the best friends of the Jews and with many other expressions of good will towards men of all creeds.'[96] By so doing, Rabbi Peretz and the Damascus Jewish communal leadership again demonstrated the high value they placed on the foreign consuls' friendship and protection.

Jewish Consuls in the Province of Aleppo

With regard to consular protection, as in other spheres, the situation in Aleppo differed from that in Damascus. Although the Jews of Aleppo were also certainly in need of consular protection, for much of the Tanzimat period they turned first to those of their co-religionists who served as consuls in the city, becoming dependent on the British and French consulates at a later date than their co-religionists in Damascus.

The reasons why various European states, beginning with the Austro-Hungarian empire, chose European Jews living in Aleppo as their consular representatives are not entirely clear.[97] Apparently, following Raphael Picciotto's appointment as consul of Austria and Tuscany in 1798, and on the basis of the services he rendered to his employers, small European nations without direct interests in Syria found the members of this respected, wealthy merchant family suitable as honorary and commercial consuls.[98] In any event, this unusual phenomenon—of several Jewish consuls being drawn from a single family—

---

[96] FO 78/2242, Green to Granville, Damascus, 29 Feb. 1872.

[97] Official reports indicate that at the time of Raphael Picciotto's appointment there was no Christian of equal wealth or reliability. See B. Le Calloc'h, 'La Dynastie consulaire', 139.

[98] See Harel, 'The Status and Image of the Picciotto Family' (Heb.), 177. Their services to the Austrian emperors over the generations included sending a shipment of thoroughbred Arabian horses to their stables, making rare book purchases, and shipping exotic animals to the royal zoo in Vienna. In exchange the Picciottos received valuable gifts, certificates of honour, and medals. In 1806 Raphael Picciotto and his descendants were granted knighthood, which allowed them to add 'von' or 'de' to their name. See the various documents in HHSTA, Adm. Reg., F4/258, especially the awarding of the cross of the Order of Franz Josef and a precious box of diamonds to Elijah de Picciotto by order of the emperor Franz Josef, Vienna, 2 Mar. 1851.

amazed Christian travellers,[99] and delighted Jewish ones such as Benjamin the Second, who noted how the Jews 'enjoy great privileges under the protection of the European Consuls, of whom some are of their own faith'.[100] To summarize, between 1840 and 1880 members of the Picciotto clan served as consular representatives of Russia and Prussia (Raphael Picciotto); of Austro-Hungary and Tuscany (Elijah Picciotto until his death on 21 October 1858, when he was succeeded by his son Moses); of the Netherlands (Daniel Picciotto); of Belgium (Hillel Picciotto); of Persia (Joseph Picciotto); of Denmark (Moses Picciotto as consul general and his son Daniel as vice consul); of Sweden (Joseph Picciotto); of the United States (Hillel Picciotto); and of Norway—Joseph Picciotto.[101]

Jewish appointments to consular positions were not restricted to Aleppo itself. Jews held various consular posts elsewhere in the *wilaya*, for example in Urfa, where Rabbi Aaron Dayan, who moved there from Aleppo to assume the post of *ḥakham bashi*, also served as the Persian consul. The traveller Wolf Schur wrote of Dayan that he 'is most honoured among them; he is the representative of the Persian government, and he is wealthy and god fearing, and constantly attends to Torah study and to work'.[102] Prior to the arrival of Emil Frank, a Jew of German extraction, to take up an appointment as consul of the United States, Britain, and Prussia in Alexandretta in the 1870s, the strong antipathy of the Greek Catholics prevented Jews from settling there.[103] But Frank 'ended the darkness, and dashed the remnants of the Greeks on the rock of strength that was his from the enlightened governments, to uproot evil and defend justice'.[104] Some twenty Jewish families, most from Syria but also including some from Europe, settled in the city in his wake and became

---

[99] Neale, *Eight Years in Syria*, ii. 105. See also Guys, *Voyage en Syrie*, 253–4; Blondel, *Deux ans en Syrie*, 277–8. The Picciottos made certain to extract a promise from the Austrian foreign ministry that the post would remain in their sons' hands. See e.g. HHSTA, Türkei, II/128, Raphael Picciotto, Aleppo, 5 Mar. 1802; Adm. Reg., F4/258, M. de Picciotto, Aleppo, 28 Oct. 1858.

[100] Benjamin, *Eight Years in Asia and Africa*, 46.

[101] These data come from Hillel de Picciotto's 29 Dec. 1854 announcement to the French consul Grasset of his appointment as Belgian consul, AECADN, Consulat de France à Alep, Cote 15; Moses de Picciotto's 24 Sept. 1863 announcement to the French consulate of the appointment of his son Daniel as Danish vice consul in the Aleppo district, AECADN, Consulat de France à Alep, Cote 21; and the 21 May 1865 announcement by Hillel de Picciotto, vice consul of the United States in Aleppo, to French consul Bertrand of President Lincoln's death, AECADN, Alep, Cote 21. See also AECCC, Alep, vol. 32, p. 17, Bentivoglio, 17 June 1858; AAIU, Syrie, III.E., Alep, 21, Behar, 22 Aug. 1870; 23, Behor, 24 Mar. 1875; *BAIU*, dernier trimestre 1864, p. cxxvi; *JC*, 21 Oct. 1859, p. 7. Much documentary material on the consular activity of the Picciottos is housed in HHSTA, Adm. Reg., F8/6, F4/258. See also Pinto, *Nivḥar mikesef*, introd. Elijah Hai Sassoon; *Hadiqat al-akhbar*, 30 Oct. 1858, 13 Apr. 1865. For a more recent treatment, see Picciotto, *The Consular History*.   [102] Schur, *Maḥazot haḥayim*, 17.

[103] His appointment as British vice consul without pay was ratified by the British Foreign Office on 26 July 1871. See FO 78/2352, Skene, Aleppo, 1 Jan. 1874.

[104] Schur, *Maḥazot haḥayim*, 6. This material was published nine years earlier in *Ḥavatselet*, 29, 16 Iyar 1875, p. 235.

his protégés. He also founded a synagogue there.[105] A third Jewish consular appointment outside Aleppo was that of Joseph Dweck, an Indian-born British subject, who was ratified as vice consul without pay in Antioch on 16 January 1869.[106] Sometimes, in the face of Ottoman objections to the stationing of foreign representatives throughout the *wilaya*, the British consulate was forced to withdraw appointments such as these; however, its interest in obtaining detailed reports on happenings throughout the *wilaya* fostered the continued appointment of Jews, mostly British subjects, as vice consuls without pay in various towns in the Aleppo district. Thus Consul Skene promoted the appointment of Abraham Samuel Dweck and Abraham Blanco as vice consuls in Urfa and in 'Ayntab respectively.[107]

Writers, poets, and travellers idealized the status and activity of these Jewish consuls, the Picciotto family in particular.[108] Captivated by their aura, the chroniclers of Aleppo's Jewish history failed to ascertain their true status in the eyes of either the population at large or the city's consular corps.[109] A more even-handed examination casts the Picciotto consuls in an entirely different, largely negative, light, especially from the early 1850s, which saw the beginning of implementation of the Ottoman reforms in Aleppo.[110] Contributing to this negative image were both the Picciottos' low consular rank and their behaviour, viewed by the surrounding non-Jewish population as narrow, self-serving, and corrupt.

With the exception of Austria and Russia, the countries employing the services of Jewish consuls were second- and third-rate European powers without direct interests in, or real political influence on, the Ottoman empire, which naturally lowered their representatives' status.[111] In addition, in contrast to the career diplomats dispatched by the powers with broad political interests in the region—Britain and France—most of the Jewish consuls served in an unsalaried, honorary capacity. Tension between the French, Russian, and Italian career diplomats who served as consuls on the one hand and the

[105] Ibid. According to the report of Jacob Obermeyer, who passed through this city in 1877, most of the families there originated in Aleppo. See *Hamagid*, 7, 11 Feb. 1880, p. 57.

[106] FO 78/2352, Skene, Aleppo, 1 Jan. 1874. Some time later a relative of Joseph Dweck was appointed dragoman for the British consulate. See FO 78/1154, Skene to Layard, Aleppo, 5 Oct. 1877.

[107] FO 78/2650, Skene to Layard, Aleppo, 17 Oct. 1877; 372/1933, 'Claim of members of the Douek Family to British nationality', Morgan, Aleppo, 31 July 1922.

[108] See e.g. Y. Abadi, *Kol rinah viyeshuah*, author's introd.; I. Sasson, *Keneset yisra'el*, pt. 1, introd. A. Sasson; Yaari, *Emissaries from Israel* (Heb.), 770; Antebi, *Mor ve'oholot*, author's introd.; Schur, *Maḥazot haḥayim*, 9; Benjamin, *Eight Years in Asia and Africa*, 46.

[109] See e.g. Lutzky, 'The "Francos"' (Heb.), 68–72; Brawer, 'New Material with Regard to the Damascus Libel' (Heb.), 263–5; Cohen-Tawil, 'The Francos in Aleppo' (Heb.), 129–35.

[110] For the period up to the 1850s, see the discussion in Harel, 'The Status and Image of the Piccioto Family' (Heb.).

[111] See FO 78/1452, Skene to Bulwer, Aleppo, 28 May 1859.

Austrian consul, Moses de Picciotto, on the other meant that in the early 1870s
Aleppo had no united consular forum through which problems affecting the
various countries' nationals could be brought before the local authorities.
Although Picciotto was ostensibly the senior diplomat in Aleppo, the other
consuls viewed him simply as a local Jewish merchant of Italian origin, finding
the idea that such a person should have a voice in a united consular body dis-
tasteful. Even though formally Picciotto's position as Austrian consul general
was higher than those of the other consuls, in actuality he was no more than a
vice consul without pay: as the other consuls noted, his appointment had come
not from the Austrian government but from the Austrian consul general in
Beirut.[112]

The other consuls, and the wider non-Jewish society of Aleppo, found little
to commend in Picciotto's behaviour. Because these Jewish consuls were
also local merchants, their actions were frequently motivated by narrow self-
interest, which was not necessarily consistent with the general good of the
region as the other consuls saw it. An instructive example comes from the British
consul Werry's anger at the Picciottos' outright objection to paying the
progressive *vergi* tax. Werry claimed that he had evidence of a self-seeking conspiracy by the Jewish consuls—in concert with wealthy land- and property-
owners—to prevent the enactment of what Werry regarded as direct, fair
taxation.[113] Describing the Jewish consuls as individuals 'who never contribute
for any public or national object a para, unless coerced',[114] Werry attributed
their obstructive behaviour to one primary motive: greed.[115]

This perception was heightened by the Jewish consuls' refusal to co-operate
in the formation of a commercial tribunal in Aleppo. Moses de Picciotto and his
sons, one of whom served as the Tuscan vice consul and the other as the United
States vice consul, informed Werry of their opposition to this step. Notwithstanding their formal claim that they had received no instructions on this matter from
their superiors in Istanbul, the British consul believed that their policy was dictated
by personal interest, rather than that of the states they represented, or indeed of the
public. Under current circumstances, their own affairs fell within the jurisdiction
of the consular court, far from the arm of Ottoman justice. The formation of a commercial tribunal would alter this situation. The Picciottos' recalcitrance aroused the
animosity of the other consuls, Werry in particular, who hoped to bring the reforms
implemented in large cities elsewhere in the empire to Aleppo. His sense of outrage
increased when the Tuscan consul employed delaying tactics, starting a petition

---

[112] FO 195/976, Skene to Elliot, Aleppo, 27 Dec. 1871. On the Aleppo consulate's answer-
ability to the Beirut consulate in the context of foreign ministry reorganization of the Austrian
representations in the Levant, see HHSTA, Adm. Reg., F8/6, Stürmer, Constantinople, 12 Aug.
1846; E. de Picciotto, Aleppo, 8 Jan. 1847.

[113] FO 78/910, Werry to Canning, Aleppo, 29 May 1852.

[114] Ibid., Werry to Stratford de Redcliffe, Aleppo, 12 June 1852.

[115] Ibid., Werry to Rose, Aleppo, 11 Sept. 1852.

opposing this tribunal's formation, signed mainly by Tuscan subjects, almost all of whom were Jews. As a result of this interference, commercial cases continued to come before the *mahkama* and the municipal *majlis*, which favoured Muslim litigants.[116]

Tension also existed between the Jewish consuls and the French consulate in Aleppo. Although the prevailing anti-Jewish prejudices of the French consular staff must be taken into account,[117] disputes and hostility between the Picciottos and the Catholic orders, which were under French protection, caused constant friction between the Jewish consuls and the French consulate up to the 1870s, when the Picciotto consulships began to come to an end.

The main charges levelled against the Picciotto consuls by their colleagues were of corruption and bribery, seen as a threat to the security and economic stability of the *wilaya*. In 1860 the Jewish consuls were accused of conspiring to compel the governor to replace Bedouin tribal heads, a step by the regime that provoked tension, rivalry, and unrest.[118] Another significant allegation was that, in conjunction with other elements in the Aleppo elites, the Jewish consuls were actually stealing from the *wilaya* treasury. According to Skene, the British consul, even though economic activity within the *wilaya* was flourishing, corruption kept the treasury empty. Skene reported that various parties, including the Picciottos, had worked out a method by which they could profit at the treasury's expense. Bribery of the *a'yan*, many of whom sat on the district *majlis*, not to collect taxes naturally led to the treasury falling into debt. Urgently needing funds to provision army troops on distant postings, the treasury was forced to borrow money to fill its coffers; treasury debts were thereby in lien even prior to their collection. As soon as any funds arrived, speculators who had purchased *wilaya*-issued government treasury bonds at about one-quarter their face value hastened to demand their redemption. In addition, whenever the treasury found itself in need of funds, the *a'yan* and council members joined forces with the moneylenders to persuade the governor to take out loans at exorbitant interest rates. Skene described the Jewish involvement in this system: 'The principal capitalists who invest money in this way are the wealthy Jews; of whom several hold the Consulates of Austria, Russia, Prussia, Tuscany, Holland, and other Powers, this official position giving them a preference over other creditors for the payment of interest due.'[119] Himself wishing primarily to advance the interests of the *wilaya* and its regime, Skene considered that the local consuls were concerned only to retain their shaky hold on their posts, to which end they were willing to fawn on whoever could buttress their

---

[116] FO 78/960, Werry to Stratford de Redcliffe, Aleppo, 28 May 1853.
[117] AECCC, Alep, vol. 30, p. 208, Guys, 10 May 1841; AECPC, Turquie, Alep, vol. 4, pp. 131–9, Bertrand, 12 July 1865; pp. 309–22, Bertrand, 12 May 1868.
[118] AECPC, Turquie, Alep, vol. 3, pp. 137–44, de Lafosse, 22 Mar. 1860.
[119] FO 78/1389, Skene to Bulwer, Aleppo, 4 Sept. 1858.

position and to act counter to the interests of the other European consuls. He asked his superiors to request that countries with Picciotto representation in Aleppo explicitly instruct the latter to co-operate with the British and French consuls for the greater good of Syria.[120]

The Muslim public and clergy shared the consuls' low estimation of the Picciottos. It is even possible that the Muslim attempt to murder Moses de Picciotto in 1859 was motivated by a general profound hatred for the Jewish consuls.[121] However, the immediate reason for the attempt is not clear, and the assailant was placed under psychiatric observation. More direct evidence of the loathing felt for the Picciottos and their associates is provided by an episode, discussed in Chapter 8, surrounding the destruction in April 1860 of the wall of a warehouse claimed for conversion to a mosque by Ezra Belilio, a relative and protégé of Moses de Picciotto. For fear of anti-Jewish riots, the Jewish consul attributed Belilio's act to insanity. Among the non-Jewish population of Aleppo, popular opinion held that the Picciottos owed their high standing with the governor to joint shady dealings, which in turn made them, and the Jewish community at large, arrogant, unlike the Jews in other regions of the empire.[122]

In the aftermath of the warehouse wall incident the '*ulama*' in Aleppo petitioned the sultan to demand the replacement of the Austrian representative to their city, claiming that the destruction of the mosque wall had been executed upon his instructions and with his full support:

Moses Picciotto is a proud man, stubborn, and overbearing. He keeps around him persons of bad fame in the town who sow the seeds of revolution in the country, and give rise to conflicts with the people. He is not influenced either by principles of justice or by the laws of the country. He acts as if he thought the Government was in his hands and that he can do what he likes. His injustice has become notorious in the town, so much so that people are disgusted with it . . . We pray, therefore, that this man may be deprived of the Consulate and kept within bounds, and that another Consul be sent by his Government as is practised by the other Powers, for those who are sent by the other Governments never act as he does.[123]

The '*ulama*' differentiated here between the behaviour and policy of foreign and local consuls, accusing the latter of combining economic interests and political intrigue, and of stirring up local intercommunal tensions. In his report to his superiors, Skene focused on one problematic point: Picciotto misuse of consular protection. He attributed popular hostility to the objectionable behaviour of Jewish consular protégés, first and foremost to the corrupt ways of

---

[120] FO 195/1153, Skene to Elliot, Aleppo, 9 Jan. 1877.   [121] *JC*, 16 Sept. 1859, p. 6.
[122] AECPC, Turquie, Alep, vol. 3, pp. 140–2, de Lafosse, 12 Apr. 1860.
[123] Translation appended to FO 78/1538, Skene to Bulwer, Aleppo, 19 Apr. 1860. See also AECPC, Turquie, Alep, vol. 3, pp. 143–4, Geofroy, 3 May 1860.

the local Jewish dragomen, asserting that they had purchased their consular protection and had been falsely registered as translators for the consulate.[124] Together, Skene submitted, the four Picciotto consuls shared ten consulates; each consulate hired more than one local Jewish dragoman without pay, even though most of these individuals had no legitimate need for protection. In Skene's opinion, the lack of a formal salary, or of any real need for their services, promoted the development of venality and attempts to corrupt the authorities.[125]

Paradoxically, because Jews represented European nations, albeit not the primary powers, this delayed the necessity for British or French intervention or protection in Aleppo until the 1870s. While British, and later French, consular protection figured significantly in bringing Damascus Jews closer to the West, only when the number and status of the Jewish consuls in Aleppo began to decline, and Alliance activity in the city became widespread, did a similar process take place there. It was not until the early 1870s, prompted by their economic and political stakes in Syria and their recognition of the need for professional consular representatives with closer ties to the country they served, that the European powers began to replace the Picciottos with career diplomats. Russia's replacement of Raphael de Picciotto by a professional diplomat in 1871 sparked the dismissal of all the other Jewish consuls, with the exception of the Austrian consul, Moses de Picciotto.[126] As the traveller Jacob Obermeyer, who visited Aleppo in 1877, commented, 'Now the wheel of fortune has turned, and the only individual still in his glory is the minister Moses [consul of Austria and Denmark] alone.'[127]

That this last Jewish consul's eminence had also waned emerges from an incident at his home in 1877. In the course of a heated argument between Turkish soldiers and a Jewish moneylender regarding the exchange rate, the soldiers began to beat the Jew, who sought refuge in Moses de Picciotto's house. Displaying no inhibitions about breaking into the house, the soldiers struck the kavass, and then the Jewish consul himself. On this occasion, even the Picciotto-hating consuls—seeing the incident as an infraction of consular status—banded together to protest to the authorities. On the other hand, it was not fortuitous that this incident took place at the home of a local, Jewish, unsalaried consul.[128] The traveller Benjamin Ze'ev Sapir Halevi provided the following description of Moses de Picciotto's weakness:

Even if God shows benevolence to the Jews there, and the majority are wealthy and respected merchants, and most of the consuls there are Jews, nonetheless, they must

---

[124] For a more comprehensive discussion, see Lutzky, 'The "Francos"' (Heb.), 56–9.

[125] FO 78/1538, Skene to Bulwer, Aleppo, 19 Apr. 1860.

[126] See AECPC, Turquie, Alep, vol. 5, pp. 124–9, Bertrand, 22 July 1871; FO 195/1113, I. de Picciotto to Skene, Aleppo, 5 Jan. 1876; AAIU, Syrie, III.E., Alep, 21, Behar, 19 Jan. 1872.

[127] *Hamagid*, 10, 3 Mar. 1880, p. 83.

[128] FO 78/2619, Skene to Elliot, Aleppo, 8 Jan. 1877.

guard their tongues, for the consul himself fears his servant the Muslim kavass, who from time to time pridefully thunders, and he fears his rebuke. What power can such a person, who fears the roar of the servant who eats his bread, have? And what good are his glorious name and splendid clothing and the glory of the government that hovers over his house if he is like a lifeless vermilion block of wood, or like a lion overcome by a foe, and how can he preserve the honour of his protégés if his honour lies in the dust?[129]

The status of the Jewish consuls was in decline prior to this date, even among the members of the Aleppo Jewish community. This process, which had its origin in the realization that the Jewish consuls no longer had the power to protect them, was exacerbated by the discovery that some of the Picciottos had personal, and not communal, interests at heart. This caused internal dissension and prevented the community from pursuing its interests as a united bloc. The Alliance emissary to Aleppo linked the Picciottos' controversial behaviour within the Jewish communal context to the decline in their consular prestige and reported that Germany, Belgium, Denmark, and the United States had revoked their trust in the Picciottos and no longer engaged them as consuls.[130]

One outcome of this changed state of affairs was the proliferation of applications by Aleppo Jews to the British and French consuls for protection. Up to the 1870s only a few Jewish families, such as the Dwecks and the Gubbays, who were able to prove their Indian origins, sought British protection.[131] This was the case even though the British consul in Aleppo saw defending the Jews and their rights as part of his job, according to the instructions of Foreign Secretary Palmerston to all the British consuls in the empire.[132] Similarly, before the 1870s French protection was extended only to one branch of the Altaras family, which had huge commercial interests linking Aleppo and Marseilles.[133] The turning point came in the early 1870s, when Jews, both as individuals and as a community, began to seek the protection of the large powers. In 1869 the local Alliance branch in Aleppo appealed to the Paris headquarters, noting that, unlike Christians, Jews did not enjoy the protection and support of European consuls, charged with implementing their governments' instructions concerning preservation of minority rights. It requested that the Alliance lobby

[129] *Halevanon*, 21, 3 Jan. 1877, p. 167. This traveller's report exaggerates the number of Jewish consuls. In that year only Moses de Picciotto and his son Daniel, who served as Danish vice consul, still held consular posts.   [130] AAIU, Syrie, III.E., Alep, 23, Behor, 19 Nov. 1877.

[131] See the testimony by the Aleppine sages and notables regarding the Dweck family's origins in Calcutta, FO 195/1154, Aleppo, 15 Dec. 1856 and 195/927, Aleppo, 5 Feb. 1869. See also Consul Werry's list of British subjects, in which the Gabbai family appears as originating in Bombay, in FO 195/207, Werry, Aleppo, 3 Jan. 1846. See also FO 195/595, Skene to Bulwer, Aleppo, 28 Sept. 1858; 195/800, Heidenstam to Bulwer, Aleppo, 29 Sept. 1864; Heidenstam to Stuart, Aleppo, 1 Dec. 1864.   [132] See FO 78/448, Werry to Palmerston, Aleppo, 28 July 1841.

[133] See AECCC, Alep, vol. 32, p. 103, de Lafosse, 10 Jan. 1860, 2 Jan. 1862; vol. 33, p. 183, Bertrand, 12 Dec. 1865.

the foreign ministers of the various powers, Britain and France in particular, officially to direct their representatives in Aleppo to oversee the implementation of the reform measures pertaining to Jews. A further request was that these consuls grant equal protection to Jews, as to Christians. Although five Picciottos still represented at least eight European nations at that point, the local Alliance committee was well aware of their status as second-rate powers, and of the communal perception that the Jewish consuls' intervention on behalf the community was not always prompted by disinterested motives.[134]

The succeeding period saw an ever-increasing number of Jews seeking British and French consular protection. Even Franco families, including branches of the Picciotto family, sought to exchange their weaker position as protégés of secondary powers for British protection. In 1876 Hillel de Picciotto himself requested British protection, on the basis that the cancellation of his long position as Belgian consul in Aleppo, which he had held for twenty-one years, and of his office as US consul, held for twenty-six years, had left him without consular protection. Forced to divest himself of his Austrian citizenship upon assuming these posts, he now sought to take advantage of the opportunity afforded to Europeans with no consular representation to designate the consular representation of their choice and to gain British protection—despite the fact that many of his colleagues, most probably family members, had offered to make him their protégé.[135] Another Franco family turned to the British at an earlier date: the Silvera family, formerly Tuscan protégés. Their 1873 petition to the British consul claimed British origins, as their grandfather had been a British subject in Gibraltar. Forced by economic considerations to transfer to Tuscan protection, they now sought to reclaim their original citizenship under British regulations.[136] The British consulate, however, though increasingly aware of the need to protect the Aleppine Jewish community as a whole, was in no hurry to grant protection to individuals.

In contrast to the British consulate, the French representatives in Aleppo maintained a strongly anti-Jewish attitude until 1878. This was dictated by Consul Victor Bertrand, whose sixteen-year term as consul began in 1862. Bertrand's hatred was grounded in a mixture of prejudice, disputes with the Picciottos in his role as defender of the Christians, and his perception of Aleppo's Jewish community as a criminal organization whose sole aim was to cheat the Ottoman authorities, the Christians, and the Muslims.[137] Although

---

[134] See AAIU, Syrie, II.E., Alep, 11, Altaras, 12 Mar. 1869, 12 July 1869.

[135] See FO 195/1113, I. de Picciotto to Skene, Aleppo, 5 Jan. 1876; Skene to Elliot, Aleppo, 12 Jan. 1876.

[136] Evidently the Silveras failed to gain British protection and became Italian protégés. See FO 78/2299, Skene to Granville, Aleppo, 27 Feb. 1873. See also the petition by the Silveras to Granville, FO 78/2299, 27 May 1873.

[137] See AECCC, Alep, vol. 34, pp. 11 ff., Bertrand, 22 Mar. 1867; AAIU, Syrie, III.E., Alep, 23, Behor, 6 Apr. 1876. Note that, despite the mutual hatred and dissension between Bertrand and

the peaking of Muslim extremism in June 1877 in the wake of war with Russia left the Alliance school in Aleppo in great need of consular protection, Moses and Daniel de Picciotto refused to complain to the authorities, asserting that their consulates were not authorized to protect the school from attack. At Daniel de Picciotto's recommendation Mordecai Behor, the Alliance emissary in Aleppo, requested that the society's central Paris committee act to have instructions issued to Bertrand to take the school under his wing.[138] In response to Bertrand's query as to how he could legitimately protect Ottoman citizens, Behor noted that the school was a French institution, that wherever such schools operated they were under French protection, and that Aleppo should be no exception. Bertrand found various pretexts for rejecting this request. Behor bitterly summed up this state of affairs: 'Décidément Mr. Bertrand est l'ennemi des Israélites, pourquoi ne fait-il pas tant de difficultés pour protéger l'école chrétienne dite la Terre-Sainte?' (Mr Bertrand is decidedly the enemy of the Israelites; otherwise, why does he not present any obstacles to protecting the Christian Terra Sancta school?)[139]

Following Bertrand's death some six months later, the consular officials, under the consular secretary Siouffi, who served temporarily as acting consul from February to March 1878, began to exhibit greater sympathy for the Jewish community and for the Alliance school.[140] The arrival of the new consul, Charles Ferdinand Destrée, who was consistently well disposed to the school and to the community, presaged even greater improvement in the French consulate's attitude towards the Jews.[141]

*

Thus the role of consular involvement in bringing Syrian Jews closer to the West proceeded at different paces in Damascus and in Aleppo. As we shall see, this was also true for the involvement of European Jewish communities in protecting the rights of their Syrian co-religionists.

the Picciottos, by virtue of his seniority Moses de Picciotto marched at the head of the consuls who attended Bertrand's funeral. Bertrand died in Aleppo on 19 Feb. 1878. See AAIU, Syrie, III.E., Alep, 23, Behor, 15 July 1878.

[138] See AAIU, Syrie, III.E., Alep, 23, Behor, 2 June 1877.   [139] Ibid., 14 July 1877.
[140] AAIU, Syrie, I.E., Alep, 1, Siouffi, 16 May 1878; III.E., Alep, 23, Behor, 16 May 1878.
[141] AAIU, Syrie, I.E., Alep, 1, Destrée, 14 Aug. 1878, 5 Sept. 1879; III.E., Alep, 23, Behor, 15 July 1878, 22 Aug. 1879; X.E., Alep, 83, Somekh, 3 May 1880, 1 July 1880; *BAIU*, 1er et 2ème sem. 1879, p. 36.

ELEVEN

'THE PRINCES OF ISRAEL'

The Turn to the Jews of the West

The preceding chapter considered the political and religious motivation for activity on behalf of Syrian Jews by the representatives of European states, the British in particular. A significant factor in this engagement was the activity of the Jewish leadership, initially in Britain and later also in France. There is a direct link between British Jewry's pre-eminent role on behalf of Middle Eastern Jewry until 1860 and Britain's part in protecting the Jews in Syria. Similarly, the beginning of Alliance activity in Syria—which increased interest among the French Jewish communities in their co-religionists there—had a direct impact on the changed attitude of the French consulates in Damascus and Aleppo towards those cities' Jewish residents.[1]

The 1840 Damascus affair represents a key turning point in this process. Before this, the Syrian Jewish communities had strong bonds with other Middle Eastern Jewish communities and only tenuous ties with European Jewry. After this episode, Syrian Jews maintained commercial links and halakhic interchanges with other Middle Eastern Jewish communities, with Erets Yisra'el in particular,[2] but increasingly turned to their European brethren for support and assistance with respect to their civil and legal status. Damascus Jewry came to recognize the salutary effect of European Jewish intervention, and their co-religionists' lobbying of their home governments, on foreign consuls' willingness to support and protect the Jewish community. Moreover, they acknowledged the role of European Jewish vigilance in preventing Jewish rights in the Middle East from being publicly disregarded. Here, as in so many other areas, there is a distinction between Aleppo and Damascus. Just as Aleppo's Jews sought the aid and protection of the British and French consuls at a later

---

[1] On the link between British policy and the activity of leading British Jews, see Baron, 'Great Britain and Damascus Jewry', 181.

[2] The Middle Eastern commercial, halakhic, and philanthropic ties of Syrian merchants and rabbis were mainly with the various communities in Erets Yisra'el, such as those of Jerusalem, Safed, Hebron, and Tiberias, and with the İzmir, Istanbul, Salonika, Baghdad, and Alexandrian communities. See e.g. Abulafia, *Lev nishbar*, 60a, no. 7.

date than their Damascus co-religionists, so they were also slower to form ties with European Jewish communities. Only with the decline in the status of the Picciotto consuls and the beginning of Alliance activity in the city in 1869 did the Jews of Aleppo begin to turn to their European brethren.

Once Syrian Jews had realized the extent of their European co-religionists' influence on their governments, they stepped up appeals, primarily to Jews in London and Paris, to act on their behalf in various spheres. In essence, Syrian Jews became dependent on European Jewry for preservation of their rights. For their part, the European Jewish communities eagerly came to their assistance—but in ways that differed from those prevailing before 1840. Now acting publicly in the name of universal, liberal-humanitarian, emancipatory principles, European Jews wielded increased moral power when they demanded intervention by their governments on behalf of Middle Eastern Jewry in the name of, and not in opposition to, these modern values. In order to achieve this end, European Jews were prepared to engage in an open, public struggle to draft European public opinion to their cause.[3] In relation to issues concerning Syrian Jews, Ottoman governors and foreign consuls alike had to take this influence into account.

The Damascus affair's focal importance to nineteenth-century Jewish history is attributable more to the shock waves it engendered in the western Jewish world than to the blood libel, itself not an unusual occurrence. The affair marks the reawakening of feelings of Jewish solidarity that had been eclipsed by European Jewish participation in the struggle for equal rights in their individual homelands. Not content with eradicating the immediate danger posed by the Damascus affair, in 1860 the European Jewish communities founded an organization devoted to protecting Jews everywhere, the Paris-based Alliance Israélite Universelle.[4]

As noted earlier, in effect the Damascus affair lasted for another twenty years following the release of the Jews accused of murdering Father Thomas, until the smashing of the epitaph in the Capuchin monastery. Those two decades saw intense activity for removal of the epitaph, in particular by the London Board of Deputies. Indeed, the board's chairman Moses Montefiore intervened on behalf of Damascus Jews whenever ritual murder accusations raised their head. His first step on this matter was to make a direct request to Cardinal Riverola, protector of the Capuchin order in Rome, that he instruct the Capuchins in Damascus to remove the epitaph. Despite promises to that effect, the cardinal did not keep his word.[5]

[3] For a comprehensive treatment, see Frankel, 'The Crisis as a Factor in Modern Jewish Politics', 51–5; id., *The Damascus Affair*, 433.

[4] See Frankel, *The Damascus Affair*, 434; Mevorah, 'Effects of the Damascus Affair' (Heb.); Rodrigue, *French Jews, Turkish Jews*, 1–25; Parfitt, '"The Year of the Pride of Israel"', 131.

[5] Nahon, *Sir Moses Montefiore*, 35.

This matter of the epitaph resurfaced in 1847 in the wake of new ritual murder accusations in Damascus and Deir al-Qamar, and Montefiore began planning a trip to Damascus.[6] But he first directed his efforts to the French government, the patron of the Capuchin order in the Middle East and in his view the sole agency capable of getting the offensive epitaph removed. Armed with promises from the British Foreign Secretary Lord Palmerston that he would reiterate his instructions to British consuls to protect the Jews, in August 1847 Montefiore left for Paris, where he met King Louis-Philippe and the French foreign minister Guizot and demanded that measures be taken against French diplomatic staff in the Middle East who were using their positions to revive blood libels. In response, both the king and the foreign minister stressed the right of Damascus' Jews to protection and disowned the activity of the French consular agent in Damascus, Beaudin. Guizot even requested clarification from the Damascus consul with regard to the local consulate's involvement in blood libel accusations.[7] Although this intervention somewhat tempered the consulate's contribution to ritual murder accusations, it did not bring about the desired result. Montefiore himself arrived in Damascus only two years later, on 3 July 1849, at the invitation of the Jewish communal leaders, and was hosted by Isaac Hayim Farhi. He hastened to the Capuchin church in order to see the epitaph for himself, as a contemporary account reports:

He proceeded on his own to the large house of worship, where he saw the stone and the epitaph inscribed there to the chagrin of every intelligent person and it was like a shaft in his heart. He spoke not a word to anyone there because they are an arrogant people, who do not obey the laws of the sultan and pay no heed to the orders of the European kings . . . Accordingly, he took this to heart and did not speak secretly, for he will neither be still nor rest until justice emerges resplendent . . . and the epitaph is removed and uprooted, without name or remnant upon the earth.[8]

These remarks clearly convey Montefiore's sense that the local authorities could not, and that the hostile French consulate would not, assist him; he therefore decided to appeal once again to the French government. First, that September, he travelled to Frankfurt, in order to consult with Jewish leaders regarding the steps necessary to effect the epitaph's removal.[9] He also petitioned the British government to put pressure on the French regime. Via the British ambassador to Paris, Palmerston urged the French government to take

[6] For the Damascus Jews' appeal to Montefiore, see AECPC, Turquie, Damas, vol. 1, pp. 263–4.

[7] A report of Montefiore's meetings with Louis-Philippe and Guizot is housed in BofD, Minute Book, ACC/3121/A/6, pp. 69–71. See also AECPC, Turquie, Damas, vol. 1, pp. 246–61; FO 195/291, Timoni to Cowley, Damascus, 1 Sept. 1847; *JC*, 17 Sept. 1847, p. 242; Loewe (ed.), *Diaries of Sir Moses and Lady Montefiore*, ii. 6–7.

[8] MC, 520, Jacob Safir Halevi, *Shemesh tsedakah*. This work was written in Elul 1849, immediately following Montefiore's visit to Damascus. For the letter of invitation, see MC, 576, Rabbi Jacob Peretz to Montefiore, Rosh Hodesh Iyar 1849.

[9] Loewe (ed.), *The Diaries of Sir Moses and Lady Montefiore*, ii. 18.

measures to ensure elimination of the epitaph, while Montefiore also issued a direct appeal to Louis Napoleon, then the President of France, to order its removal.[10]

These tireless efforts by Montefiore and others, such as James de Rothschild, who assisted him in his contacts with the French regime,[11] did not escape the attention of Damascus' Jewish, or even its Christian, population. The French consul de Ségur perceived this international Jewish lobbying as endangering France's image and status in Syria. He stated that he had no difficulty personally explaining to Gustave de Rothschild, during the latter's visit to Damascus, the futility of Damascus Jewry's untiring efforts to recruit their influential European brethren to lobby for the epitaph's removal.[12]

In April 1855, in preparation for a return trip to Damascus, Montefiore requested a letter from Napoleon III instructing French officials there to assist in the epitaph's removal. Apparently, no such letter was forthcoming: Montefiore's letter to the emperor was forwarded to the foreign ministry without clear instructions either to help or to hinder him. When this letter came to the attention of the French consul in Damascus, Outrey, not only did he fail to initiate steps for its removal, he raised counter-reasons as to why the epitaph should remain in place.[13] Montefiore did not actually visit Damascus again, but he and the London Board of Deputies continued to work to achieve this goal on behalf of Damascus Jewry. The contemporary Jewish press noted the opening of a window of opportunity with the European powers' decision to dispatch armed forces to Syria to restore calm after the July 1860 massacre:

The chosen representatives of the Jews in Britain, located in London, decided to demand that the British government take action on behalf of the Damascus Jews . . . Now, when the European kings decided to send armed forces to Syria to restore order and to avenge the innocent Christian blood shed cruelly like water, this was also an opportune moment to have the above-mentioned epitaph removed from its place, so that there will no longer be a witness to the purported sin of the innocent Israelites.[14]

But, as the epitaph had already been smashed by the Muslim mob that destroyed the city's churches during the riots, no further steps turned out to be necessary.[15]

The years after 1860 saw increased involvement by European Jews both in rescuing their Syrian co-religionists from new accusations of active partici-

---

[10] See AECPC, Turquie, Damas, vol. 2, p. 98, Palmerston to the Marquess of Normandy, 8 Mar. 1850; pp. 95–6, Montefiore to Prince Louis Napoleon, President of the Republic of France, 1850. [11] See BofD, Minute Book, ACC/3121/A/6, p. 71.
[12] AECPC, Turquie, Damas, vol. 2, pp. 132–5, de Ségur, 12 Dec. 1850.
[13] Montefiore's letter to the emperor of 26 Apr. 1855 is housed in AECPC, Turquie, Damas, vol. 3, pp. 268–72. See also AECPC, Turquie, Damas, vol. 3, p. 279, Palais de Tuileries, 1 June 1855.
[14] *Hamagid*, 34, 29 Aug. 1860, p. 133. [15] *JC*, 29 Mar. 1861, p. 5.

pation in murder and plunder during the massacre and in effecting their release from the burdensome fine imposed on all non-Christian residents of Damascus. Motivated by the expectation that a new Christian recognition of the danger religious fanaticism posed to them, as well as to Jews, would help restrain and extinguish antisemitism in Europe, European Jews initiated fundraising drives to help the victims of the massacre. In France, Adolphe Crémieux, who was in the forefront of these efforts, used the press to appeal to the Jews to found a society to help the unfortunate Christians, in hopes that this would initiate a worldwide movement of mutual aid for victims of religious persecution and also strengthen the principle of freedom of worship.[16] In England, Moses Montefiore not only issued a similar call but also donated £200 to the cause, facilitating the foundation of the British Syrian Relief Fund, of which Lord Stratford de Redcliffe served as president, and Montefiore as chairman.[17] Donations to this cause began to arrive from Jewish communities in Austria, France, Britain, Hungary, Russia, The Netherlands, and elsewhere.[18]

Not only Catholic antisemitism but also Jewish–Protestant friction in Syria attracted European Jewish intervention on behalf of Syrian Jews. As patrons of the Protestants in the Middle East, the British consuls tended to side with the Protestants in these disputes, perhaps truly convinced that Protestant missionary activity was to Jewish benefit. For their part, the leaders of the Damascus Jewish community sought relief from Protestant missionary pressure and besought the leading members of British Jewry to exert their influence to this end. In the early 1870s, bitter disputes and power struggles broke out between the Damascus Jewish community and Protestant activists headed by Frankel (as described in Chapter 9). One threat, aimed at forcing the rabbis to cancel their ban on anyone co-operating with Frankel, was that the missionaries would relay reports of the Jewish anti-Protestant campaign to the European press, which could set off renewed persecution of the Jews. The Damascus rabbis hastened to enlist the help of their Paris and London co-religionists and the Alliance referred to the matter to the London Anglo-Jewish Association. Its president Henry de Worms brought the threats made by the envoys of the London Society for Promoting Christianity amongst the Jews to the attention of the Earl of Shaftesbury, chairman of the latter organization. Following Shaftesbury's unhesitating condemnation of the missionaries' actions and his commitment that his society would not take steps against the Jews in the future, the Protestant mission in Syria withdrew their threats and the rabbis withdrew their ban.[19]

[16] Leven, *Cinquante ans d'histoire*, ii. 395–6.

[17] *Hamagid*, 29, 25 July 1860, p. 114; 32, 15 Aug. 1860, p. 127.

[18] See *Hamagid*, 32, 15 Aug. 1860, p. 127; 33, 22 Aug. 1860, p. 131; 38, 27 Sept. 1860, p. 152; 40, 16 Oct. 1860, p. 159.

[19] *JC*, 14 Mar. 1873, p. 730; 21 Mar. 1873, p. 750; *BAIU*, 1er sem. 1873, p. 65; AAIU, Syrie, XI.E., Damas, 94, Halfon au Président de l'AIU, 8 June 1873.

British Jews also helped their Syrian brethren by providing the necessary documentation for acquisition of British protection. British law stipulated that only individuals who could prove British origins were eligible to become British protégés. Depositions from London Jews stating that certain Syrian Jews were indeed of British origin facilitated this process.[20]

English Jews, Moses Montefiore in particular, also engaged in purely philanthropic activity on behalf of their Damascus co-religionists. During his 1849 visit to Damascus, Montefiore disbursed substantial sums to the poor and to scholars, and even donated £50 towards the founding of a modern school. In return, the Damascus Jews designated him their president.[21] Over the years, the city's Jews continued to turn to Montefiore when under duress, requesting his intervention to lighten their tax burden and support the needy. In 1875, during a cholera outbreak, the rabbis forwarded a request to Montefiore for aid, reminding him: 'There are many sick and even more poor, and some widows and orphans. Even earlier, during the days of the libel, you saved several Jews and now, with God's help, our restoration will be at your hands.'[22]

By far the most significant European Jewish contribution to the security of Syrian Jews lay in protecting them from hostile consuls. Montefiore's and Crémieux's successful campaign against Ratti-Menton, the French consul during the Damascus affair, unmistakably demonstrated their political influence. Thereafter, the Jewish communities in both Aleppo and Damascus did not hesitate to request European Jewish intervention whenever a particular consul took an antagonistic, anti-Jewish stand, at times even going so far as to seek the assistance of their western brethren in effecting the recall of a particularly hostile consul—as, for example, in the case of the British consul in Damascus from 1870 to 1871, Richard Burton.

From the moment of his arrival in Damascus, this consul had an adversarial relationship with the Jews. Burton himself attributed this to his antipathy towards extortionate Jewish moneylending, claiming that this activity had bankrupted many *fallahin*, causing entire villages to collapse. It is more likely, however, that his hostility was grounded in antisemitism and in his belief that the Jews had indeed murdered Father Thomas in 1840 to acquire blood for ritual purposes.[23]

---

[20] See e.g. FO 78/1751, Rogers to Bulwer, Damascus, 8 May 1863; 78/2242, Skene to Granville, Aleppo, 9 May 1872.

[21] MC, 520, Jacob Safir Halevi, *Shemesh tsedakah*. See also Loewe (ed.), *The Diaries of Sir Moses and Lady Montefiore*, ii. 14. For appeals during Montefiore's visit to Damascus in 1849, see many undated documents in MC, 576 and 577.

[22] MC, 551, the scholars of Damascus to Moses Montefiore, 2 Av 1875.

[23] After leaving Damascus, Burton penned a book condemning the Jews entitled *Human Sacrifice amongst the Sephardim or Eastern Jews or the Murder of Padre Tomaso*. This book remained in manuscript, and was brought to press only in the 1890s by his heirs. By purchasing the manuscript, the English and French Jewish leaders successfully prevented its publication. See AAIU,

The opening clash between Burton and the Jewish community came in June 1870, when the consul reported on what he viewed as the destructive activity of Jewish moneylenders to the British ambassador to Istanbul. Burton strongly condemned the practice of the most prominent moneylenders—David Harari, Isaac Tobi, and Jacob Stambouli, all British protégés—using the services of the Damascus consulate for debt collection. Burton proclaimed that British protection would be granted solely to secure its protégés' lives and property, and that the consulate would not assist Jewish moneylenders in collecting debts from either the government or the *fallahin*. A notice to this effect was posted on the consulate gate on 20 June 1870.[24] Burton justified this step by claiming that the moneylenders' use of the consulate in debt collection was attracting the debtors' anger towards the representatives of Britain in Syria, thus harming British status in the region.[25] Especially vexing to Burton was his sense that the Jewish moneylenders viewed the British consul as their leading agent for debt collection. In a letter to the regional Alliance emissary, Charles Netter, Burton accused the Jewish moneylenders of being totally corrupt, alleging that they forged seals, documents, and receipts, deceitfully doubled their demands, and enserfed the farmers, all of which Burton regarded as a curse on the land. He further asserted that the moneylenders had no qualms about employing criminal or violent means for debt collection.[26]

Burton's steps undoubtedly had a deleterious effect on the profits of the Jewish moneylenders. Unable to rely on the Ottoman authorities for collection, without British support they faced the threat of heavy losses. Additional

Angleterre, II.D., 36, London Committee of Deputies of the British Jews, London, 15 Apr. 1897. Nonetheless, Burton's condemnatory conclusions were published in his *The Jew, the Gypsy and el Islam* (1898). In his introduction, the book's editor William Henry Wilkins noted that he chose to omit Burton's inquiry into Father Thomas's death because of its extreme antisemitic nature. Burton's wife Isabel also believed the Jews to be guilty of the murder. See FO 78/2259, Burton to Granville, Damascus, 29 Nov. 1870. Even though she claims not to be antisemitic, her own book is replete with antisemitic sentiments. See e.g. I. Burton, *The Inner Life of Syria*, i. 41, 58. Her use of Shylock as a designation for a Jewish moneylender is indicative of her stereotypical view of Jews. See FO 78/2260, Burton to Granville, Damascus, 28 Nov. 1870; I. Burton, *The Inner Life of Syria*, i. 336.

[24] I. Burton, *The Inner Life of Syria*, i. 333–4; FO 78/1751, Rogers to Bulwer, Damascus, 8 May 1863.

[25] Charles Malcolm Kennedy, the special envoy sent from the British Foreign Office to investigate the matter, explained that the behaviour of Jewish moneylenders was actually *more* humane than that of moneylenders under the protection of other consulates. Kennedy attributed the problem to the fact that most of the moneylenders were British Jewish protégés, thereby creating the impression that these were British claims. These Jews were also accused of bribing the police to arrest their creditors without informing the British consulate in whose name the arrests were carried out. See Hyamson (ed.), *The British Consulate in Jerusalem*, ii. 350; Brawer, 'The Jews of Damascus', 105.

[26] FO 78/2260, Burton to Netter, Damascus, 4 Oct. 1870; 406/12, Burton to Elliot, Damascus, 21 Nov. 1870.

factors further hampered their freedom of action. Because the British consulate did not entirely retract its protection, they were barred from becoming protégés of other consulates. Moreover, even had they been able to acquire alternative protection, the law prohibited collection of a claim submitted under the jurisdiction of one consulate under that of another.[27] But in itself, the economic damage to this small, albeit important, group within the Jewish community did not yet suffice to prompt an appeal for European Jewish intervention. For the present, the Damascus Jewish leadership proceeded to act on the local level, lobbying Burton to change his approach.[28] But as soon as Burton's quarrel with the Jews acquired antisemitic, life-threatening overtones, the Damascus Jewish leaders demanded that their European coreligionists work towards his dismissal, as well as that of two consular dragomen involved in anti-Jewish incitement.[29]

The impetus for this appeal came in the wake of an accusation in August 1870 that the Jews were fomenting a Muslim attack on Christians like that of 1860. Allegations of incitement in the present were coupled with the revival of the charge that Jews had played a role in the July 1860 massacre.[30] The appearance of signs—such as crosses drawn in the street and on the mosque walls—similar to the ones that had presaged the riots a decade earlier created panic among the Christians of Damascus. On the basis of a brief inquiry, Burton deduced that Jewish children had drawn the crosses at the bidding of their employers, the brothers Donemberg, Jews of Russian origin under British protection. Burton attributed the interest of Damascus Jews in inciting Muslim–Christian conflict to their desire to enrich themselves, as in the aftermath of the 1860 massacre, by selling booty. By way of demonstrating to the Christians that the perpetrators had been punished, Burton temporarily withdrew British protection from the Donembergs, whom he held responsible for the children's actions.[31] It was after this episode that the Jews of Damascus began a concerted

---

[27] Brawer, 'The Jews of Damascus' (Heb.), 106.

[28] According to Burton, these attempts to influence him included bribery and bars of silver. See FO 78/2260, Burton to Granville, Damascus, 28 Nov. 1870.

[29] FO 78/2259, Rabbis Aaron Jacob and Jacob Peretz to Rabbi Nathan Ahler [Adler] Hakohen, 17 Elul 1870. On these two dragomen, see Brawer, 'The Jews of Damascus' (Heb.), 106–7.

[30] See FO 78/2260, Burton to Granville, Damascus, 28 Nov. 1870; I. Burton, *The Inner Life of Syria*, i. 108, 305; Hyamson, *The British Consulate in Jerusalem*, ii. 352. Evidently, Burton used direct influence to ensure the publication in the London *Times* on 31 Oct. 1870 of a letter sent from Damascus, signed by three British clergymen, in which they too accused the Jews of stirring up trouble in Damascus and of assisting the Muslims during the 1860 massacre. The similarity between the wording of the letter and the language of Burton and his wife on these matters supports the surmise that Burton inspired its publication. Montefiore swiftly responded with a reply in the same newspaper. For a more extended discussion, see Loewe (ed.), *The Diaries of Sir Moses and Lady Montefiore*, ii. 233–4.

[31] See FO 195/965, Burton to Elliot, Damascus, 1 Sept. 1870. Note that the consular dragoman, Nasif Mishaqa, claimed that Muslims were responsible, either directly or indirectly, for the

campaign to get Burton removed from his post and from their city. As Burton's wife Isabel interpreted the situation, the Jewish moneylenders took advantage of the circumstances to avenge themselves on her husband and to have him dismissed.

So strong was the belief of Damascus Jewry in their British co-religionists' power to bring about Burton's recall that Jews made public declarations in the streets that Burton's days as consul were numbered.[32] Letters written by the Damascus rabbis to Moses Montefiore, Francis Goldsmid, and Rabbi Adler in London, and to Charles Netter, the Alliance emissary to the Middle Eastern Jewish communities, reveal their unfolding relationship with Burton from his arrival in Damascus. In particular, they single out his fixed antagonism to Jews, which distinguished him from all previous British consuls: 'For the previous consuls from England before this one showed love and affection. The former consuls were singularly loving towards the people of Israel who gathered under the protection of the aforementioned consulate, may it be exalted, and encouraged their proximity and fulfilled their wishes and helped them with their affairs, and this Senor Burton is their opposite.'[33]

The rabbis accused Burton of torturing the children in order to extract a confession that their employers had set them to inflame religious tensions in the city, recounted the anti-Jewish acts carried out by him under the aegis of the British consulate and described his contemptuous attitude towards them personally. Further ammunition for his removal, grounded not in his attitude towards the Jews but in his incompetence as a consul, took the form of allegations of inadequate performance of his duties. Because Burton took extended trips—returning to Damascus only for a day or two before setting out again— instead of dealing with pressing matters, he was unable properly to attend to consular affairs and this, the complainants argued, was to the detriment of British interests. In explaining why they, and not Jews under British protection, had penned the complaint, Rabbis Jacob Peretz and Aaron Jacob stressed the British Jewish protégés' fear of retaliation.[34]

Montefiore and Goldsmid forwarded the rabbis' letters to the British Foreign Secretary, who asked Burton to respond to these charges.[35] Burton's

drawing of the crosses. He indicated that they hoped that unrest would lead to cancellation of the conscription of Muslim men, which left many families without breadwinners. Burton preferred to stick to his conception of the Jewish interest in stirring up unrest, even to the extent of inciting Muslims to massacre Christians. See Hyamson (ed.), *The British Consulate in Jerusalem*, ii. 352; I. Burton, *The Inner Life of Syria*, i. 305–6; Brawer, 'The Jews of Damascus' (Heb.), 106.

[32] I. Burton, *The Inner Life of Syria*, i. 335, 340.

[33] FO 78/2259, Rabbis Aaron Jacob and Jacob Peretz to Rabbi Nathan Ahler [Adler] Hakohen, 17 Elul 1870.

[34] Ibid. See also FO 78/2259, Rabbis Aaron Jacob and Jacob Peretz to Moses Montefiore, Elul 1870; 78/2260, Weisskopf to Sir Francis Goldsmid, Beirut, 12 Sept. 1870.

[35] FO 78/2260, Montefiore to Granville, London, 25 Oct. 1870; Goldsmid to Hammond,

defence reiterated his accusations of Jewish corruption and Jewish crimes against the villagers of Syria under Her Majesty's protection and in her name. It also reflects his awareness that he had incurred the enmity of influential Jews worldwide; he in turn blamed these Jews for the arrogance of Damascus Jewry, further claiming that even the chief rabbi addressed him insolently, as if Burton were his servant.[36] According to Burton, the Jewish moneylenders had become the most powerful group in Damascus, not only because they were British protégés, but mainly because 'they enjoy the confidence of influential friends in England—they are leagued together by the Alliance Israélite universelle—and they are by no means scrupulous, as their writings prove, when they determine to gain a point.'[37]

Evidently fearing that his position was in danger, Burton tried to draft the Foreign Secretary, Lord Granville, to his side. He wrote: 'The Chief Rabbis unhesitatingly demand my recall and the dismissal of the two Dragomans of this Consulate; they evidently expect that on their simple assertion, an officer of 28 years standing should be disgraced, and that similar dishonour should be extended to two Syrian Christian gentlemen of high local standing, who have long served the British Government.'[38] Burton asserted that Damascus Jews had in the past employed the strong influence of their European co-religionists to work towards the dismissal of consuls who refused to act on their behalf. According to Burton, William Wrench, acting British consul from 1860 to 1861, who had served under Wood, had been forced out by the lobbying of Jewish moneylenders, and others among his predecessors had kowtowed to the Jews.[39] Isabel Burton alleged that, despite her husband's predecessor's accession to all Jewish demands, rumours and complaints were spread in order to effect Rogers' dismissal; she also claimed that, for years after Rogers' departure, the Damascus Jews boasted of having obtained his services through bribery.[40] She further claimed that the Jews now sought to restore Rogers to

London, 24 Oct. 1870; Russell to Burton, London, 3 Nov. 1870. Burton and his wife Isabel were angered in particular by Sir Francis Goldsmid, who submitted that Burton's attitude towards the Jews was influenced by his wife, whom he termed a 'bigoted Roman Catholic'. Isabel Burton responded to these remarks in a letter to the British Foreign Secretary. See FO 78/2259, Isabel Burton to Granville, Damascus, 29 Nov. 1870; FO 78/2260, Burton to Granville, Damascus, 28 Nov. 1870; *JC*, 3 Feb. 1871, p. 2; I. Burton, *The Inner Life of Syria*, i. 336.

[36] FO 78/2260, Burton to Granville, Damascus, 6 Dec. 1870; 406/12, Burton to Elliot, Damascus, 21 Nov. 1870.

[37] FO 78/2260, Burton to Granville, Damascus, 28 Nov. 1870; 78/2259, Burton to Granville, Damascus, 15 Dec. 1870; I. Burton, *The Inner Life of Syria*, i. 340; Hyamson (ed.), *The British Consulate in Jerusalem*, ii. 365. After receiving letters of complaint from Damascus Jews, Charles Netter also attempted to have the Christian dragomen dismissed from the British consulate. See FO 78/2260, Netter to Burton, 14 Jan. 1870. This is not the original letter and the date should read September and not January, as the cross-drawing incident took place in August. As personal friends, Netter and Burton corresponded frequently.

[38] FO 78/2260, Burton to Granville, Damascus, 6 Dec. 1870.   [39] Ibid.

[40] FO 78/2259, I. Burton to Granville, Damascus, 29 Nov. 1870.

his post so that he could continue to serve them, also reporting the existence of rumours that, because of business connections with the Jews, Rogers himself was behind the Jewish intrigues against her husband.[41] Even assuming that the Burtons exaggerated, this summary of their allegations illustrates the complex nature of the relationship between the British consulate and the Damascus Jewish community: a relationship governed by sympathy and personal hatred, by business ties, international intrigues, and economic manipulation, and coloured by European Jews' willingness to protect their Damascus co-religionists.

Charles Malcolm Kennedy, dispatched to Syria by the British Foreign Office as a special envoy to look into the roots of the situation described by Burton with respect to Jewish moneylending and alleged Jewish attempts to incite the Muslim masses against the Christians, by and large supported Burton's version of the situation.[42] Notwithstanding Kennedy's support, Burton was recalled to England on 16 August 1871. Conciliatory overtures to the Damascus Jewish leadership through Burton's wife Isabel met with no success.[43]

This raises the question of the weight played by Jewish complaints in Burton's recall and whether additional factors also played a role in his dismissal. Isabel Burton attributed her husband's dismissal to the governor, Rashid Pasha, whereas William Henry Wilkins, editor of one of Burton's books, blamed it on Jewish hostility to Burton, provoked by his accusation that they used human blood for ritual purposes.[44] Closer investigation shows that the Christian population of Damascus disliked Burton as well; indeed, his intense interest in Islam and Middle Eastern culture, and his demonstrative fondness for Muslims, led Damascus Christians to conclude that he was a secret convert to Islam. One traveller in the East described Burton, probably on the basis of local Christian informants, as 'L'ennemi déclaré des chrétiens' (the declared enemy of the Christians).[45] Evidently, complaints regarding Burton reached the Sublime Porte as well, which also requested his replacement. In summing up the

---

[41] See also Consul Burton's remarks regarding Rogers in FO 78/2260, Burton to Granville, Damascus, 28 Nov. 1870.

[42] For further detail on Kennedy's activity, see Hyamson (ed.), *The British Consulate in Jerusalem*, ii. 350–64.

[43] In her book Isabel Burton conveys the impression that this peacemaking initiative was a Jewish one. She alleges that the Jews suggested that they pen a statement, signed by six rabbis, to the effect that all the letters dispatched with the aim of bringing about her husband Richard Burton's recall were written in the heat of the moment. Evidently, in her attempt to prove her husband's claims, Isabel Burton diverged from the facts. The Jews never penned any letters of regret. It is entirely possible that Isabel Burton made this suggestion after a last-ditch attempt to explain to the Jews that her husband had acted only against the moneylenders and was not motivated by hatred of the Jewish community as a whole. See I. Burton, *The Inner Life of Syria*, ii. 263–4.

[44] Ibid. ii. 280–1; Burton, *The Jew, the Gypsy and el Islam*, p. viii.

[45] Bost, *Souvenirs d'Orient*, 85. On Richard Burton as traveller and geographer, see Trench, *Arabian Travellers*.

reasons for Burton's recall for the Porte, the British ambassador to Istanbul, Henry George Elliot, noted his own dissatisfaction with the Damascus consulate's functioning. Burton, in his opinion, had failed to win the trust either of the British subjects, whether Christian missionaries or Jews, or of the Ottoman authorities. The Porte's complaint focused on Burton's frequent warnings of an impending massacre of Christians, an allegation that had reached Elliot's ears from other, probably Jewish, sources. Elliot also noted the grumbling about Burton's frequent absences from the consulate. Although these complaints were in themselves insufficient to bring about Burton's dismissal, nonetheless Elliot concluded: 'I consider . . . that his presence tends to unsettle the public mind at Damascus, and to keep alive a sentiment of insecurity, which may at any time become a source of danger, and that it would be very desirable that he should be removed whenever an opportunity for it might offer.'[46] The Foreign Office adopted his recommendation and began implementing the steps that led to Burton's recall.[47]

Reviewing this evidence, it is probable that complaints by Damascus Jews, which came to the Foreign Secretary's attention through the agency of their influential English co-religionists, played a crucial role in verifying and strengthening the Sublime Porte's grievance against Burton and in his recall. The successful outcome of their campaign against the British representative in their city, with the assistance of their European brethren, enhanced the power and image of Damascus Jews not only in their own eyes but also in that of their neighbours. This episode marks the apex of Damascus Jewry's political influence, which evaporated with its economic collapse in 1875 upon the Ottoman empire's declaration of bankruptcy.

During the mid-1870s Aleppo too saw an attempt to manipulate consular appointments through European Jewish influence. By this time, aware that the power of their traditional protectors—the Jewish consuls from the Picciotto family—was waning, Aleppo's Jews were newly appreciating the power of their western co-religionists to exercise political influence on their behalf.

As described in Chapter 10, anti-Jewish hostility was a prevailing feature of French consul Bertrand's sixteen-year tenure in Aleppo from 1862 to 1878.[48] Bertrand persistently schemed against the Jews, in particular the Altaras family, who held French citizenship. Initial complaints by members of this family, forwarded directly to the French foreign ministry, referred to infringement of their rights not as Jews but as French citizens.[49] However, when it became apparent that Bertrand was motivated by simple hatred of Jews, Aleppo's Jews

[46] FO 406/12, Elliot to Granville, Constantinople, 22 Apr. 1871.

[47] Ibid., Granville to Elliot, London, 25 May 1871.

[48] See AAIU, Syrie, V.E., Alep, 62, Nerson, 21 Oct. 1864.

[49] AECCC, Alep, vol. 34, pp. 11 ff., Bertrand, 21 Mar. 1867. It was Bertrand who raised the Jewish issue by portraying the Jewish merchants as a crooked 'mafia'.

began to seek ways to rid themselves of this malicious presence. Because Bertrand's powerful position hampered any attempts at achieving his dismissal, the Jews sought instead to have one Alexander Lucciana—a merchant favourably disposed towards the Jews—appointed consular secretary.[50] In conjunction with the Alliance emissary to Aleppo, the leaders of the Jewish community and its rabbis appealed to the Alliance head office in Paris to lobby the French foreign ministry for Lucciana's appointment.[51] These efforts were successful, and Lucciana served as consular secretary until 1877. At the end of his tenure in office, Lucciana received letters of approbation from the leaders of the Jewish community in recognition of his support.[52]

European Jews' achievements on behalf of their eastern brethren led to their being exalted as protectors and saviours among Syrian Jewry. Because these influential Jews lived in enlightened countries, the Syrian Jews thought, they alone could spur their governments to persuade the Ottoman regime to act favourably towards its Jewish subjects. As early as 1847, after a rash of forced conversions of Jews and Christians to Islam in Damascus, a rumour spread that the converts would be allowed to return to their original religion through a Rothschild's intervention with the sultan. Rabbi Hayim Maimon Tobi provided the following description of this event:

One of the Rothschilds came to Istanbul and was hosted by the English ambassador. According to established custom, they went to the court to see the sultan, who, knowing that there was a Rothschild among the guests, said, 'Let Senor Rothschild come before me.' He came before him [the sultan], who honoured him and said, 'You are one of the large Rothschild family, beloved of all kings, and I love you as well. Now ask a favour of me on behalf of the Jews and I will do it in your honour.' He replied, 'I ask for nothing, just a minor request and that is that you not force any convert to Islam to remain Muslim against his wishes; let each person do as he sees fit.' And he responded, 'Let it be so.'[53]

More expansive glorification of their European co-religionists was expressed in a letter of Elul 1860 from the Jewish leaders in Damascus to Baron James de Rothschild:

Glory of Israel, the crown of our heads, the summit of our stronghold, whose splendour and majesty stand in the breach, of worldwide fame . . . and may God preserve him and raise his star in battle and grant him favour in the eyes of the mighty kings

[50] Lucciana served as French consular secretary in Mosul in the 1840s. On him, see AECCC, Alep, vol. 31, pp. 287 ff., Geofroy, 22 Oct. 1853.

[51] AAIU, Syrie, I.B., Alep, 1, Rabbi Moses Sutton to Crémieux, 3 Adar 1875.

[52] Ibid., III.E., Alep, 23, Behor, 15 June 1876. See also the letters of approbation from the Aleppo rabbis, 11 Nisan 1877, and from the members of the local Alliance branch in Aleppo, 26 Mar. 1877, ibid., IV.E., 50, Gubbay.

[53] NLIS, DA, V-736/28, Hayim Maimon Tobi to Abraham Hayim Gagin, Damascus, 5 Sivan 1847.

and in the eyes of princes, may they be exalted, and may Judah be saved in his day, and may Israel dwell in safety . . . and we constantly praise God that he has not abandoned us, nor will he abandon us; and for not denying us a saviour: you are our saviour.[54]

In this specific instance the Jewish leadership was asking that the baron request that the head of the French task force sent to Syria in 1860 be instructed to protect the Jews, 'for we, the Israelites who live in Damascus take refuge in the might . . . of Senor Rothschild'.[55] The Jews of Damascus sought to evoke an image of a united Jewish people, in which harm to them would be equated with harm to the Jews of France and would at the same time detract from Baron de Rothschild's honourable status. In their effort to draft European Jews to the aid of eastern Jews, the Damascus community also dispatched a special envoy to the London Board of Deputies.[56]

The ability of European Jews to assist their Middle Eastern co-religionists filtered into public awareness, both in Syria and in the West. This awareness is exemplified by an incident that took place in the Beirut region involving an assault with robbery on five Jews. At first it was ignored by the Ottoman authorities, 'but because of our close loving link with our brethren worldwide, it came to pass, with God's help, that they awakened the hearts of all the representatives of the kingdoms in Turkey regarding this foul deed, and upon their instructions the government made efforts to trace the robbers and murderers'.[57] On the other hand, the non-Jewish population of Syria took a jaundiced view of the intervention of western Jews on behalf of their Middle Eastern co-religionists, as did the foreign consuls, who felt threatened by Jewish influence in the national corridors of power. In planning their own policies and strategies, the consuls stationed in Syria were forced to consider the power and influence of Jews in London and Paris, lest this be turned against them in support of the Jews in Syria. Some consuls ill-disposed to Jews saw in this state of affairs a worldwide Jewish conspiracy in favour of Syrian Jewry that would come to the latter's aid even when it was in the wrong—a perception fostered by the development of a myth of world Jewish dominion in the decades following the Damascus affair.[58] In this respect, the political power of European Jews at least equalled, and was even said to exceed, that of the foreign consuls in Syria. Richard Burton's report of July 1871 regarding European protection obtained by the various sects—in which he noted that 'the Jews either obtain the protection of foreign passports or they rely upon the influence of their

---

[54] *Hamagid*, 39, 5 Oct. 1860, pp. 154–5.

[55] Ibid. See also their letter to Montefiore dated 7 Tishrei 1860, in BofD, Minute Book, ACC/3121/A/9, pp. 101–5.   [56] *JC*, 1 Nov. 1861, p. 5.

[57] *Hamagid*, 19, 14 May 1862, p. 148. For reports of similar attacks and European Jewry's desire to intervene on behalf of their co-religionists, see *BAIU*, 2ème sem. 1873, 33, 62, 74–5; 1er sem. 1874, 41; BofD, Minute Book, ACC/3121/A/9, p. 154.

[58] For the development of this myth, see Frankel, *The Damascus Affair*, 435.

co-religionists throughout the civilized world'[59]—draws a parallel between European Jewry's protective power and that of local foreign consulates in the Syrian context.

Enhancing this image of a manipulative international Jewish organization was the introduction of another layer of European Jewish involvement with the Jewish communities of Syria: activity among the Jews of Damascus and Aleppo by the Alliance Israélite Universelle. Jews in the Syrian cities, and to an even greater extent those in small towns, envisaged the Alliance as an international Jewish government, and as the legitimate representative of the Jews with regard to any issue, anywhere. They imagined the Alliance president Adolphe Crémieux to be the king of the Jews; in practical terms, this made them confer on the school principals, the Alliance envoys, the status of 'consuls of the Kingdom of the Alliance'.[60] A variety of appeals for help, both individual and communal, were sent to the Alliance, on matters ranging from the minor and personal—such as a complaint that the mufti of Aleppo had built a khan opposite the house of a Jew, thereby disturbing its residents and lowering its property value—to communal issues of urgent import, such as rescuing Jews from the Ottoman system of justice, whose anti-minority bias could be life-threatening. The Alliance became *the* address to which all Syrian Jewish hopes for rectification of wrongs were directed. This is how the Damascus rabbis described the status of their community under Ottoman justice and the hopes and trust they placed in the Alliance:

Oh heavens! The pain of the distressed. He who has a father will live; he who has no father will die. Alas, what has befallen us? We have become orphans, fatherless [Lam. 5: 3]; we have no help and no support. We lie prostrate in the dust; our body clings to the ground [Ps. 44: 26]. Where shall we turn for help ... We are downtrodden and trampled under their feet, despised and oppressed, wretched and unhappy; from being taunted and reviled humiliation covered our faces [Jer. 51: 51], and we have not the audacity to lift our heads ... And this is our comfort, thank God, who has not withheld a redeemer from us [paraphrase of Ruth 4: 14], for Israel was not widowed [Jer. 51: 5], for he has sent us a cure for our ills and healing for our blows, the princes of Israel from the honourable holy society, may God preserve them, who are in charge of [Num. 7: 2] ... saving the people of Israel, they are the people of God to save them from every ambush and enemy [Ezra 8: 31].[61]

From the outset, the Alliance did not define itself as a philanthropic society, and providing help for the needy was not among its goals. Nonetheless, the

[59] FO 406/12, Burton to Elliot, Damascus, 15 July 1871; 195/965, Burton to Elliot, Damascus, 1 Sept. 1870.

[60] See e.g. AAIU, I.B., Alep, 1, the Khafif brothers to the Alliance, 25 Oct. 1877, and the letter of the Aleppo rabbinical court to the Alliance, Erev Shavuot 1875. See also Rodrigue, *Images of Sephardi and Eastern Jewries*, 201–3.

[61] AAIU, Syrie, I.B., 5, Damas, Damascus rabbis to AIU, Rosh Hodesh Heshvan 1876.

society did not refuse material assistance to the Syrian communities in times of need. Requests for financial aid sent to the Alliance and to wealthy French Jews, some of whom were descendants of Syrian families that had emigrated from Syria to France or vice versa, were viewed sympathetically. Thus, for example, a donation from Isaac Altaras of Marseilles, who obtained funds from Baron Rothschild and David Sassoon, financed the renovation of the Aleppo synagogue.[62] The Antioch Jewish community appealed to the Alliance for aid in renovating its synagogue and for the poor.[63] During the severe regional famine of 1880, the Aleppo community and the surrounding communities of 'Ayntab, Antioch, Tadef, and Kilis were beneficiaries of massive Alliance aid.[64]

In sum, although political lobbying formed the main thrust of western Jewish assistance to Syrian Jewry, the 'Princes of Israel' did not neglect the Syrian Jewish communities' basic needs.

Migration to the West

The process whereby the Syrian Jewish communities drew closer to their western co-religionists not only had an impact on their self-image and way of life, but also served as a catalyst for their exodus to the West. Ultimately, reliance on western Jewish communities and recognition of the superiority of the western Jewish lot to that of Middle Eastern Jewry under Ottoman rule triggered emigration by young people and families from Syria to the new world of the United States and South America.

This phenomenon was not restricted to Jews. Syrian emigration in general began with the Egyptian conquest, at which time the main destination was Egypt.[65] Gaining momentum in the late 1870s, by the mid-1880s migration had become an all-encompassing mass movement, penetrating each and every Syrian community and social stratum. The proportionally greater involvement of the Christian and Jewish minorities during its early stages points to religious and sectarian motives for leaving Syria.[66] In the aftermath of the 1860 mas-

---

[62] See Moses Sutton, *Kehilat mosheh*, 299b–300.

[63] AAIU, Syrie, I.B., 4, Antioche, the Antioch Jewish community to the Alliance, received 8 Jul. 1872.

[64] See e.g. AAIU, Syrie, III.E., Alep, 32, Cohen, Rabbi Moses Hakohen to the chief rabbi of France, Rabbi Isidor, 7 Apr. 1880; 'Compte-rendu des secours de Paris pour les pauvres israélites d'Alep', 19 July 1880.

[65] For Jewish emigration under Egyptian rule, See e.g. Antebi, *Mor ve'oholot*, 94a, 'Ḥoshen mishpat', no. 13; M. Labaton, *Nokhaḥ hashulḥan*, 112b, 'Ḥoshen mishpat', no. 39; fo. 77b, 'Ḥoshen mishpat', no. 24.

[66] The literature on the late nineteenth- and early twentieth-century migration from Syria deals mainly with Christians, and to a lesser extent with Muslims, rather than with Jews. Thus, because he views them as belonging to the Jewish, and not to the immigrant Syrian, community, Philip Hitti excludes the Syrian Jewish communities from his discussion of the religious condition of Syrian immigrants to the United States. See Hitti, *The Syrians in America*, 109. For a mar-

sacre, surviving Christians sought safer places to live.[67] For Jews, who remained unharmed during the riots, security issues became a more pressing issue at a later date, when they too became disillusioned with the Ottoman attempts at reform. Notwithstanding official secularization of the regime and the judiciary, the continued lack of personal safety in Syria, as well as continuing religious and political restrictions and discrimination, fostered Syrian Jewish fears that Muslim society would never internalize the principles of equality and would make them the targets of the next anti-minority outbreak. Swept along in the Christian wave of emigration, Jewish emigration was fuelled by the increasing regional political instability.[68]

Even so, in considering Jewish emigration from Syria specifically, it is important to acknowledge the dominant role of economic factors.[69] As early as the 1850s, Jews from Aleppo began to migrate to western commercial centres and to found branches of their commercial houses there.[70] The opening of the Suez Canal, which took the main axis of east–west trade outside Syria, dealt a harsh blow to the Syrian economy, impoverishing many merchants, and recurrent regional financial crises climaxed with the Ottoman empire's declaration of bankruptcy in 1875.

The shrinking distances between continents as a result of improvements in travel by both land and sea also facilitated emigration for those seeking their future in the new world. Egypt remained the prime destination during the 1870s and early 1880s, but by then often as a way station en route to America.[71]

Alongside the primary economic, political, and religious reasons for emigration, we must note some secondary causes. European missionary activity in Syria fostered Christian emigration; similarly, Alliance activity promoted

ginal consideration of the migration of Jews from Syria to Egypt, see Philipp, *The Syrians in Egypt*. On the other hand, until recently even Jewish historians of the nineteenth century almost totally ignored the Syrian Jewish migration to the West, most probably because of its small numbers as compared to the east European migration. In the past few years, however, interest in this topic has grown. See Hamui de Halabe, *Los Judíos de Alepo*; J. A. D. Sutton, *Aleppo Chronicles*; id., *Magic Carpet*; Harel, 'The First Jews from Aleppo'; Chira, *From Aleppo to America*; Zenner, *A Global Community*; Rodgers, 'The Aleppan Jews of Buenos Aires' (Heb.), 129–30.

[67] See Ma'oz, *Ottoman Reform*, 241; Tibawi, *A Modern History of Syria*, 175.

[68] See e.g. AECPC, Turquie, Damas, vol. 11, pp. 89–90, Guys, 2 May 1877; Hitti, *The Syrians in America*, 50–2. With the declaration of a constitution in 1909, which made conscription compulsory for non-Muslims as well, this stream of migration became a flood. See AENS, Turquie (Syrie–Liban), vol. 112, p. 210, Laronce, 28 Oct. 1909; *Ha'or*, 20, 5 Heshvan 1912, p. 3. See also Harel, 'The Encounter of Exiles' (Heb.), 184–6.

[69] Some scholars argue that socio-economic decline was also the main factor sparking emigration among the Christian public. See Karpat, 'The Ottoman Emigration to America', 176–80.

[70] On the founding of the Aleppine Jewish commercial community in Manchester, see Harel, 'The First Jews from Aleppo'.

[71] See Avni, *The History of Jewish Immigration to Argentina* (Heb.), 112; Hitti, *The Syrians in America*, 49–50; J. A. D. Sutton, *Magic Carpet*, 5–7; Saul Dweck Hakohen, *Emet me'erets*, 44b, no. 34; Sukary, *Yoru mishpateikha leya'akov*, 19–20; Abulafia, *Penei yitsḥak*, ii. 54a.

Jewish emigration. Although Christian missionaries and Alliance envoys made
no efforts, in the 1870s at least, to encourage emigration from Syria to the West,
the education they provided opened a window on a new world and showed the
opportunities awaiting young Syrian Christians and Jews in the West. Like
the missionaries who preached against Christians leaving Syria, the Alliance
saw its main goal as the integration of Middle Eastern Jews as equal citizens in
their homelands. But because the study of French, and of western history, geography, literature, and culture, was perceived as superior to traditional eastern
studies, these subjects acted as a magnet, drawing young people to seek their
future outside Syria. Through their reading and through the staging of plays
and performances, they tasted the flavour of the West and of western culture.[72]
While still living in Syria, these young people adjusted their political aspirations and cultural values to what was accepted in the West, essentially becoming a foreign implant in local society, not just in religious terms but also
culturally.

The political power and improved status of European and American Jewry
also encouraged emigration from Syria. Visitors to the region from these lands
offered assistance to Syrian Jews and spoke of the wonders of the West; subsequently, the first emigrants' letters back to their relatives spoke of western
wealth and the ease with which it could be obtained. These became some of
the most prominent factors encouraging emigration. As Philip Hitti put it,
'the pen of the emigrant', as he dubbed the emigrants' letters to their families,
'became mightier than the sword of the persecutor'.[73]

In 1886 the Alliance envoy to Damascus, Isaac Astruc, gave apt expression
to the Alliance's drive to turn the eyes of Syrian Jewish youth to the West:

Déjà il existe ici un commencement d'émigration vers l'Egypte. Six de nos élèves
y ont trouvé des emplois fort honorables. Je suis presque sûr que cet exemple sera
suivi, et que notre jeunesse, qui était jusqu'à ce jour si casanière et si peu tentée de
s'établir dans des nouveaux pays, verra qu'il n'y a pour elle d'autre moyen de gagner
sa vie qu'en émigrant vers des pays plus vivants, plus actifs, et qui offrent des
ressources variées.[74]

[At present, there are the beginnings of emigration towards Egypt. Six of our pupils
have found honourable employment. I am almost certain that this example will be imitated, and that our young people, until now stay-at-homes, displaying little tendency
to settle in new lands, will realize that they have no alternative means of earning a living except by emigrating to more lively, active lands, which offer varied resources.]

[72] As early as 1875 the students of the Alliance school in Aleppo staged Molière's *Le Malade
imaginaire*. These performances generally attracted not only a Jewish audience but also many
individuals from the consular staffs stationed in Aleppo, and even Ottoman civil servants, who
came to enjoy French culture. See e.g. AAIU, Syrie, III.E., Alep, 23, Behor, 24 Mar. 1875. For
the missionaries' policy on emigration, see Hitti, *The Syrians in America*, 55.

[73] Hitti, *The Syrians in America*, 52.   [74] *BAIU*, 2ème sem. 1886, p. 66.

His prediction was to be fulfilled. From the 1880s the emigration of their vital young people to the West depleted the Syrian Jewish communities.[75] The last years of the nineteenth century mark the height of the Syrian Jewish shift from fatalistic acceptance of their lot in the Middle Eastern Muslim society to assumption of responsibility for their own fate by taking the radical step of migrating to the West.

[75] See Harel, 'The Encounter of Exiles' (Heb.), 184–6; Hourani, *Minorities in the Arab World*, 84–5.

AN ERA OF TRANSITION

THE TIME SPAN of this examination of the Jewish minority in Syria, the period beginning in 1840, when the Damascus affair took place, and ending with 1880, when economic disaster overtook Damascus Jewry, overlaps with what is known in the history of the Ottoman empire as the Tanzimat era. A key phenomenon of this era was the ever-widening encounter between East and West. This led to profound changes in Ottoman imperial rule and society in general, and in Syria specifically from 1840, when Ottoman rule was reinstated. In this book the shifts in Jewish society have been examined against the broad background of the political, social, and economic changes taking place in Syria during the period in question.

As delineated here, the two main Jewish communities differed with regard to social structure, economic endeavour, communal leadership and organization, and education, essentially retaining their heterogeneity through these years. The identity of each community was grounded not in a shared Syrian Jewish awareness, but rather in a unique local character. While the Damascus Jewish community was characterized by a wide gap between a small elite of extremely affluent families, wealthy by any standard, and an overwhelming majority who were among the most underprivileged in Syrian society, that in Aleppo was dominated by a thriving middle class that bridged the gap between rich and poor. Aleppo was also distinguished by a small social elite—dubbed Francos—composed almost entirely of descendants of eighteenth-century European Jewish settlers. Although these Jews were neither members of the Jewish community nor bound by its taxation or communal regulations, they exercised considerable influence on that community. During the period under consideration, the nucleus of this European Jewish elite was in a process of decline, causing it to focus inwardly and to concentrate on the preservation of its status and privileges, as evinced through its desire to create a separatist, modern education system for its children and through its lessened support for communal institutions.

Alongside the Francos, a new Syrian Jewish elite developed. Drawing its strength and status from the acquisition of modern education, it became more closely linked, spiritually and culturally, to Europe than to the Muslim East.

Notwithstanding some identifiably maskilic tendencies in this stratum, we should not mistake it for a full-blown Haskalah movement in the European sense; it was based, rather, on an admiration of western culture, which it considered superior to the traditional culture of the East, and a recognition of the practical importance of general education. The failure of this group's attempt to inculcate its values in the community at large, generally through efforts to synthesize tradition and modernization, was one factor behind the decision of most of this cultural elite to leave Syria, starting in the late 1870s. This emigration had far-reaching social ramifications for the Syrian Jewish communities. In the short term, these communities lost their most talented young people. In the long term, because of the absence of those young people, the group best qualified to move the community towards progress and the twentieth century, the Jewish communities declined.

During the period under study here, the two main Syrian Jewish communities were also distinguished by their respective fields of economic activity, which in both cases were closely tied to, and influenced by, the Ottoman economy. Up to the 1840s Jewish merchants in both Damascus and Aleppo engaged mainly in international trade via the camel caravans that travelled between the Persian Gulf and the Mediterranean Sea. From the 1840s onwards Damascus traders largely abandoned this pursuit and turned to the business of extending credit, both to the government and, primarily, to the rural *fallahin*. Aleppo's merchants, on the other hand, continued to engage in trade, concentrating on western imports, while the city's middle class engaged mainly in small business enterprises, moneychanging, and commercial intermediation; in Damascus the majority of the Jewish community were either craft workers or pedlars. These differences in the patterns of economic activity gave rise to different effects when the Suez Canal opened. Although Aleppo's trade and communal functioning were certainly affected by the opening of the canal at the time, they were able to adapt and survive. The Damascus Jewish community, on the other hand, barely affected at the time, crashed a few years later when the Ottoman empire declared bankruptcy in 1875.

The Ottoman fiscal crisis was another substantive cause of immigration to the West. The economic success enjoyed by the first migrants to the new world, in contrast to the increasingly straitened circumstances of the Syrian economy, played a role in drawing others in their wake, further shrinking the Jewish communities. It was not only educated youths who emigrated for economic reasons but also members of the younger generation who were in line to inherit the small and medium-sized businesses. Many of these young people, even those who had not studied in modern schools, imitated their better-educated contemporaries in seeking their fortunes abroad, first in Egypt and then in the West. This dilution of the community further compounded the economic decline. The fall in the numbers of marriageable men also created a social problem in the rising number of unmarried women, whose need for support further strained communal resources. The economic damage caused by emigration was partly repaired when the successful emigrants began to support their relatives who remained in Syria; nonetheless, this financial subsidy was not sufficient fully to rehabilitate the communal economy.

There were also differences between the two main communities with respect to patterns of leadership. In Damascus, the leadership consisted of two chief rabbis, of whom one, the *ḥakham bashi*, liaised between the regime and the community while the other acted as the leading spiritual authority for the community. Functioning alongside them was a committee composed of high-status Damascus Jews. The power struggles between these notables and the *ḥakham bashi* for control of the community, and among the notables themselves regarding the appointment of local rabbis, fostered the importation of rabbis from other communities to Damascus and even, on occasion, involvement by the local Ottoman regime in the choice of the *ḥakham bashi*. In Aleppo, on the other hand, the *ḥakham bashi* was also the supreme spiritual authority, which endowed him with a higher and more stable status among most of the community's Jews. Nonetheless, the 1870s saw the beginning of a decline in the status of the rabbinate in Aleppo as well, and the eventual adoption of the two-rabbi pattern operating in Damascus. The declining status of the rabbinate and of rabbinic scholars in Syria, which began earlier in Damascus than in Aleppo, motivated a wave of emigration by this class from Syria in the 1880s. Unlike the younger population, which left in search of economic opportunities, the Torah scholars chose to move to Jerusalem, which they viewed as the most suitable place for preservation of the traditional framework and of Torah scholarship. Scholars began to emigrate overseas only after substantial numbers of Syrian Jews had established themselves abroad and sought to import religious functionaries to assist in the organization of a traditional Jewish communal framework.

Any consideration of why the Syrian Jewish communities turned westward must take into account the significant role played by the introduction of modern education through the agency of the Alliance Israélite Universelle. The shift from traditional to modern education proceeded slowly, but largely without polemic and with minimal friction between traditionalists and modernizers. This was due not only to Syrian Jewish admiration for the Alliance as a world Jewish leadership, but also to the wisdom of the policy pursued by the Alliance envoys to Syria in integrating secular and religious studies within the curriculum. Opposition to Alliance activity began only in the late nineteenth century, with the weakening of religion in the Syrian Jewish communities. Whereas in Damascus this was the result of a general process of secularization, in Aleppo it emerged from an ideology with maskilic overtones, which questioned rabbinic status and the legitimacy of the halakhah and even culminated in an attempt at introducing some elements of Reform Judaism.

Alliance influence in Syria extended beyond the academic sphere. Certainly the Alliance made intensive efforts to found schools, whose graduates comprised the new elite mentioned earlier. But this society's greatest influence was vested in a realm outside its expressed aims: that of emigration. Consistently with its principles, the Alliance at first sought to improve the situation of Syrian Jews in their homeland and to facilitate their integration into the local economy and administration, on the European pattern. But local conditions—the ever-deteriorating economic situation, the Jews' continued low social status in Syrian society, and the Alliance students' Francophone tendencies—led Alliance envoys to support and encourage the immigration of young Jews to the West.

Even though the Tanzimat era saw an alteration in the Muslim Ottoman empire's formal legal treatment of its non-Muslim minorities, these minorities did not achieve integration into Muslim society. Although a string of reforms touching upon all spheres of life abolished discriminatory signs, granted broader freedom to exercise religion, outlawed forced conversion, and introduced measures aimed at establishing equality and integrating the minorities into the administrative and judicial networks, because their implementation required not only the issuing of firmans but also preparation, education, and a change in Muslim public opinion, in many areas the reforms remained unrealized. The Muslims, the dominant element of Syrian society, could not simply jettison a millennium of tradition governing minority treatment. In essence, continued Muslim religious zealotry stifled any real change in minority status. The Ottoman regime did not require its Jews either to become integrated into Muslim society or to change how they organized their own communities; nor did it demand a clear statement by the Jewish community of its attitude towards the regime. For their part, Jews were not eager to seek integration into the Ottoman frameworks. The Jewish leadership feared that such a trend would diminish its judicial autonomy and also lead to disintegration of the Jewish communal framework if individual Jews no longer needed its services. At the same time, it was wary of arousing Muslim fanaticism, which viewed equality between believers and infidels with suspicion and hostility. Initially, Syrian Jews sought no privileges, and remained passive with regard to the reforms and their implementation. Only towards the end of the period do we find some alteration in the Jewish attitude beyond the educated stratum. Representatives of the Alliance encouraged the rabbinic leadership to consider the advantages of implementation of the letter of the reform law. Moreover, as the rabbis' status declined within their own communities, they sought Ottoman authorization for their leadership. This support brought with it increased government involvement in the internal affairs of the Syrian Jewish communities.

In the sensitive relationship between the Muslim majority and the religious minorities the Jews were more vulnerable than the Christians, and in consequence maintained a lower political profile. Although as a result they did not enjoy most of the privileges promised by the reforms, they also avoided arousing the anger of the Muslim populace. In this they differed from the Christians, who, in seeking to realize their privileges, offended Muslim religious sensibilities. This provocation, coupled with the Muslim perception of local Christians as collaborators with west European Christian powers, led on more than one occasion to outbreaks of anti-Christian violence, while the Jews remained largely unharmed. Thus the Muslim majority adhered to its traditional attitude towards its Jewish minority, as required by Islamic law, but its attitude towards Christians shifted sharply. Growing Muslim closeness to Jews prompted an extreme manifestation of Christian hatred for Jews: the ritual murder accusation by Catholics in Damascus in February 1840. After the Damascus affair, there were repeated blood libel accusations in Damascus and Aleppo until the July 1860 massacre of the Christians. Although this was carried out by Muslims, the Christian public manufactured claims of Jewish participation. Because of the Christian communities' loss of economic and social clout in the wake of the massacre, there was a significant decline in the frequency of blood libel accusations. Towards the late nineteenth century, however, as Jewish economic power in turn declined, the Jewish–Christian balance of power shifted again and new ritual murder accusations were heard once more.

While animosity between Jews and Catholics was of long standing, the arrival of Protestants on the Syrian scene exposed Jews to a less hostile Christian denomination. Protestant backing during the Damascus affair, coupled with the fact that the Catholics persecuted them as well, endowed them with the image of friends of the Jews. But this amity was transformed into suspicion and even antagonism once their primary motivation of converting the Jews became apparent.

On the complex interreligious Syrian social scene, contacts between Muslim Arabs and Jews remained restricted to interaction on the daily level. The processes of modernization and accompanying change detailed here did not alter the basic relationship between the two religious groups. Notwithstanding the alterations in nearly all areas of Syrian Jewish life, from education to the economy, no substantive shift took place in the Jewish attitude towards the majority population. Jewish society neither aspired nor demanded to become part of the larger society. Although there was pronounced acculturation, there was no assimilation. Among Syrian Jews, acculturation was not the result of a desire to resemble a surrounding society perceived as superior; it is better defined more as a protective means of camouflage. Syrian Jewish and Syrian Arab intellectuals did not meet or engage with one another in pursuit of either

socio-cultural or national ends. Even though the Jews were formally granted
equality with Muslims, Muslim Syrian society did not easily absorb this exter-
nally imposed notion. Consequently, notwithstanding their improved legal
status, Jews did not perceive themselves as equal citizens in a changing state,
and did not view emancipation as an achievable and desirable end. We do find,
however, a passive aspiration for equality that grew out of an understanding of
emancipation as a means of release from discriminatory oppression on a religious basis. This came to the fore in the latter half of the nineteenth century,
which saw the formation of two political movements in Syria. Because the first
called for an Arab Muslim identity, and the second for a secular Syrian identity, neither was accessible to Jews, and the walls of Jewish solidarity and separatism remained unbreached. In addition, the closer relationship between
Syrian and European Jews, which enhanced Jewish national feelings and solidarity, prevented the formation of either a local Syrian, or an all-Ottoman,
identity among Jews. Thus Jews retained in their own eyes, and in the eyes of
the surrounding society, the identity of a separate and separatist national and
religious collective. The emergence of a Syrian national identity in which Jews
had no place was another element encouraging Jewish immigration to the
West.

The new westward inclination of Syrian Jews was fostered by their recognition of the ability of European powers to lobby the Ottoman regime to improve
its treatment of its non-Muslim minorities. In the context of active European
intervention in Ottoman affairs, the various minorities acquired consular protection. France protected the Catholics, while Britain, which had no large
Protestant communities in the region in need of protection, took the Jews
under its wing. In the Catholic–Jewish conflict the French consulate sided with
its protégés and took a hostile approach towards the Jews with antisemitic overtones. With Britain backing the Jews, this local Catholic–Jewish tension
became a disputed patch of international diplomatic turf. The positive shift in
the French consulate's attitude in Damascus towards the Jews which came
about in the wake of the 1860 massacre of Christians was the outcome of several confluent factors: the weakened position of the Christians, the founding
of the Alliance in France, and the fact that the French consul in Damascus was
a Judaeophile. Although Prussia, Austria, and Persia also granted protection
to the Syrian Jews, nonetheless, throughout the period in question Britain
remained their primary protector, much to the Jews' political and economic
benefit. The western consuls safeguarded the rights and security of the non-
Muslim minorities, mainly by urging the implementation of Ottoman reforms.
Through coming to the aid of the Jews in instances of ritual murder accusations, and by mediating between Jews and Protestants, British involvement
with the Syrian Jewish community crossed the boundaries of the complex intercommunal map.

During the period under consideration the Picciottos, members of the Franco elite, served as consular representatives for most of the European powers in Aleppo, with the exception of Britain and France. Paradoxically, the fact that local Jews of European extraction served as consuls in Aleppo delayed the need for British and French protection there and delayed the westernization of Aleppine Jews. Only in the early 1870s, with the declining status of the Picciottos and the recognition of the weakness of their consular protection, did Aleppo's Jews begin to seek to become protégés of the major European powers. Moreover, the failure of the Francos consistently to defend the communal good where this conflicted with their own interests alienated many of Aleppo's Jews and contributed to a decline in the number who sought consular protection from the Picciottos. The Jewish consuls were also held in low esteem by both the Muslim public and other, professional, consuls on account of their low consular status, their failure to co-operate with the other consuls, their self-serving activity, and their imputed corruption.

Contacts with European Jewish communities, and Syrian Jewish awareness of the ability of their European co-religionists to persuade their governments to act on behalf of Middle Eastern Jewry, were of supreme importance to the Syrian Jewish communities and encouraged them to look to the West. Syrian Jews were no longer divorced from events in the wider Jewish world, and concern for their safety and welfare became part of the west European Jewish agenda. The ties initiated with the 1840 Damascus affair were not simply maintained but also widened. From this perspective, Damascus was the corridor through which renewed Jewish solidarity and western Jewish interest in the Jews of the Middle East penetrated the entire Mediterranean basin. These bonds were strengthened when the Jews of Damascus required European Jewish assistance to escape accusations of involvement in the 1860 massacre of Christians. Although Syrian Jews rarely travelled to the West, a fair number of European Jews visited the Middle Eastern Jewish communities, either for that specific purpose or en route to Erets Yisra'el. European Jewish engagement with the Syrian Jewish communities encompassed such spheres as the anti-mission struggle, philanthropic activity, and confrontation of hostile consuls, and the willingness of west European Jews to come to the aid of their Middle Eastern co-religionists endowed them with the status of leaders and heroes in Syrian Jewish eyes. Accordingly, Syrian Jewry drew closer to the emerging spirit of Jewish revival and renewed Jewish solidarity in the wake of the Damascus affair. Among non-Jews this phenomenon gave rise to a negative image of an international Jewish conspiracy, always prepared to come to the aid of Syrian Jews, rescuing them from every complaint, even those that were justified. Increasing Alliance involvement in Syria reinforced this perception, with Jews and non-Jews alike viewing this society as the 'government of the Jewish people'.

Syrian Jewry was not stagnant during the period in question. Indeed, until the 1870s the picture is one of slow but consistent progress. The economy flourished, Jewish social status saw some minor improvement, and the winds of modernization and enlightenment began to blow through at least some sectors of Jewish society. The downturn, which began with the opening of the Suez Canal in 1869 and intensified when the Ottoman empire declared bankruptcy in 1875, spiralled downward with Sultan 'Abd al-Hamid's suspension of the constitution in 1878, which heralded retrograde steps with regard to the status of the non-Muslim minorities. Despairing of improvement in either their socio-political status or the economic situation within Syria, and recognizing the superiority of western culture and the chance of a better future in the new world, many young Syrian Jews emigrated overseas in the 1880s.

Despite the changes charted in Syrian Jewish society during the years from 1840 to 1880, westernization and modernization were not fully realized in this period. Moreover, the surrounding Muslim society's attachment to its overarching world-view made it more difficult for Jews to free themselves entirely from traditional perspectives. They could not act in accord with modern criteria when the surrounding society had not yet absorbed this conceptual change. Thus it was not the Jewish communities in Syria that reaped the fruits of change but rather their new satellite communities overseas, which were built and flourished on the ruins of the traditional Jewish communities in their homeland. But here too we find an intriguing phenomenon. Despite a high degree of economic integration into the modern world, in socio-cultural terms the migrant communities chose to remain in the old world, voluntarily founding communal frameworks similar to the traditional ones under rabbinic religious leadership. Unable to break out of the *harat al-yahud* and become citizens in Syria, emigration alone made this feasible. Nevertheless, this escape was not accompanied by abandonment of tradition; rather, the Syrian Jewish immigrants chose to recreate the Jewish quarter in their new centres. In addition to the sociological factors that prompt migrants to seek the warmth of the familiar, there was also a desire on the part of Syrian Jews to preserve the foundations of their old world. The introduction of modern education and other changes, which had begun to detach Syrian Jews from the East, had not yet turned them into citizens of the West. Thus, for years to come, they did not assimilate to their new homelands, but zealously guarded their identity as Damascus or Aleppo Jews living outside Syria.

Emigration from Syria ebbed and flowed, according to circumstances, until 1949, when Syrian Jews became hostages in their land of residence. Only in 1992 did the Syrian regime, under Hafiz al-Asad, allow the remnants of the Jewish community to emigrate. Most of its members took this opportunity to leave Syria, bringing the history of the most ancient Jewish diaspora to a close.

Glossary

ahl al-dhimma (Arab.)   See *dhimmi*

ahl al-kitab (Arab.)   People of the book, namely Jews and Christians

Aleppo Codex   A tenth-century manuscript copy of the Bible held by the Aleppo Jewish community

aliyah (Heb.)   Immigration to Erets Yisra'el

amir al-mu'minin (Arab.)   Commander of the faithful; the sultan

arikhah (Heb.)   Assessment of worth of members of the Syrian Jewish communities

Ashkenaz   Germany and the surrounding region

Ashkenazi   Jew originating from Germany and the nearby lands

ashraf (sing. *sharif*) (Arab.)   Lineal descendants of the Prophet Muhammad

av beit din (Heb.)   Head of the rabbinic court

a'yan (Arab.)   Muslim notables, especially those participating in local government

bedel-i 'askeri (Turk.)   Military service commutation tax

bikur holim (Heb.)   Jewish communal health fund

capitulation   Contract between the Ottoman empire and a European power conferring on citizens of that power rights and privileges in respect of residence in, and trade with, Ottoman dominions

daftardar (Arab.)   Senior Ottoman provincial treasury official

dayan (pl. *dayanim*) (Heb.)   Rabbi qualified to serve as a judge on a rabbinic court

dhimmi (Arab.)   Member of the Jewish or Christian minority, allowed to live under Muslim authority with some degree of communal and religious autonomy in return for payment of the poll tax (*jizya*) and other measures reinforcing subordinate status

diwan (Arab.)   Council

fallahin (Arab.)   Peasant farmers

ferde (Turk.)   Personal tax, levied by the Egyptians on the Syrian population and left in place when the Ottomans returned

firman   Edict of the Ottoman sultan

Francos   Jews of Italian origin who settled in Syria

gabilah (Heb.)   Indirect Jewish communal tax on meat, wine, and other commodities

gemilut hasadim (Heb.)   Jewish charitable fund

hajj (Arab.)   Yearly pilgrimage to Mecca

hakham bashi   Chief rabbi, officially appointed by the sultan (the term is a combination of the Hebrew *hakham* (sage), and the Turkish *basi* (chief)

halakhah (Heb.)   The legal code of Judaism, which embraces personal, social, national, and international relationships, as well as the practices and observances of Judaism

halakhist (Heb.)   Sage versed in the intricacies of halakhah

harat al-yahud (Arab.)   The Jewish quarter

Haskalah (Heb.)   The Jewish 'enlightenment': an eighteenth-century intellectual movement among east European Jews that attempted to acquaint the masses with European languages and Hebrew and to introduce secular education and culture to supplement talmudic studies

Hatt-i Hümayun (Turk.) (1856)   The second stage of the Tanzimat reforms initiated with the promulgation of the Hatt-i şerif of Gülhane

Hatt-i şerif of Gülhane (Turk.) (1839)   A royal decree that set in motion within the Ottoman empire a governmental reorganization known as the Tanzimat

hazan (Heb.)   Prayer leader in the synagogue

hekdesh (pl. *hekdeshot*) (Heb.)   Endowment in the Jewish community, created by the dedication of property for a charitable public cause

'id al-adha (Arab.)   Muslim Feast of Sacrifice

iltizam (Arab.)   Tax-farming

jizya (Arab.)   Poll tax levied by the Ottoman authorities on the *dhimmi*

kashrut (Heb.)   Jewish dietary laws

kavass (Turk.)   A guard for important individuals in the countries of the eastern Mediterranean

ketubah (pl. *ketubot*) (Heb.)   Jewish marriage contract

kharaj (Arab.)   Tax levied on land or its produce

kohen (Heb.)   Lit. 'priest'; a member of one of the families or clans descended from the high priest Aaron, possessing certain hereditary privileges

kuttab (Arab.)   Elementary school; *see also talmud torah*

mahkama (Arab.)   Religious court

mahmal (Arab.)   Muslims' annual caravan to Mecca

majidi   A Turkish coin or medal bearing the portrait of the sultan 'Abd al-Majid

majlis (Arab.)   Council or court

majlis al-'adliyya (Arab.)   Supreme court

majlis baladiyya (Arab.)   Municipal council

majlis idara (Arab.)   Provincial council

maskilic   In line with the Haskalah movement

maskil (pl. *maskilim*) (Heb.)   Follower of the Haskalah

matzah (pl. *matzot*) (Heb.)   Unleavened bread eaten on the Passover holiday

melamed (pl. *melamedim*) (Heb.)   Teacher of young children

mezuzah (Heb.)   A piece of parchment inscribed on one side with Deut 6: 4–9 and 11: 13–21 and on the other with the name *shadai*, rolled up in a scroll and placed in a case or tube affixed to the doorpost of Jewish homes as a reminder of faith in God

mihrab (Arab.)   Prayer niche in a mosque

millet   A non-Muslim group or community in the Ottoman setting organized under a religious head of its own who also exercises civil functions of importance

minyan (Heb.)   Prayer quorum in synagogue

mufti (Arab.)   Chief arbiter in Muslim religious law

mukhtar (Arab.)   Neighbourhood headman

Musar   A nineteenth-century Jewish ethical and religious movement stressing the practice of strict moral discipline and piety

Mustarib (pl. Mustaribun) (Arab.)   Local Jew of eastern origin

muwali (Arab.)   Honorary religious title

parnas (pl. *parnasim*) (Heb.)   Elected lay leader in the Jewish community

Passover   Annual spring Jewish religious festival, celebrating the Exodus from Egypt

pesak (pl. *pesakim*) (Heb.)   Jewish legal ruling; also the judgment in a court case

posekim (sing. *posek*) (Heb.)   Jewish halakhic authorities; also the adjudicative literature produced by these authorities

qadi (Arab.)   Judge in a Muslim community whose decisions are based on Islamic law

ra'aya (Arab.)   Lit. 'flock': non-Muslim subjects in the Muslim state

Rosh Hashanah   Jewish new year

Rosh Hodesh   The beginning of the month in the Jewish calendar, marked by a special liturgy

rosh harabanim (Heb.)   Chief rabbi, as described within the Jewish community

rosh haruhaniyim (Heb.)   Spiritual head

sarraf (Arab.)   Cashier of the treasury

Sephardi   Jew of Spanish origin

ser'asker (Turk.)   Chief provincial military official

seray (Arab.)   Government building

shari'a (Arab.)   Islamic law

sharif (Arab.)   President; eminent individual; name for a lineal descendant of the Prophet Muhammad *shaykh* (Arab.)   Head of a guild, village, or tribe; also title of respect

Shulḥan arukh (Heb.)   Widely accepted code of Jewish law

sijill   Muslim court register

Simhat Torah (Heb.)   Jewish festival celebrating the completion of the cycle of reading the Torah in synagogue; last day of the festival of Tabernacles

sukot (sing. *sukah*) (Heb.)   Temporary booths in which Jews live during the festival of Tabernacles, the last of the three major pilgrim festivals

talmud torah (pl. *talmudei torah*) (Heb.)   Jewish elementary schools, also known as *kuttab*s

Tanzimat   Lit. 'reorganization': Ottoman governmental reforms beginning with the promulgation of the Hatt-i şerif of Gülhane

takanot (Heb.)   Regulations governing the internal life of Jewish communities and congregations

tsitsit (Heb.)   Ritual fringes worn by religious Jews on an undergarment

'ulama' (Arab.)   Members of the Muslim religious establishment, including legal experts, teachers, scholars, and mosque functionaries

umma (Arab.)   Muslim community of believers

vergi   Tax on immovable property which replaced the *ferde*

wali (Arab.)   District governor

waqf (Arab.)   Muslim endowment, created by the dedication of property for a charitable public cause or for the support of the donor's family

wilaya (Arab.)   District; province

yeshiva (pl. yeshivas) (Heb.)   Traditional Jewish academy primarily devoted to the study of the Talmud and rabbinic literature

Yom Kippur (Heb.)   Jewish Day of Atonement

Bibliography

ARCHIVAL SOURCES

Government Archives

Affaires Etrangères, Centre des Archives Diplomatiques de Nantes (AECADN)
 Constantinople, Correspondance avec les Echelles, Damas, 1846–53
 Consulat de France à Alep, Cotes 15, 21
 Damas, 01, Cote A/18/54
 Damas, 5, Cote A/18/19
 Damas, 27, Cote A/18/42
 Damas, 66

Archives du Ministère des Affaires Etrangères, Paris
 Correspondance Consulaire et Commerciale (AECCC), Alep, vols. 26, 30–6
 Correspondance Consulaire et Commerciale (AECCC), Damas, vols. 1–7
 Correspondance Politique du Consul (AECPC), Turquie, Alep, vols. 1, 3–5
 Correspondance Politique du Consul (AECPC), Turquie, Damas, vols. 1–4, 7, 8,
  10–11
 Nouvelle Série (AENS), Turquie (Syrie–Liban), vol. 112

Österreichisches Staatsarchiv, Haus-, Hof-, und Staatsarchiv, Vienna (HHSTA)
 Administrative Registratur (Adm. Reg.): F4, 82, 258; F8, 6, 38; F60, 25
 Politisches Archiv (PA): XIII, 3 (Constantinople); XXXVIII, 93, 98, 134, 139, 183
 Türkei: II, 128–9; VI, 74
 Türkei, Politisches Archiv (PA): XII, 42, 51, 70–1

National Archives, Foreign Office Archives, London (FO)
FO 78 Vols. 379, 447–8, 498–9, 538, 579, 622, 660A–B, 686, 714, 761, 782, 802,
  836, 837, 872–3, 910, 912, 959–61, 1028–9, 1118, 1154, 1220, 1297, 1388, 1389,
  1452, 1538, 1686, 1688–9, 1751, 1829, 1869, 1877, 1934, 2051–2, 2103, 2242,
  2259–60, 2282, 2299, 2352, 2375A, 2619, 2650, 2850

FO 195 Vols. 207, 226, 291, 368, 416, 458, 595, 601, 800, 902, 927, 965, 976, 1113,
  1153–4, 1262, 1305, 1514

FO 372 Vol. 1933

FO 406 Vols. 10, 12

Other Archives and Libraries

Archives de l'Alliance Israélite Universelle, Paris (AAIU)

Angleterre, II.D., 36

Syrie, I.B., Alep: 1, Comités locaux et communautés (1868–1913)

Syrie, I.B., 4, Antioche, Comités locaux et communautés (1872–1908)

Syrie, I.B., 5, Damas, Comités locaux et communautés (1862–1938)

Syrie, I.C., Damas: 5, Situation générale interieure des juifs (1869–1936)

Syrie, I.E., Alep: 1, Divers concernant les écoles

Syrie, II.E., Alep: 11, Altaras

Syrie, III.E., Alep: 21, Behar; 23, Behor; 32, Cohen

Syrie, IV.E., Alep: 50, Gubbay

Syrie, V.E., Alep: 62, Nerson

Syrie, VIII.E., Alep: 68, Moïse de Picciotto

Syrie, X.E., Alep: 83, Somekh

Syrie, XI.E., Damas: 94, Divers concernant les écoles; 96, Aboulafia

Syrie, XV.E., Damas: 146, Fresco

Syrie, XVI.E., Damas: 151c, Loupo

Syrie, XVII.E., Damas: 160, Heymann

Syrie, XXI.E., Damas: 222, Weisskopf

Archives of the Chief Rabbinate, Istanbul (ACRI)

TR/Is-162a (CAHJP no. HM2 8636)

Benayahu Collection, Jerusalem

Ḥet 79, *Pinkas ḥalab* [Record Book of Aleppo] (Jewish National University Library, Institute of Microfilmed Hebrew Manuscripts, JER BENAYAHU, no. 43753)

Ḥet 86, *Pesakim* (Jewish National University Library, Institute of Microfilmed Hebrew Manuscripts, JER BENAYAHU, no. 43765), uncatalogued documents

Ben-Zvi Institute, Jerusalem

MS 3724, *Pinkas rabi mosheh suton* [Record Book of Rabbi Moses Sutton]

British Library, London

Gaster Collection

Or. 10709, 933, Solomon ben Yom Tov Sutton [copyist?]: Prayer, *Piyutim* (Jewish National University Library, Institute of Microfilmed Hebrew Manuscripts, no. 8024)

Central Archives for the History of the Jewish People, Jerusalem (CAHJP)

INV/521D, Damascus

Central Zionist Archive, Jerusalem (CZA)

J-41, Mikveh Yisra'el Archive: 83

Columbia University Library, New York

893 M6847, Joseph ben Nissim Harari (owner): Responsa and sermons (Jewish National University Library, Institute of Microfilmed Hebrew Manuscripts, no. 27385)

Jewish National and University Library, Department of Manuscripts and Archives, Jerusalem (JNUL, DMA)

Arc. 4° 1271, Rabbi Jacob Shaul Elyashar papers: 607, 608a

8° 5655, *Shut umafte'aḥ aharon ya'akov* [Responsa and Index of Aaron Jacob]

V-736, Rabbi Abraham Hayim Gagin papers: 28, 64, 72, 99, 101, 215, 217, 218, 248, 261, 272

Jewish Theological Seminary Library, New York (JTSL)

Mic. 3102, Diwan, organized according to melodies/tunes (Jewish National University Library, Institute of Microfilmed Hebrew Manuscripts, no. 29139)

Jews' College, London
Montefiore Collection (MC)

520, Jacob Sapir Halevi, *Shemesh tsedakah* [Account of Montefiore's journey to Jerusalem and Damascus in 1849] (JNUL, IMHM no. 6142)

551, *Talmidei ḥakhamim bedamesek lemontefiori* [Letter from the scholars of Damascus to Montefiore] (Jewish National University Library, Institute of Microfilmed Hebrew Manuscripts, no. 6173)

576, *Igerot me'erets yisra'el* [Letters from the Land of Israel] (Jewish National University Library, Institute of Microfilmed Hebrew Manuscripts, no. 6192)

577, *Igerot me'erets yisra'el* [Letters from the Land of Israel] (Jewish National University Library, Institute of Microfilmed Hebrew Manuscripts, no. 6193)

Metropolitan Archives (London)
Board of Deputies of British Jews (BofD): Minute Book
ACC/3121/A/5/4
ACC/3121/A/6
ACC/3121/A/9

NEWSPAPERS AND JOURNALS

Bulletin de l'Alliance Israélite Universelle, Paris
Hadiqat al-akhbar, Beirut
Halevanon, Jerusalem, Paris, Mayence
Hamagid, Lyck, Berlin, Krakow
Ha'or, Jerusalem
Havatselet, Jerusalem

Hed hamizraḥ, Jerusalem
L'Impartial, İzmir
Jewish Chronicle, London
Jewish Intelligence, London
Sha'arei tsiyon, Jerusalem
The Times, London
Voice of Jacob, London

PRINTED PRIMARY SOURCES

ABADI, MORDECAI, *Divrei mordekhai* [hymns] (Aleppo: Sasson, 1873).

—— *Ma'ayan ganim* [responsa], vol. i (repr. Jerusalem: Mekhon Haketav, 1986).

—— *Melits na'im* [ethical literature] (Jerusalem: Tsiyon, 1927).

—— *Vikuah na'im* [polemic] (Jerusalem: Tsiyon, 1927).

ABADI, YESHUAH, *Kol rinah viyeshuah* [sermons] (Leghorn: Belleforte, 1853).

ABOUD, HAYIM SHAUL, *Habakashot leshabat* [hymns] (Jerusalem: n.p., 1995).

ABULAFIA, ISAAC BEN MOSES, *Lev nishbar* [responsa] (İzmir: Shevet Ahim, 1879).

—— *Penei yitshak* [responsa and sermons], 6 vols.: vol. i (Aleppo: Sasson, 1871); vols. iii–vi (İzmir: Pontrimoli, 1887).

ADLER, ELKAN N., *Jews in Many Lands* (Philadelphia: Jewish Publication Society, 1905).

ALTARAS, ISAAC RAPHAEL, *Yitshak yeranen* [hymns] (Jerusalem: Beck, 1855).

ANDERSON, JOHN, *Wanderings in the Land of Israel and through the Wilderness of Sinai, in 1850 and 1851* (Glasgow: W. Collins, 1853).

ANTEBI, ABRAHAM, *Hokhmah umusar* [ethical literature] (Leghorn: Ottolenghi, 1850).

—— *Mor ve'oholot* [responsa] (Leghorn: Ottolenghi, 1843).

—— *Yoshev ohalim* [sermons] (Leghorn: Sa'adon, 1825).

ASHKENAZI, HAYIM, *Ginzei hayim* [responsa] (1st pub. 1941–2; repr. Jerusalem: Mekhon Haketav, 1985).

ASHWORTH, JOHN, *Walks in Canaan* (Manchester: Tubbs & Brook, [1869]).

ATTIAH, ISAIAH BEN HAYIM, *Bigdei yesha* [responsa] (Leghorn: n.p., 1827).

AZRIEL, AARON, *Kapei aharon*, pt. 1 [responsa] (Jerusalem: Beck, 1874).

BASILI, KONSTANTIN, *Memories from Lebanon* [Zikhronot milevanon], trans. Ari Avner, intr. and ann. Mosheh Ma'oz (Jerusalem: Ben-Zvi Institute, 1983).

BELGIOJOSO-TRIVULZIO, CRISTINA, *Asie Mineure et Syrie: Souvenirs de voyages par la princesse de Belgiojoso* (Paris: M. Levy, 1861).

BELL, GERTRUDE L., *The Desert and the Sown* (1st pub. 1907; repr. New York: Arno, 1973).

BENJAMIN, ISRAEL JOSEPH, *Eight Years in Asia and Africa: From 1846 to 1855* (Hanover: pub. by author, 1859).

BLONDEL, EDUARD, *Deux ans en Syrie et en Palestine (1838–1839)* (Paris: Durfart, 1840).

BONAR, ANDREW A., and ROBERT M. M'CHEYNE, *Narrative of a Mission of Inquiry to the Jews from the Church of Scotland in 1839*, 3rd edn. (Philadelphia: Presbyterian Board of Publication, 1845).

BOST, JEAN A., *Souvenirs d'Orient* (Paris: Sandoz & Fischbacher, 1875).

BURTON, ISABEL, *The Inner Life of Syria, Palestine, and the Holy Land*, 2 vols. (London: H. S. King, 1875).

CHURCHILL, CHARLES H., *Mount Lebanon*, vol. i (London: Saunders & Otley, 1853).

CURTIS, GEORGE W., *The Howadji in Syria* (New York: Harper, 1852).

DAYAN, AARON, *Beit aharon* [responsa] (Aleppo: Isaiah Dayan, 1887).

DAYAN, ABRAHAM BEN ISAIAH, *Holekh tamim* [ethical literature] (Leghorn: Ottolenghi, 1850).

—— *Po'el tsedek* [responsa] (Leghorn: Ottolenghi, 1850).

—— *Tuv ta'am* [commentary and ethical literature] (Leghorn: n.p., 1864; repr. Jerusalem: Mekhon Haketav, 1984).

—— *Vayosef avraham* [responsa] (Leghorn: Ben Amozeg, 1884).

—— *Zikaron lanefesh* [ethical literature] (Leghorn: n.p., 1842; repr. Jerusalem: Mekhon Haketav, 1985).

DAYAN, ISAIAH, *Imrei no'am* [responsa] (Aleppo: Isaiah Dayan, 1898).

—— *Zeh ketav yadi* [responsa] (Aleppo: n.p., 1872; repr. Jerusalem: Mekhon Haketav, 1986).

DAYAN, MOSES, *Yashir mosheh* [commentary] (Leghorn: Belleforte, 1879).

DWECK HAKOHEN, JACOB SAUL, *Derekh emunah* [ethical literature] (Aleppo: Isaiah Dayan, 1914).

—— *She'erit ya'akov* [sermons] (Aleppo: Isaiah Dayan, 1925).

DWECK HAKOHEN, SAUL, *Emet me'erets* [responsa] (Jerusalem: Azriel, 1910).

DWECK HAKOHEN, SIMEON BEN SAMUEL, *Rei'ah sadeh* [responsa] (Constantinople: Yonah ben Ya'akov Ashkenazi, 1738).

ELYASHAR, JACOB SAUL, *Simhah le'ish* [responsa] (Jerusalem: Zuckermann, 1888).

—— *Yisa ish* [responsa] (Jerusalem: Zuckermann, 1896).

FRANKL, LUDWIG A., *The Jews in the East*, trans. Patrick Beaton, 2 vols. (London, 1859; repr. Westport, Conn.: Greenwood, 1975).

GAGIN, SHALOM MOSES HAI, *Yismah lev* [responsa] (Jerusalem: n.p., 1878; repr. Monroe, NY: Copy Corner, 1991).

GALANTE, MORDECAI, *Divrei mordekhai* [responsa] (Leghorn: Ben Amozeg, 1860).

GUYS, HENRI, *Voyage en Syrie: Peinture des mœurs musalmanes, chrétiennes et israélites* (Paris: J. Rouvier, 1855).

HADAYA, SHALOM, *Shalom la'am* [sermons] (Aleppo: Isaiah Dayan, 1896).

HAMWAY, ABRAHAM, *Beit el* [prayers] (Leghorn: Ben Amozeg, 1878).

—— *Beit habehirah* [prayers] (Leghorn: Israel Kushta, 1875).

—— *Zeman beit din* [prayers] (Leghorn: Ben Amozeg, 1899).

HAZZAN, HAYIM DAVID, *Nediv lev: Orah hayim vehoshen mishpat* [responsa] (Jerusalem: Shemuel Ashkenazi, 1866).

JESSUP, HENRY H., *Fifty-three Years in Syria*, 2 vols. (New York: Revell, 1910).

KASSIN, JUDAH BEN YOM TOV, *Mahaneh yehudah* [responsa] (Leghorn: Falorni, 1803).

KEAN, JAMES, *Among the Holy Places: A Pilgrimage through Palestine* (London: T. F. Unwin, 1894).

KESTELMANN, YEHIEL, *Expeditions of the Emissary from Safed in the Lands of the East* [Masot sheliaḥ tsefat be'artsot hamizraḥ], ed. Abraham Yaari (Jerusalem: Tarshish, 1942).

LABATON, ISAAC, *Oseh ḥayil* [responsa] (Jerusalem: Zuckermann, 1926; bound with Mordecai Labaton, *Ben ya'ir* [sermons]).

LABATON, MORDECAI, *Nokhaḥ hashulḥan* [sermons] (İzmir: De Ciégura, 1868).

LANIADO, RAPHAEL SOLOMON BEN SAMUEL, *Beit dino shel shelomoh* [responsa] (Istanbul: Shemuel Ashkenazi, 1775; repr. Jerusalem: Mekhon Haketav, 1982).

—— *Kise shelomoh* [responsa] (Jerusalem: Zuckermann, [1901]).

—— *Hama'alot lishelomoh* [sermons] (Istanbul: Shemuel Ashkenazi, 1775).

LOEWE, LOUIS (ed.), *Diaries of Sir Moses and Lady Montefiore*, 2 vols. (London: Griffith, Farran, Okeden, & Welsh, 1890).

LYNCH, WILLIAM F., *Narrative of the United States' Expedition to the River Jordan and the Dead Sea* (1st pub. 1849; repr. New York: Arno, 1977).

MADOX, JOHN, *Excursions in the Holy Land, Egypt, Nubia, Syria . . .*, 2 vols. (London: R. Bentley, 1834).

MARGOLIOUTH, DAVID S., *Cairo, Jerusalem and Damascus: Three Chief Cities of the Egyptian Sultans* (London: Chatto & Windus, 1907).

MARGOLIOUTH, MOSES, *A Pilgrimage to the Land of my Fathers*, 2 vols. (London: Bentley, 1850).

MARTINEAU, HARRIET, *Eastern Life: Present and Past*, new edn. (1st pub. 1848; London: E. Moxon, 1875).

MISHAQA, MIKHAYIL, *Eye-witness Account of Events in Syria and Lebanon* [Mashhad al-a'yan bi-hawadith suriya wa-lubnan], ed. Mulhim Khalil 'Abduh and Andrawus Hanna (Cairo: n.p., 1908).

—— *Murder, Mayhem, Pillage, and Plunder: The History of the Lebanon in the 18th and 19th Century*, trans. W. M. Thackston, Jr (Albany: State University of New York Press, 1988).

Mishmeret haḥodesh [prayers] (Safed: Kara, 1863).

MURRAY, JOHN, *Handbook for Travellers in Syria and Palestine*, 2 vols. (London: J. Murray, 1868).

NEALE, FREDERICK A., *Eight Years in Syria, Palestine and Asia Minor, from 1842 to 1850*, 2nd edn., 2 vols. (London: Colburn & Co., 1852).

NEUMARK, EPHRAIM, *A Journey in the Old Land* [Masa be'erets hakedem], ed. Abraham Yaari, Sifriyat Levi Halevi 2 (Jerusalem: Levin-Epstein, 1947).

PALAGI, HAYIM BEN JACOB, *Ḥayim veshalom* [responsa] (İzmir: Ben-Zion Roditi, 1857.)

—— *Ḥikekei lev* [responsa], 2 vols. (Salonika: Shemuel Ashkenazi, 1848).

—— *Ḥukot haḥayim* [responsa] (İzmir: Deshen, 1868).

PATON, ANDREW A., *The Modern Syrians: Native Society in Damascus, Aleppo, and the Mountains of the Druses . . .* (London: Longman, Brown, Green, & Longmans, 1844).

PINTO, JOSIAH, *Nivḥar mikesef* [responsa] (Aleppo: Sassoon, 1869).

PORTER, JOSIAS L., *Five Years in Damascus*, 2 vols. (London: J. Murray, 1855).

—— *The Giant Cities of Bashan and Syria's Holy Places* (London: T. Nelson, 1867).

POUJADE, M. E., *Le Liban et la Syrie, 1845–1860* (Paris, 1861).

POUJOULAT, BAPTISTIN, *La vérité sur la Syrie* (Paris: Gaume & J. Duprey, 1861).

REISCHER, MOSES BEN MENAḤEM MENDL, *Sha'arei yerushalayim* (Warsaw: Lebensohn, 1872).

SASSON, ISRAEL, *Keneset yisra'el* [responsa], pt. 1 (Leghorn: Belleforte, 1856).

SAULCY, LOUIS FÉLICIEN JOSEPH CAIGNART DE, *Narrative of a Journey Round the Dead Sea and in Bible Lands, in 1850 and 1851*, 2 vols. (London: Bentley, 1854).

SCHAFF, PHILIP, *Through Bible Lands* (New York: American Tract Society, 1878).

SCHUR, WOLF (WILLIAM), *Maḥazot haḥayim* [travels] (Vienna: Brög, 1884).

SEGALL, JOSEPH, *Travels through Northern Syria* (London: Society for Promoting Christianity amongst the Jews, 1910).

SHNEOUR, ZALMAN, *Zikhron yerushalayim* [travels] (Jerusalem: Beck, 1876).

SHREM, ISAAC, *Hadar ezer* [commenteary] (İzmir: De Ciégura, 1865).

STEWART, ROBERT WALTER, *The Tent and the Khan: A Journey to Sinai and Palestine* (Edinburgh: W. Oliphant & Sons, 1857).

SUKARY, JACOB, *Vayeḥi ya'akov* (Leghorn: Ben Amozeg, 1901)

—— *Vayikra ya'akov* (Leghorn, 1880)

—— *Yoru mishpateikha leya'akov* [ethical literature] (Calcutta: n.p., 1882).

SUKARY, SOLOMON, *Ateret shelomoh* (Jerusalem: Ma'arekhet ha-hashqafa, 1902).

SUTTON, JOSEPH, *Vayelaket yosef* [laws] (Aleppo: Isaiah Dayan, 1915).

SUTTON, MENASHEH, *Kenesiyah leshem shamayim* [ethical literature] (Jerusalem: Sasson, 1874).

—— *Maḥberet pirḥei shoshanim* [ethical literature] (Aleppo: Hashalem, 1910).

—— *Mateh menasheh* [responsa] (New York, 2007).

SUTTON, MOSES, *Kehilat mosheh* [sermons] (Aleppo: Eliyahu Sasson, 1873).

TARAB, EZRA BEN ELIJAH, *Milei de'ezra* [responsa] (Jerusalem: Rohold, 1924).

—— *Sha'arei ezra* [responsa] (Jerusalem: n.p., 1906).

TAWIL, EZRA ELI HAKOHEN, *Et sofer* [responsa] (Jerusalem: Zuckermann, 1928).

THOMSON, ANDREW, *In the Holy Land* (London: T. Nelson, 1874).

TILT, CHARLES, *The Boat and the Caravan: A Family Tour through Egypt and Syria*, 5th edn. (London: D. Bogue, 1851).

TWAIN, MARK, *The Innocents Abroad, or The New Pilgrims' Progress* (New York: Heritage Press, 1962).

WELD, AGNES G., *Sacred Palmlands or, The Journal of a Spring Tour* (London: Longmans, Green, 1881).

WILSON, JOHN, *The Lands of the Bible*, 2 vols. (Edinburgh: Whyte, 1847).

WOOD, WILLIAM S., *An Eastern Afterglow* (Cambridge: Deighton, Bell & Co., 1880).

WOODCOCK, WILLIAM J., *Scripture Lands* (London: Longman, Brown, Green, &
Longmans, 1849).

WORTABET, GREGORY M., *Syria and the Syrians* (London: J. Madden, 1856).

YADID HALEVI, ELIEZER RAHAMIM BEN YOM TOV, *Shivḥei moharam* [accounts of
Rabbi Mordecai Labaton] (Jerusalem: Anav, 1932).

YADID HALEVI, JOSEPH, *Yemei yosef batra* [responsa] (Brooklyn, NY: Balshon, 1972).

SECONDARY SOURCES

ABU ʿIZZ AL-DIN, SULAYMAN, *Ibrahim Basha in Syria* [Ibrahim basha fi suriya]
(Beirut: n.p., 1929).

ABU-MANNEH, BUTRUS, 'The Genesis of Midhat Pasha's Governorship in Syria
1878–1880', in Thomas Philipp and Birgit Schaebler (eds.), *The Syrian Land:
Processes of Integration and Fragmentation*, Berliner Islamstudien 6 (Stuttgart: F.
Steiner, 1998), 251–67.

ADES, ABRAHAM, *Derekh erets* [The way of the land] (Benei Berak: Hamakhon
Lehafatsat Erkhei Hamasoret Shel Yahadut Aram Tsova, 1990).

ANTÉBI, ELIZABETH, *Les missionnaires juifs de la France 1860–1939* (Paris: Calmann-
Lévi, 1999).

AL-ASADI, KHAYR AL-DIN, *Districts and Markets of Aleppo* [Ahya' halab wa-
aswaquha] (Damascus: Dar qutayba li-al-tibaʿa wa-al-nashr wa-al-tawziʿ, 1990).

AVNI, HAIM, *The History of Jewish Immigration to Argentina, 1810–1950* (Mibitul
ha'inkvizitsiyah ve'ad 'ḥok hashevut'] (Jerusalem: Magnes, 1982).

ʿAWAD, ʿABD AL-ʿAZIZ MUHAMMAD, *Ottoman Administration of the Province of Syria
1864–1914* [Al-idara al-ʿuthmaniyya fi wilayat suriya 1864–1914] (Cairo: Dar al-
maʿarif, 1969).

BACQUÉ-GRAMMONT, JEAN-LOUIS, and PAUL DUMONT (eds.), *Economie et sociétés
dans l'Empire Ottoman*, Colloques internationaux du Centre National de la
Recherche Scientifique (Paris: Centre National de la Recherche Scientifique,
1983).

BAER, GABRIEL, *Introduction to the History of Agrarian Relations in the Middle East,
1800–1970* [Mavo letoledot hayaḥasim ha'agrariyim bamizraḥ hatikhon, 1800–
1970] (Tel Aviv: Hakibuts Hame'uhad, 1971).

—— 'Landlord, Peasant and the Government in the Arab Provinces of the Ottoman
Empire in the 19th and Early 20th Century', in Jean-Louis Bacqué-Grammont
and Paul Dumont (eds.), *Economie et sociétés dans l'Empire Ottoman*, Colloques
internationaux du Centre National de la Recherche Scientifique (Paris: Centre
National de la Recherche Scientifique, 1983), 261–74.

BAGIS, ALI I., 'The Impact of Beralti Tuccari on 18th and 19th Century Aleppo and its Social Effects', in Abdeljelil Temimi (ed.), *La Vie social dans les provinces arabes à l'époque ottomane*, 3, 266 (Zaghouan: Centre d'Etudes et de Recherches Ottomans, Morisques, de Documentation et d'Information, 1988).

BAR-DEROMA, HAYIM, *A Unique Conquest* [Kibush yaḥid], Sifriyat Yeruham (Jerusalem: Be'er, 1968).

BARDIN, PIERRE, *Algériens et Tunisiens dans l'empire Ottoman de 1848 à 1914* (Paris: Centre National de la Recherche Scientifique, 1979).

BARNAI, JACOB, '"Blood Libels" in the Ottoman Empire of the Fifteenth to the Nineteenth Centuries', in Shmuel Almog (ed.), *Antisemitism through the Ages*, trans. Nathan H. Reisner (Oxford: Pergamon for the Vidal Sassoon International Center for the Study of Antisemitism, The Hebrew University of Jerusalem, 1988), 189–94.

—— 'The Jews in the Ottoman Empire' (Heb.), in Shmuel Ettinger (ed.), *The History of the Jews in the Islamic Countries* [Toledot hayehudim be'aratsot ha'islam], pt. 2: *From the Middle of the Nineteenth to the Middle of the Twentieth Century* [Me'emtsa hame'ah hatesha-esreh ad emtsa hame'ah ha'esrim] (Jerusalem: Zalman Shazar Centre, 1986), 181–297.

BARON, SALO W. 'Great Britain and Damascus Jewry in 1860–61', *Jewish Social Studies*, 2/2 (1940), 179–208.

—— 'The Jews and the Syrian Massacres of 1860.' *Proceedings of the American Academy for Jewish Research*, 4 (1932/3), 3–31.

BAT YE'OR, *The Dhimmi: Jews and Christians under Islam*, rev. and enlarged English edn. (London and Toronto: Associated University Presses, 1985).

BENAYAHU, MEIR, 'The Jews of Damascus and the Galilee in the Days of the Druze Attacks in the Year 1860' (Heb.), *Sinai*, 24 (1948), 91–105.

BEN-ZVI, IZHAK, *Remnants of Ancient Jewish Communities in the Land of Israel* [She'ar yashuv], rev. edn. (Jerusalem: Ben-Zvi Institute, 1965).

BOCQUET, JÉRÔME, 'Un example de minorité au Levant a la fin de l'empire ottoman: les chretiens du quartier de Bâb Tûma a Damas', *Revue des Mondes Musulmans et de la Méditerranée*, 107–10 (2005), 33–59.

BOSWORTH, C. E., 'The Concept of Dhimma in Early Islam', in Benjamin Braude and Bernard Lewis (eds.), *Christians and Jews in the Ottoman Empire* (New York: Holmes & Meier, 1982), i. 37–51.

BOUCHAIN, JULIE D., *Juden in Syrien: Aufstieg und Niedergang der Familie Farḥi von 1740 bis 1995*, Hamburger Islamwissenschaftliche und Turkologische Arbeiten und Texte 9 (Hamburg: Lit, 1996).

BOWRING, JOHN, *Report on the Commercial Statistics of Syria* (1st pub. 1840; repr. New York: Arno, 1973).

BRASLAVY (BRASLVSKY), JOSEPH, 'Elijah Caves from Cairo to Aleppo' (Heb.), *Yeda am*, 7/25 (1961), 49–57.

BRAUDE, BENJAMIN, and BERNARD LEWIS, *Christians and Jews in the Ottoman Empire*, 2 vols. (New York: Holmes & Meier, 1982).

BRAWER, ABRAHAM J., 'The Jews of Damascus after the Blood Libel of 1840' (Heb., Eng. abstract), *Tsiyon*, 11 (1945/6), 83–108.

—— 'New Material with Regard to the Damascus Libel' (Heb.), in *Jubilee Volume for Professor Shmuel Krauss* [Sefer yovel leprofesor shemuel kraus] (Jerusalem: Rubin Mass, 1937), 260–302.

—— 'Notes on the Damascus Blood-Accusation' (Heb., Eng. abstract), *Tsiyon*, 5 (1940), 294–7.

BURTON, RICHARD F., *The Jew, the Gypsy and el Islam*, ed. W. H. [William Henry] Wilkins (London: Hutchinson, 1898).

BUZPINAR, S. TUFAN, 'The Question of Citizenship of the Algerian Immigrants in Syria, 1847–1900', in Moshe Ma'oz, Joseph Ginat, and Onn Winckler (eds.), *Modern Syria: From Ottoman Rule to Pivotal Role in the Middle East* (Brighton: Sussex Academic Press, 1999), 135–49.

CASSUTO, DAVID, 'The Ancient Synagogue of Aleppo and its History' (Heb., Eng. abstract), *Pe'amim*, 72 (1997), 84–105.

CHEVALLIER, DOMINIQUE, 'Western Development and Eastern Crisis in the Mid-Nineteenth Century: Syria Confronted with the European Economy', in William R. Polk and Richard L. Chambers (eds.), *Beginnings of Modernization in the Middle East*, Publications of the Center for Middle Eastern Studies 1 (Chicago: Chicago University Press, 1968), 205–22.

CHIRA, ROBERT, *From Aleppo to America* (New York: Rivercross, 1994).

CIOETA, DONALD J., 'Ottoman Censorship in Lebanon and Syria, 1876–1908', *International Journal of Middle East Studies*, 10 (1979), 167–86.

CLAY, CHRISTOPHER, 'The Origins of Modern Banking in the Levant: The Branch Network of the Imperial Ottoman Bank, 1890–1914', *International Journal of Middle East Studies*, 26 (1994), 589–614.

COHEN, AMNON, 'Damascus and Jerusalem' (Heb., Eng. abstract), *Sefunot*, NS, 2/17 (1983), 97–104.

—— *A World Within: Jewish Life as Reflected in Muslim Court Documents from the* Sijill *of Jerusalem (XVIth Century)*, 2 vols., *Jewish Quarterly Review* suppl. (Philadelphia: Center for Judaic Studies, 1994).

COHEN, HAYYIM J., *The Jews of the Middle East, 1860–1972*, trans. Z. and L. Alizi (Jerusalem: Israel Universities Press, 1973).

COHEN-TAWIL, A., 'The Francos in Aleppo' (Heb.), *Shevet va'am*, 2nd ser., 10 (1984), 129–35.

COMMINS, DAVID, 'Religious Reformers and Arabists in Damascus, 1885–1914', *International Journal of Middle East Studies*, 18 (1986), 405–25.

—— 'Social Criticism and Reformist Ulama of Damascus', *Studia Islamica*, 78 (1993), 160–80.

CUNNINGHAM, ALLAN, 'Dragomania: The Dragomans of the British Embassy in Turkey', *St Antony's Papers* 2 (1961), 81–100.

DAHIR, MAS'UD, 'The Settlement Movement in the Arab East at the End of the

Ottoman Period: A Study of Migration to Beirut in the Nineteenth Century' (Arab.), in ʿAbd al-Jalil al-Tamimi (ed.), *Social Life in the Arab Provinces in the Ottoman Period* [Al-haya al-ijtimaʿiyya fi al-wilaya al-ʿarabiyya athnaʾ al-ʿahd al-ʿuthmani], 2 vols. (Zaghwan: Markaz al-dirasat wa-al-buhuth al-ʿuthmaniyya wa-al-murisikiyya wa-al-tawthiq wa-al-maʿlumat, 1988), 461–76.

DAVIS, FANNY, *The Ottoman Lady: A Social History from 1718 to 1918*, Contributions in Women's Studies 70 (New York: Greenwood, 1986).

DAVISON, RODERIC H., 'The *Millets* as Agents of Change in the Nineteenth-Century Ottoman Empire', in Benjamin Braude and Bernard Lewis (eds.), *Christians and Jews in the Ottoman Empire* (New York: Holmes & Meier, 1982), i. 319–37.

—— *Reform in the Ottoman Empire: 1856–1876* (Princeton, NJ: Princeton University Press, 1963).

—— 'Turkish Attitudes Concerning Christian–Muslim Equality in the Nineteenth Century', *American Historical Review*, 59/4 (1954), 844–64.

DEGUILHEM, RANDI, 'State Civil Education in Late Ottoman Damascus: A Unifying or a Separating Force?', in Thomas Philipp and Birgit Schaebler (eds.), *The Syrian Land: Processes of Integration and Fragmentation*, Berliner Islamstudien 6 (Stuttgart: F. Steiner, 1998), 221–50.

DERINGIL, SELIM, '"There Is No Compulsion in Religion": On Conversion and Apostasy in the Late Ottoman Empire: 1839–1856', *Comparative Studies in Society and History*, 42 (2000), 547–75.

DESHEN, SHLOMO, and WALTER P. ZENNER (eds.), *Jews among Muslims: Communities in the Precolonial Middle East* (Basingstoke: Macmillan, 1996).

AL-DIMASHQI, MIKHAʾIL, *History of Events in Syria and Lebanon* [Tarikh hawadith al-sham wa-lubnan] (Beirut: n.p., 1912).

DINABURG, BEN-ZION, 'The Political Nature of the Damascus Libel' (Heb.), *Hashiloʾaḥ*, 41 (1924), 518–28.

DOTHAN, ALEXANDER, 'On the History of the Ancient Synagogue in Aleppo' (Heb., Eng. abstract), *Sefunot*, 1 (1956), 25–61.

DOUWES, DICK, *The Ottomans in Syria: A History of Justice and Oppression* (London: I. B. Tauris, 2000).

DUPARC, PIERRE, *Turquie*, Recueil des instructions données aux ambassadeurs et ministres de France 29 (Paris: Centre National de la Recherche Scientifique, 1969).

ELIAV, MORDECHAI, *Die Juden Palästinas in der deutschen Politik: Dokumente aus dem Archiv des deutschen Konsulats in Jerusalem, 1842–1914* (Tel Aviv: Tel Aviv University, 1973).

—— *The Land of Israel and its Jewish Settlement in the 19th Century (1777–1917)* [Erets yisraʾel viyishuvah bameʾah ha-19] (Jerusalem: Keter, 1978).

—— with BARBARA HAIDER, *Österreich und das Heilige Land: Ausgewählte Konsulatsdokumente aus Jerusalem, 1849–1917*, Fontes Rerum Austriacarum, Österreichische Geschichtsquellen, pt. 2: Diplomataria et Acta 91 (Vienna: Verlag der Österreichischen Akademie der Wissenschaften, 2000).

ELMALEH, ABRAHAM, *The Jews in Damascus and their Economical and Cultural Situation* [Hayehudim bedamesek umatsavam hakalkali vehatarbuti] (Jaffa: Hapo'el Hatsa'ir, 1912).

—— 'Nouvelles sources sur la grandeur et l'influence politique et économique de la famille Farhi en Syrie' (Heb.), in Abraham Elmaleh (ed.), *In Memoriam: Hommage à Joseph David Farhi* (Jerusalem: Farhi, 1948), 40–51.

ESTABLET, COLETTE, and JEAN-PAUL PASCUAL, 'Damascene Probate Inventories of the 17th and 18th Centuries: Some Preliminary Approaches and Results', *International Journal of Middle East Studies*, 24 (1992), 373–93.

FARAH, CAESAR E., 'Necip Paşa and the British in Syria, 1841–1842', *Archivum Ottomanicum*, 2 (1970), 115–53.

—— *The Politics of Interventionism in Ottoman Lebanon, 1830–1861* (Oxford: Centre for Lebanese Studies with I. B. Tauris, 2000).

—— 'Protestantism and British Diplomacy in Syria', *International Journal of Middle East Studies*, 7 (1976), 321–44.

—— 'Protestantism and Politics: The 19th Century Dimension in Syria', in David Kushner (ed.), *Palestine in the Late Ottoman Period: Political, Social and Economic Transformation* (Jerusalem: Ben-Zvi Institute, 1986), 320–40.

FAUR, JOSÉ, *Rabbi Yisrael Moshe Ḥazzan: The Man and his Works* [Harav yisra'el mosheh ḥazan] (Jerusalem: n.p., 1977).

FAWAZ, LEILA, 'The Beirut–Damascus Road: Connecting the Syrian Coast to the Interior in the Nineteenth Century', in Thomas Philipp and Birgit Schaebler (eds.), *The Syrian Land: Processes of Integration and Fragmentation*, Berliner Islamstudien 6 (Stuttgart: F. Steiner, 1998), 19–27.

—— *An Occasion for War: Civil Conflict in Lebanon and Damascus in 1860* (London: Centre for Lebanese Studies, 1994).

FINDLEY, CARTER V., 'The Acid Test of Ottomanism: The Acceptance of Non-Muslims in the Late Ottoman Bureaucracy', in Benjamin Braude and Bernard Lewis (eds.), *Christians and Jews in the Ottoman Empire* (New York: Holmes & Meier, 1982), i. 339–68.

—— *Ottoman Civil Officialdom: A Social History* (Princeton, NJ: Princeton University Press, 1989).

FIRRO, KAIS M., 'The Impact of European Imports on Handicrafts in Syria and Palestine in the Nineteenth Century', *Asian and African Studies*, 25 (1991), 31–53.

FLORENCE, RONALD, *Blood Libel: The Damascus Affair of 1840* (Madison: University of Wisconsin Press, 2004).

FRANCO, MOISE, *Essai sur l'histoire des Israélites de l'Empire Ottoman depuis les origines jusqu'à nos jours* (1st pub. 1897; repr. Hildesheim: G. Olms, 1973).

FRANKEL, JONATHAN, 'The Crisis as a Factor in Modern Jewish Politics, 1840 and 1881–1882', in Jehuda Reinharz (ed.), *Living with Antisemitism: Modern Jewish Responses*, Tauber Institute for the Study of European Jewry 6 (Hanover, NH: University Press of New England for Brandeis University Press, 1987), 42–58.

—— *The Damascus Affair: 'Ritual Murder,' Politics, and the Jews in 1840* (New York: Cambridge University Press, 1997).

—— 'A Historiographical Oversight: The Austrian Consul-General and the Damascus Blood Libel (with the Laurin–Rothschild Correspondence, 1840)', in Ada Rapoport-Albert and Steven J. Zipperstein (eds.), *Jewish History: Essays in Honour of Chimen Abramsky* (London: Halban, 1988), 285–317.

—— '"Ritual Murder" in the Modern Era: The Damascus Affair of 1840', *Jewish Social Studies*, 3/2 (Winter 1997), 1–16.

FRENKEL, MIRIAM, 'The Jewish Community of Aleppo According to Geniza Fragments' [Kehilat yehudei ḥalab al pi kitei hagenizah], MA diss., Hebrew University, Jerusalem, 1990.

FRIEDMAN, ISAIAH, 'The System of Capitulations and its Effects on Turco-Jewish Relations in Palestine, 1856–1897', in David Kushner (ed.), *Palestine in the Late Ottoman Period: Political, Social and Economic Transformation* (Jerusalem: Ben-Zvi Institute, 1986), 280–93.

GAON, MOSES DAVID, *The Jews of the East in the Land of Israel* [Yehudei hamizraḥ be'erets yisra'el], 2 vols. (Jerusalem: privately printed, 1938).

—— *The Sages of Jerusalem: A Selection of Articles* [Ḥakhmei yerushalayim: mivḥar ma'amarim] (Jerusalem: Va'ad Adat Hasefaradim Ve'edot Hamizrah Biyerushalayim, 1976).

GERBER, HAIM, 'Jews and Money-Lending in the Ottoman Empire', *Jewish Quarterly Review*, 72 (1981/2), 100–18.

—— '"Palestine" and Other Territorial Concepts in the 17th Century', *International Journal of Middle East Studies*, 30 (1998), 563–72.

—— and NACHUM T. GROSS, 'Inflation or Deflation in Nineteenth-Century Syria and Palestine', *Journal of Economic History*, 40 (1980), 351–8.

AL-GHAZZI, KAMIL, *The Golden River of Aleppine History* [Nahr al-dhahab fi tarikh halab], 3 vols. (Aleppo: n.p., 1923–6).

GIDNEY, WILLIAM T., *The History of the London Society for Promoting Christianity amongst the Jews (from 1809 to 1908)* (London: London Society for Promoting Christianity amongst the Jews, 1908).

GOREN, HAIM, and YEHOSHUA BEN-ARIEH, 'Catholic Austria and Jerusalem in the Nineteenth Century: The Beginnings', in Marian Wrba (ed.), *Austrian Presence in the Holy Land in the 19th and Early 20th Century: Proceedings of the Symposium in the Austrian Hospice in Jerusalem on March 1–2, 1995* (Tel Aviv: Austrian Embassy, 1996), 7–24.

GREHAM, JAMES, *Everyday Life and Consumer Culture in 18th-Century Damascus* (Seattle: University of Washington Press, 2007).

GROSS, MAX L. 'Ottoman Rule in the Province of Damascus, 1860–1909', Ph.D. diss., Georgetown University, Washington, DC, 1979.

GROSSMAN, AVRAHAM, 'From Father to Son: The Inheritance of the Spiritual Leadership of the Jewish Communities in the Early Middle Ages' (Heb., Eng. abstract), *Tsiyon*, 50 (1985), 189–220. A revised version appeared in English in

David Kraemer (ed.), *The Jewish Family: Metaphor and Memory* (New York: Oxford University Press, 1989), 115–32.

AL-HALIL, AHARON, 'An Important Document Source about the Damascus Blood Libel' (Heb.), *Mizraḥ uma'arav*, 3 (1929), 34–49.

HALLIDAY, FRED, 'The Millet of Manchester: Arab Merchants and Cotton Trade', *British Journal of Middle East Studies*, 19 (1992), 159–76.

HAMUI DE HALABE, LIZ, *Los Judíos de Alepo en México* (Mexico City: Maguen David, 1989).

HAREL, YARON, *Between Intrigues and Revolution: The Appointment and Dismissal of Chief Rabbis in Baghdad, Damascus and Aleppo 1744–1914* [Bein tekhakhim lemahapekhah: minui rabanim rashiyim vehadaḥatam bekehilot bagdad, damesek, veḥaleb] (Jerusalem: Ben-Zvi Institute, 2007).

—— *The Books of Aleppo: The Rabbinic Literature of the Scholars of Aleppo* [Sifrei erets: hasifrut hatoranit shel ḥakhmei aram tsova] (Jerusalem: Ben-Zvi Institute, 1997).

—— 'The Citizenship of the Algerian-Jewish Immigrants in Damascus', *Maghreb Review*, 28 (2003), 294–305.

—— 'Conflict and Agreement: Sephardis and Mustarabs in Aleppo' (Heb.), *Ladinar: Studies in the Literature, Music and the History of the Ladino Speaking Sephardic Jews*, 1 (1998), 119–38.

—— 'Le Consul de France et l'Affaire de Damas à la lumière de nouveaux documents', *Revue d'histoire diplomatique*, 2 (1999), 143–70.

—— 'The Controversy over Rabbi Ephraim Laniado's Inheritance of the Rabbinate in Aleppo', *Jewish History*, 13/1 (Spring 1999), 83–101.

—— 'The Damascus Jewish Community and its Customs in the Notes of Eliezer Rivlin' (Heb., Eng. abstract), *Pe'amim*, 74 (1998), 131–55.

—— 'The Edict to Destroy *Em lamikra*: Aleppo 1865' (Heb., Eng. abstract), *Hebrew Union College Annual*, 64 (1993), 27–36.

—— 'The Encounter of Exiles from Palestine with Damascus Jewry in the Twentieth Century' (Heb., Eng. abstract), *Tsiyon*, 61 (1996), 183–207.

—— 'The First Jews from Aleppo in Manchester: New Documentary Evidence', *Association for Jewish Studies Review*, 23 (1998), 191–202.

—— 'From Opening to Closing: The Motives for Change in the Attitude of the Rabbinic Elite in the Middle East towards Modernity' (Heb.), *Association for Jewish Studies Review*, 26 (2002), 1–58.

—— '"Great Progress": The Committee of Deputies and the Community of Damascus—Surveys, Programs and Actions' (Heb.), *Pe'amim*, 67 (1996), 57–95.

—— 'The Influence of the Books *Penei yitsḥak*, *Yismaḥ lev*, and *Lev nishbar* on the Struggle around the Rabbinic Office in Damascus' (Heb.), *Asufot*, 11 (1998), 211–43.

—— 'Jewish–Christian Relations in Aleppo as Background for the Jewish Response to the Events of October 1850', *International Journal of Middle East Studies*, 30 (1998), 77–96.

—— 'Latakia: A Forgotten Colony of the First Aliyah' (Heb., Eng. abstract), *Katedrah*, 74 (1994), 62–85.

—— 'Midhat Pasha and the Jewish Community of Damascus: Two New Documents', *Turcica*, 28 (1966), 339–45.

—— 'The Overthrow of the Last Aleppan Chief Rabbi' (Heb.), *Pe'amim*, 44 (1990), 110–31.

—— 'The Rise and Fall of the Jewish Consuls in Aleppo', *Turcica*, 38 (2006), 233–50.

—— 'A Spiritual Agitation in the East: The Founding of a Reform Community in Aleppo in 1862' (Heb.), *Hebrew Union College Annual*, 63 (1992), 19–35.

—— 'The Status and Image of the Picciotto Family as Perceived by Aleppo's French Colony (1784–1850)' (Heb., Eng. abstract), *Mikha'el*, 14 (1997), 171–86.

HARKAVY, ALBERT (ABRAHAM E.), *New and Old: Sources and Research in the History of Israel and its Literature* [Ḥadashim gam yeshanim; mekorot umeḥkarim betoledot yisra'el uvesifruto], 2nd edn. (Jerusalem: Carmiel, 1970).

AL-HASANI, ʿA., *The Economic History of Syria* [Tarikh suriya al-iqtisadi] (Damascus: n.p., 1923).

HIRSCHBERG, HAYIM ZEʾEV, 'The Jews under Islam' (Heb.), in Hava Lazarus Yafeh (ed.), *Studies in the History of the Arabs and Islam* [Perakim betoledot ha'aravim veha'islam] (Tel Aviv: Reshafim, 1975), 262–315.

HITTI, PHILIP K., *The Syrians in America* (New York: Doran, 1924).

HOFMAN, ITZHAK, 'Muhammed Ali in Syria' [Pe'alo shel muhamad ali besuryah], Ph.D. diss., Hebrew University, Jerusalem, 1963.

HOURANI, ALBERT, *A History of the Arab Peoples* (London: Faber & Faber, 1991).

—— *Minorities in the Arab World* (London: Oxford University Press, 1947).

HUREWITZ, JACOB C. (comp., trans., and ed.), *The Middle East and North Africa in World Politics: A Documentary Record*, 2nd edn., 2 vols. (New Haven, Conn.: Yale University Press, 1975).

HYAMSON, ALBERT M., 'The Damascus Affair–1840', *Transactions of the Jewish Historical Society of England*, 16 (1952), 47–71.

—— (ed.), *The British Consulate in Jerusalem in Relation to the Jews of Palestine, 1838–1914*, 2 vols. (London: Jewish Historical Society of England, 1939, 1941).

IDELSOHN, ABRAHAM ZVI, 'The Jewish Community in Damascus' [Kehilat yisra'el bedamesek], *Luaḥ erets yisra'el*, 16 (Jerusalem: A. M. Luncz, 1910–11), 86–107.

INALCIK, HALIL (trans.), 'The Hatt-i Şerif of Gülhane', in J. C. Hurewitz (ed.), *The Middle East and North Africa in World Politics: A Documentary Record* (New Haven: Yale University Press, 1975), i. 269–71.

ISH-SHALOM, MICHAEL, *Christian Travels in the Holy Land: Descriptions and Sources on the History of the Jews in Palestine* [Masa'ei notserim le'erets yisra'el], 2nd edn. (Tel Aviv: Am Oved, 1979).

ISSAWI, CHARLES, 'British Trade and the Rise of Beirut, 1830–1860', *International Journal of Middle East Studies*, 8 (1977), 91–101.

JAFFE, BENJAMIN, *A Portrait of the Land of Israel, 1840–1914* [Diyokenah shel erets yisra'el] (Tel Aviv: Dvir, 1983).

KARAGILA, SVI, *The Jewish Community in Palestine ('Yishuv') during the Egyptian Rule (1831–1840): Social and Economic Patterns* [Hayishuv hayehudi be'erets yisra'el bitekufat hakibush hamitsri (1831–1840)], Publications of the Diaspora Research Institute 77 (Tel Aviv: Tel Aviv University and the Ministry of Defence, 1990).

KARAL, ENVER Z., 'Non-Muslim Representatives in the First Constitutional Assembly, 1876–1877', in Benjamin Braude and Bernard Lewis (eds.), *Christians and Jews in the Ottoman Empire* (New York: Holmes & Meier, 1982), i. 387–400.

KARPAT, KEMAL H., 'The Ottoman Emigration to America, 1860–1914', *International Journal of Middle East Studies*, 17 (1985), 175–209.

—— *Ottoman Population, 1830–1914* (Madison: University of Wisconsin Press, 1985).

—— 'Ottoman Population Records and the Census of 1881/82–1893', *International Journal of Middle East Studies*, 9 (1978), 237–74.

KASABA, RESAT, *The Ottoman Empire and the World Economy: The Nineteenth Century*, State University of New York Series in Middle Eastern Studies (Albany: State University of New York Press, 1988).

KAYALI, HASAN, 'Jewish Representation in the Ottoman Parliaments', in Avigdor Levy (ed.), *The Jews of the Ottoman Empire* (Princeton, NJ: Darwin, 1994), 507–17.

KEDEM, MENACHEM, 'Mid-Nineteenth-Century Anglican Eschatology on the Redemption of Israel' (Heb.), *Cathedra*, 19 (1981), 55–71.

KEDOURIE, ELIE, *England and the Middle East: The Destruction of the Ottoman Empire, 1914–1921*, 2nd edn. (Hassocks, Sussex: Harvester, 1978).

KHOURY, PHILIP S., *Urban Notables and Arab Nationalism: The Politics of Damascus, 1860–1920* (Cambridge: Cambridge University Press, 1983).

KIWAN, MA'MUN, *The Jews in the Middle East: The Final Exodus from the New Ghetto* [Al-yahud fi al-sharq al-awsat: al-khuruj al-akhir min al-jitu al-jadid] (Amman: Al-ahliyya li-al-nashr wa-al-tawzi', 1996).

KUSHNER, DAVID (ed.), *Palestine in the Late Ottoman Period: Political, Social and Economic Transformation* (Jerusalem: Ben-Zvi Institute, 1986.)

KUSHNIR [KUSHNER], DAVID, 'The Firman of the Ottoman Sultan Rejecting Blood Libels against the Jews' (Heb., Eng. abstract), *Pe'amim*, 20 (1984), 37–45.

LAMDAN, RUTH, 'Female Slaves in the Jewish Society of Palestine, Syria and Egypt in the Sixteenth Century' (Heb.), in Minna Rozen (ed.), *The Days of the Crescent: Chapters in the History of the Jews in the Ottoman Empire* [Yemei ha-sahar: perakim betoledot hayehudim be'imperiyah ha'otemanit], Publications of the Diaspora Research Institute 111; Publications of the Chair for the History and Culture of the Jews of Salonika and Greece, NS, 2 (Tel Aviv: Tel Aviv University, 1996), 355–71.

—— *A Separate People: Jewish Women in Palestine, Syria and Egypt in the Sixteenth Century*, trans. Yaffa Murciano, Brill's Series in Jewish Studies 26 (Leiden: Brill, 2000.)

LANDAU, JACOB M., and Moshe Ma'oz, 'Jews and Non-Jews in 19th Century Egypt and Syria' (Heb., Eng. abstract), *Pe'amim*, 9 (1981), 4–13.

LANIADO, DAVID-SION, *For the Sake of the Holy Ones in Aleppo* [Likedoshim asher ba'arets] (Jerusalem: Itah, 1952; 2nd edn. Jerusalem: published by the author's sons, 1980). Appeared in English translation as David Sutton (ed.), *Aleppo, City of Scholars: Based on LiKedoshim Asher Ba'Aretz by Hacham David-Sion Laniado*, trans. David Kirzner, Artscroll Sefardic Heritage Series (Brooklyn, NY: Mesorah, 2005).

LASKIER, MICHAEL M., 'The Alliance Israélite Universelle and the Social Conditions of the Jewish Communities in the Mediterranean Basin (1860–1914)', in Simon Schwarzfuchs (ed.), *L''Alliance' dans les communautés du basin méditerranéen à la fin du 19ème siècle et son influence sur la situation sociale et culturelle: Actes du deuxième Congrès international de recherché du patrimoine des Juifs Sépharades et d'Orient* [Ha'alians bikehilot agan hayam hatikhon besof hame'ah ha-19 vehashpa'ato al hamatsav haḥevrati vehatarbuti] (Jerusalem: Misgav Yerushalayim, 1987), pp. lxxi—lxxxviii.

LAURENT, ACHILLE, *Relation historique des affaires de Syrie depuis 1840 jusqu'en 1842: Statistique Général du Mont-Liban, procédure complète dirigée en 1840 contre des Juifs de Damas à la suite de la disparition du Père Thomas*, vol. ii (Paris: Gaume Frères, 1846).

LAZARUS-YAFEH, HAVA, *Muslim Authors on Jews and Judaism* [Soferim muslemim al yehudim veyahadut] (Jerusalem: Zalman Shazar Centre, 1996).

LE CALLOC'H, B., 'La Dynastie consulaire des Picciotto (1734–1894)', *Revue d'histoire diplomatique*, 1–2 (1991), 135–72.

LEVEN, NARCISSE, *Cinquante ans d'histoire: L'Alliance Israélite Universelle (1860–1910)*, 2 vols. (Paris: F. Alcan, 1911–20).

LEVI, AVNER, 'Changes in the Leadership of the Main Spanish Communities in the Nineteenth-Century Ottoman Empire' (Heb.), in Minna Rozen (ed.), *The Days of the Crescent: Chapters in the History of the Jews in the Ottoman Empire* [Yemei hasahar: perakim betoledot hayehudim be'imperiyah ha'otemanit], Publications of the Diaspora Research Institute 111; Publications of the Chair for the History and Culture of the Jews of Salonika and Greece, NS, 2 (Tel Aviv: Tel Aviv University Press, 1996), 237–71.

LEVTZION, NEHEMIA, 'Conversion to Islam in Syria and Palestine and the Survival of Christian Communities', in Michael Gervers and Ramzi J. Bikhazi (eds.), *Conversion and Continuity: Indigenous Christian Communities in Islamic Lands, 8th to 18th Centuries*, Papers in Mediaeval Studies 9 (Toronto: Pontifical Institute of Mediaeval Studies, 1990), 289–312.

LEVY, AVIGDOR (ed.), *The Jews of the Ottoman Empire* (Princeton, NJ: Darwin, 1994).

LEWIS, BERNARD, *The Emergence of Modern Turkey* (1st pub. 1961; repr. London: Oxford University Press, 1966).

—— *Islam in History: Ideas, People, and Events in the Middle East*, new rev. and expanded edn. (Chicago: Open Court, 1993).

LEWIS, BERNARD, *The Jews of Islam* (Princeton, NJ: Princeton University Press, 1984).

—— *The Middle East: 2000 Years of History from the Rise of Christianity to the Present Day* (London: Weidenfeld & Nicolson, 1995).

LUTZKY, A., 'The "Francos" and the Effect of the Capitulations on the Jews in Aleppo' (Heb., Eng. abstract), *Tsiyon*, 6 (1940–1), 46–79.

AL-MAGHRIBI, MUHAMMAD, 'The Jews of Syria in the Last Hundred Years' (Arab.), *Majallat al-majma' al-'ilmi al-'arabi*, 11–12 (1929), 641–53.

MAKOVETSKI, L. BORNSTEIN, 'The Jewish Economic Elite in Aleppo during the Ottoman Period (16th–18th Centuries)' (Heb.), *East and Maghreb*, 8 (2008), 185–217.

MALACHI, ELIEZER R., 'The Jews in the Druze Revolt' [Hayehudim behitkomemut haderuzim], *Horeb*, 1 (1934), 105–16.

MALUL, NISSIM, 'The Arabic Press' [Ha'itonut ha'aravit], *Hashiloah*, 31 (1914–15), 364–74, 439–50.

MA'OZ, MOSHE, 'Changes in the Status of Jews in the Ottoman Empire' (Heb.), *Mikedem umiyam*, 1 (1981), 11–28.

—— 'Communal Conflict in Ottoman Syria during the Reform Era: The Role of Political and Economic Factors', in Benjamin Braude and Bernard Lewis (eds.), *Christians and Jews in the Ottoman Empire* (New York: Holmes & Meier, 1982), ii. 91–105.

—— 'Intercommunal Relations in Ottoman Syria during the Tanzimat Era: Social and Economic Factors', in Osman Okyar and Halil Inalcik (eds.), *Social and Economic History of Turkey (1071–1920)* (Ankara: Meteksan, 1980), 205–10.

—— *Modern Syria: Political and Social Changes in the Process of Creating a National Community* [Suryah hehadashah: Temurot politiyot vehevratiyot betahalikh hakamat kehiliyah le'umit] (Tel Aviv: Reshafim, 1974).

—— *Ottoman Reform in Syria and Palestine, 1840–1861: The Impact of the Tanzimat on Politics and Society* (Oxford: Clarendon Press), 1968.

—— 'Society and State in Modern Syria' (Heb.), in Menahem Milson (ed.), *Society and Political Structure in the Arab World* [Hevrah umishtar ba'olam ha'aravi] (Jerusalem: Van Leer Institute, 1977), 24–81.

—— 'The 'Ulamā' and the Process of Modernization in Syria during the Mid-Nineteenth Century', in Gabriel Bar (ed.), *The 'Ulamā' in Modern History: Studies in Memory of Professor Uriel Heyd, Asian and African Studies* 7 (special issue) (Jerusalem: Israel Oriental Society, 1971), 77–88.

—— Joseph Ginat, and Onn Winckler, *Modern Syria: From Ottoman Rule to Pivotal Role in the Middle East* (Brighton: Sussex Academic Press, 1999).

MARCUS, ABRAHAM, *The Middle East on the Eve of Modernity: Aleppo in the Eighteenth Century* (New York: Columbia University Press, 1989).

MARINO, BRIGITTE, 'Cafés et cafetiers de Damas aux XVIIIᵉ et XIXᵉ siècles', *Revue du Monde Musulman et de la Méditerranée*, 75–6 (1995), 275–94.

MASTERS, BRUCE A., 'Aleppo: The Ottoman Empire's Caravan City', in Edhem Eldem, Daniel Goffman, and Bruce Masters (eds.), *The Ottoman City between East and West: Aleppo, İzmir, and Istanbul*, Cambridge Studies in Islamic Civilization (Cambridge: Cambridge University Press, 1999), 17–40.

—— *Christians and Jews in the Ottoman Arab World*, Cambridge Studies in Islamic Civilization (Cambridge: Cambridge University Press, 2001).

—— 'The 1850 Events in Aleppo: An Aftershock of Syria's Incorporation into the Capitalist World System', *International Journal of Middle East Studies*, 22 (1990), 3–20.

—— *The Origins of Western Economic Dominance in the Middle East: Mercantilism and the Islamic Economy in Aleppo, 1600–1750*, New York University Studies in Near Eastern Civilization 12 (New York: New York University Press, 1988).

—— 'The Sultan's Entrepreneurs: The *Avrupa Tüccaris* and the *Hayriye Tüccaris* in Syria', *International Journal of Middle East Studies*, 24 (1992), 579–97.

MERIWETHER, MARGARET L., 'Women and Economic Change in Nineteenth-Century Syria: The Case of Aleppo', in Judith E. Tucker (ed.), *Arab Women: Old Boundaries, New Frontiers* (Bloomington: Indiana University Press, 1993), 65–83.

MEVORAH, BARUCH, 'Effects of the Damascus Affair upon the Development of the Jewish Press, 1840–6' (Heb., Eng. abstract), *Tsiyon*, 23–4 (1958–9), 46–65.

MOREH, SHMUEL, and PHILIP SADGROVE, *Jewish Contributions to Nineteenth-Century Arabic Theatre: Plays from Algeria and Syria. A Study and Texts, Journal of Semitic Studies*, suppl. 6 (Oxford University Press for University of Manchester, 1996).

AL-MUKHALLISI, AL-KHURI QUSTANTIN AL-BASHA (ed.), *Historical Memoirs* [Mudhakkarat tarikhiyya] (Harisa: n.p., n.d.).

MUNDY, M., and R. SAUMAREZ SMITH, *Governing Property, Making the Modern State: Law, Administration and Production in Ottoman Syria* (London: I. B. Tauris, 2006).

NAHON, UMBERTO S., *Sir Moses Montefiore, Leghorn 1784–Ramsgate 1885: A Life in the Service of Jewry* (1st pub. 1965; repr. Jerusalem: World Zionist Organization, 1985).

NINI, YEHUDA, *Western Cultural Assimilation among Jews of the Mediterranean Basin* [Yehudei agan hayam hatikhon nokhaḥ hitbolelut ve'imut im tarbut hama'arav], Study Circle on Diaspora Jewry in the Home of the President of Israel (Jerusalem: Shazar Library, 1979).

PAMUK, SEVKET, *A Monetary History of the Ottoman Empire*, Cambridge Studies in Islamic Civilization (Cambridge: Cambridge University Press, 2000).

—— *The Ottoman Empire and European Capitalism, 1820–1913: Trade, Investment, and Production*, Cambridge Middle East Library 12 (Cambridge: Cambridge University Press, 1987).

PARFITT, TUDOR, '"The Year of the Pride of Israel", Montefiore and the Damascus Blood Libel of 1840', in Sonia Lipman and Vivian D. Lipman (eds.), *The Century of Moses Montefiore* (Oxford: Oxford University Press for The Littman Library of Jewish Civilization, 1985), 131–48.

PERRY, YARON, *British Mission to the Jews in Nineteenth-Century Palestine* (London: Frank Cass, 2003).

PHILIPP, THOMAS, 'Bilad al-Sham in the Modern Period: Integration into the Ottoman Empire and New Relations with Europe', *Arabica*, 51 (2004), 401–18.

—— 'The Farhi Family and the Changing Position of the Jews in Syria, 1750–1860', *Middle Eastern Studies*, 20/4 (1984), 37–52.

—— 'French Merchants and Jews in the Ottoman Empire during the Eighteenth Century', in Avigdor Levy (ed.), *The Jews of the Ottoman Empire* (Princeton, NJ: Darwin, 1994), 315–25.

—— 'Identities and Loyalties in Bilad al-Sham at the Beginning of the Early Modern Period', in Thomas Philipp and Christoph Schumann (eds.), *From the Syrian Land to the States of Syria and Lebanon* (Beirut and Wurzburg: Ergon in Kommission, 2004), 9–26.

—— *The Syrians in Egypt, 1725–1975* (Stuttgart: F. Steiner, 1985).

—— and BIRGIT SCHAEBLER (eds.), *The Syrian Land: Processes of Integration and Fragmentation*, Berliner Islamstudien 6 (Stuttgart: F. Steiner, 1998).

PICCIOTTO, EMILIO, *The Consular History of the Picciotto Family, 1784–1895* (Milan: privately published, 1998).

POLK, WILLIAM R., and RICHARD L. CHAMBERS (eds.), *Beginnings of Modernization in the Middle East: The Nineteenth Century*, Publications of the Center for Middle Eastern Studies 1 (Chicago: University of Chicago Press, 1968).

QARALI, BULUS, *The Most Important Events in Aleppo* ['Ahamm hawadith halab] (Cairo: n.p., n.d.).

AL-QATTAN, NAJWA, 'The Damascene Jewish Community in the Latter Decades of the Eighteenth Century: Aspects of Socio-Economic Life Based on the Registers of the *Sharīʿa* Courts', in Thomas Philipp (ed.), *The Syrian Land in the 18th and 19th Century*, Berliner Islamstudien 5 (Stuttgart: F. Steiner, 1992), 196–216.

—— 'Dhimmīs in the Muslim Court: Legal Autonomy and Religious Discrimination' *International Journal of Middle East Studies*, 31 (1999), 429–44.

—— 'Litigants and Neighbors: The Communal Topography of Ottoman Damascus', *Comparative Studies in Society and History*, 44 (2002), 511–33.

QUATAERT, DONALD, *Ottoman Manufacturing in the Age of the Industrial Revolution*, Cambridge Middle East Library 30 (Cambridge: Cambridge University Press, 1993).

RAFEQ (RAFIQ), ABDUL-KARIM, 'The Damascus Economy and its Confrontation with the Economy of Europe in the Nineteenth Century' (Arab.), *Dirasat tarikhiyya*, 17 (1984), 115–59.

—— 'The Impact of Europe on a Traditional Economy: The Case of Damascus, 1840–1870', in Jean-Louis Bacqué-Grammont and Paul Dumont (eds.), *Economie et sociétés dans l'Empire Ottoman*, Colloques internationaux du Centre

National de la Recherche Scientifique (Paris: Centre National de la Recherche Scientifique, 1983), 420–32.

—— 'Land Tenure Problems and their Social Impact in Syria around the Middle of the Nineteenth Century', in Tarif Khalidi (ed.), *Land Tenure and Social Transformation in the Middle East* (Beirut: American University of Beirut, 1984), 371–96.

—— 'Manifestations of the Craft System in the Levant in the Ottoman Period' (Arab.), *Dirasat tarikhiyya*, 6 (1981), 30–62.

—— 'Manifestations of Ottoman Military Life in the Levant from the Sixteenth to the Beginning of the Nineteenth Century' (Arab.), *Dirasat tarikhiyya*, 1 (1980), 66–90.

—— *The Province of Damascus, 1723–1783* (Beirut: Khayats, 1966).

—— 'The Social and Economic Structure of Bāb-al-Muṣallā (al-Midān), Damascus, 1825–1875', in George N. Atiyeh and Ibrahim M. Oweiss (eds.), *Arab Civilization: Challenges and Responses: Studies in Honor of Constantine K. Zurayk* (New York: State University of New York Press, 1988), 272–311.

—— 'The Syrian Pilgrimage Caravan and its Importance in the Ottoman Period' (Arab.), *Dirasat tarikhiyya*, 6 (1981), 5–28.

RAYMOND, ANDRÉ, *The Great Arab Cities in the 16th–18th Centuries: An Introduction*, Hagop Kevorkian Series on Near Eastern Art and Civilization (New York: New York University Press, 1984).

RAYYAN, MUHAMMAD RAJA'I, 'French Economic Interests in Syria (1535–1920)' (Arab.), *Dirasat tarikhiyya*, 27–8 (1987), 33–65.

REILLY, JAMES A., 'From Workshops to Sweatshops: Damascus Textiles and the World Economy in the Last Ottoman Century', *Review: A Journal of the Fernand Braudel Center*, 16 (1993), 199–213.

—— 'Shariʿa Court Registers and Land Tenure around Nineteenth-Century Damascus', *Middle East Studies Association Bulletin*, 21 (1987), 155–69.

—— 'Status Groups and Propertyholding in the Damascus Hinterland, 1828–1880', *International Journal of Middle East Studies*, 21 (1989), 517–39.

RIVLIN, ELIEZER, and JOSEPH JOEL RIVLIN, 'Chronicles of the Jews in Damascus in the Second Half of the 16th and the First Half of the 17th Century' (Heb.), *Reshumot*, 4 (1926), 77–119.

RIVLIN, JOSEPH JOEL, 'First Names as a Reflection of the Situation of the Jews in Syria in the Previous Century' (Heb.), *Hed hamizraḥ*, 32, 29 Dec. 1944, 6.

RODED, RUTH M., 'Tradition and Change in Syria during the Last Decades of Ottoman Rule: The Urban Elite of Damascus, Aleppo, Homs and Hama, 1876–1918', Ph.D. diss., University of Denver, 1984.

RODGERS, SUSANA BRAUNER, 'The Aleppan Jews of Buenos Aires (1920–60): Their Leadership and Religious Identity' (Heb., Eng. abstract), *Pe'amim*, 80 (1999), 129–42.

RODRIGUE, ARON, *French Jews, Turkish Jews: The Alliance Israélite Universelle and the Politics of Jewish Schooling in Turkey, 1860–1925*, The Modern Jewish Experience (Bloomington: Indiana University Press, 1990).

RODRIGUE, ARON, *Images of Sephardi and Eastern Jewries in Transition: The Teachers of the Alliance Israélite Universelle, 1860–1939* (Seattle: University of Washington Press, 1993).

ROGAN, EUGENE, 'Instant Communication: The Impact of the Telegraph in Ottoman Syria', in Thomas Philipp and Birgit Schaebler (eds.), *The Syrian Land: Processes of Integration and Fragmentation*, Berliner Islamstudien 6 (Stuttgart: F. Steiner, 1998), 113–28.

—— 'Sectarianism and Social Conflict in Damascus: The 1860 Events Reconsidered', *Arabica*, 51 (2004), 493–511.

ROSANES, SOLOMON, *Chronicles of the Jews in Togarmah* [Divrei yemei yisra'el betogarmah], 5 vols. (Sofia: Amischpat, 1934–8). Vols. ii—v appeared under the title *Chronicles of the Jews in Turkey and the Lands of the East* [Korot hayehudim beturkiyah ve'artsot hakedem].

ROZEN, MINNA, 'The Archives of the Chamber of Commerce of Marseilles' (Heb.), *Pe'amim*, 9 (1981), 112–24.

—— 'The Fattoria: A Chapter in the History of Mediterranean Commerce in the 16th and 17th Centuries' (Heb.), *Mikedem umiyam*, 1 (1981), 101–31.

—— *In the Mediterranean Routes: The Jewish-Spanish Diaspora from the Sixteenth to Eighteenth Centuries* [Binetivei hayam hatikhon: hapezurah hayehudit-sefaradit bame'ot ha16–18], Publications of the Chair for the History and Culture of the Jews of Salonika and Greece, NS, 1 (Tel Aviv: Tel Aviv University Press, 1993).

—— (ed.), *The Days of the Crescent: Chapters in the History of the Jews in the Ottoman Empire* [Yemei hasahar: perakim betoledot hayehudim be'imperiyah ha'otemanit], Publications of the Chair for the History and Culture of the Jews of Salonika and Greece, NS, 2 (Tel Aviv: Tel Aviv University Press, 1996).

RUSTUM, ASAD, *The Arab Roots of Syrian History at the Time of Muhammad Ali* [Al-usul al-'arabiyya li-tarikh suriya fi 'ahd muhammad 'ali], vol. v (Beirut: Al-matba'a al-amirkaniyya, 1933).

SALEH, SHAKHIB, *History of the Druzes* [Toledot haderuzim] (Jerusalem: Ministry of Defence, 1989).

SALIBA, NAJIB E., 'The Achievements of Midhat Pasha as Governor of the Province of Syria 1878–1880', *International Journal of Middle East Studies*, 9 (1978), 307–23.

SALIBI, KAMAL S., 'The 1860 Upheaval in Damascus as Seen by Al Sayyid Muhammad Abu'l-Su'ud al Hasibi, Notable and Later Naqib al Ashraf of the City', in William R. Polk and Richard L. Chambers (eds.), *Beginnings of Modernization in the Middle East*, Publications of the Center for Middle Eastern Studies 1 (Chicago: University of Chicago Press), 1968, 185–202.

SALOMONS, DAVID, *An Account of the Recent Persecution of the Jews at Damascus: With Reflections Thereon; and an Appendix, Containing Various Documents Connected with the Subject* (London: Longman, 1840).

SCHILCHER, LINDA SCHATKOWSKI, *Families in Politics: Damascene Factions and Estates of the 18th and 19th Centuries*, Berliner Islamstudien 2 (Wiesbaden: F. Steiner, 1985).

SCHLICHT, ALFRED, 'The Role of Foreign Powers in the History of Lebanon and Syria from 1799–1861', *Journal of Asian History*, 14 (1980), 97–126.

SCHROETER, DANIEL J., 'Jewish Quarters in the Arab-Islamic Cities of the Ottoman Empire', in Avigdor Levy (ed.), *The Jews of the Ottoman Empire* (Princeton, NJ: Darwin, 1994), 287–300.

SCHWARZFUCHS, SIMON, 'Aliyah from North Africa after the French Conquest of Algeria' (Heb., Eng. abstract), *Pe'amim*, 38 (1989), 109–23.

—— 'Jews, Druzes, Muslims and Christians in Damascus in 1860' (Heb.), *Mikha'el*, 7 (1981), 431–44.

—— 'The Jews of Algeria in Northern Erets Yisra'el and the French Protection' (Heb., Eng. abstract), *Shalem*, 3 (1981), 333–49.

—— 'La "Nazione Ebrea" Livornaise au Levant', *Rassegna Mensile di Israel*, 50/9–12 (1984), 707–24.

—— (ed.), *L'Alliance' dans les communautés du bassin méditerranéen à la fin du 19ème siècle et son influence sur la situation sociale et culturelle: Actes du deuxième Congrès international de recherché du patrimoine des Juifs Sépharades et d'Orient* [Ha'alians bikehilot agan hayam hatikhon besof hame'ah ha-19 vehashpa'ato al hamatsav haḥevrati vehatarbuti] (Jerusalem: Misgav Yerushalayim, 1987).

SEROUSSI, EDWIN, 'On the Origin of the Custom of Chanting *Bakashot* in Jerusalem in the Nineteenth Century' (Heb., Eng. abstract), *Pe'amim*, 56 (1993), 106–24.

SHALIT, YORAM, 'European Foreigners in Damascus and Aleppo during the Late Ottoman Period', in Moshe Ma'oz, Joseph Ginat, and Onn Winckler (eds.), *Modern Syria: From Ottoman Rule to Pivotal Role in the Middle East* (Brighton: Sussex Academic Press, 1999), 150–69.

SHAMIR, SHIMON, *A Modern History of the Arabs in the Middle East* [Toledot ha'aravim bamizraḥ hatikhon be'et haḥadashah] (Tel Aviv: Reshafim, 1987).

—— 'The Modernization of Syria: Problems and Solutions in the Early Period of Abdülhamid', in William R. Polk and Richard L. Chambers (eds.), *Beginnings of Modernization in the Middle East: The Nineteenth Century*, Publications of the Center for Middle Eastern Studies 1 (Chicago: University of Chicago Press, 1968), 351–81.

SHAMOSH, AMNON, *The 'Keter': The Story of the Aleppo Codex* [Haketer: sipuro shel keter aram tsova] (Jerusalem: Ben-Zvi Institute, 1987).

SHAW, STANFORD J., 'The Ottoman Census System and Population, 1831–1914', *International Journal of Middle East Studies*, 9 (1978), 325–38.

SHOCHETMAN, ELIAV, 'The Murder of the "Minister" Hayim Farhi in Akko and the Affair of his Inheritance' (Heb.), *Asufot*, 6 (1992), 161–209.

—— 'New Sources with Regard to the Affair of the Inheritance of the "Minister" Hayim Farhi' (Heb.), *Asufot*, 11 (1998), 281–308.

SOMEL, SELÇUK AKSIN, 'Christian Community Schools during the Ottoman Reform Period', in Elisabeth Özdalga (ed.), *Late Ottoman Society: The Intellectual Legacy* (New York: Routledge Curzon, 2005), 254–73.

STRAUSS-ASHTOR, ELIYAHU, *History of the Jews in Egypt and Syria: Under the Rule of the Mamluks* [Toledot hayehudim bemitsrayim vesuryah taḥat shilton hamamelukim], 3 vols. (Jerusalem: Mosad Harav Kuk, 1944–70).

'Sultan ʿAbdülmecid's *Islahat Fermani*', in J. C. Hurewitz (ed.), *The Middle East and North Africa in World Politics: A Documentary Record*, 2nd edn. (New Haven, Conn.: Yale University Press, 1975), i. 316–17.

SUNAR, ILKAY, 'State and Economy in the Ottoman Empire', in Hurī Islamoğlu-Inan (ed.), *The Ottoman Empire and the World Economy*, Studies in Modern Capitalism (Cambridge: Cambridge University Press, 1987), 63–87.

SUTTON, DAVID (ed.), *Aleppo, City of Scholars: Based on LiKedoshim Asher Ba'Aretz by Hacham David-Sion Laniado*, trans. David Kirzner, Artscroll Sefardic Heritage Series (Brooklyn, NY: Mesorah, 2005).

SUTTON, JOSEPH A. D., *Aleppo Chronicles: The Story of the Unique Sephardeem of the Ancient Near East in their Own Words* (New York: Thayer-Jacoby, 1988).

—— *Magic Carpet: Aleppo-in-Flatbush* (New York: Thayer-Jacoby, 1979).

AL-TABBAKH, MUHAMMAD RAGHIB, *Eminent Nobles in the History of Aleppo* [Aʿlam al-nubala' bi-tarikh halab al-shahba'], vol. iii (Aleppo: Dar al-qalam al-ʿarabi, 1924).

TIBAWI, ABDUL L., *American Interests in Syria, 1800–1901: A Study of Educational, Literary and Religious Work* (Oxford: Clarendon Press, 1966).

—— *A Modern History of Syria: Including Lebanon and Palestine* (London: Macmillan, 1969).

THOMPSON, ELIZABETH, 'Ottoman Political Reform in the Provinces: The Damascus Advisory Council in 1844–45', *International Journal of Middle East Studies*, 25 (1993), 457–75.

TOLEDANO, EHUD R., *The Ottoman Slave Trade and its Suppression, 1840–1890* (Princeton, NJ: Princeton University Press, 1982).

TRENCH, RICHARD, *Arabian Travellers* (London: Macmillan, 1986).

TUCKER, JUDITH E., *In the House of the Law: Gender and Islamic Law in Ottoman Syria and Palestine* (Berkeley: University of California Press, 1998).

AL-TUNJI, MUHAMMAD, 'Social Interaction between the Ottomans and the Arabs in the Province of Syria' (Arab.), in ʿAbd al-Jalil al-Tamimi (ed.), *Social Life in the Arab Provinces in the Ottoman Period* [Al-haya al-ijtimaʿiyya fi al-wilaya al-ʿarabiyya athna' al-ʿahd al-ʿuthmani], vols. i–ii (Zaghwan: Markaz al-dirasat wa-al-buhuth al-ʿuthmaniyya wa-al-murisikiyya wa-al-tawthiq wa-al-maʿlumat, 1988), 213–27.

VERETÉ, MAYIR, 'The Restoration of the Jews in English Protestant Thought, 1790–1840', *Middle Eastern Studies*, 8 (1972), 3–50.

WALLERSTEIN, IMMANUEL, HALE DECDELĪ, and REŞAT KASABA, 'The Incorporation of the Ottoman Empire into the World-Economy', in Hurī Islamoğlu-Inan (ed.), *The Ottoman Empire and the World Economy*, Studies in Modern Capitalism (Cambridge: Cambridge University Press, 1987), 88–97.

—— and REŞAT KASABA, 'Incorporation into the World Economy: Change in the Structure of the Ottoman Empire, 1750–1839', in Jean-Louis Bacqué-Grammont and Paul Dumont (eds.), *Economie et sociétés dans l'Empire Ottoman*, Colloques internationaux du Centre National de la Recherche Scientifique (Paris: Centre National de la Recherche Scientifique, 1983), 335–54.

YAARI, ABRAHAM, 'Additions to "Hebrew Printing at Aleppo"' (Heb.), *Kiryat Sefer*, 11 (1934), 401–2.

—— *Emissaries from Israel: History of* Sheliḥut *from the Land of Israel to the Diaspora* [Sheluḥei erets yisra'el: toledot hasheliḥut meha'arets lagolah] (Jerusalem: Mosad Harav Kuk, 1951).

—— 'Hebrew Printing at Aleppo' (Heb.), *Kiryat Sefer*, 10 (1933), 100–18.

AL-YASHUʿI, FARDINAN TAWTAL, *Historical Documents about Aleppo* [Watha'iq tarikhiyya ʿan halab], 3 vols. (Beirut: n.p., 1958–62).

YELLIN, AVINOAM, 'About the Biblical Codices in Damascus' [Al haketarim bedamesek], *Mizraḥ uma'arav*, 1 (1919/20), 19–26, 117–26.

ZACHS, FRUMA, *The Making of a Syrian Identity: Intellectuals and Merchants in Nineteenth-Century Beirut* (Leiden: Brill, 2005).

ZENNER, WALTER P., *A Global Community: The Jews from Aleppo, Syria* (Detroit: Wayne State University Press, 2000).

—— 'Jews in Late Ottoman Syria: Community, Family and Religion', in Shlomo Deshen and Walter P. Zenner (eds.), *Jews among Muslims: Communities in the Precolonial Middle East* (Basingstoke: Macmillan, 1996), 173–86.

—— 'Syrian Jewish Identification in Israel', Ph.D. diss., Columbia University, New York, 1965.

—— 'Syrian Jews and their Non-Jewish Neighbors in Late Ottoman Times', in Shlomo Deshen and Walter P. Zenner (eds.), *Jews among Muslims: Communities in the Precolonial Middle East* (Basingstoke: Macmillan, 1996), 161–72.

ZIMMELS, H. J., *Magicians, Theologians, and Doctors: Studies in Folk-Medicine and Folk-Lore as Reflected in the Rabbinical Responsa (12th–19th Centuries)* (London: Goldstone, 1952).

ZOHAR, ZVI, 'Militant Conservatism: On the Socio-Religious Policy of Rabbis of Aleppo in Modern Times' (Heb., Eng. abstract), *Pe'amim*, 55 (1993), 57–78.

—— 'Quelques réflexions sur l'influence de l'Alliance sur les communautés juives en pays d'Islam et son caractère missionaire' (Heb., Fr. abstract), in Simon Schwarzfuchs (ed.), *L''Alliance' dans les communautés du bassin méditerranéen à la fin du 19ème siècle et son influence sur la situation sociale et culturelle: Actes du deuxième Congrès international de recherché du patrimoine des Juifs Sépharades et d'Orient* [Ha'alians bikehilot agan hayam hatikhon besof hame'ah ha-19 vehashpa'ato al hamatsav haḥevrati vehatarbuti] (Jerusalem: Misgav Yerushalayim, 1987), 31–5.

—— *Tradition and Change: Halakhic Responses of Middle Eastern Rabbis to Legal and Technological Change (Egypt and Syria, 1880–1920)* [Masoret utemurah: hitmodedut ḥakhmei yisra'el bemitsrayim uvesuryah im etgarei hamodernizatsiyah, 1880–1920] (Jerusalem: Ben-Zvi Institute, 1993).

Index

Printed and bound by CPI Group (UK) Ltd, Croydon, CR0 4YY

09/06/2025

14685812-0004